INTERNET EXPLORER PLUG-IN AND ACTIVEX COMPANION

INTERNET EXPLORER PLUG-IN AND ACTIVEX COMPANION

Written by Krishna Sankar with

Geoffrey Baird • Don Doherty, Ph.D. • Rob Falla • Brian Farrar
Jerry Honeycutt, Jr. • Jim O'Donnell

Internet Explorer Plug-In and ActiveX Companion

Credits

PRESIDENT
Roland Elgey

PUBLISHER
Stacy Hiquet

PUBLISHING MANAGER
Jim Minatel

TITLE MANAGER
Steven M. Schafer

EDITORIAL SERVICES DIRECTOR
Elizabeth Keaffaber

MANAGING EDITOR
Sandy Doell

DIRECTOR OF MARKETING
Lynn E. Zingraf

ACQUISITIONS MANAGER
Cheryl D. Willoughby

ACQUISITIONS EDITOR
Stephanie Gould

SENIOR EDITORS
Patrick Kanouse
Caroline D. Roop

PRODUCT DIRECTOR
Steven M. Schafer

PRODUCTION EDITORS
Jade Leah Williams
Susan Ross Moore

EDITORS
Jim Bowie
Sean Dixon
Patricia R. Kinyon
Tonya Maddox
Bill McManus

PRODUCT MARKETING MANAGER
Kristine Ankney

ASSISTANT PRODUCT MARKETING MANAGERS
Karen Hagen
Christy M. Miller

STRATEGIC MARKETING MANAGER
Barry Pruett

TECHNICAL EDITOR(S)
Russ Jacobs
Jim O'Donnell

TECHNICAL SUPPORT SPECIALISTS
Nadeem Muhammed

ACQUISITIONS COORDINATOR
Jane K. Brownlow

SOFTWARE RELATIONS COORDINATOR
Susan D. Gallagher

BOOK DESIGNER
Ruth Harvey

COVER DESIGNER
Barbara Kordesh

PRODUCTION TEAM
Michael Beaty
Jason Carr
Erin M. Danielson
Anjy Perry

INDEXER
Craig Small

Composed in *Century Old Style, Franklin Gothic,* and *MCPdigital* by Que Corporation.

To all the intranet practitioners—Administrators, Business Analysts, Developers, and Webmasters—who, in spite of the galloping technologies, are delivering strategic business systems that work.

About the Authors

Krishna Sankar is the cofounder of U.S. Systems & Services, a Silicon Valley intranet systems and Java technology company. He has worked on strategic business systems, ranging from real-time process control applications to client/server and groupware systems, for companies such as HP, GM, AT&T, U.S. Air Force and Navy, Pratt & Whitney, Testek, Ford, TRW, Caterpillar, Quantas Airlines, and Air Canada. He still believes in information reengineering and development of competitive business systems and is excited about the possibilities of intranet applets and servlets in those areas. He is a Microsoft Product Specialist as well as a Lotus Notes Certified Professional. Occasionally, you can find him at the corridors of venture capitalists and banks promoting products "for whose lives are not Internet but want to leverage the Net to enjoy it."

"Jerry" Honeycutt, Jr. provides business-oriented technical leadership to the Internet community and software development industry. He has served companies such as The Travelers, IBM, Nielsen North America, IRM, Howard Systems International, and NCR. Jerry has participated in the industry since before the days of Microsoft Windows 1.0 and is completely hooked on Windows 95 and the Internet.

Jerry graduated from the University of Texas at Dallas in 1992 with a B.S. degree in computer science. He currently lives in the Dallas suburb of Frisco, Texas with Becky, two Westies, Corky and Turbo, and a cat called Scratches. Jerry is an avid golfer with a passion for fine photography. Feel free to contact Jerry on the Internet at **jerry@honeycutt.com** or visit his Web site at **http://rampages.onramp.net/~jerry**.

Geoffrey Baird graduated from the University of Michigan in 1991. Joining Metamor Technologies in 1992, he worked in application development and systems support before leaving to head up marketing operations. In 1994, he helped form the Internet and intranet practice at Metamor, and has consulted for, trained, and developed Internet applications for some of the world's largest companies.

Dr. Donald Doherty is a brain scientist and a computer expert. His research into signal processing in both brains and computers keeps him pushing technology to its fullest capacity. Don enjoys sharing some of his adventures through writing about computers and the Internet.

Rob Falla is a computer author, professional Web developer, freelance writer, and speculative fiction writer. He is the author of the book *HTML Style Sheets Quick Reference* (published by QUE) and recently won first place for a speculative fiction short story titled "The October Comet." Rob is currently living in Nanticoke, Ontario with his wife Kathy and their two daughters. Rob is available for any questions or comments through e-mail at **rfalla@netroute.net**.

Brian Farrar received his B.A. in English and economics from Wabash College in 1985, and his M.B.A. from Indiana University in 1987. He began his career at GTE and progressed through a series of positions until 1994, when he left to start an Internet and intranet consulting practice for Metamor Technologies. Through this consulting practice, Brian has helped some of the largest companies in the world decide on and deploy Internet technologies to solve business problems.

Jim O'Donnell, was born on October 17, 1963, (you may forward greetings to **odonnj@rpi.edu**) in Pittsburgh, Pennsylvania. After a number of unproductive years, he began his studies in electrical engineering at Rensselaer Polytechnic Institute. He liked that so much that he spent 11 years there getting three degrees, graduating for the third (and final) time in the summer of 1992. He can now be found plying his trade at the NASA Goddard Space Flight Center. He's not a rocket scientist, but he's close.

Acknowledgments

My first thanks go to you, the reader. You gave me the motivation and the guidance to write this book. I always had you and your best interests in mind when I was contemplating the topics to be covered. Now that you are looking at this book, please do let me know how I did—what went right and what went wrong. If I was able to assist you in developing business logic and true n-tier Weblications across your intranet or if I motivated you to developed a date entry with drop-in calendar and users love you for it, then I have succeeded in my task.

Next, I wish to thank all the people at Que for their excellent work. Most of them I do not know, but they played an important role in getting this book into your hands. Of the people I dealt with directly at Que, Stephanie Gould was, is, and will be a motivating force for me. I thank Steve Schafer for his vision and ideas in shaping this book. Jade Williams literally ignored a harsh winter with temperatures approaching −40° F, to spend time editing this book, and of course, did an excellent job. To the coauthors of this book, I wish to record my thanks for their contributions and want to proudly share with them the credit for a book well done.

On the home front, my eternal gratitude goes to my wife, Subbalakshmi, "Usha," who is also my friend, philosopher, guide, and debate partner. She suffered through many hours of loneliness and my near-maniacal discussions about ActiveX. The encouragement given by my mother and Usha's parents was very valuable, not only in writing this book but also in keeping my sanity (which is still a question mark in the minds of many). My younger siblings, Jyothi and Prakash, and Usha's siblings, Suresh and Vaishali, always asked me how the chapters were going and I would mumble something about not getting time and inspiration. Now I can tell them truthfully that the book is finished! And lastly, I wish my late father was with us to see my book in print.

We'd Like to Hear from You!

As part of our continuing effort to produce books of the highest possible quality, Que would like to hear your comments. To stay competitive, we *really* want you, as a computer book reader and user, to let us know what you like or dislike most about this book or other Que products.

You can mail comments, ideas, or suggestions for improving future editions to the address below or send us a fax at (317) 581-4663. For the online inclined, Macmillan Computer Publishing has a forum on CompuServe (type **GO QUEBOOKS** at any prompt) through which our staff and authors are available for questions and comments. The address of our Internet site is **http://www.quecorp.com** (World Wide Web).

In addition to exploring our forum, please feel free to contact me personally to discuss your opinions of this book at **sschafer@que.mcp.com** on the Internet.

Thanks in advance—your comments will help us to continue publishing the best books available on computer topics in today's market.

Steven M. Schafer
Product Development Specialist
Que Corporation
201 W. 103rd Street
Indianapolis, Indiana 46290
USA

N O T E Although we cannot provide general technical support, we're happy to help you resolve problems you encounter related to our books, disks, or other products. If you need such assistance, please contact our Tech Support department at 800-545-5914, ext. 3833.

To order other Que or Macmillan Computer Publishing books or products, please call our Customer Service department at 800-835-3202, ext. 666.

Contents at a Glance

Table of Contents

Introduction

What is ActiveX? Quoting Microsoft from its Web page, "ActiveX is a set of technologies that integrate software components in a networked environment, regardless of the language in which they were created. This integration of components enables content and software developers to easily create interactive applications and Web sites. As a leading commercial object model, ActiveX has been widely adopted by corporate MIS and ISV communities and is used by millions of application and content developers today."

This book is a reference for the ActiveX technology with emphasis on the actual controls—the thrills and chills of corporate systems development. You should keep this book near your computer and refer to it when developing controls and Web pages. ■

ActiveX and This Book

The ActiveX technology does not lack information; instead, it lacks *structured* information that can be accessed readily when required by a developer. Although there are many controls available, it takes time to download, install, try out, and categorize each available control before you can use it. That is where this book comes in by providing structured information on the properties, methods, and events of a set of ActiveX controls to help you create interactive, useful Web pages for your Internet or intranet Web applications.

The ActiveX controls do not stand in a vacuum. They are best understood in COM, OLE, and other contexts. Hence there are chapters on related technologies that will put the ActiveX controls in perspective.

Even though not directly, this book targets Web developers of three-tier to n-tier business processes across corporate intranets. Static Web pages are almost a relic. Dynamic Web pages, which perform some kind of business function over and beyond corporate information publishing, are becoming a norm. You should be developing Weblications—client/server applications over the intranet.

What Is This Weblication Anyway?

Weblication is the short form for a Web-based application—a new systems development paradigm or approach. Weblications consist of HTML pages, probably generated dynamically as the client requests them, as opposed to the current client/server forms-based applications. In essence, they are HTML-based, TCP/IP protocol-backboned client/server applications with the Web browser as the client presentation layer. The logic and objects in a Weblication span operating systems and interfaces across many systems geographically separated in many time zones and countries. Weblications are more dynamic in nature and can have richer multimedia content, and they are more widely distributed and follow mostly the fat server/thin client architecture.

You should be able to prototype strategic business applications (Weblications) across the Web to show effective systems. Once approved, you can turn them into solid industrial-strength Weblications using rapid application development (RAD) techniques and tools. This strategy calls for components and component-based development, and this is where you can begin to use ActiveX controls and the Visual Basic Control Creation Edition.

History of ActiveX

After Windows 3.1 became popular as a desktop environment, developers were scrambling to develop products with the graphical user interface (GUI). The products that embraced the GUI paradigm survived, while those late-to-market were almost left behind.

The first development tools were using mostly assembly languages, such as C, with the Windows API. You needed to be an expert in handles as hWND and message loops—and then came Visual Basic. The arrival of Visual Basic was the beginning of true RAD environments.

Visual Basic pioneered (popularized might be a more accurate choice, but for many, pioneered is accurate) not only the visual development of Windows applications, but also the component development. The component development was done by Visual Basic (VBX) controls. A cottage industry sprang up developing and supporting VBX. Even Borland's Delphi and Powersoft's PowerBuilder development products began supporting the VBX components. The architecture for buying components, including them into your GUI, and controlling them from your code was a dream come true for the RAD practitioners.

For all their glory, VBX controls were not perfect. They had many limitations, the foremost of which was their 16-bit nature. They were also closed-aligned with the architecture of the BASIC language.

At this time, Microsoft started introducing the new technology called OLE. In 1991, OLE succeeded DDE (dynamic data exchange) as a technique by which different applications communicate with each other on the desktop system. OLE 1.0 had its humble origin from inserting objects usable by one program into another program. The original expansion of the OLE acronym was object linking and embedding. By 1993, OLE 2.0 metamorphosed from an acronym to just OLE—a name for the COM implementation (COM is a binary specification for interoperable objects). The component-based systems architecture began to take shape.

A Note from the Author

This is not a complete explanation of OLE and COM. This is to give you a perspective on the technologies. If you plan to embrace the ActiveX technology, you should at some point read through some material on OLE and COM.

Also, there are other competing and equally capable technologies like CORBA, IIOP, and so on, from OMG and other groups.

Microsoft started supporting the COM and OLE vigorously after the VBX industry turned its VBX controls into 32-bit OLE controls and then came the Internet. The rest, as they say, is history.

One outcome of the Internet revolution is that the pre-Internet OLE controls became ActiveX controls in the post-Internet era. These controls gained on-demand automatic downloading capability (through the Web browser) with authenticode verification and scripting programmability from the Web pages. The controls are easy to use and are true drop-in components. The dropped-in components can be connected using straightforward scripts to develop dynamic Web pages resulting in reduced development and deployment times. That is where the ActiveX controls are useful to Webmasters and developers like yourself. Your motto should be, "Buy, not build, and when you build, reuse."

What's in This Book

This book consists of four parts.

Part I, "Understanding ActiveX," introduces you to the world of ActiveX.

Part II, "ActiveX Technology," gives you a perspective of the use of ActiveX components. Here you will find information on security, using ActiveX with the Netscape Web browser, Microsoft Office, databases, and more. You will also find chapters on Visual Basic, Java, and server-side ActiveX.

Part III, "ActiveX Control and Plug-In Reference," constitutes the bulk of the content, categorizing controls and plug-ins with descriptions of each property, method, and event. The controls range from GUI-related form element controls (Chapter 12) to Web navigation (Chapter 13) and database controls (Chapter 14). On the multimedia side, there are controls dealing with images and animation (Chapters 15 and 16), VRML controls (Chapter 17), conferencing controls (Chapter 18) and finally, audio and video controls (Chapters 19 and 20). In Chapter 21, you will come across a bunch of controls like the FTP, MIME, NNTP, and the UUEncode/Decode that cannot be categorized in any other chapters. And finally, we end this book with Chapter 22, "The Future of ActiveX."

Part IV, "Appendixes," contains the index of ActiveX controls found in this book and the contents of the companion CD-ROM.

When I was approached by Stephanie Gould of Que to write this book, I grabbed the idea with reckless abandon. I knew I would learn more about this exciting technology and that, itself, was reason enough to write this book. Now that I am done with the book, I can surely say that the journey was worthwhile. That big software giant in Seattle is capable of developing nifty technology when awakened, as it did with the Internet.

Understanding ActiveX

CHAPTER 1

Introducing ActiveX Controls

A lot of people are wandering around mumbling something like "ActiveX; what is ActiveX?" Nobody knows for sure. You can check day to day with Microsoft to see what the latest definition of ActiveX is, but you'll soon tire of doing so.

ActiveX is a big umbrella that Microsoft uses to encompass all of its Internet-related technology. It's not a product. It includes technologies that programmers can use to build Internet-enabled applications, products that end-users can use to access the Internet, and technologies that content developers can use to build terrific Web sites.

One of the most exciting ActiveX technologies is ActiveX controls. These controls let you add diverse functionality to your Web site by inserting a control right in the Web page. You can insert a control that pops open a menu, for example, or you can insert a control that performs a query on a database and displays the result. There are thousands of controls available; you need only find one to fit your needs. ∎

Tour an ActiveX Web site

This chapter walks you through an ActiveX Web site, pointing out all the ActiveX touches along the way.

Understand how ActiveX controls evolved

You'll learn to appreciate the elegance of ActiveX controls by learning how they have evolved.

What do ActiveX controls do for you?

You'll see. ActiveX controls help you build a dynamic and exciting Web site, with little effort.

What about all the other ActiveX technology?

So you don't walk away confused, this chapter gives you a brief introduction to related technology.

ActiveX is another example of a buzzword gone awry. Microsoft serfs do not pronounce the X in ActiveX. It's silent. Instead of saying active-x-controls, for example, say active-controls.

The Evolution of ActiveX Controls

In the November 1, 1996, edition of *Windows Magazine*, Fred Langa traced the lineage of ActiveX controls back to the early days of cut-and-paste. Do you remember how cool that seemed back then? Cut-and-paste was touted as one of the major benefits of Windows because you could now share data between different applications.

OLE

Next comes OLE (object linking and embedding). This technology allows objects to be inserted into containers. In layperson terms, OLE allows a document from one application to be embedded within a document in another application. When you insert an Excel spreadsheet into a Word document, you are using OLE. You are also using OLE when you insert a picture into a Word document.

The first step was OLE 1.0. OLE 1.0 only provided the ability to share documents, not the ability to actually work with a document that's embedded within another. OLE 2.0 came along and allowed users to work on a document while embedded within another. For example, if you embed a spreadsheet in a Word document, as shown in Figure 1.1, you can work with that spreadsheet within the Word document. Thus, you can even use Excel's toolbars and menus while working with the spreadsheet in the Word document.

Following OLE 2.0 is OLE 2.5, or Distributed OLE. Distributed OLE lets you work with documents and links across a network. Thus, you don't have to worry about the location of documents on a network (even the Internet), as they all appear to be local.

ActiveX Controls

Now Microsoft has breathed new life into OLE and called it ActiveX controls. In reality, both OLE and ActiveX controls are based upon COM (Component Object Model). OLE is still alive and kicking. You use it all the time in the applications you know and love. ActiveX controls, on the other hand, are a trimmer version of OLE that's built for distribution on the Internet and is optimized for size and speed. You can insert an ActiveX control into any ActiveX container, such as Internet Explorer, Microsoft Office 97, and even the Windows desktop (with the help of Internet Explorer 4.0).

FIG. 1.1
Choose Insert, Object from Word's main menu to see the types of objects you can insert into a Word document.

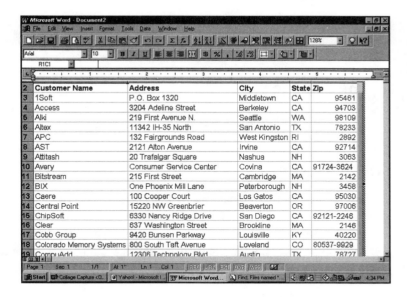

N O T E On the Internet, the availability of technology across all platforms is a key to that technology's success. As a Web developer, it doesn't make sense for you to rely on technology that is only available for the Mac, does it? Likewise, Microsoft knows that if UNIX and Mac users do not have support for VBScript and ActiveX objects, no one will develop Web pages with it because they can't reach the largest possible audience. All those UNIX and Mac users will be left out in the cold. Thus, Microsoft intends to make ActiveX available across all of the popular platforms you find on the Internet. ■

What ActiveX Controls Mean to You

If ActiveX is a technological umbrella, then ActiveX controls represent the umbrella's handle. They are the basic building blocks of ActiveX.

As you read, ActiveX controls are based upon COM (Component Object Model). They are a refinement of what you know as OLE custom controls. Any program that is a container for ActiveX controls can host them. Thus, you can stick ActiveX controls in a Web page since Internet Explorer is a container. You can also stick ActiveX controls in a Visual Basic application since Visual Basic forms are containers.

Currently, there are already more than a thousand ActiveX controls available because ActiveX is based upon a technology—OLE—that's been around for quite a while. Whereas it'll take time to build strong developer support for Java or Netscape plug-ins, ActiveX controls have immediate developer support from millions of programmers all over the world. Microsoft has been working with this technology for years using a different name.

ON THE WEB
You can get a good idea as to what types of ActiveX controls are available by opening **http://www.microsoft.com/activex/gallery** in your browser.

Working with Data

Remember what Web pages were like a few years back? They were static. The Web browser displayed what it was given: a fancy text file that contained information (HTML) about how the browser should display it. Once the browser had displayed the Web page, nothing changed. It just sat there. Great for reading the Unabomber's Manifesto, but not very useful or productive.

ActiveX controls let the content developer build Web pages that actually work with data they're given. The Web page is not static. It changes depending on the data the controls are working with and input from the user. That's starting to sound like what a program does, work with input and provide output. In fact, you can actually distribute programs, as ActiveX controls, via the Web page.

Here are a few examples of the types of things an ActiveX control can do with data:

- Allows the user to input information on the Web page using a wide variety of metaphors (drop-down lists, outline views, spinner buttons, and so on)
- Queries a database on the server and displays the results of the query on the Web page
- Works with a spreadsheet or grid inside the Web page. You'll find an example of a grid at ProtoView's Web site: **http://www.protoview.com**.
- Reports on information in a database. For example, the Crystal Reports Viewer Control lets you view reports via the Web (see **http://www.protoview.com**).

Integrating with Windows

Since ActiveX controls are fully conversant in COM, they can work closely with the other COM objects on the user's computer. For example, an ActiveX control can manipulate a document in Microsoft Word or it can work with the user's Windows 95 desktop (a container).

> **CAUTION**
>
> ActiveX controls are not limited as Java applets. They have full access to your computer, including your file system, when they run. Make sure you install only those controls that come from vendors you trust. For more information, take a look at Chapter 5, "Understanding Authentication and Security."

Provide Building Blocks

You should think of ActiveX controls as building blocks that you can assemble from a bunch of small building blocks into a much larger structure. You can combine a variety of ActiveX controls to build a solution that you distribute on the Web page. Here are some ideas of the types of things you can build with ActiveX controls:

- You can combine a handful of data-entry controls to provide a robust input for the user.

- You can use a combination of controls, such as Popup Menu and Popup Window controls, to provide advance navigation and help on your Web site. Figure 1.2 shows you such an example.

FIG. 1.2
Microsoft's NT Web pages use the Popup Menu Control to provide navigational tools.

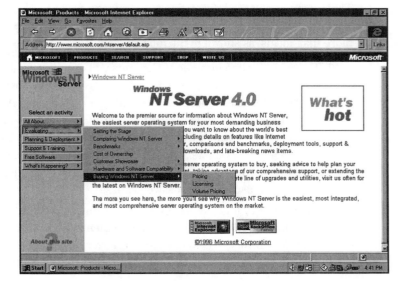

- You can build a mean game of checkers and distribute it on a Web page using ActiveX controls. Each piece may be a control, while the board is a container, such as the HTML Layout Control.

- You can build a complete interface to a corporate database using ActiveX controls for the user interface and the database access.

ActiveX versus Everything Else

From time to time, you may have heard a bit of confusion about what ActiveX is and is not. I've heard questions such as, "Why do I need ActiveX when I can use Java? What's so great about ActiveX controls when compared to Netscape plug-ins?" The sections that follow will answer many of these questions for you.

ActiveX and Forms

ActiveX controls do not supplant forms. Forms have their lot in life. They collect basic data from the user, as text boxes, check boxes, lists, and so on, and submit that information to the server. Scripts on the server do as they see fit with the information. The script can add the information to a database, for example, or verify a user's logon to a Web site. ActiveX controls let you collect information from the user, but they do much more than forms, as shown in the following list:

- There is a limited number of elements you can put on a form. You can use text boxes, lists, text areas, and so on. They are all geared towards collecting information from the user. There are currently over a thousand ActiveX controls; however, only a handful are actually geared toward user input. You can do things with controls that you can't with forms, including inserting complete programs into a Web page. For example, you can insert a control on the Web page that queries a database on the server and displays the results of the query. You can insert a control that lets the user play a crossword puzzle.

- You have very little control over how a form's elements appear on the Web page. You can change the size of a form's elements, but you can't control much else. ActiveX controls give you total control over how they appear on the Web page. For example, you can rotate a text label and change its color to your liking.

Even though ActiveX controls are not really related to forms, you can still submit the contents of a control with a form. You learn how to do this in Chapter 2, "Inserting ActiveX Controls on the Web Page."

ActiveX and Plug-Ins

Are ActiveX controls comparable to Netscape plug-ins? Yes and no. You can use both ActiveX controls and plug-ins to enhance the content of a Web page. For example, you can use an ActiveX control to display a video just as well as you can use a plug-in. Here are some of the biggest differences between ActiveX controls and plug-ins:

- The biggest difference is in the philosophy. With plug-ins, you are distributing data. When you embed a data file in a Web page, the plug-in behaves as a browser extension by displaying or otherwise doing something with the data. Thus, the primary purpose of a plug-in is to handle data embedded in the Web page that the browser can't normally handle by itself.

- With ActiveX controls, you are actually distributing smallish programs that have a specific purpose. You can associate some data with the program, but the primary purpose of an ActiveX control is to add some sort of functionality to the Web page, such as input a bit of information from the user or display a menu from which the user can make a choice.

- ActiveX controls install themselves automatically. The controls don't require the user to stop right in the middle of a Web page, download an installation program, and run it. However, the user does have to install plug-ins manually. Many times the user has to shut down the browser altogether to install a plug-in.

- Another difference is plug-ins are not based upon COM (Component Object Model). ActiveX controls are based upon COM. Thus, ActiveX controls have a life apart from the Web page.

ActiveX and Java

Microsoft contends that ActiveX and Java are not competing technologies—they're complimentary. You don't have any reason to disbelieve them, either. Here are some of the bigger differences between ActiveX controls and Java applets:

- Java is an Internet language that's great for distributing simple applications on the Internet. ActiveX is a much larger group of technology that integrates a variety of objects from a variety of sources.

- ActiveX controls have a life apart from the Web page. Since the controls are based on COM, they can also be used in Visual Basic applications.

- Java applets are secure because they have no life apart from the Web page and, thus, have no direct access to the user's computer. ActiveX controls, however, do have direct access to the user's computer and are therefore not as secure.

■ The biggest difference between ActiveX controls and Java applets is how they behave on the user's computer. Java applets run in a Java Virtual Machine (JVM). They are interpreted, so they run slower than ActiveX controls. ActiveX controls, on the other hand, are compiled into native code that is not interpreted. Therefore, they run much faster. However, with the recent addition of just-in-time compilers (JIT) for Java, this difference will eventually go away.

Other ActiveX Technologies

ActiveX controls are not the only thing Microsoft has stuffed under the ActiveX umbrella. In reality, ActiveX is a magic buzzword that encompasses a lot of different products and technologies. The sections that follow describe the products that are add-ons for Internet Explorer and the ActiveX technologies which Microsoft has produced.

N O T E Microsoft has transferred "stewardship" for ActiveX to an independent group called the ActiveX Working Group. You can get more information at **http://www.activex.org**. ■

ActiveX Products

There is more to Internet Explorer than just a Web browser. It also has add-on products that let you conference, exchange e-mail messages, chat on IRC, and more. Here are some of the products that are available:

Internet Explorer	Internet Explorer is the actual browser. Internet Explorer has support for all of the latest HTML tags, scripting, Netscape plug-ins, and much more.
NetMeeting	NetMeeting, shown in Figure 1.3, is Microsoft's answer to online conferencing. This program lets you share programs and files; chat with audio or the keyboard; use a virtual white-board; and much more.
Internet Mail & News	Internet Mail is a much simpler mail client than Exchange. It'll provide most of your needs. Internet News is a great newsreader that competes well with most of the newsreaders on the market.
Comic Chat	Comic Chat is a unique IRC client. Instead of seeing line after line of text, you see a comic strip with characters that represent each person in the chat room as seen in Figure 1.4.

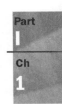

FIG. 1.3
Microsoft Netmeeting
enables a productive
conference with associates
all over the world.

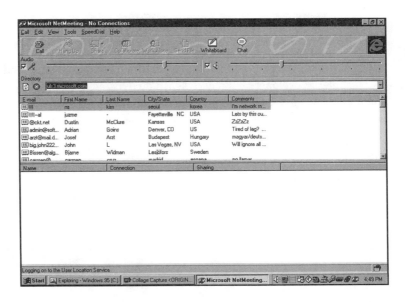

FIG. 1.4
Comic Chat uses a comic
strip metaphor to make IRC
a bit more interesting than it
already is (wink).

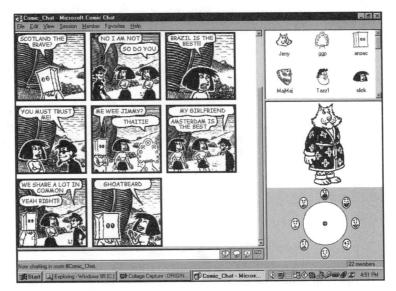

ActiveX Technologies

ActiveX contains a number of technologies for both programmers and content developers (Web authors). Programmers can take advantage of the technology, such as the CryptoAPI to add encryption capabilities to their Internet programs. Content developers can take advantage of ActiveX scripting to build dynamic Web pages. The following sections give you a brief look at the types of technologies that ActiveX encompasses.

ActiveX Controls   ActiveX controls, which you have learned about in this chapter, let content developers build and distribute dynamic applications on the Web page. The controls themselves are part of this technology. The tools that Microsoft provides for programmers to build ActiveX controls are also a part of it.

ActiveX Documents   ActiveX documents allow a user to view documents other than HTML files over the Internet. For example, a user can view a Word document or Excel spreadsheet over the Internet. Microsoft provides technology to programmers so that they can make their application's documents distributable in this manner. Figure 1.5 shows you an example of a Word document in the Web browser.

FIG. 1.5

You can use all of Microsoft Word's features when you're editing a document within Internet Explorer 3.0.

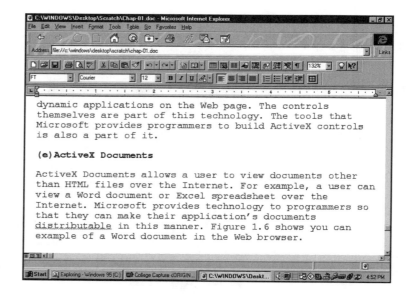

ActiveX Scripting   ActiveX Scripting includes Microsoft's VBScript and JScript (Microsoft's version of JavaScript). These scripting languages allow a Web developer to glue together the controls and forms on a Web page so that each individual object becomes a bit player in a bigger solution.

Microsoft also provides technology under this umbrella that allows programmers to build ActiveX Scripting into their own applications or to add new scripting languages to the browser. Watch out—you may see a FortranScript one day.

Java Virtual Machine   The Java Virtual Machine (JVM) allows an ActiveX-enabled browser to run Java applications over the Internet. Microsoft also provides a tool called Visual J++, shown in Figure 1.6, that programmers and content developers can use to build Java applets.

FIG. 1.6
Visual J++ uses the Visual Developer Studio similar to Microsoft's other Visual developer products.

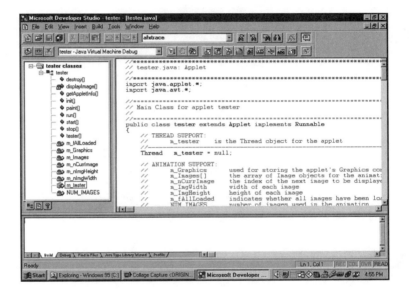

ActiveX Server Framework   The ActiveX Server Framework provides technology for security, cryptography, and database access on the server. Also, the server is extensible through ISAPI (Information Server Application Programmer Interface).

Using ActiveX Controls

This chapter presented you with a lot of background information about ActiveX controls. The following chapter, "Inserting ActiveX Controls on the Web Page," shows you how to put these controls in your Web page. Once you are familiar with how to put a control on your Web page, you can browse Parts II and III of this book to learn about some of the controls available for your use. And don't forget all the controls included on this book's CD-ROM. ●

CHAPTER 2

Inserting ActiveX Controls on the Web Page

What is an ActiveX control?

Learn what ActiveX controls are provided by Microsoft for Internet Explorer 3.0, and how to use them.

Inserting controls in your Web page is easy

You can insert ActiveX controls in your Web pages using the OBJECT tag and can set properties using the PARAM tag.

Interact with ActiveX controls using scripts

You can make controls interact with each other with scripting. This chapter shows you how you can connect scripts to controls.

An example of ActiveX controls

You learn more about ActiveX controls by trying out the real-world example at the end of this chapter. Enjoy.

You use ActiveX controls (the objects formerly known as OLE controls or OCXs) to add a variety of features to your Web page. For example, you can add a Timer Control to your Web page that periodically updates the page's content, or you can use a Popup Window Control to display tooltip-style help when the user holds the mouse pointer over a link. Considering that there are more than a thousand ActiveX controls available for you to use, the possibilities are just about endless.

Simply dropping ActiveX controls onto your Web page isn't enough for you to build a dynamic and exciting Web page. You have to make all those controls work together. That's where scripting comes in. You associate scripts with the events and values of the controls you put on a Web page so that you can make them interact. You can update the contents of a TextBox Control when the user clicks a button, for example, or you can open a Web page in a frame when the user chooses an item from a Popup Menu Control.

Although this chapter describes how to connect scripts to controls, this book isn't about scripting languages. It is about using ActiveX controls and plug-ins with Internet Explorer. However, this book is a perfect companion to several of Que's books on scripting languages, such as:

> *VBScript by Example*
>
> *JavaScript by Example*
>
> *Special Edition Using VBScript*
>
> *Special Edition Using JavaScript*
>
> *Using JScript*

 T I P Find out more about these books and other Que Internet titles by visiting Que's Web page at **http://www.quecorp.com**.

Getting Microsoft's ActiveX Controls

Microsoft provides a basic collection of ActiveX controls with Internet Explorer 3.0. You need only install Internet Explorer 3.0 to get them. However, Microsoft packages some controls only with the complete installation of Internet Explorer 3.0, while providing other controls through its ActiveX Gallery Web site at **http://www.microsoft.com/activex/gallery**. Table 2.1 briefly describes each control and how you get it. The sections that follow show you working examples of some of these controls.

Table 2.1 Microsoft's ActiveX Controls	
Name	**Description**
Provided by the Minimum, Typical, and Complete Installs of Internet Explorer 3.0	
Web Browser	Displays HTML files, ActiveX controls, and ActiveX documents
Timer	Executes a script at specific intervals
Marquee	Scrolls an HTML file horizontally or vertically
Provided by the Complete Install of Internet Explorer 3.0	
ActiveMovie	Displays streaming and nonstreaming video and audio
HTML Layout	Displays 2-D HTML regions created with the ActiveX Control Pad

Name	Description
Provided by the Complete install of Internet Explorer 3.0	
Forms 2.0 Label	Displays a text label
Forms 2.0 Textbox	Prompts the user for text
Forms 2.0 Combo Box	Displays a drop-down list of options
Forms 2.0 List Box	Displays a scrollable list of options
Forms 2.0 CheckBox	Displays a check box option
Forms 2.0 Option Button	Displays an option button
Forms 2.0 Toggle Button	Displays a button that the user can toggle on and off
Forms 2.0 CommandButton	Displays a basic command-style button
Forms 2.0 Tabstrip	Displays multiple pages of controls that the user selects by clicking a tab
Forms 2.0 ScrollBar	Displays vertical and horizontal scroll bars
Forms 2.0 Spin Button	Displays a spin button with arrows that can be pushed up or down
Image	Displays a progressive image from a JPG, GIF, or BMP file
Hotspot	Adds a transparent hotspot to a layout
Provided at http://www.microsoft.com/activex/gallery	
Animated Button	Displays an AVI file on a button
Chart	Draws various types of charts
Gradient	Shares an area with a range of colors
Label	Displays a text label with a given angle, color, and font
Menu	Displays a button that pops up a standard menu which triggers an event when the user chooses an item
Popup Menu	Displays a pop-up menu that triggers an event when the user chooses an item
Popup Window	Displays an HTML file in a pop-up window
Preloader	Downloads the file at the given URL into the user's cache
Stock Ticker	Displays data from a text file at regular intervals
View Tracker	Triggers events when the control enters or leaves the browser's viewing area

Part

I

Ch

2

N O T E Many of the ActiveX controls you find on the Internet are not digitally signed. By default, Internet Explorer 3.0 will not install unsigned controls (signed controls provide information about their publisher)—it doesn't even give you the chance to override it. Thus, Internet Explorer will ignore many of the controls that the Web page authors are using. Check your security configuration to make sure you have a choice: choose View, Options from the main menu; click the Security tab; click the Safety Level button; and make sure that you select Medium. Internet Explorer 3.0 will then ask you before installing an unsigned control. If you choose not to install the control, the Web page may not work as the author intends. On the other hand, if you do install the control, you open yourself up to troubles that come from running controls from unknown sources, such as bugs that cause the browser to crash or, worse, controls that damage your system. For more information, see Chapter 5, "Authentication and Security." ▓

Label Control

The ActiveX Gallery shows an example of the use of the ActiveX Label Control, shown in Figure 2.1. Using this control, you can display text within a Web page using any installed font with any style or color, and at any arbitrary angle you choose. In this example, the two regions change—either color, text, or orientation—whenever you click them.

FIG. 2.1
The Label Control gives you the ability to place text on the Web page without resorting to graphics.

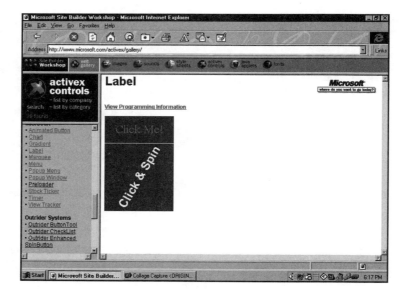

Preloader Control

The ActiveX Preloader Control makes your Web site seem to work faster than normal. It's a slight-of-hand, however, because the Preloader Control quietly caches files (graphics, video, audio, and HTML) from the Web site while the user is reading the current Web page. You can see an example of the Preloader Control at Microsoft's ActiveX Gallery.

Timer Control

The Timer Control lets you periodically run a script which you can use to change the content of a Web page or perform some other task. Figure 2.2 shows a Web page that uses a timer to change the size and color of the two labels (each implemented with the Label Control) over time. Both labels change at different intervals because this Web page uses two different Timer controls.

FIG. 2.2
You use the Timer Control to execute a script at preset intervals, such as every second or every ten seconds.

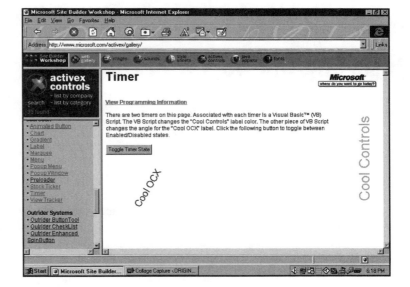

Menu Control

You use the Menu Control to put a button on your Web page that, when clicked by the user, displays a menu. When the user chooses a menu item, the control fires an event which you can handle with a script. Figure 2.3 shows you the example from Microsoft's ActiveX Gallery. It contains two Menu controls; each one displays a different submenu.

FIG. 2.3
You can use the Menu
Control to add menu-driven
navigation to your Web site,
like Microsoft's Site Builder
Workshop.

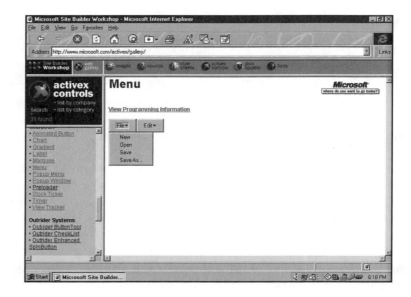

Inserting Controls with the *OBJECT* Tag

You've seen the controls, now you need to know how to insert them into your Web pages.
You use the OBJECT tag to do just that. With regard to ActiveX controls, the OBJECT tag
identifies the control you're using. The OBJECT tag identifies which control on the user's
computer (the browser downloads and installs the control on the user's computer) you
want to use and gives that instance of the control a name, which you can use in scripts.
That's all.

In the sections that follow, you learn much more about each of the OBJECT tag's attributes.
Before moving on, take a look at how you use the OBJECT tag in a Web page. In its simplest
form, the OBJECT tag looks similar to the following:

```
<OBJECT
        classid="clsid:1A771020-A28E-11CF-8510-00AA003B6C7E"
        id=Track1
        width=400
        height=2
        align=left>
<IMG SRC="noobject.gif">
<PARAM NAME="Image" VALUE="image.gif">
</OBJECT>
```

The CLASSID attribute uniquely identifies, on the computer, the control you're using. Every control installed on the user's computer is installed in the Registry. The control's CLASSID is the number that Windows uses to identify that control. You can think of the CLASSID as a name that is guaranteed to be unique. You'll learn more about this attribute later. In this case, I'm using the View Tracker Control. You use the id attribute to identify the control to the scripts in your Web page. width, height, and align work the same as with other types of tags; they specific the size and location of the control on the Web page.

The OBJECT tag provides a way out for those browsers that don't support the OBJECT tag. Browser's that do support the OBJECT tag ignore anything between <OBJECT> and </OBJECT> that isn't a PARAM tag (you learn about this in the next section). Browser's that don't support the OBJECT tag will ignore it and the PARAM tags, and use the sandwiched <OBJECT> and </OBJECT> tags instead. In this case, if the user's Web browser supports the OBJECT tag, she sees the View Tracker Control inserted into her Web page. Otherwise, she sees an IMAGE.GIF image inserted using the IMG tag.

> **N O T E** Some sources refer to the tags sandwiched between the <OBJECT> and </OBJECT> tags as the apology section. As in: I'm sorry you don't support this object; here, try these tags instead. ▓

Setting a Control's Properties with the *PARAM* tag

You will need to set the properties of the ActiveX controls you put on the Web page to control its appearance or functionality. For example, you need to give the Stock Ticker Control the URL of the text file it should use for data. You need to provide the Label Control the text it should display. The only way to know for sure which properties each control requires is to check in the control's documentation. You can also use the ActiveX Control Pad to set a control's properties, as described in Chapter 3, "Creating Web Pages with the ActiveX Control Pad & Layout Control."

So how do you set these properties? You use the PARAM tag to assign a value to a named property within the control. This works very much like Visual Basic property sheets. Note that the PARAM tag has no closing </PARAM> tag. Table 2.2 describes the attributes you use with the PARAM tag. You frequently need to use only the NAME and VALUE attributes.

Table 2.2   Attributes of the *PARAM* Tag

Attribute	Description
NAME	Defines the name of the property. An ActiveX control may treat the name as case-sensitive
VALUE	Specifies the value of the property identified in NAME
VALUETYPE	Can be one of REF, OBJECT, or DATA
TYPE	Refers to Internet Media Type (RFC 1590) of the item referred to in the VALUE field when VALUETYPE = REF

NAME, VALUE, and TYPE are self-explanatory. Table 2.3 describes the settings you can use with VALUETYPE.

Table 2.3   Values for *VALUETYPE* Attribute

Value	Meaning
REF	VALUE contains a URL
OBJECT	VALUE contains URL of another OBJECT
DATA	VALUE contains string data

The following is an example of inserting an ActiveX control using the OBJECT tag. The CLASSID attribute specifies the Popup Menu Control, and each PARAM tag adds a menu item to the menu.

```
<OBJECT
      id=iemenu1
      classid="clsid:0482B100-739C-11CF-A3A9-00A0C9034920"
      width=1
      height=1
      align=left
      hspace=0
      vspace=0
   >
   <PARAM NAME="Menuitem[0]" VALUE="First Choice">
   <PARAM NAME="Menuitem[1]" VALUE="Second Choice">
   <PARAM NAME="Menuitem[2]" VALUE="Third Choice">
   <PARAM NAME="Menuitem[3]" VALUE="Fourth Choice">
   <PARAM NAME="Menuitem[4]" VALUE="Firth Choice">
</OBJECT>
```

More About the *OBJECT* tag

The OBJECT tag has a number of attributes that you can use. The sections that follow describe each attribute. In reality, however, you'll find yourself using only a few: classid, id, height, width, align, and, possibly, codebase.

ALIGN You use the ALIGN attribute to specify where to place the object. You can position an object relative to the text line or on its own on the left, right, or center of the page. Table 2.4 describes the settings you can use to align the object with the text line. Table 2.5 describes the settings you can use to align the object with the page.

Table 2.4   Aligning the Object with the Text Line

Setting	Description
TEXTTOP	Aligns the top of the object with the top of the current font
MIDDLE	Aligns the middle of the object with the baseline of the text line
TEXTMIDDLE	Aligns the middle of the object with the middle of the text line
BASELINE	Aligns the bottom of the object with the baseline of the text line
TEXTBOTTOM	Aligns the bottom of the object with the bottom of the current font

Table 2.5   Aligning the Object with the Web Page

Setting	Description
LEFT	Aligns the object with the left side of the Web page with text flowing around the right side of the object
CENTER	Aligns the object in the center of the Web page with the text starting on the line following the object
RIGHT	Aligns the object with the right side of the Web page with text flowing around the left side of the object

BORDER When you use an object as part of a hypertext link, you can specify whether or not the object has a border. The BORDER attribute specifies the width of the border around the object. If you don't want a border around the object, set this attribute to 0, such as: BORDER=0.

CLASSID and CODEBASE   You use CLASSID to refer to the ActiveX control to be placed within the object's borders. There are several different ways to indicate the object to be inserted here. ActiveX uses the clsid: URL scheme to specify the ActiveX class identifier.

ON THE WEB

For further information on the clsid: URL scheme see **http://www.w3.org/pub/WWW/ Addressing/clsid-scheme**.

The best way to obtain the CLSID for an ActiveX control is to look at the control's documentation. You can look up Microsoft's ActiveX controls at Microsoft's ActiveX Gallery. Alternatively, use the ActiveX Control Pad to insert an ActiveX control in your Web page so that you don't have to worry about the CLSID (see Chapter 3, "Creating Web Pages with the ActiveX Control Pad & Layout Control"). If the CLASSID attribute is missing, ActiveX data streams will include a class identifier that can be used by the ActiveX loader to find the appropriate control.

The CODEBASE attribute can be used to provide an URL from which the control can be obtained. If the control is already installed on the user's computer, the browser will do nothing with this attribute. If the control isn't installed on the user's computer, however, the browser will try to download the control from the URL in CODEBASE and install it.

Getting a *CLASSID* from the Registry

You can also get the CLASSID for an ActiveX control from the Windows Registry. Follow these steps:

1. Open the Registry Editor, choose <u>R</u>un from the Start menu, type **regedit**, and press Enter.

2. Locate a control under HKEY_CLASSES_ROOT, such as Internet.Gradient or Internet.Label.

3. Note the default value of the CLSID subkey for that control. This is the string you use in the CLASSID attribute.

You can learn more about CLSIDs in *Special Edition Using the Windows 95 Registry* or *Windows Registry Handbook* by Que.

CODETYPE   The CODETYPE attribute is used to specify the Internet Media Type for the code pointed to by the CLASSID attribute. Browsers use this value to check the type of code before downloading it from the server. Thus, the browser can avoid a lengthy download for those objects which it doesn't support.

Currently, the CODETYPE attribute is supported in a limited fashion in Internet Explorer 3.0. Microsoft has indicated that TYPE will be implemented for all relevant MIME types.

DATA   The DATA attribute contains a URL that points to data required by the object, for instance a GIF file for an image. Internet Explorer 3.0 currently supports the DATA attribute.

DECLARE   You'll use the DECLARE attribute to tell the browser whether to instantiate the object or not. If the DECLARE attribute is present, it indicates that the object should not be instantiated until something references it. The browser will note the declaration of the object, but won't actually load it until you reference it.

HEIGHT   The HEIGHT attribute defines the height in pixels to make available to the ActiveX control when rendered by the browser. The Web browser might use this value to scale an object to the requested height.

HSPACE   The HSPACE attribute defines the amount of space in pixels to keep as white space on the left and right as a buffer between the ActiveX control and surrounding page elements. The Web browser might use this value to allocate white space.

ID   The ID attribute defines a document-wide identifier. This can be used for naming positions within documents. You also use the control's ID to reference it in scripts.

NAME   You use the NAME attribute to indicate whether an object wrapped in a FORM tag will be submitted as part of the form. If you specify NAME, the Web browser submits the VALUE property of the object to the host. If you don't specify NAME, the ActiveX control is assumed to be decorative and not functional in the form.

STANDBY   STANDBY is short string of text that the browser displays while it loads the ActiveX control.

TYPE   The TYPE attribute is used to specify the Internet Media Type for the data specified by the DATA attribute.

ON THE WEB

You can learn more about Internet Media Types by referring to RFC 1590. You can get RFC 1590 from the Internet at **ftp://ds.internic.net/rfc/rfc1590.txt**.

USEMAP   The value in USEMAP specifies a URL for a client-side image map.

VSPACE   The VSPACE attribute defines the amount of space in pixels to keep as white space on the top and bottom as a buffer between the ActiveX control and surrounding page elements. The Web browser might use this value to allocate the requested white space.

Part

I

Ch

2

WIDTH   The WIDTH attribute defines the width in pixels to make available to the ActiveX control when rendered by the browser. The Web browser might use this value to scale an object to the requested width.

Using ActiveX Controls in Netscape (NCompass)

NCompass Labs provides a Netscape plug-in called ScriptActive that makes ActiveX controls work in Netscape. It requires Netscape Navigator 3.0 or later. To install the ScriptActive plug-in, download ScriptActive from **http://www.ncompasslabs.com**, saving it into a temporary folder. In Windows Explorer, double-click the file that you downloaded to start the setup program. Follow the instructions you see on the screen.

As always, there are a few caveats. These caveats should make you wary in choosing the ScriptActive plug-in. For example, you won't have much luck using Microsoft's new development tools with ScriptActive, because ScriptActive doesn't support ActiveX Controls with the OBJECT tag. Here's more information about these caveats:

- ScriptActive only supports VBScript if it's stored in a separate file. Thus, if you want both Internet Explorer and Netscape users to be able to use your Web page, you must store your scripts in files with the ALX extension and refer to that script using the EMBED tag, such as:

  ```
  <EMBED SRC="myscript.axs" WIDTH=1 HEIGHT=1 LANGUAGE="VBScript">
  ```

- ScriptActive doesn't directly support the OBJECT tag. It only supports the EMBED tag. Thus, if you're authoring a Web page that you want to be compatible with both Internet Explorer and Netscape, you must insert a comparable EMBED tag inside of each OBJECT tag. Otherwise, Netscape users won't be able to use your Web page, regardless of whether or not they have ScriptActive. Internet Explorer will use the OBJECT tag, ignoring the EMBED tag, and Netscape will use the EMBED tag, ignoring the OBJECT tag.

N O T E   For more information, and more caveats, about using ScriptActive with Netscape, I recommend that you read NCompass Lab's FAQ. It's at **http://www.ncompasslabs.com/faq_main.htm**. ▇

Connecting Controls to Scripts

Now, we're getting to the meat of the matter. You learned how to insert ActiveX controls into your Web page using the OBJECT tag. Now you need to learn how to interact with those controls using a scripting language. In the sections that follow, you learn how to handle the events that are triggered by a control. You also learn how to get and set a control's properties from your scripts. Incidentally, the scripting language of choice is VBScript for these examples. The JavaScript versions of these examples aren't much different, however.

ActiveX controls act like and quack like the elements on a form. You interact with each ActiveX control's properties, methods, and events in exactly the same way in which you interact with a form's elements. You handle a control's events when the control needs attention, you call a control's methods, and you get and set the control's properties.

Handling an Event

In a Web page, an object causes events in response to the messages the object receives from Windows. When you click inside of an object, Windows sends a message to the object telling it that you clicked the mouse. In turn, the object causes a click event, and the browser looks for a special script procedure or function called an event-procedure to handle that event.

You can use a couple of different methods of handling events for forms and elements (event-procedures, inline event-handlers, and so on), but there's really only one way to handle an ActiveX control's events: using the FOR/EVENT attributes of the SCRIPT tag.

The FOR and EVENT attributes let you associate a script with any named object in the HTML file and any event for that object. Take a look at the following:

```
<SCRIPT LANGUAGE="VBScript" FOR="btnButton" EVENT="Click">
<!--
 window.alert( "Ouch! You clicked on me." )
-->
</SCRIPT>
<OBJECT ID="btnButton" WIDTH=96 HEIGHT=32
        CLASSID="CLSID:D7053240-CE69-11CD-A777-00DD01143C57">
        <PARAM NAME="Caption" VALUE="Click Me">
        <PARAM NAME="Size" VALUE="2540;847">
</OBJECT>
```

This defines a button (with an ID of btnButton) that executes the script when the user clicks it. Take a look at the <SCRIPT> tag. It contains the FOR and EVENT attributes which define the object and event associated with that script. FOR="btnButton" EVENT="Click" says that when an object named btnButton triggers the Click event, every statement in this script is executed.

Some events pass arguments to the event handlers. How do you handle arguments when you're handling the event using the FOR/EVENT syntax? Like the following:

```
<SCRIPT LANGUAGE="JavaScript" FOR="btnButton" EVENT="MouseMove(shift,
➥button, x, y)">
```

The enclosed script can then use any of the parameters passed to it by the `MouseMove` event.

 TIP Once you've specified a language in your HTML file, you don't need to do it again. Your browser defaults to the most recently used language in the HTML file. You can put `<SCRIPT LANGUAGE="VBScript"></SCRIPT>` at the very beginning of your HTML file one time and forget about it. The rest of the scripts in your file will use VBScript.

You just saw the `Click` event. ActiveX controls support a wide variety of other events. The only way to know for sure which events a control supports is to consult the control's documentation or the ActiveX Control Pad's documentation. For your convenience, however, the following list describes the most prevalent and useful events:

- `BeforeUpdate` occurs before data in a control changes.
- `Change` occurs when the value property in a control changes.
- `Click` occurs when the user either clicks the control with the left-mouse button or selects a single value from a list of possible values.
- `DblClick` occurs when the user clicks twice with the left-mouse button rapidly.
- `DropButtonClick` occurs when a drop-down list appears or disappears.
- `KeyDown` occurs when a user presses a key.
- `KeyUp` occurs when a user releases a key.
- `KeyPress` occurs when the user presses an ANSI key.
- `MouseDown` occurs when the user holds down a mouse button.
- `MouseUp` occurs when the user releases a mouse button.
- `MouseMove` occurs when the user moves the mouse pointer over a control.
- `Scroll` occurs when the user changes a scroll bar.

N O T E Often, the easiest way to see the events, properties, and methods that an ActiveX control supports is to insert the control into a Web page using the ActiveX Control Pad, and pop open the Script Wizard. The Script Wizard lists all of the control's events in the left pane. It lists all of the control's properties and methods in the right pane. See Chapter 3, "Creating Web Pages with the ActiveX Control Pad & Layout Control," for more information. ■

Changing an Object's Properties

Many objects let the user input data. For example, the user can choose an item from a list, type text in an edit box, or click a check box. What good are objects if you can't get and set their value? Not much. You read the value of most elements using the object's `value` property in an assignment or logical expression. The following example assigns the text that the user typed into the `txtTextBox` Control to a variable called `str`. The next example compares the text that the user typed into the `txtTextBox` with the word "Howdy."

```
str = txtTextBox.value
If txtTextBox.value = "Howdy" Then
```

You can also set the value of an element by assigning a string to the element's value, as follows:

```
txtTextBox.value = "New Contents of the Text Box"
```

The `value` property is the default property for most ActiveX controls which accept user input. Thus, you can use the control's value in an expression without explicitly using the `value` property, such as:

```
alert txtTextBox
txtTextBox = "New Contents of the Text Box"
```

Tying It All Together with an Example

You learned a lot in this chapter. You learned about the variety of ActiveX controls you can put in your Web page. You learned about using the OBJECT and PARAM tags to insert controls in your Web page. You also learned how to associate scripts with controls.

Working through a quick example might make things clearer for you. This example in particular is a simple Web page that prompts the user for his name and displays a greeting to him when he clicks a button. Use these steps to create this example:

1. Start with an empty HTML file. All you really need in this file are the `<HTML>` and `</HTML>` tags.

2. Insert a TextBox Control called `txtName` into your Web page using the following OBJECT tag. This is where the user will type his name. You don't need to set any properties for the text box. You can change the size of the text box by experimenting with the WIDTH and HEIGHT attributes. You must type the CLASSID attribute exactly as shown.

```
<OBJECT ID="txtName" WIDTH=160 HEIGHT=24
  CLASSID="CLSID:8BD21D10-EC42-11CE-9E0D-00AA006002F3">
</OBJECT>
```

3. Insert a CommandButton Control named `cmdDisplay` into your Web page using the following OBJECT tag. The `Caption` property determines what the user sees on the

button. The `Size` attribute determines the size of the button. The `ParagraphAlign` property aligns the caption in the middle of the button, because it's set to 3.

```
<OBJECT ID="cmdDisplay" WIDTH=60 HEIGHT=24
 CLASSID="CLSID:D7053240-CE69-11CD-A777-00DD01143C57">
    <PARAM NAME="Caption" VALUE="Display">
    <PARAM NAME="Size" VALUE="2455;846">
    <PARAM NAME="ParagraphAlign" VALUE="3">
</OBJECT>
```

4. Add the following script to the HTML file. The `FOR` attribute associates this script with the `cmdDisplay` object you created in step 3. The `EVENT` attribute associates this script with the `Click` event of the CommandButton Control. When the user clicks the button, Internet Explorer executes every line in this script, which displays a message box with the user's name in it.

```
<SCRIPT LANGUAGE="JavaScript" FOR="cmdDisplay" EVENT="Click()">
<!--
 window.alert( "Hello " + txtName)
-->
</SCRIPT>
```

5. Save the HTML file and open it in Internet Explorer 3.0. Type your name in the text box, and click the button. You should see a message box similar to Figure 2.4.

FIG. 2.4
The user can't interact with Internet Explorer 3.0 as long as the message box is displayed.

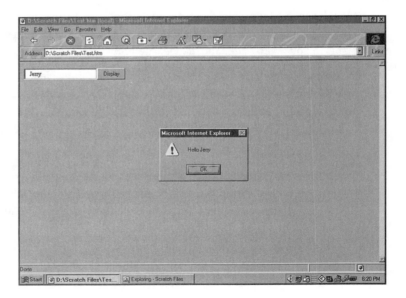

N O T E There is an easier way to insert controls into your Web pages; however, this chapter has been a useful exercise because there are times that you'll want to work with these controls by hand. Although you can continue to work with ActiveX controls by hand, I don't recommend that you do so. Microsoft's ActiveX Control Pad makes inserting ActiveX controls into a Web page far too simple for you to continue whacking yourself with the OBJECT tag. See Chapter 3, "Creating Web Pages with the ActiveX Control Pad & Layout Control," for more information. ■

Using the Internet Explorer Logo

No doubt, you've seen the Netscape logo on just about every page on the Web. Did you know that you can also put the Internet Explorer logo on your Web page? Microsoft has a few more requirements than Netscape, however, they are different for each of the logos you can use:

 This is a static logo. It doesn't contain any animation. If you use any of Internet Explorer's HTML extensions, such as background sounds, frames, and tables, you qualify to use this logo on your site. Microsoft also recommends, but doesn't require, that you showcase some of the more advanced HTML features like ratings and style sheets.

 This is the animated logo that you frequently see on Microsoft's Web site. All you have to do to use this logo is use one or more ActiveX controls on your Web site. Since you bought this book for that purpose, you shouldn't have any problems qualifying, right?

You can apply for and download the logo at **http://www.microsoft.com/powered/pbbo.htm**. There is a short questionnaire that you must complete to use the logo. After you've answered the questions, click Accept & Register, at the bottom of the page, to download the file.

Don't Manually Insert Controls

This chapter has showed you how to manually insert controls into a Web page. You need this information. Understanding the OBJECT and PARAM tags makes it easier to understand what tools, such as the ActiveX Control Pad, are doing to your Web page.

On the other hand, you shouldn't make a habit of manually inserting controls into your Web page. Why? Well, because it's a bit tedious and it's certainly error prone. The next chapter, "Creating Web Pages with the ActiveX Control Pad & Layout Control," shows you how to use this great tool to automatically insert a control into your Web page, creating all the necessary tags as it works. ●

CHAPTER 3

Creating Web Pages with the ActiveX Control Pad

In Chapter 2, you learned how to insert ActiveX controls into your Web pages using the OBJECT and PARAM tags, but doing this by hand is nasty, tedious work. First, you have to find the control's CLSID. Then, you have to type the OBJECT by hand and, worse yet, set all those properties using those PARAM tags. If you're inserting more than a few ActiveX controls in your Web page, you'll quickly become frustrated.

The ActiveX Control Pad (from Microsoft, of course) makes the process a whole lot easier. It has three primary features, as follows:

■ The Control Pad lets you easily insert ActiveX objects into your HTML files using a graphical user interface. This means that you don't have to mess around with those <OBJECT> tags at all. Point the Control Pad at a control, fill in the property sheet, and the Control Pad inserts all the required HTML into your Web page.

- The Control Pad provides the Script Wizard, which lets you create event handlers by associating events with actions. You can make these associations by using a graphical user interface, too. That means that you can avoid as many of those <SCRIPT> tags as possible, but you might still need to write them when working on more complicated scripts.

- The Control Pad lets you graphically edit Layout Controls. That means that you can take full, two-dimensional control of where objects are placed on your Web page. You can actually place and edit controls just like the form editor in Visual Basic. ■

 The ActiveX Control Pad contains the complete VBScript reference and a complete HTML reference. It also contains a reference for all of Microsoft's ActiveX controls and the Internet Explorer Object Model. Unfortunately, it doesn't include a JScript reference. To access these references, choose Help from the Control Pad's main menu. Choose either VBScript Reference or HTML Reference.

Downloading and Installing the ActiveX Control Pad

Before you can take advantage of all this wonderment, you need to download the ActiveX Control Pad onto your computer. It's a free download available through Microsoft's Site Builder Workshop at **http://www.microsoft.com/workshop/author/cpad/download-f.htm**.

Click Download (in the middle of the Web page) to download the self-extracting, self-installing file that contains the ActiveX Control Pad (SETUPPAD.EXE) into a temporary directory on your hard drive. Then run SETUPPAD.EXE and follow the instructions you see on the screen.

Getting Acquainted with the HTML Editor

The Control Pad uses VBScript by default. If you want to use JScript, you need to set it up to do so. Run the Control Pad. Then, choose Tools, Options, Script from the main menu. Select JavaScript, and click OK to save your changes. The Script Wizard (described later in this chapter) will now generate JScript language scripts instead of VBScript language scripts.

Figure 3.1 shows you the Control Pad's HTML editor with an HTML file in it. You can open many HTML files in Control Pad because it's an MDI (Multiple Document Interface) application. You switch between each open HTML file using the Window menu.

FIG. 3.1
The Editor window shows you only the contents of your HTML. Save the file to disk and open it in your Web browser to preview what the Web page looks like.

Object Icon ⟶

Script Icon ⟶

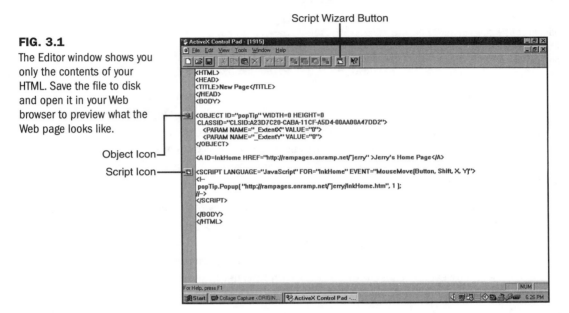

Script Wizard Button

The HTML file you see in Figure 3.1 contains an object. You see an <OBJECT> tag. You also see the object icon in the margin of the Editor window. Click this icon to change the object next to it in the Editor window. Just below the object, you see a script. You can also see the script icon in the margin of the Editor window. You can edit the script using the Script Wizard by clicking this button.

You can type any text you like in the Editor window. You can add forms to the file, for example. You can also add everyday text and tags, such as headings, lists, and so on. If you're really into punishment, you can add objects to your HTML by typing them in the Editor window. Considering the features you will learn in the next section, you are strongly discouraged from doing the preceding steps.

Placing Objects into Your HTML File

Inserting an object into an HTML file is easy. Position your mouse pointer to the point at which you want to insert an object, then right-click. Choose Insert ActiveX Control, and you'll see a dialog box similar to the one shown in Figure 3.2. The Insert ActiveX Control dialog box lets you pick one of the many controls that are available on your computer.

FIG. 3.2

The usable ActiveX controls'
names start with Microsoft
ActiveX or Forms 2.0. Do
not use the objects whose
names end with Ctl.

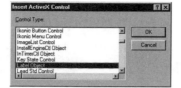

Select one of the controls, such as the Label Object, and click OK. The Control Pad opens up the Object Editor and property sheet for the control, as shown in Figure 3.3. You can change each of the control's properties using the property sheet shown in the figure. You can also adjust the size of the control by grabbing one of its handles in the Object Editor and dragging it.

Using a control in this manner is called using it at *design time*. You're designing how the control is going to look on your Web page. The user uses the control at *run-time*, since all he is doing is using a page built with that control. Many controls require that you have a license to use them at design time. The controls you see in this chapter do not require a license, however, because they all come with Internet Explorer.

Select a property here

Change its value here

FIG. 3.3

Select a property, change it
at the top of the property
sheet, and click Apply to
save your changes.

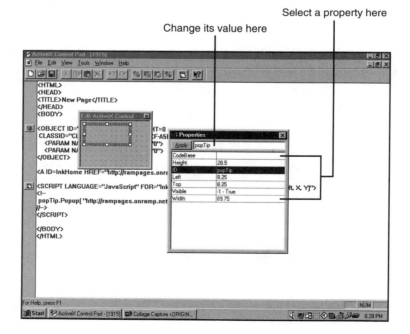

After you have made your changes to the control's property sheet, close both windows. After you close both windows, the Control Pad inserts the <OBJECT> and <PARAM> tags into your HTML file which match how you filled in the property sheet.

You can change the control's properties in the HTML (PARAM tags) using the Control Pad's text editor. The next time you open that control's property sheet, the property sheet will reflect any changes you made.

 The Control Pad has its own way to format the <OBJECT> and <PARAM> tags. You may as well make all of your tags consistent with the way the Control Pad formats them, as shown in this chapter's figures, so that your scripts will be easier to read.

Editing Scripts Using the Control Pad's Script Wizard

The Visual Basic and Visual C++ integrated development environments make the process of writing code as pleasant as possible. They provide text editors, graphical editors, and other tools to make managing objects much easier. If you have ever used these environments, you'll appreciate the Control Pad's features.

The Control Pad's Script Wizard helps you point and click your way to some terrific scripts. The best part about it is that you don't have to know anything about the browser's object model, a control's properties, methods and events, or even the run-time functions the browser provides. The Script Wizard displays them for you, so that you can automatically insert statements in your scripts that use them by pointing and clicking.

To call it a wizard is a bit misleading, since it doesn't act or quack like other wizards in Windows 95. It does give you a smooth interface for editing the events of each object in your HTML file, though. It lets you edit an object's events in two different ways, as follows:

- The List view lets you associate an event with a list of actions. You give arguments for those actions by answering questions in the Script Wizard.
- The Code view is more of a traditional programming approach. You select an object's event and edit the code in the window.

The following sections show you how to use both methods for editing event handlers in your HTML file. You cannot use the Script Wizard to edit other types of scripts, such as support functions and subprocedures, that are not event handlers. You can create event handlers that call your JScript or VBScript functions, however.

Part
I
Ch
3

TIP Are you unsure which properties, methods, and events a particular object in your HTML file supports? Click the Script Wizard button in the toolbar, and select that object in the left pane to see its events. Select that object in the right pane to see its properties and methods.

List View

The Script Wizard's List view lets you edit an event handler with the greatest of ease. Click the Script Wizard button in the toolbar to open the Script Wizard. Then click the List View button at the bottom of the window. See the window shown in Figure 3.4.

FIG. 3.4
In most cases, the List view is all you ever need to create exciting Web pages.

Here's how it works. You associate an object's event with another object's methods and properties by taking the following steps:

1. Expose the events for an object in the left pane by clicking the plus sign (+) next to the object. Select an event that you want to handle. You can select the window object's onLoad event, for example.

2. Expose the methods and properties for an object in the right pane by clicking the plus sign (+) next to the object. Select a method or property that you want to associate with the event you selected in the left pane. For example, you can click the plus sign next to the document object, and select the bgColor property.

3. Click the Insert Action button below the bottom pane. If you select a property, Control Pad prompts you for the value you want to assign to that property in the event handler. If you pick a method that has arguments, Control Pad prompts you for the arguments you want to use. If you pick a method that does not have

arguments, Control Pad doesn't prompt you for anything at all. After you have answered any questions that Control Pad asks, it inserts the association in the bottom pane. For example, if you insert an action for the document object's bgColor property, the Control Pad prompts you for the value to which you want to set bgColor.

4. You can rearrange the order of the actions in the bottom pane by selecting an action, and clicking the up and down arrow buttons to move it around in the list. You can also remove an action by selecting it and clicking the Delete Action button.

5. When you're happy with the way you're handling that particular event, you can move onto another object and another event, or close the Script Wizard by clicking OK.

Part

I

Ch

3

N O T E The Control Pad creates a script block with the FOR and EVENT tags for each event that you handle. Alternatively, you can write a VBScript or JScript function that handles an event the way you want, and then associate an event with the function using the Script Wizard. ■

Code View

If you're more comfortable with the traditional programmer view of life (optimistic about everything), you can use the Script Wizard's Code view. This works just like the List view, except that you don't see a list of associated events and actions in the bottom pane. You see the actual code the Script Wizard creates, instead.

Click the Script Wizard button in the toolbar to open the Script Wizard. Then click the Code View button at the bottom of the window. See the window shown in Figure 3.5.

FIG. 3.5
You have to use the Code view if you want to use compound statements, such as If in your scripts.

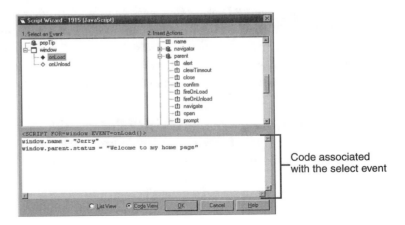

Code associated with the select event

You can insert actions into the bottom pane of the Code view—just as you do in the List view—by selecting an event in the left pane and choosing an action in the right pane. This view does not have an Insert Action button, so you double-click the action in the right-hand pane to add it to the bottom pane.

After you have added a few actions to the event handler by double-clicking them in the right pane, you can edit the code in any way you like. You can add or change the arguments for each method you use, add conditional and looping statements, or whatever you want.

When you're happy with the way you are handling a particular event, you can move on to another event, or close the Script Wizard by clicking OK.

 Keep your Web browser running with the Web page you're working on open in it. Then, you can save the changes, flip to the browser, and refresh the Web page to see your changes while you're working in Control Pad.

Controlling Page Layout with the HTML Layout Control

Web browsers position the content of an HTML file in a stream. The Web browser reads the contents of an HTML file—left to right, top to bottom—and displays its contents in the order it encounters it. The only real control you have over the placement of an HTML file's content is through tags such as TABLE, PRE, and so on. Even these require that you understand the stream orientation of HTML.

On the other hand, 2-D placement gives you complete control over the positioning of objects on a Web page. You have seen 2-D placement in many different kinds of products. Visio, Micrografx Designer, and most publishing tools give you complete placement control. You can position text so that it wraps around a graphic object in Microsoft Publisher, for example. In fact, the exception to 2-D placement seems to be HTML and the Web browsers that display it.

Microsoft created the ActiveX Layout Control expressly for this purpose. It gives you complete control over how you place objects on a Web page. You can place an object at a specific coordinate, for example. You can also overlap objects and make parts of some objects transparent so that objects in the background show through.

The Layout Control is similar to all the other objects you've seen in this book. You insert the Layout Control into your Web page using the OBJECT tag. It's a container, however, that can host other objects. You learn more about this later in this chapter.

W3C to the Rescue

In the meantime, W3C (World Wide Web Consortium) is developing a standard for HTML that will give you complete control over how you position objects in a Web page. You will be able to specify the exact horizontal (x) and vertical (y) positions (coordinates) of each object on a Web page. Until its release, use the Layout Control.

You should know that the Layout Control is a temporary solution. It will go away eventually. Thus, when the W3C defines its standard, and browsers such as Internet Explorer and Netscape support it, you will not need to use the Layout Control to have 2-D placement of objects.

Microsoft has committed to providing a utility that you can use to convert your ActiveX Layout Control layouts to the new HTML standard for 2-D layouts when that standard becomes available. You can get more information about this standard at **http://www.w3.org/pub/ WWW/TR/WD-layout.html**.

Understanding the Layout Control

The Layout Control is a container. This is the primary concept you need to understand about this object. It's an object you put in your Web page that can contain other objects. If you think of your Web page as a grocery bag, the controls you put in it are the groceries. With a Layout Control, you're going to put your groceries inside plastic bags (the Layout Control); then you drop the plastic bag into your grocery bag. Bet you didn't think of the Layout Control as produce, did you?

Another way to think of the Layout Control is as a form. It works just like forms you create in Visual Basic or in Visual C++. You drop a Layout Control on the Web page, and then you can arrange objects within it in any way you like. You can use the Layout Control to create virtually any form using the Visual Basic form editor.

Following are some of the other things the Layout Control brings to the party:

- You can overlap the objects you put on a Layout Control. Try that in HTML and you'll be very frustrated.

- You can control the Z-order of each object you overlap by controlling which objects are in front and which objects are in back.

■ You can make parts of some objects transparent so that the objects in the background show through.

■ You can use WYSIWYG environment to place and arrange objects on a Layout Control.

N O T E   If you don't really need to control the exact location of the objects you're putting on a Web page, don't use the Layout Control. It comes with a heavy price (download time, compatibility with other browsers, and so on) that's hard to justify if you're just trying to be cute. ■

Inserting the Layout Control into an HTML File

A layout has two components. First, you insert the actual Layout Control in your Web page using the <OBJECT> and <PARAM> tags. This tag looks similar to the following:

```
<OBJECT CLASSID="CLSID:812AE312-8B8E-11CF-93C8-00AA00C08FDF"
➥ID="example" STYLE="LEFT:0;TOP:0">
<PARAM NAME="ALXPATH" REF VALUE="file:example.alx">
 </OBJECT>
```

The other component is the layout itself. You store a layout in a separate text file that has the .ALX file extension. The ALXPATH property that you see in the previous example tells the Layout Control where to find this file. You can set this property to any valid URL, including a Web server. You do have to copy the ALX file onto the Web server with all of your other files. You learn more about the contents of the ALX file later in this chapter.

You don't have to insert the OBJECT tag or create the ALX file by hand, since the ActiveX Control Pad does it automatically. This tag simply loads an ActiveX object into your Web page that defines a region in which you can place other ActiveX objects or a layout. You don't use the Insert ActiveX Object menu item; you do use the Insert HTML Layout menu item by taking the following steps:

1. Position your mouse pointer where you want to use a Layout Control, right-click, and choose Insert HTML Layout.

2. When the Control Pad asks you for a file name, type the name of the file in which you want to store the layout, and click Open. If the file doesn't exist, Control Pad will ask you if you want to create it.

As a result, the Control Pad inserts an OBJECT tag in your HTML file. Take a look at Figure 3.6 to see what the tag looks like.

FIG. 3.6
Insert the Layout Control
using a plain old OBJECT
tag.

Layout Button

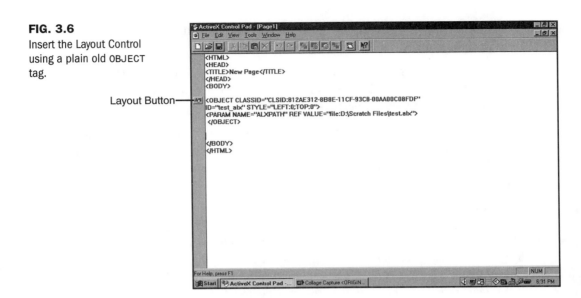

Editing the Layout

After you have inserted a Layout Control into your Web page, you can open it for editing.
This allows you to place other ActiveX objects inside the Layout Control. Remember the
Layout button in Figure 3.6? Click this button, and the Control Pad opens the layout in the
Layout Editor, as shown in Figure 3.7.

FIG. 3.7
The Layout Editor is very
similar to VBScript's Form
editor.

Layout

Toolbox

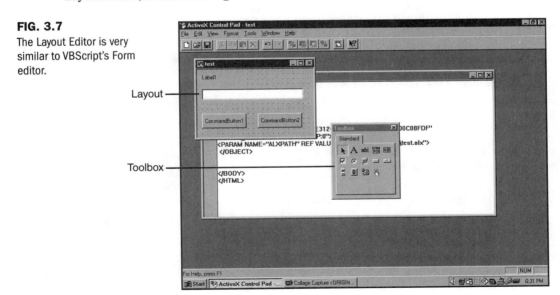

The Layout Editor lets you drag controls from the toolbox to the layout. Then you can rearrange the controls, write event handlers for controls, and so on.

Understanding What's in the ALX File   As you've seen, the Control Pad stores layouts in separate files with the .ALX file extension. It gives the name of a layout file to the Layout Control using the ALXPATH property.

The contents of the layout file aren't too mysterious. Each layout region begins and ends with the DIV and /DIV tags. You can give a region a name using the ID attribute, and you specify the style of the region using the STYLE attribute. Following is what the tag looks like:

```
<DIV STYLE="LAYOUT:FIXED;WIDTH:240pt;HEIGHT:180pt;">
</DIV>
```

What you do between the DIV tags is your business. You can insert objects into the layout by putting an OBJECT tag inside the layout's DIV tag. Inserting an object into a layout is not very different from inserting an object directly into your HTML file. The only difference is that you can specify the location of the object using the properties inherited from the Layout Control. The following is what a Label Control looks like in a layout file:

```
<DIV STYLE="LAYOUT:FIXED;WIDTH:423pt;HEIGHT:265pt;">
    <OBJECT ID="MyLabel" CLASSID="CLSID:978C9E23-D4B0-11CE-BF2D-
00AA003F40D0"
➥STYLE="TOP:83pt;LEFT:74pt;WIDTH:72pt;HEIGHT:18pt;ZINDEX:0;">
        <PARAM NAME="Caption" VALUE="MyLabel">
        <PARAM NAME="Size" VALUE="2540;635">
        <PARAM NAME="FontCharSet" VALUE="0">
        <PARAM NAME="FontPitchAndFamily" VALUE="2">
        <PARAM NAME="FontWeight" VALUE="0">
    </OBJECT>
</DIV>
```

You do not need to worry about understanding or setting the DIV tag's attributes or the attributes of the objects you put in the Layout Control; the Control Pad does it for you. It is not recommended to edit a layout by hand anyway. It just doesn't make sense considering the tools that are available to you.

N O T E   You can also put scripts in an ALX file. You can put them before or after the <DIV> tag, but not inside the tag. ■

Adding Controls to a Layout   Adding controls to a layout is easy. You drag a control from the toolbox and drop it on the layout in the Layout Editor. The following steps show you how to create a simple form using the Layout Editor:

1. Insert an HTML Layout Control into an HTML file and click the Layout button next to it. You'll see the Layout Editor, as shown in Figure 3.8.

FIG. 3.8
You now have two files: an HTML file (in the background) and an ALX file.

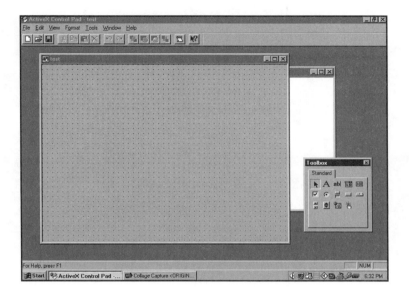

2. Drag a control from the toolbar and drop it onto the layout. Change the control's ID and any other properties for your use of the control. If the control's property sheet isn't open, you can open it quickly by double-clicking the control. This property sheet is the same one you learned about earlier in this chapter.

3. Repeat step 2 for each control you want to add to your layout.

4. Save the layout by clicking the Save button. Then, open the Web page in your browser. Figure 3.9 shows you what a layout looks like in Internet Explorer.

 TIP You can create control templates in the Layout Editor. Create a new page in the toolbox, right-click a tab, and choose New Page. Drag a control from your layout onto the new page. You can then use this template at any time by dragging it onto a layout.

Adding Scripts to Your Layout You can add scripts to a layout just as you would add scripts to an HTML file. You use these scripts to handle the events fired by the objects in the layout. You can validate that the user has entered valid text in each field, for example. Click the Script Wizard button in the Control Pad's toolbar. In this case, the Script Wizard works exactly as you learned it would in the previous chapter.

Part

I

Ch

3

FIG. 3.9
The fruits of your labor.

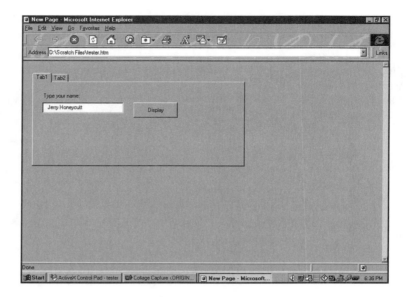

N O T E ActiveX controls that you put on a Layout Control have many more events, properties, and methods than the ActiveX controls you use directly on the Web page. Also, when you open the Script Wizard in an HTML Layout control, you don't see the events, properties, and methods for ActiveX controls on your Web page or the browser's object model. ▪

Changing a Layout's Tab Order When you create a form using the HTML Layout Control, the user can't tab between each field if you have not set up the tab behavior for each tab box. First, double-click each control in the layout, and set the TabStop property to True and TabKeyBehavior to False (if the control supports it). Then, change the TabIndex property for each control in the layout. Set TabIndex to 0 for the first control in the tab order. Set TabIndex to 1 for the next control in the tab order, and so on.

 You can leave the property sheet open all the time. When you select a different object on the layout, the property sheet changes to the one for that object.

Learning by Doing

As always, the best way to learn the Control Pad is to try an example. This section contains a few examples that will help you become an expert at using Control Pad to create classy Web pages. Here are the examples you will find in this section:

- You'll re-create the example from Chapter 2, "Inserting ActiveX Controls on the Web Page," using the Control Pad. This will give you a whole new appreciation for how much trouble the Control Pad saves you.

- You'll learn how to add tooltips and scripts to your Web page that pop up a little Help window when the user hovers over a link.

Hello Jerry

Remember the example in Chapter 2, "Inserting ActiveX Controls on the Web Page"? You'll create this example using the ActiveX Control Pad. In this example, the user types his name in a textbox, clicks the Display button, and receives a warm greeting from the browser. In Chapter 2, you had to insert the OBJECT and PARAM tags into the HTML file yourself—kind of a pain in the browser. However, creating this Web page using the Control Pad is a snap using the following steps:

1. Open the ActiveX Control Pad and create a new HTML by clicking the New button, choose Internet Document (HTML) from the list, and click OK.

2. Position the cursor inside the BODY tags, and insert a Microsoft Forms 2.0 TextBox Control by right-clicking in the area inside the BODY tags, choose Insert ActiveX Control, choose Microsoft Forms 2.0 TextBox from the list, and click OK. You'll see the Control Editor, as shown in Figure 3.10.

Part I

Ch 3

FIG. 3.10
You learned about the Control Editor in "Placing Objects into Your HTML File" earlier in this chapter.

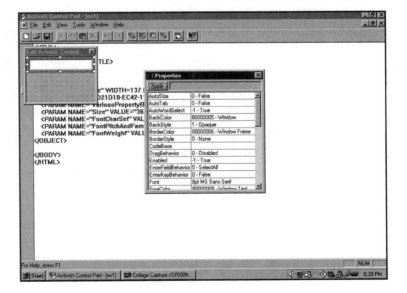

3. In the Control Editor, select TextBox Control and stretch it, by dragging the control's handles, so that it's long enough to accept a user's name. In the property sheet, change the ID property of the TextBox Control to `txtName`. Then close the Control Editor. Your HTML file should look similar to Figure 3.11.

FIG. 3.11

Become familiar with the way the Control Pad formats OBJECT and PARAM tags, because you cannot change it.

4. Position the cursor inside the BODY tags again, and insert a Microsoft Forms 2.0 CommandButton Control by right-clicking in the area inside the BODY tags, choose Insert ActiveX Control, choose Microsoft Forms 2.0 CommandButton from the list, and click OK.

5. In the Control Editor, select the CommandButton Control. In the property sheet, change the ID property to `cmdDisplay` and change the Caption property to `Display`. Then close the Control Editor. Your HTML file should look similar to Figure 3.12.

6. Add a script that handles the button's Click event, displaying a message box when the user clicks it. Click the Script Wizard button in the toolbar, and change to the Code view. Select the Click event for the cmdDisplay object in the left pane, double-click the alert method for the Window object in the right pane, and change window.alert(msg) to window.alert("Hello " + txtName) in the bottom pane. Your Script Wizard window should look very similar to Figure 3.13. Click OK to save your changes.

FIG. 3.12

The Control Pad inserts more PARAM tags than you did in Chapter 2, "Inserting ActiveX Controls on the Web Page."

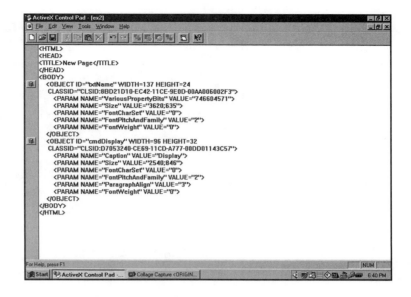

FIG. 3.13

After you've edited an event using the Script Wizard's Code view, you cannot go back to the List view.

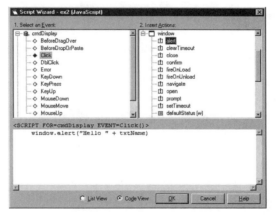

N O T E In the Script Wizard, the only way to see absolutely all of the methods and properties for a control is to change to the Code view. The List view hides many methods and properties of most controls. ▪

7. Save your HTML file and open it in Internet Explorer 3.0. Although your Web page may not look exactly like Figure 3.14, it should resemble the page.

FIG. 3.14

You can resize the CommandButton Control so that it looks better beside the TextBox Control.

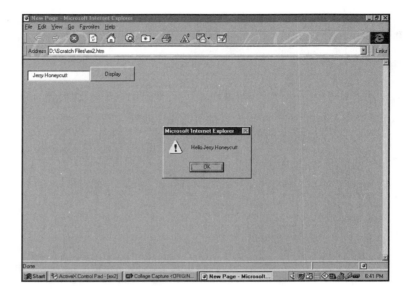

Pop-Up Help (Tooltips)

If you're not sure what tooltips are, try this little experiment: pop open WordPad and hold the mouse pointer over one of the buttons in the toolbar. What do you see? A little window that displays the purpose of the button. Microsoft calls these *tooltips*. You can use tooltips on your Web pages to provide additional help to users when they hold their mouse pointer over a link. To add tooltips, take the following steps:

1. Open the Control Pad and create a new HTML file. Call it TOOLTIP.HTM. Add a link to the body of the HTML file.

2. Add an ID to the link using the ID attribute for anchors by adding ID=Name to the A tag. Figure 3.15 shows this example with a link that contains an ID of lnkHome.

3. Insert the Microsoft IE30 Popup Windows Control to your HTML file (if you don't have this control, see Chapter 2 to learn how to get it) by right-clicking above the link you added in step 2, choose Insert ActiveX Control, select Microsoft IE30 Popup Windows Control from the list, and click OK. Change its ID to popTip using the control's property sheet. Change its size so that it has no height and no width. Close the Control Editor.

4. Add the following script to your HTML file. This handles the MouseMove event for the link called lnkHome. In this case, it pops up the Popup Window with the contents of LNKHOME.HTM found on my Web site. You can replace this with an HTML file on your Web site as described in the next step.

```
<SCRIPT LANGUAGE="JavaScript" FOR="lnkHome" EVENT="MouseMove(Button, Shift,
➥X, Y)">
<!--
 popTip.Popup( "http://rampages.onramp.net/~jerry/lnkHome.htm", 1 );
//-->
</SCRIPT>
```

FIG. 3.15

You can also add tooltips for images, objects, and forms.

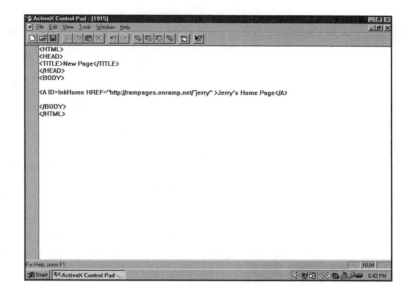

5. Create a file called LNKHOME.HTM that contains the formatting and text you want to display in the tooltip. You need to provide only the HTML and BODY tags, as well as the text you want to display in the Window. You can use the BODY tag's TOPMARGIN, LEFTMARGIN, BGCOLOR, and TEXT attributes to change the size of the tooltip window and its colors. Here's what the file you created looks like:

```
<HTML>
<BODY TOPMARGIN=0 LEFTMARGIN=0 BGCOLOR=YELLOW TEXT=BLACK>
Click this link to go to Jerry's home page
</BODY>
</HTML>
```

6. Save your new HTML file, TOOLTIP.HTM, and load it in Internet Explorer 3.0. Move the mouse pointer over the link, and you should see a small window pop up that contains the words "Click this link to go to Jerry's home page," as shown in Figure 3.16. When you click the mouse pointer outside the pop-up window, the pop-up window goes away.

Part

I

Ch

3

FIG. 3.16
The Popup Window Control only works with files using HTTP. You cannot use this control with local files.

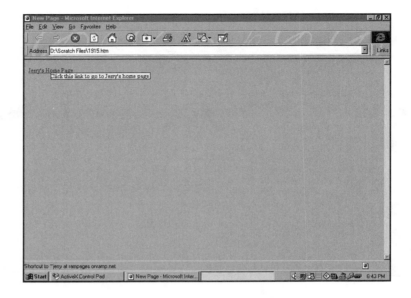

N O T E Microsoft's HTML Wizard is a very simple tool that enables you to use a folder's context menu to create brand-new HTML files using a template of your choice. You can get your own copy from Microsoft's Web site at **http://www.microsoft.com/intdev/download.htm**. ■

Learn by Doing

The best way to learn more about ActiveX controls and the ActiveX Control Pad is to play. I mean it. Create an empty Web page and start slapping controls into it. Change the properties, one at a time, and watch how each change affects the control when you load it in the browser. Be sure to keep this book open to Parts II and III when creating your Web page, so you can look up what each control's property does. ●

CHAPTER 4

Understanding ActiveX: The Technology

This chapter covers the ActiveX technology from a design abstraction point of view. You will get a firsthand glimpse at the framework and infrastructure leading to the ActiveX controls. The underlying foundations, including OLE, are very involved and complex topics with a dozen books and volumes of information available on CD-ROM. Hopefully, you will explore further to get more insight into the various components of the ActiveX infrastructure. ■

What is the Active Platform?

Learn about the technology and architecture of the Active Platform and the interactions between the components that make up the Active Platform.

Component Object Model (COM)

The ActiveX components are based on the COM model, the vtable indirection, the COM interfaces including the IUnknown, and the marshalling and remoting of COM objects.

ActiveX framework

The ActiveX framework consists of the ActiveX containers, ActiveX documents, and ActiveX controls. The scripting model elaborates how you can connect the objects using programs written in VBScript.

Creating ActiveX controls

You learn about the various tools that can be used to create ActiveX controls.

Definition

ActiveX technology is a component-based architecture that enables a developer to leverage the hundreds of available components and build upon them rather than starting from scratch. The ActiveX components can interoperate across networks with clients and servers and communicate over the intranet/Internet.

ActiveX technology can be used to create, integrate, and reuse software components or "controls" over the Internet or intranets. ActiveX software components, can be integrated into Web pages or any host that supports ActiveX controls. The ActiveX controls are, technologically, in-process COM objects. As they are COM objects, the controls can be integrated together with scripting to dynamically interact with users—at the client side and at the server side.

If the above definition looks like a marketing brochure, don't worry. It is easy to define ActiveX by its capabilities and technology and, as you read on, you will see glimpses of the actual inner workings.

N O T E ActiveX controls have the file name extension .OCX. Almost all the ActiveX controls are 32-bit implementations. The 16-bit controls are obsolete and, unless there is a compelling reason, you should refrain from using them. ▪

Before you dive into the ActiveX Controls, take a look at the Active Platform. The Active Platform consists of three core technologies: Active Desktop, Active Server, and ActiveX Components. Figure 4.1 shows a diagram of the Active Platform.

FIG. 4.1
The Active Platform consists of the Active Server and Active Desktop with ActiveX, HTML, Scripts, Components, and System Services.

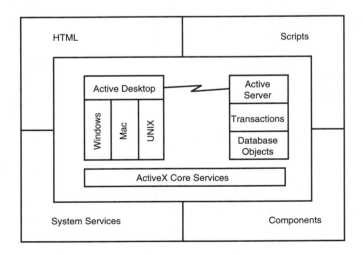

The Active Platform is based on three core technologies:

- **Active Desktop** The Active Desktop (or Active Themes as it will be called in future versions of Windows) is the client-side component. It runs on top of an operating system. Any operating system that hosts the Active Desktop can get all the client-side ActiveX features.

- **Active Server** The Active Server is built on the Microsoft Internet Information Server (IIS) and the Windows operating system. Windows NT is the most suited OS for the Active Server components. The services include transaction services, data access, and more.

- **ActiveX Core Services** ActiveX Core Services include COM, DCOM, MS-RPC, Structured Storage, Registry, ActiveX controls, Monikers, and so on. The major part of the ActiveX Core Services is the ActiveX controls. Now, the ActiveX Core Services are under an open body called the Open Group.

What Is This COM Anyway?

COM is the acronym for Component Object Model. It is a binary specification that describes an infrastructure for component-based system interactions. Because the COM is binary, it is platform and programming language independent. COM is the foundation for the ActiveX technologies and OLE automation that are the foundations of the ActiveX Platform. One of the advantages of the COM specification is that it uses the same model for interobject-process communication—whether the objects are in the same execution space, in the same computer system, or in different systems across a network. It allows for dynamic loading and unloading of components as well as shared memory management between components/objects.

ON THE WEB

http://www.microsoft.com/oledev/olecom/com_modl.htm   A good overview of the COM technology.

http://www.microsoft.com/oledev/olecom/title.htm   The COM reference and related documentation.

It might be drastic to say that all the ActiveX technologies are based on the COM and OLE technologies since the COM is the basis for the ActiveX technology. It is the COM basics that make the ActiveX controls scalable and capable of being distributed on systems across a network.

vtable Indirection

The COM objects can exist anywhere in the network, in the namespace of a program, or in a separate server. From a client program perspective, the COM objects reference as a pointer to a virtual table in the memory called vtables. These vtables contain interface or function pointers to various registered COM objects. Figure 4.2 is a representation of this double indirection.

FIG. 4.2
The COM Virtual Function Table (vtable) double indirection philosophy is that the client programs have the pointer to the virtual function table, which in turn points to specific functions in the COM object.

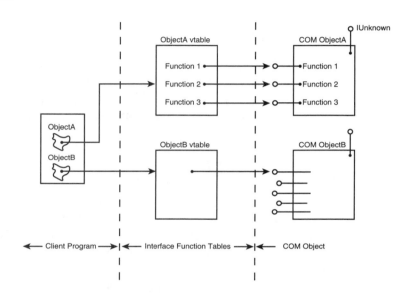

The advantage of the vtable double indirection is that COM objects can be shared between various programs and processes. The COM object is capable of handling the data belonging to each process. Thus, you do not need a separate COM object instance to share the objects, minimizing resource requirements while maintaining data independence.

COM Interfaces

The COM objects interact with the outside world through interfaces. COM interfaces are accesses from the outside world through the interface pointers. Interfaces are a group of functions that can act as properties, methods, or events in the traditional sense. You cannot call a method directly; you can only invoke a method using the interface pointer to that method. All these double indirection and function pointers are handled by the ActiveX code transparently. The program code required to handle all the COM interactions is already built into the developer tools and DLLs. Figure 4.3 shows how a COM object can be represented in a diagram.

FIG. 4.3
Schematic representation of
a COM object shows the
interface pointers and the
`IUnknown` interface.

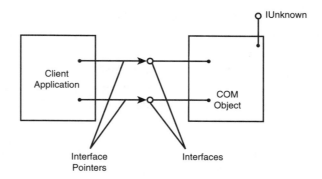

The CLSID

Now that you know there are COM objects registered in local or remote systems, how do you identify them? Even though names would be a good choice, duplicate names will occur frequently so you may be unable to uniquely identify a COM object. COM objects are identified by a 128-bit integer called GUID (Globally Unique Identifier) or UUID (Universally Unique Identifier). The GUIDs are created using the OSF DCE algorithm, which guarantees universal uniqueness (hopefully, aliens on Mars are not using the same algorithm). The GUIDs, which are guaranteed to be unique in space and time, are generated by an algorithm that takes the 48-bit network adapter ID and the current date and time.

N O T E GUIDs are written in hexadecimal digits as [12345678-1234-1234-1234-123456789ABC]. ▓

A CLSID is the GUID for the class in a COM object. You use the CLSID in the Web pages to refer to a COM object. There are also IIDs (Interface Identifiers) to refer to the interfaces for a given COM object.

The *IUnknown* Interface

`IUnknown` actually is the only known COM interface. Conceptually, it is the handle to all the functionalities of the COM object. When an external program or object wants to create a vtable for a COM object, the program invokes the `QueryInterface` function of the `IUnknown` handle. The `QueryInterface` procedure of the `IUnknown` interface takes the name of a function and returns information about whether it supports the function or not. If the COM object supports the requested function, the `QueryInterface` will return the function pointer. Your program will then use this function pointer to call that function. One point to be mentioned is that using the `IUnknown` handle, you can dynamically query the capabilities of a COM object.

Part
I

Ch
4

The IUnknown also contains the AddRef and Release procedures. These control the lifetime of the COM object. AddRef adds the user counter by one and you will use the AddRef procedure to inform the object that you are using the object. When you are done with the object, you should call the Release procedure that will decrement the usage counter in the COM object. When the counter is zero, the object can be safely unloaded from the system, if required. This reference counting technique is called *life-cycle encapsulation* in the COM specification.

NOTE For those technically minded folks, the UUID or GUID for the IUnknown interface is [00000000-0000-0000-C000-000000000046].

Data Marshalling and Remoting of COM Objects

COM objects can live anywhere in the network and they can be activated with proper registration and security. The buzzword for this concept is *location transparency*. There are three scenarios:

- **In-process COM object**   The COM object is in the namespace of the calling process.
- **Out-of-process COM object**   The COM object is in the same system as the client but will be running as a separate process.
- **Remote COM object**   The COM object is within the client's reach in the network.

Data marshalling is the name given to pass the data between the client and the COM object. The marshalling functions build the required data structures and data packets to COM objects as they unpack the data packets received from objects. The data packets contain the information necessary to interact with the COM object. In-process data marshalling is simple and is usually memory mapped. There is no need to resort to any special data marshalling schemes other than the vtable, interface pointers, and so on.

Out-of-process data marshalling is done using lightweight RPC; remote marshalling requires true RPC communication. In both cases, the client will access the local object proxy or the remote object proxy. The proxy will interact with the COM stub using the RPC method.

Proxy and Stub

The proxy for a COM object resides in the local program namespace. When an interface is called, the proxy packages the required information and sends it to the stub that resides in the system where the COM object is. The stub receives the data packet, unpacks it, and calls the COM object with the unpacked data.

When the COM object wants to send some information or data to the client, it sends the data to the stub, which packs the data and ships the packet to the proxy. The proxy unpacks the packet and gives the data to the client.

Conceptually, the proxy provides the virtual COM interface pointers and the real COM interface implementations are with the stub. But, to the client and the object, the proxy-stub mechanisms are transparent.

The proxy-stub mechanism enables the COM objects to reside anywhere. On local machines, the proxy-stub communication is through LRPC and on the network through DCE RPC.

More ActiveX

Now you'll concentrate on the ActiveX objects and tools. Figure 4.4 shows the ActiveX framework in the Windows environment.

FIG. 4.4
The ActiveX framework for the Windows environment is layers of objects as the ActiveX containers and ActiveX controls over the COM and the operating system layers.

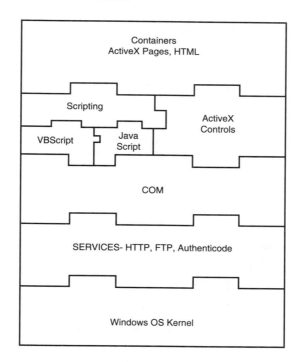

Part
I
Ch
4

The ActiveX containers, like the HTML Viewer, embed the ActiveX controls. The COM services and finally the Windows OS kernel support the framework with the required facilities. The three main pieces of the ActiveX architecture are ActiveX documents, ActiveX controls, and ActiveX scripting.

Figure 4.5 shows the interaction between these pieces hierarchically and also as COM objects with interfaces.

FIG. 4.5

The ActiveX architecture hierarchy is a set of interacting COM objects.

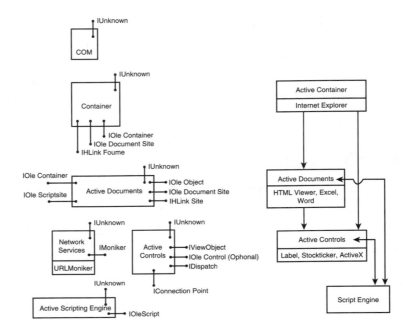

N O T E   To put COM and ActiveX in perspective, ActiveX controls are lightweight COM Objects that are reusable and programmable at the HTML level. ■

ActiveX Containers

An ActiveX container is the controlling application, usually the Internet Explorer. It can also be a Web browser object in your Visual Basic application.

From a COM implementation point of view, the container must support the IOleContainer, IOleDocumentSite, and the IHLinkFrame interfaces. The IOleDocumentSite interface will interact with the embedded document or objects.

The ActiveX container can also be viewed as an ActiveX document server because it acts as a container for multiple documents and objects. The ActiveX container offers full-fledged support to the application that creates and manipulates the object. For example an embedded object with the .DOC extension, when activated, will launch the WORD.EXE application and give control to the application. Objects with .VBD extension (Visual Basic Document) will involve the VB5_XXX.DLL or VB5_XXX.EXE application.

ActiveX Documents

ActiveX documents are actually objects that can be browsed and edited in-place by the applications. ActiveX documents can also be a collection inside another document, like the Microsoft Binder.

From a COM implemetation point of view, the ActiveX documents should support the IUnknown, IOleObject, IOleDocument, and IHLinkSite interfaces. The IOleContainer interface will connect with the IOleContainer interface of the document container and the IOleScript interface will connect with the IOleScript of the scripting engine.

ActiveX Controls

An ActiveX control is an object that can be embedded in an ActiveX container. It is activated by the container and is not a freestanding object. It requires the context of the container to function. ActiveX controls are not limited to Web applications. They can be embedded in traditional applications developed by the C, BASIC, or Pascal languages.

An ActiveX control is COM object with the IUnknown interface and should export the DLLRegisterServer and DLLUnRegisterServer procedures. The properties, methods, and events it supports will be exposed via the IUnknown interface. The parent ActiveX document can control the ActiveX control via scripting.

Part

I

Ch

4

N O T E ActiveX controls are the updated versions of the OLE controls. For those who are familiar with older OLE controls, the main differences are

- The ActiveX controls require fewer interfaces than older OLE controls.
- They are always in-place activated.
- They can be windowless controls.

ActiveX Scripting

ActiveX controls expose their properties, events, and methods to the container. Dynamic manipulation of these is done by ActiveX scripting. The scripting languages can be VBScript or JavaScript.

Scripting Object Model

Scripts are added to the HTML page using the <SCRIPT> tag. The general usage of the <SCRIPT> tag is as follows:

```
<SCRIPT language="VBScript/JavaScript">
...Script Statements ...
 </SCRIPT>
```

The scripting language can be VBScript or JavaScript—you cannot mix the languages. The scripts can be part of the <OBJECT> tag also. A full example of a script is as shown in Listing 4.1.

Listing 4.1   Script Example

```
<HTML>
<HEAD>
<TITLE>New Page</TITLE>
</HEAD>
<BODY>
    <OBJECT ID="ComboBox1" WIDTH=120 HEIGHT=30
 CLASSID="CLSID:8BD21D30-EC42-11CE-9E0D-00AA006002F3">
    <PARAM NAME="VariousPropertyBits" VALUE="746604571">
    <PARAM NAME="DisplayStyle" VALUE="3">
    <PARAM NAME="Size" VALUE="2540;635">
    <PARAM NAME="MatchEntry" VALUE="1">
    <PARAM NAME="ShowDropButtonWhen" VALUE="2">
    <PARAM NAME="FontCharSet" VALUE="0">
    <PARAM NAME="FontPitchAndFamily" VALUE="2">
</OBJECT>
    <SCRIPT LANGUAGE="VBScript">
<!--
Sub cmdAddComboBoxItem_Click()
ComboBox1.AddItem("Another Item ")
end sub
-->
    </SCRIPT>
    <OBJECT ID="cmdAddComboBoxItem" WIDTH=120 HEIGHT=40
     CLASSID="CLSID:D7053240-CE69-11CD-A777-00DD01143C57">
        <PARAM NAME="Caption" VALUE="Add Item">
        <PARAM NAME="Size" VALUE="2540;847">
        <PARAM NAME="FontCharSet" VALUE="0">
        <PARAM NAME="FontPitchAndFamily" VALUE="2">
        <PARAM NAME="ParagraphAlign" VALUE="3">
    </OBJECT>
</BODY>
</HTML>
```

The built-in objects accessible through the ActiveX script are Anchor, Document, Element, Frame, Form, History, Link, Location, Navigator, Script, and Window. The Window is the top-level object that contains Frame, History, Navigator, Location, Script, and Document objects. The next level is the Document object that contains Links, Anchors, and Form objects. The Form object is the most elemental built-in object in the hierarchy. The Form object contains the Element object. Actually, the Element objects are the ActiveX controls in the form.

Creating ActiveX Controls

You can develop ActiveX control using the Microsoft Foundation Classes (MFC) using C++ and distributing the DLLs. To create an ActiveX using the MFC/C++, you will first use the AppWizard to create an ActiveX control project. Then you will proceed to add properties, methods, and events to your control using the visual wizards and adding C++ code as required. The end user will need the MFC4x.DLL, as well as your control DLL, to run your ActiveX control.

> **N O T E** Because the MFC developed controls require the MFC4x.DLL to run, you should think about distributing the MFC runtime DLLs. They are approximately 1M in size. Internet Explorer 3.0 and Windows NT 4.0 ship with the MFC Version 4.2 DLLs. If you develop your controls with VC++ 4.2, your users need not download the DLLs. If you do need other versions or even the 4.2 DLLs, use the cab file at **http://www.microsoft.com/visualc/download/mfc42cam.htm**. It takes about five minutes to download this compressed file with a 28.8Kbps modem. ∎

A second method for creating ActiveX controls is to use the ActiveX Template Library (ATL) that will generate an .OCX file the end user can download. On a technical level, the ActiveX Template Library is a set of C++ template classes for COM object development. The current version is ATL 2.0. More information is available at the URL **http:// www.microsoft.com/visualc/prodinfo/atlhowto.htm**.

The third method for creating ActiveX controls is to create, customize, or assemble an ActiveX control using the Visual Basic Control Creation Edition.

Part

I

Ch

4

ActiveX and Existing OLE Controls

The new ActiveX controls are optimized for code size and downloading time. The older OLE controls were implemented with all the mandatory interfaces and possibly contain things, like property pages, which are not required. They will work fine in the ActiveX environment but will be bulkier. Actually, with respect to OLE and older controls, there are three types of ActiveX controls—the older OLE controls that can be used across the intranets and Internets, the true ActiveX controls that function similar to the older desktop OLE controls, and the Internet-specific ActiveX controls which have new functionality as the Stock Ticker Control, News Reader, and so on.

Internet-Abling Currently Available OLE Controls

To make the existing controls Internet-friendly, Microsoft suggests the following tips:

- Most of the users will be using the controls over low transmission bandwidth medium. So be asynchronous and try to download code and properties in the background.

- Don't block other programs.

- Become user-interface active as quickly as possible.

- Be efficient.

- Keep code size small.

- Keep persistent data storage to a minimum. Store large BLOBs of data (graphics or audio or video) only if necessary. If large data storage is required, you should search for alternate methods.

- And always communicate delays and progress to the user.

Other Object Technologies

Even though we are deeply into ActiveX and related technologies, we should not forget that there are other competing equal or more powerful object-oriented technologies available. CORBA and IIOP are two of the main technologies which parallel the ActiveX capabilities.

Another recent development is JavaBeans from Sun. The good news is that JavaBeans includes an ActiveX bridge that will act as an ActiveX component with JavaBeans events and properties mapped as COM interfaces, as shown in Figure 4.6.

Using JavaBeans you could interact with other object systems from your ActiveX world.

FIG. 4.6
ActiveX Bridge for JavaBeans
enables the COM world to
interface with JavaBeans
components.

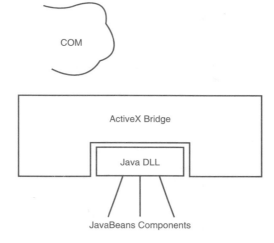

ActiveX Technology

CHAPTER 5

Understanding Authentication and Security

In consumer goods, one way a buyer can access a product's quality is by looking at who made the product. Of course, the term quality has a lot of different features when applied to different types of goods. Goods, such as Hewlett Packard laser printers, Sony TVs, or Panasonic telephones and answering machines, are bought by people for their reliability, for the support received in case something goes wrong, and for their utility values.

The code signing technology from Microsoft, called Authenticode, is the electronic equivalent of labeling. Microsoft positions the Authenticode as "digital shrink-wrap for the Internet software."

Security and Internet Explorer 3.0

You learn about the High, Medium, and None security options and their implications on the execution of components downloaded from the Web.

Inner workings of the Authenticode

The Authenticode technology is built upon the accepted cryptography algorithms and standards including X.509 and PKCS #10 certificates request.

Steps to sign your components

You will gain a good understanding about the Authenticode process from applying for a developer certificate to signing your components with this certificate.

Are there any guidelines?

There are certain guidelines to be followed when you use the Authenticode technology with your components including the trademark reference and symbol and the graphic usage.

The software authentication is similar to the labeling in concept. The software makers label their software components with a digital signature that has the developer's digital ID or digital certificate. This digital signature is tamper-proof and very difficult to duplicate. (It is believed that a 1,024-bit key will take a lot of effort to break.) The electronic label not only identifies the component maker but also verifies that the software is not tampered with after it has left the "docks."

The Microsoft Authenticode works with the Internet Explorer 3.0 and later versions. The technology can apply to ActiveX controls, plug-in components, dynamic-link libraries (DLLs), or Java applets. ■

What Authentication Can and Cannot Do

Now, a legitimate question to ask is: Why do you need this designer or brand name software? Why can't you use generic software? More importantly, what do these schemes give us?

The short answer is authenticity, accountability, integrity, and a tamper-proof seal.

The long answer is that it offers a level of protection to your system from viruses, Trojan horses, and other malicious pieces of software.

NOTE Trojan horses are malicious codes that lie masqueraded in a normal program. For example, a cracker can add code to delete all your files when you press a Next Page command button in an ActiveX control. ■

If you start downloading software with reckless abandon and running it as if there were no tomorrow, you will end up with components that delete files in your hard disk or render your data files useless. Anyone who has a lot of work stored in a computer is vulnerable to destruction. Another threat to your data is the publication of personal data, such as credit card numbers that can lead directly to monetary loss.

On a corporate level, an efficient virus can bring down an entire business and damage can be in the millions of dollars. Another area is espionage, where the software could start sending company secrets to its competitors.

Going back to the previous question, the authentication scheme and code signing do not guarantee protection from any of the above. It is a foolproof system of identifying the software or component maker. After you download a component, the browser will call Windows CryptoAPI to verify the signature.

If the code is not signed, it will tell you so.

If the signature is invalid or is revoked, it will let you know.

If it finds a valid signature, it will give you the component developer's name and the certifying authority.

Whether you want to run the component or not is up to you. Note the phrase, "a level of protection." The Authenticode schemes take the anonymity out of the security equation. You will know for sure who created the component if it is digitally signed. If not, you will know that the component is unsigned. Considering your experience with the certifying authority and the component maker, you can decide either to reject the component or download and run it.

The identity provides trust and accountability. Also, as the signing process keeps a digital fingerprint of the component, digitally signed software is tamper-proof. If somebody modifies the software, by including a Trojan horse code for example, the fingerprint will be different. This will alert the user that the software, even if signed by Microsoft, does not pass the fingerprint test. The user will be better off either downloading the software again or abandoning the Web page. It is also a good practice to report this kind of error to the company who signed the code.

CAUTION

The Authenticode is not a full security solution.

The Authenticode technology does not assure a bug-free product.

The Authenticode technology is not a replacement for anti-virus software or a copy-protection scheme.

It only provides the identity of the component developer and assures the component's integrity across the network.

Part
II

Ch
5

Security Options in Internet Explorer

Now you can see how this is achieved from a user perspective. The Microsoft Internet Explorer (version 3.0 and above) has configurable security settings. Figure 5.1 shows the Security Property Page for the Internet Explorer 3.0 with the various options. You can get to the Options property pages from the View-Options-Security choice in the Internet Explorer 3.0. The emphasis here is the Active Content frame.

FIG. 5.1
There are settings to control certificates as well as ActiveX controls. Take a look at each one of them.

Certificate List

The browser can keep a list of trusted certificates—personal, Web site, or publishers—which can be given security clearance to be downloaded and run as shown in Figure 5.2. Once an entity is in this list, the browser will not query you as to whether to download or run components signed by these entities.

To activate, choose the View-Options-Security choice in the Internet Explorer 3.0. Then press the Publishers button in the Certificates frame (refer to Figure 5.1) from the Options property pages.

FIG. 5.2
This figure shows the list of certificates you have indicated to be trusted by your browser.

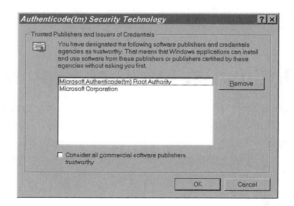

ActiveX Controls' Security

In the Security property page, you can allow or disallow the downloading of ActiveX controls, enable or disable the controls, or run or do not run ActiveX and JavaScripts as shown previously in Figure 5.1.

As a lot of the Web functionality comes from ActiveX controls and scripts, it is a good idea to enable all the preceding settings. You can control how these are downloaded and executed by the safety level page, as shown in Figure 5.3. You can get to this list by pressing the Safety Level button in the Active content frame (refer to Figure 5.1) from the Options property pages, from the View-Options-Security choice in Internet Explorer 3.0.

FIG. 5.3
This is the list of Active Content Safety Level Options when downloading components from the Web.

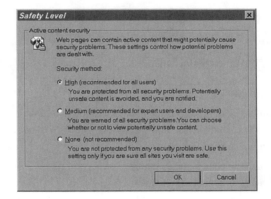

The three Safety Level Options settings for handling the active content to be downloaded from the Web are None, Medium, and High. As you can see in Figure 5.3, High is suitable for normal users. With the High setting, when the browser encounters an unsigned control or if the entity who signed the control is not in the list, the browser will notify you that an unsafe control has been encountered. It will not give you a chance to download or execute that control or component. See Figure 5.4 for the message.

FIG. 5.4
This Message is displayed when Internet Explorer encounters an unsigned control with the Safety Level set on High.

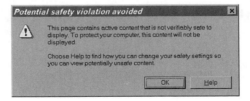

Part
II

Ch
5

In case of Medium security, the system will notify you (as shown in Figure 5.5) if an un-signed component or a component that is signed by an entity is not in the list. Unlike the high option, you can choose to download and run the component.

FIG. 5.5

Here is the Information Message and options Medium Safety Level and an unsigned control.

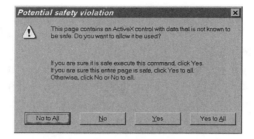

If the safety level is None, the browser will download and run the component. This option should be used with care and is recommended only for developers.

For Corporate Administrators

Using the Microsoft Internet Explorer Administrator's Kit (IEAK), administrators can configure the security level to control the code download across the enterprise. The administrator can also prevent a user from changing this setting.

With the current level of security across the Internet, a good setting is to not allow any unsigned component to download. In the case of signed components, a default list of trusted vendors should be used for automatic download, and if the component maker is not on the list, the user can choose on a case-by-case basis.

In the future, IEAK will have the capability to block any download from distrusted or unsigned sources.

Anatomy of a Certificate

When the browser encounters a new component signed by an entity not in the list, and the safety level option is Medium, the browser will display the certificate as shown in Figure 5.6. You can see the link for details of the component as well as the Certifying Authority's Web site.

The certificate has the component name with a link to an URL, which contains more de-tails about the control. Also shown is the name of the developer, commercial or individual, and finally, the certifying authority and a link to the CA Web site.

The Internet Explorer also gives you choices (via check boxes) to add the publisher or the certifying authority to the trusted list.

FIG. 5.6
The Component certificate is displayed by Internet Explorer 3.0 when it encounters a signed component.

Exploder Control

The Exploder Control is an ActiveX control developed by Fred McLain and is available at **http://www.halcyon.com/mclain/ActiveX/**. It is labeled as a nonviolent demonstration of the Authenticode security limitations—just because software is signed, that doesn't mean it is safe. This control, when activated, will shut down Windows 95 and turn the power off on computers that have the power conservation or green BIOS capability. Fred McLain has signed the Exploder Control using his individual software publisher certificate.

The Exploder Control could have easily done a dozen things, from deleting all files in the hard disk to corrupting files. This is a control that is properly signed and will pass the Windows trust verification services. On the other hand, it could be a malicious control.

Actually, Fred McLain did a service to all the users by developing this control. The Authenticode technology does not protect the system from malicious programs—it just makes developer anonymity impossible. You will only know from whom the code came. You have the ultimate responsibility to decide whether or not to run the component.

Part
II

Ch
5

How Does It All Work?

The major pieces of the Authenticode are:

1. Certifying Authority
2. Cryptographic Technology
3. `WinVerifyTrust()` calls in the Windows Trust Verification Services

Certifying Authority (CA)

Conceptually, the certifying authorities are the electronic equivalent of the notary public. A certifying authority (CA) is an organization that specializes in providing security services, such as issuing and managing certificates, authenticating identities, checking registrations, handling legal and liability issues for broken security, and so on. The two major CA companies are Verisign and GTE.

> **N O T E**   What happens if the certificate is stolen or a company or individual uses the Authenticode to sign malicious code? The CA will maintain a list of revoked keys. If a certificate or key is stolen, the developer will immediately notify the CA, who will issue another certificate and revoke the original certificate.
>
> A user can periodically refresh a revoked key list to get the current list of revoked keys. As the digital certificate has a site link to get more information, the developer can also display alert messages at their site in case of revoked certificates. ■

Cryptography Technology Used in Authenticode

X.509 Certificate   The X.509v3 is data structure and standard for the binary representation of a digital certificate. It is an OSI/ITU-T standard. The X.509 certificate includes information, such as the public key of the developer's name, issuer, the serial number, the lifetime (start and end date) of the certificate, the algorithm, parameters for the signature and keys, and so on. This standard is officially called CCITT, Recommendation X.509, Directory-Authentication Framework.

PKCS#7—Cryptographic Message Syntax Standard   This standard contains the representation of a signature block to data. This standard is officially called PKCS #7—Cryptographic Message Syntax Standard.

PKCS#10—Certification Request Syntax Standard   This standard details an "electronic form" to request a certificate from a certifying authority. The request includes information, such as the requester's public key, signature algorithm ID, version, requester's distinguished name, and so on. The data packet is signed using the requester's private key. The CA will transform the request to a X.509 certificate after proper verifications and will send the certificate to the requester.

Aren't There Export Controls on Encrypted Software?

Yes. The United States government is very strict about the key lengths and algorithms when it comes to exporting secure software products.

In the case of Authenticode, this is not a problem, as you are only encrypting the hash or digest of the software. The U.S. government allows the export of software that contains encrypted signatures. There are no export controls for encrypted message digests.

RSA Encryption Standard   The RSA standard MD5 algorithm generates a one-way hash or message digest for a binary stream. The hash is also called a message authentication code, or MAC. The digest has the property to be unique for a binary stream, so a generated digest is a signature for the component. If the signature does not match with the component, it is sure that the component byte stream is not the same.

WinVerifyTrust() Function

The `WinVerifyTrust()` API is the Windows call to ascertain the subject's trustworthiness. In this case, the call will first check for the PKCS #7 data structure in the signature block. If it finds the data structure, it will extract the X.509 certificate block and verify the certificate and then the software digest, for any tampering. This is contained in the WINTRUST.DLL file.

N O T E   The Windows system now has more support for cryptography. The Microsoft CryptoAPI is a set of routines to handle cryptographic functions, such as encoding, certificate authentication, encryption, and the like. It contains a rich set of functions and allows a Cryptographic Service Provider to add cryptographic services. The current version is 2.0. You can find more information on the CryptoAPI at **http://www.microsoft.com/intdev/security/ misf6-f.htm**. ■

The Authenticode Process

Now that you know the pieces, you can see how it all works. First the CA, after verifying the credentials, issues a software publishing certificate (in the X.509v3 format) to the developer. When the component is developed, debugged, and ready for shipping, the developer will produce a fingerprint using the one-way hashing algorithm. The hash is then encrypted using the private key of the developer—effectively signing the software. The signature and the certificate are then appended to the software component in the

PKCS #7 signed data object format. When a user wants to verify the authenticity, the `WinVerifyTrust()` call is made. This call first checks the certificate and then recreates the hash. When the hash is verified, the user is assured that the software is developed by the developer and has not been changed after the developer has signed the component.

Steps to Sign Your Own Components

Figure 5.7 shows the steps in the signing process. The first step is to apply for a software publishing certificate from a CA. Currently, only Verisign is acting as a CA. GTE and other companies are slowly getting into the arena. The CA requires a few pieces of information, including the Dunn & Bradstreet rating for a Class 3 Certificate. During this process, you will have to generate a pair of keys and send the CA a copy of your public key. You should safekeep the private key. For a Class 3 Certificate, the hardware safekeeping is required.

The CA will do credential checking, including a financial verification. After the verification process, and if you meet policy criteria, the CA will issue a software publisher certificate. The certificate will conform to the X.509v3 format.

As a software publisher, you will have to take a pledge that you will take all precautions required to make sure that your code is not malicious.

FIG. 5.7
These are the steps needed to get a software publisher's certificate and to sign components developed by you.

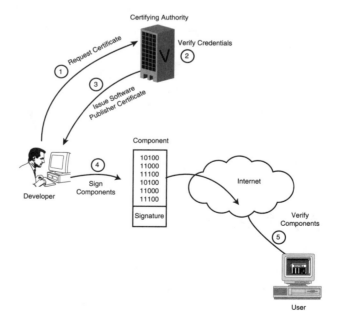

Commercial and Individual Certificates

There are two classes of certificates issued by a certifying authority—Class 3 Commercial Certificates and Class 2 Individual Certificates.

Class 3 Commercial certificates are for companies that develop a lot of controls and involve rigorous identity and financial stability checking by the certifying authority. The commercial certificate holder should have a Dunn & Bradstreet rating, and should maintain their private keys in some hardware form, a PCMCIA device, a BBN SafeKeyper, or a Spyrus EES LYNX Privacy Card, for example.

Class 2 Individual certificates do not require the hardware key storage and the DUNN & BRADSTREET rating. Therefore, the Class 2 certificate has a lesser degree of identity verification and is aimed at individual software publishers.

Verisign charges $400 per year for a Class 3 certificate and $20 per year for a Class 2 certificate.

Once you get the certificate, you can start signing your code using the certificate. The tools for signing the code are available with the ActiveX SDK, which can be downloaded from the Microsoft Web site **http://www.microsoft.com/msdownload/activex.htm**. The ActiveX SDK contains the program SignCode. This program takes the program name, credentials, the privatekeyfile, and so on as input parameters and generates the signed component as output.

Microsoft Authenticode Trademark Usage Guidelines

As you may have guessed by now, the Authenticode is a trademark. As with all trademarks, there are guidelines to properly use the trademark. Microsoft has the guidelines at the Web link **http://www.microsoft.com/intdev/security/authcode/ tmguidline.htm**.

For easy reference, I am including these major points:

DO use Microsoft trademarks in a proper referential manner.

For example, phrases such as "works with," "compatible with," or "for" Microsoft® Authenticode™ technologies are proper.

DO use proper trademark symbols: When you use the Authenticode trademark, be sure to include the following references:

Authenticode™ is a trademark of Microsoft Corporation.

DO use Microsoft trademarks or product names as proper adjectives.

Part
II

Ch
5

Don't use Microsoft trademarks or product names as part of your product name.

Don't use any language that implies Authenticode "certifies" or "verifies" your company, product, or the way in which your product is distributed. Do not use the mark in a manner that suggests that Microsoft is warranting or has tested your product.

Don't use Microsoft trademarks or product names as possessives or in plural forms.

Don't abbreviate.

Don't use Microsoft trademarks or product names with your company name.

Don't create a graphic or design out of the Authenticode trademark and do not include this trademark in any logos. ●

CHAPTER 6

Using Netscape Plug-Ins in Internet Explorer 3.0

Microsoft wants you to use ActiveX. They want you to use Internet Explorer 3.0 and all the related tools. They want you to put ActiveX controls in your Web page. If you are a loyal Internet Explorer user, you're probably really eager to do so, too.

Microsoft isn't stupid, however. They know the trick to making Internet Explorer successful is nabbing all those Netscape Navigator users. Do you think they could do that if they didn't provide some way to hang on to all those plug-ins? Nope. Microsoft knows that. So they made sure that Internet Explorer can use any plug-ins installed on your computer, as well as any plug-ins you might want to install in the future.

Using a plug-in with Internet Explorer is very simple. In reality, you don't have to do much at all. Internet Explorer automatically detects it. You learn more about that in this chapter. For all you loyal Internet Explorer fans, this chapter also introduces you to plug-ins and shows you how to use them in your own Web pages. ■

What is a Netscape plug-in?

Plug-ins are old hats to Netscape users, but they are new to Internet Explorer users.

Downloading and installing Netscape plug-ins

Getting to and installing Netscape plug-ins is like downloading and installing any other program.

Using Netscape plug-ins with Internet Explorer 3.0

You can use plug-ins if you're an Internet Explorer 3.0 user.

Inserting Netscape plug-ins into your Web page

If you want to use plug-ins in your Web page, you need to learn how to insert them.

What Is a Plug-In?

Plug-ins are programs that extend or add features to Netscape and Internet Explorer. These features usually appear as a small window within the Web page (*embedded*); but it can take over the browser's entire window (*full-screen*) or be altogether invisible (*hidden*). Web authors put tags into a Web page that cause the browser to load and use the plug-in within the page. For example, a Web author might put tags into a Web page that embeds a Shockwave video file. Your browser, when seeing this tag, would load the plug-in and insert it in the Web page with the appropriate data file. Thus, you can think of a plug-in as a program that knows how to handle embedded data files, such as images and videos, that the browser doesn't know how to handle on its own.

N O T E You'll find several different plug-ins for each type of file. It's not important that you use a specific plug-in with a specific type of file. For example, if a Web page contains an embedded AVI video, the browser will use any plug-in associated with that type of file. ■

In many ways, plug-ins are similar to ActiveX controls. They add features to Web pages. They are platform specific with a version for each operating system that you may want to use. There are a few differences between plug-ins and ActiveX controls. You have to download and install plug-ins yourself; whereas with ActiveX controls, the browser can automatically download and install a control when needed. Also, plug-ins primarily extend the browser. They allow the browser to handle types of data, such as videos or animations, that the browser can't handle by itself. ActiveX controls, on the other hand, are not really extensions to the browser. They are more like Java applets since their programs are distributed within a Web page.

The chapters in part III, "ActiveX Control and Plug-In Reference," describe a countless number of plug-ins that you can use with Internet Explorer. These chapters also show you how to insert these plug-ins into a Web page. The sections that follow describe some of the types of plug-ins you'll find in these chapters.

Animation

Animation plug-ins include browser extensions that play animations created by a Web author. The author usually purchases an authoring package to create the animation. The viewer, which you install on your computer, is usually free of charge or very inexpensive.

The types of animations you'll see on the Web vary. In some cases, authors use animations as a navigational tool: menus, fly-over help, and so on. Figure 6.1 shows an example of a

Shockwave animation. The graphic in the middle of the page fades in when you load the Web page and each menu item in the center of the page is highlighted as you move the mouse cursor over it. In other cases, authors use animations to jazz up the Web page.

FIG. 6.1
Shockwave is one of the most popular plug-ins on the Internet.

Shockwave plug-in display area

Chapter 16, "Animation Controls," documents the plug-ins that are available. You can use the information in this chapter to download the plug-in for use with other Web pages. You can also use this information to add animation plug-ins to your own Web page.

VRML

VRML (Virtual Reality Modeling Language) allows a Web author to create virtual 3-D worlds. Then, the author distributes those worlds on a Web page. As a user, you view those VRML worlds by using a VRML plug-in. Chapter 17, "VRML Controls," describes the VRML plug-ins that you can use with Internet Explorer 3.0. You'll also find information about building and distributing your own VRML worlds in this chapter.

Conferencing

Conferencing plug-ins, such as IChat, let you hold a chat session right there in the Web browser. You'll also find conferencing plug-ins that rely on other means, however.

Part
II

Ch
6

Chapter 18, "Conferencing Controls," describes the plug-ins you can use in Internet Explorer. Figure 6.2 shows what IChat looks like in the browser window.

FIG. 6.2

Conferencing tools, such as IChat, let you conference within an environment you're already familiar with.

IChat plug-in display area

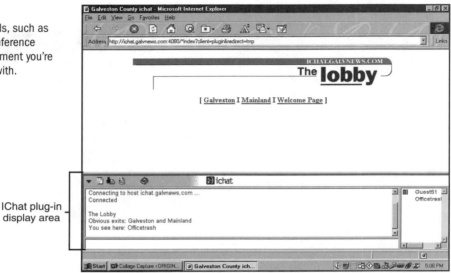

Database

Database plug-ins allow you to query databases over the Web. For example, you can provide hit statistics for your Web site by embedding a database plug-in in a Web page that queries a hit database.

Chapter 14, "Database Controls," describes these types of plug-ins. PowerBuilder Datawindow is a plug-in that lets the user view and navigate a database right on the Web page. Chapter 14 also describes plug-ins that are generally useful for database access, such as Citrix winFrame ICA and Dynamic Cube.

Form Elements

Form elements are data entry fields, buttons, and lists that you can use on the Web page to collect information from the user. Since a plug-in requires a data file from the Web server, you won't find any plug-ins suited to this purpose. Chapter 12, "Form Elements Controls," describes a variety of ActiveX controls you can use for user input, however.

 TIP You can submit ActiveX controls to the server as part of a form. See Chapter 2, "Inserting ActiveX Controls on the Web Page," for more information.

Imaging

Internet Explorer and Netscape directly support most of the popular image formats. They support GIF, JPG, and BMP, for example. However, the Web contains a lot of image files that use formats that Internet Explorer or Netscape does not directly support. PNG (Portable Network Graphics), which is a new graphics format with features similar to GIF, comes to mind.

You can install a plug-in for those types of graphics files that extend the browser so it can display the image in the Web page. A PNG plug-in allows you to view a Web page that contains a PNG image file. When new graphics standards emerge, you will see plug-ins that support those, too.

Chapter 15, "Imaging & Portable Document Controls," describes the imaging plug-ins that you can use with Internet Explorer. This chapter also shows you how to create and distribute great graphics on your own Web pages by using these plug-ins.

Video

Video is one of the biggest uses for plug-ins you will find. There are a number of video formats on the Internet—MOV, AVI, and MPG, for example. Neither Internet Explorer nor Netscape support these video formats directly. In Netscape, you have to use a plug-in to extend the browser so it can play videos. In Internet Explorer, you can either use a plug-in or an ActiveX control for each type of video. Figure 6.3 shows what a video looks like in the browser window.

FIG. 6.3
Sometimes, you will see controls in the plug-in that let you play, pause, stop, or fast-forward the video.

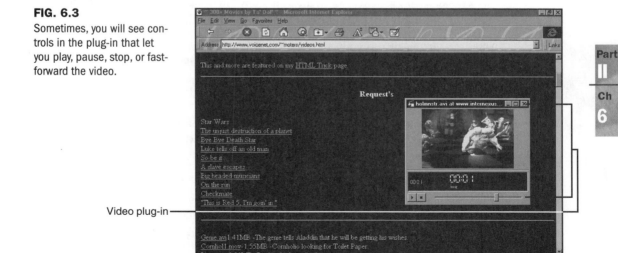

Video plug-in

Part
II

Ch
6

Chapter 20, "Video Controls," describes the video plug-ins available for use with Internet Explorer. If you're interested in distributing videos on your own Web pages, you can get information from this chapter about creating videos and embedding them in the page.

Web Site Navigation

Plug-ins that help the user better navigate your Web site are becoming more common these days. In fact, many of the animation plug-ins, described earlier, can be used to create fancy menus and fly-over help. Other plug-ins make it possible to put menus on the Web page or create pop-up windows.

Chapter 13, "Web Navigation Controls," describes the plug-ins you can use to help your users better navigate your Web site.

Downloading and Installing Plug-Ins

The best place to get for plug-ins is Netscape's Web site (Internet Explorer users should feel guilty). Open **http://www.netscape.com/comprod/products/navigator/version_2.0/plugins/index.html** in your Web browser, and you'll see a list of the plug-in types available. Click one of the links to see all the plug-ins available for that category. You can also find plug-ins at BrowseWatch. Open **http://www.browserwatch.com** in your browser, and click the Plug-In Plaza button.

When you find a plug-in you want, download it into a temporary folder. For example, create a scratch folder on the Windows desktop and download a plug-in into it. After you install the plug-in, simply nuke the scratch folder to clean up the mess.

Once you have downloaded the file, double-click it. The file is almost always an executable file, which will either be a compressed file or a self-installing file:

- If you double-click the file and it extracts all of its contents into the scratch folder, you need to look for a program called Setup.exe (in some cases, Install.exe). Double-click Setup.exe to start the setup program and answer any questions it asks you. If the program asks you for the path in which you want to install the plug-in, accept the default.

- If you double-click the file, you may see the setup program immediately. This is a self-extracting, self-installing compressed file. Again, answer any questions that the setup program asks you, accepting the default path, which is usually the location of your other Netscape plug-ins, even if it lets you change it.

TIP You'll almost always find instructions for downloading and installing a plug-in on the Web page on which you downloaded the plug-in.

Using Plug-Ins with Internet Explorer 3.0

By now, you have to be wondering why you would install a plug-in when you can install a comparable ActiveX control. For example, you can install the Shockwave plug-in as well as the Shockwave ActiveX Control. Why not just install the control? You need the ActiveX control to view Web pages that use it. You also need the plug-in to view Web pages designed for use with Netscape.

In Netscape, if you open a Web page that uses a type of embedded file for which Netscape does not have a plug-in, Netscape will help the user locate and install that plug-in. Internet Explorer does not do this. Figure 6.4 shows you a Web page looks in Internet Explorer that contains an embedded file for which Internet Explorer cannot find a plug-in. Notice how it uses placeholders to represent the missing plug-ins.

FIG. 6.4
Internet Explorer can't find the correct plug-in, so it uses placeholders instead.

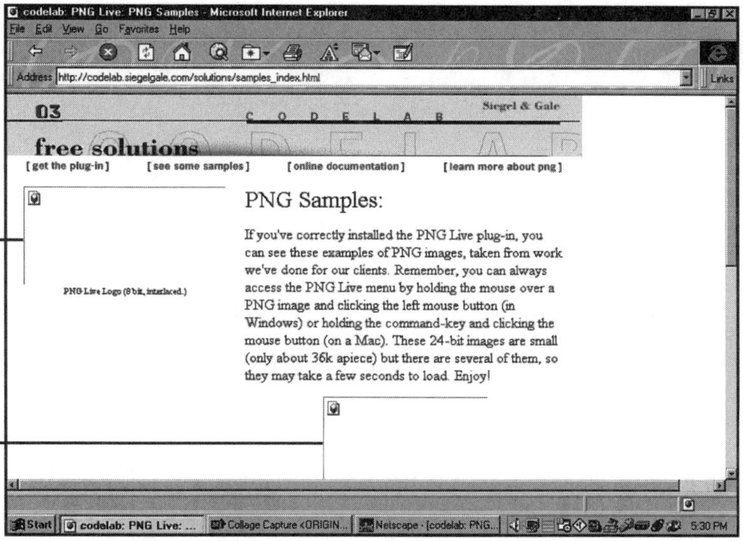

Unknown plug-in ——

Unknown plug-in ——

Using Plug-Ins if You Have Netscape

Netscape comes with many different plug-ins—out of the box. If Netscape is currently installed on your computer, Internet Explorer 3.0 will use those plug-ins without you having to do anything. Internet Explorer 3.0 will also use any plug-ins that you install later using Netscape. You'll typically find these plug-ins under C:\Program Files\Netscape\ Navigator\Program\Plugins.

Table 6.1 describes the plug-ins you'll find after you first install Netscape Navigator 3.0. Live3D is a plug-in that knows how to display VRML worlds. QuickTime is a plug-in that places Apple QuickTime movies, a very popular video format, on the Web. LiveAudio plays a variety of sound formats, including the two most popular formats for Windows: WAV and MID. Lastly, NPAVI32 is a Netscape plug-in that plays the Windows AVI video format.

Table 6.1   Default Netscape Plug-Ins

Name	Description
Live3D	Displays VRML worlds (WRL)
QuickTime	Plays QuickTime movies (MOV)
LiveAudio	Plays sounds by using a variety of formats (AU, AIFF, WAVE, and MIDI)
NPAVI32	Plays AVI videos (AVI)

N O T E   Netscape also installs a default plug-in that handles any embedded objects for which Netscape cannot locate a matching plug-in. Netscape also refers to this as a Null plug-in. ▨

Using Plug-Ins if You Don't Have Netscape

Just because you don't have Netscape, doesn't mean you can't use plug-ins with Internet Explorer. You just need to install those plug-ins in a different folder, that's all. Install them in the plugins folder, that is under the folder in which you have installed Internet Explorer. Typically, that path will be C:\Program Files\Plug!\Microsoft Internet\Plugins. Internet Explorer will then load and use the plug-ins you install when it opens a Web page that refers to them.

Inserting a Plug-In in a Web Page

When you install a Netscape plug-in, it registers itself on your computer as a program that can handle a particular type of file. For example, the CoolTalk plug-in registers itself to handle embedded files with the ICE file extension.

To use a plug-in on your Web page, you create a data file for that plug-in and embed it on the page by using the EMBED tag. When the browser opens the Web page and sees the EMBED tag, it locates the plug-in associated with that data file. Then, it launches the plug-in with the data file. Depending on how the author created the plug-in, it'll either run embedded in the Web page (for instance, LiveVideo), take over the entire browser window (such as PointCast Network), or remain hidden in the background (like LiveAudio).

Using the *EMBED* Tag

The EMBED tag is quite simple to use. It's not nearly as complicated as the OBJECT tag, which you learned about in Chapter 2, "Inserting ActiveX Controls on the Web Page." You don't have to worry about those nasty numbers that identify a control (clsid), for example. To embed a plug-in, you have to know three bits of information:

- The file extension that the plug-in associates with itself on the user's computer. This file extension associates a data file that you embed in the Web page with the plug-in on the user's computer.

- The filename of the data file that you created to use with the plug-in. Most plug-ins require that you provide a data file for that plug-in to play.

- The size of the plug-in as you want it to appear on the Web page. The WIDTH and HEIGHT attributes of the EMBED tag specify the width and height, in pixels, that the browser gives to the plug-in.

Armed with this information, you can embed a data file into the Web page by using the EMBED tag. This tag requires the name of the data file and the size of the area that the browser will use to display the plug-in. For example, the following tag will embed a data file called Vacation.avi with a width of 320 and a height of 200. If the user has installed the LiveAudio plug-in, Netscape will download Vacation.avi and pass it to the plug-in.

```
<EMBED SRC=vacation.avi WIDTH=320 HEIGHT=200>
```

The EMBED tag supports a few more Param tags than given in the previous example. Table 6.2 describes each tag it supports.

Table 6.2 *EMBED* Attributes

Attribute	Description
HEIGHT=*N*	Specifies the height of the plug-in's display area
NAME=*Text*	Provides a name by which to refer to the plug-in
PALETTE=*#rgb*|*#rgb*	Sets the color palette for the foreground and background color

continues

Part
II

Ch
6

Table 6.2 Continued	
Attribute	**Description**
SRC=*URL*	Specifies the URL of the data file
UNITS=PIXELS|EN	Specifies the unit of measurement you are using for HEIGHT and WIDTH. EN is half the point size
WIDTH=*N*	Specifies the width of the plug-in's display area

You can also use custom attributes that are specific to some plug-ins. For example, a video plug-in may need to know if it's to play-back the data file at full speed or half speed. In this case, you might add another attribute to the EMBED tag as in the following example. Note that custom attributes are specific to each plug-in; thus, you need to refer to the plug-in's documentation for more information.

```
<EMBED SRC=vacation.avi WIDTH=320 HEIGHT=200 PLAYBACK=FULL>
```

Supporting Internet Explorer 3.0 and Netscape

Netscape does not directly support ActiveX controls. You can use the NCompass Labs plug-in, as described in Chapter 6, or you can support both ActiveX controls and plug-ins on your Web page. If you're using a Shockwave animation on your Web page, for example, you can insert the ActiveX control on the Web page by using the OBJECT tag. Then, you can sandwich the Shockwave plug-in between the beginning and ending OBJECT tag. Netscape users will use the plug-in, while Internet Explorer users will use the ActiveX control.

In the following example, Internet Explorer 3.0 will use the FutureSplash ActiveX Control, and ignore the EMBED tag, because it supports ActiveX controls. It'll load the control indicated by the CLASSID attribute and set its parameters as defined by each PARAM tag. Since Netscape does not support ActiveX controls, it'll ignore the OBJECT and PARAM tags, while using the EMBED tag to load the FutureSplash plug-in. Notice the custom attributes, LOOP and PLAY, which are specific to the FutureSplash plug-in.

```
<OBJECT ID=mine CLASSID="clsid:D27CDB6E-AE6D-11cf-96B8-444553540000"
        CODEBASE=http://www.myserver.com/fsplash.cab
        HEIGHT=25
        WIDTH=200>
<PARAM NAME=Movie VALUE=mine.spl>
<PARAM NAME=Loop VALUE=True>
<PARAM NAME=Play VALUE=True>
<EMBED SRC=mine.spl HEIGHT=25 WIDTH=200 LOOP=TRUE PLAY=TRUE>
</OBJECT>
```

TIP You can also detect the type of browser being used, and direct the user to a Web page that uses ActiveX controls or Netscape plug-ins.

N O T E In many cases, Internet Explorer users will not get to choose between using an ActiveX control or a Netscape plug-in. Many Web sites check which browser the user is using and directs them to a Web page that uses an ActiveX control for Internet Explorer users or a plug-in for Netscape users. If the user is using Internet Explorer, Internet Explorer automatically downloads and installs the control, if it's not already present. If the user is using Netscape, Netscape helps the user locate and install the plug-in—again, if it's not already present. ■

Part

II

Ch

6

ActiveX and Visual Basic

Microsoft declares the Visual Basic Control Creation Edition to be one of the most significant Internet/intranet products. VBCCE (as it is affectionately called) makes the creation of an ActiveX control easy, especially for Webmasters and content creators. The VBCCE is positioned as a Visual Rapid Application Development tool for creating ActiveX controls. One can always use Visual C++ to create a complex control. To develop a reusable business function ActiveX object that can be embedded into a Web page by assembling a few available ActiveX controls, VBCCE is the preferred choice.

VBCCE is available for downloading from the URL **http://www.microsoft.com/vbasic/**. Microsoft will include VBCCE as a part of the Visual Basic 5.0 family of products.

VBCCE requirements

You will encounter files that consist of the VBCCE product including the main program, help and documentation files, and the minimum system requirements to run the VBCCE program.

Ways of building ActiveX controls using VBCCE

You will learn the three ways to build an ActiveX control by creating a new control from scratch, customizing an existing ActiveX control, and assembling a composite control by combining a set of ActiveX controls.

Elements of the VBCCE system

You will find information on the user interface, the editor, the wizards, and more.

ActiveX control licensing, design guidelines, and steps

You will find valuable information on designing, developing, and deploying ActiveX controls.

VBCCE Functionality in a Nutshell

The focus of VBCCE is on reusability and development speed. The VB IDE with the forms package, intelligent, color-coded syntax, type-ahead editor with syntax reference and object model reference (Microsoft calls this intellisense technology), and object browser is the best in the market. The debugging facilities offered by the IDE are excellent.

For starters, you can create new controls from scratch or customize existing ActiveX controls to fit an application or business problem. However, most of the developers will combine a set of existing ActiveX controls to develop a new ActiveX control module that implements a business function.

You need not be an expert programmer to assemble a set of ActiveX controls to develop a single function using the VBCCE.

In this chapter, you cover the basics of the VBCCE. In-depth coverage requires a full book. This chapter should give you the courage, and possibly the motivation, to delve into the realms of control creation. While downloading the VBCCE from the Web, download the documentation also. The files are CCEDOC01.EXE, CCEDOC02.EXE, CCEDOC03.EXE, CCEDOC04.EXE, CCEDOC05.EXE, CCEDOC06.EXE, and CCEHELP.EXE.

Where and What to Look for in the VB Help Files

The VBCCE help files and manuals contain exhaustive information varying from explaining variables and constants to descriptions on polymorphism, interfaces, type libraries, and GUIDs. You will find detailed information in the following chapters.

- General Principles of Component Design
- Creating an ActiveX Control
- Building ActiveX Controls
- Deploying Controls on the Web

VBCCE Requirements, Control Usage, et al

The VBCCE is a typical Internet product—it is free, it can be downloaded from the URL, and it is a full product. One limitation is that it can be used to create only ActiveX components and not a full application.

To run the VBCCE, you need a computer with the following configuration:

- 486 or higher processor running Windows 95 or Windows NT Workstation version 4.0 or later
- 12M of memory (16M recommended)
- VGA or better yet Super VGA display and card
- A mouse or similar pointing device
- Hard Disk with 20M of free disk space (10M will be freed after installation)

The controls created using the VBCCE are complete ActiveX controls that can be used in any ActiveX-supported environments including the Microsoft Internet Explorer, Netscape Navigator (using the ActiveX plug-in from Ncompass Labs), MS Office 97 components (Word, Excel, Access), and Lotus Notes.

Visual Basic Virtual Machine

The VBCCE does not create a fully compiled code. It actually produces a pCode. This means that to run the controls on a client machine, you need the Visual Basic Virtual Machine.

If a Web client does not have the VBVM in the system, it will be downloaded. This is a one-time event. But it does take time, and every client has to download the VBVM files. Also, whenever newer versions become available, clients should download them. If you are Web mastering an intranet, you should local host the VBVM and the base control DLLs. This allows Web clients to download the infrastructure files quicker over your faster network rather than from the Internet over proxy servers.

The VBCCE comes with an Application Setup Wizard. When you create the deployment version, you have the choice of pointing to your internal server as the source for the VBVM and other required files. The required run time CAB files are listed in Table 7.1.

Table 7.1   VBCCE Controls Client Files

File Name	Description
MSVBVMB5.CAB	Expands to MSVBVM50.DLL—The Visual Basic Virtual Machine required to run the controls created by the VBCCE.
CMCTLB32.CAB	Expands to COMMTB32.DLL—The common controls such as Tab, Toolbar, ProgressBar, StatusBar, TreeView, ListView, Slider, and ImageList.
CMDLGB32.CAB	The Common Dialog controls.

Part

II

Ch

7

Ways of Building an ActiveX Control

There are three ways to build an ActiveX control:

Creating a new control

Customizing an existing ActiveX control

Assembling a composite control by combining a set of ActiveX controls

Creating a New Control from Scratch

This is the least common method of creating an ActiveX control. If possible, you should leave this task to the commercial control developers due to the time and effort required to create a brand new control. There will usually be a control commercially available or a shareware control that does at least part of what you want to do.

On the other hand, if you have a situation where you need to create a brand new control, do not hesitate to create one. You will need to take care of handling painting and displaying your control (called user-drawn control), managing the various states, events, and so on.

Customizing an Existing ActiveX Control

In this case, usually, the painting of the control, its states, and so on, will be handled by the control itself. Your job will first be to set default values for properties, methods, and events. Secondly, you need to come up with a design to expose some of these properties, events, and methods to the control user. You may add some interfaces as well to suit your business needs. This method is called sub-classing existing ActiveX controls.

Assembling a Composite Control by Combining A Set of ActiveX Controls

In this case, you will be aggregating multiple controls, possibly some user input controls, some display controls, and add program logic specific to a particular business process or function. The result is a single control "assembly" with its own interfaces, properties, and methods defined by you.

To cite an example, you can build an expense report control with an aggregation of calendar control for data entry, currency control for dollar entry, and memo control for description entry. Of course, you will add a couple of image controls for your corporate logo and possibly a help control to add some online help. Once this expense report control is developed, many departments can use it to develop their own Web pages for expense reporting. If you add some properties and methods for routing the expense record, depending on the amount and so on, you have a full-fledged ActiveX control "assembly."

Elements of VBCCE

The VBCCE environment is an integrated editor, property inspector, project explorer, object browser, debugger, and wizard for tasks.

Main Window and Features

When you start the VBCCE program, you will be greeted with a screen like the one shown in Figure 7.1. You can either start a new control project or open an existing project. The existing and recent tabs add a nice touch to the interface.

FIG. 7.1
The VBCCE Project Creation Window allows the user to start a new project or open an existing one.

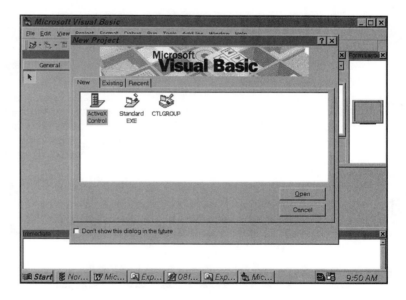

Once you open or create a new project, you will see the VBCCE IDE as displayed in Figure 7.2. As you can see, the IDE is an MDI (Multiple Document Interface).

Part
II

Ch
7

FIG. 7.2
VBCCE IDE shows the
toolbox, project explorer,
properties, and the form
layout windows. The menu
options and the toolbar
provide the interface for
various operations.

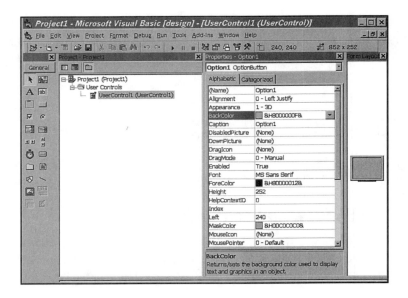

The various elements of the IDE are as follows:

Table 7.2   VBCCE IDE Elements

Element	Description
ToolBox	Contains all the registered controls in the current session that you can use. The toolbox not only contains the built-in common controls as the list box, text box, options, and check box, but you can also add other ActiveX controls. By right-clicking the toolbox, you can customize and organize it.
Project Explorer	The project explorer displays a hierarchical expandable tree of all the objects in your project including resources, code and class modules, user controls, and forms. This helps organization and also allows you to jump directly into any object.
Properties Window	This window displays the properties of the currently selected object. You can change the properties in this window. Notice the alphabetical and categorized views of the properties.
Forms Layout	This window helps you position the form in the control.

Figure 7.3 shows the main control window with the objects in the control.

FIG. 7.3

The Control Window-Object View shows the option buttons enclosed in a Frame, the DriveListBox, and the TextBox in the current project.

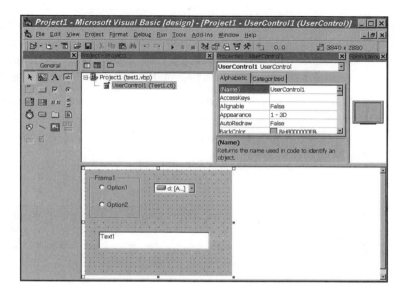

You can either view the object window or the code window. Figure 7.4 shows the code window.

FIG. 7.4

The Control Window-Code View shows the Visual Basic program window for the controls in the current project.

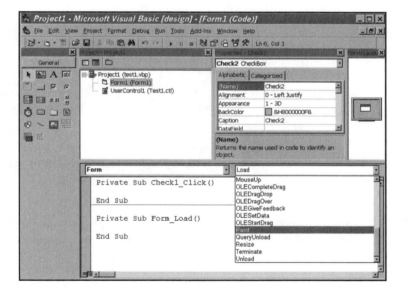

The intellisense technology (on-the-fly syntax and programming assistance and reference) employed in the code editor is worth mentioning more than once. It automatically detects the programming objects as you type and displays a drop-down list of the available properties. The intellisense functionality includes word completion, a quick information tip for a procedure or method name, a pop-up list of properties and methods for any ActiveX control in the project, and a pop-up list of constants for a property.

You will find this technology very useful as you develop programs. In the beginning, it might take a little while to get used to the pop-up property/list windows, but it is worth the effort, especially when you want to develop controls rapidly.

The ActiveX object browser, as shown in Figure 7.5, is another feature helpful for developers.

FIG. 7.5

The ActiveX Object Browser shows the properties and methods of the ActiveX controls installed in the development system with the DBEngine class highlighted.

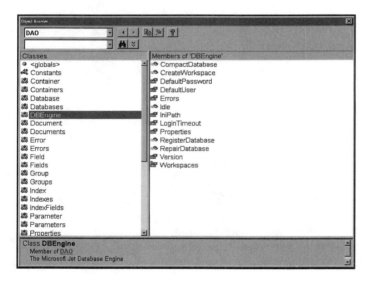

You can see the objects available with their properties, events, and methods. The Object Browser window can help you find and include in your program the right object properties, methods, and events across the various object model libraries installed in your system.

VBCCE has extensive debugging facilities, including a Locals Window with a call stack browser and current variable display, a Watch window, and the Immediate Window.

Task Wizards

The VBCCE comes with a set of task wizards to make control creation and deployment easy. The primary ones are the Setup Wizard, Property Page Wizard, and the ActiveX Control Interface Wizard.

The Setup Wizard   The setup wizard makes it easy to make a deployment configuration. This wizard runs through the project file and makes a dependency INF file. It then creates the CAB files with the required files, OCXs, and so on. An important note is that the downloading of the dependent files is done only on an as-needed basis when the client invokes your control. The loader will look at the INF file and the installed components in the client system. It will then download the files that are not in the client system and run your control.

The Property Page Wizard   This wizard enables you to add property pages to your control. Users will invoke this page at design time by clicking the right mouse button. This allows user customization capability to your control. The property page can also include a preview of your controls after the various properties are set. This preview gives your users valuable feedback as it designs the Web pages using your control.

The ActiveX Control Interface Wizard   This wizard helps expose the methods, events, and properties to the control user. You should run this wizard after you have placed all the controls. The wizard will examine all the controls in the project and list all the properties, events, and methods. You can then select the ones you want to expose in your control. Once you have selected the list, the wizard will generate stubs for procedures and functions.

ActiveX Controls Licensing

Now that you are assembling third-party controls to make your own controls, you should be aware of the licensing implications. To use a third-party control during development, you will normally get the Design Time Control. After you have created your control assembly, you will be distributing the runtime of the third-party tools you have used. Usually, the design and runtime are controlled by license files. Some companies give two versions—design time and the runtime version.

ActiveX Component Design Guidelines

Here are some good practices and guidelines to remember when you create your own controls. The Visual Basic Manual contains more detailed information under the Appendix ActiveX Component Standards and Guidelines. Also, you should keep looking for information on good development practices, naming conventions, and so on, in the Web, as well as in books. For your controls to be reusable, first they should be easy to use.

1. Use entire words to name an object.

   There is no need to abbreviate object names. It will create more confusion for the users and even for you. For example, the ActiveX control for an Expense report function is better if called ExpenseReport, rather than ExpRep or EReport.

2. Use mixed case for object names.

   In the preceding example, the name ExpenseReport is more readable than expensereport or Expensereport.

3. Use consistent terminology.

   The ActiveX controls will be used by many people, and you should not expect all of them to be full-fledged computer programmers. In fact, the ActiveX controls should be easily usable by the Webmasters and content developers whose primary competence is the knowledge of business requirements and user interactions. You should use normal names (the names your users will normally use to describe a property, method, or event) for interfaces, properties, and methods. For example, you should name the print method as PrintReport rather than HPRep or some other scheme. Microsoft suggests not using Hungarian notation for ActiveX controls' properties, methods, and events.

4. Use the correct plural for collection class names.

   It is possible that your ActiveX controls will have object collections, such as Line Items in a purchase order or expense lines in an expense report. Call them with the correct, normal grammar, such as LineItems or ExpenseLines.

5. Use Consistent methods names.

   When naming methods, use either the verb/object or the object/verb and keep it consistent. For example, InsertALineItem or DeleteExpenseLine is a good choice.

ActiveX Component Design Steps

This is a good time to iterate the steps you will go through to develop an ActiveX control. These steps are based on recommendations by Microsoft in their manuals. The following steps will help you put all you've seen in this chapter into proper perspective.

- Create a feature list for your control
- Divide the features into logical groups and assign each logical unit to one or more components—most probably the components are third-party ActiveX controls
- Design the GUI form
- Design the interface—properties, methods, and events—you want to expose in your control
- Use VBCCE to create and develop the control project
- Use the ActiveX Interface Wizard to add the interfaces
- Debug and test the control as much as possible
- Use the Setup Wizard to make the deployment Cab files
- Test the installation and running of your control using some sample Web pages
- Identify some beta users and do beta testing including usability testing
- Incorporate the inputs received from the beta testing
- Do final setup CAB file and preshipping testing
- Ship the version to your users
- Start working on the next version

CHAPTER 8

Server-Side ActiveX

Microsoft's ActiveX technology is not limited to the browser clients; its foundations are extended to the Web server, as well. The Active Server consists of the Active Server pages, components, and the scripting (VBScript and JScript) engine. The Active Server operates on Windows NT 4.0 system services and the Internet Information Server (IIS) Web services. You can write server-side scripting, connecting server objects and accessing databases, that outputs HTML code to the client browser. The Active Server's capability varies from simple scripting to enterprise data access and scalable transaction management functions. ■

An overview of the Active Server

For an effective Web application, you need the capability to separate the server processes into components. The Active Server technology, in a broad sense, enables you to develop server-side processing using the ActiveX technologies.

Active Server pages

The Active Server pages are HTML files with an .ASP extension live in the Web server containing ActiveX controls and VBScript or JScript programs to process client requests, interact with databases, and more.

Active Server components

The Active Server components you learn about are ActiveX data objects (ADO), the Advanced Data Connector, the Information Retrieval System, the transaction server, Active Messaging, and ActiveEDI.

Active Server—An Overview

Microsoft's mission statement for the ActiveX Server system (or Active Server, as it is called now) is "to address the development and deployment requirements for robust and scalable line-of-business server applications for the Web and beyond." This sums up the Active Server's capabilities and functionality.

The Active Server architecture supports the component-based scripting and adds data access facilities. It also adds scalability and data concurrency by transaction services. The Active Server components are built on the n-tier client/server application development paradigms.

Active Server Case Study (MSN)

The Microsoft Network (MSN) home page was originally developed using traditional methods—mostly Visual C++ code. It took Microsoft 4-person months to develop the initial working system. At that point, the bottleneck was development and not content.

As the Active Server products began popping up, the developers at Microsoft changed to the Active Server architecture and it took them one-person week to develop the system. Now, it is the graphic designers and Web page HTML authors who take up the time because system development no longer creates a bottleneck. In the process, Microsoft gained a flexible system that is adaptable and upgradable.

As a development time rule-of-thumb, Active Server will take the same amount of design time as traditional methods, but you will be able to code, test, and roll out the Web pages in a fraction of the time taken for traditional Web design models. However, HTML authors and graphic designers should be familiar with HTML, graphic packages like the Photoshop, and, on the programming end, VBScript and JScript. On the configuration end, you should place all Web servers in a remote "Web farm" and replicate the contents from the content master to the Web servers several times a day.

As an additional note, you can do the same thing even if you are a small business, as many of the ISPs offer the Web farm service.

From a Web application, one of the main components is the Active Server pages. The Active Server pages' capabilities are extended by ActiveX Server components—examples are database access, transaction processing, messaging, and so on. Most, if not all, of these extensions are built on the OLE automation. Figure 8.1 shows the hierarchy of the Active Server components.

FIG. 8.1

Active Server building blocks consist of the Active Server pages, HTML code, and the ActiveX components controlled through scripting with the system services such as the network, directory, and security provided by the Windows operating system.

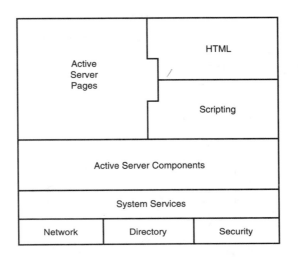

Active Server Pages

In a simplistic sense, Active Server pages (code named "Denali") are nothing but server-based HTML pages with ActiveX controls and VBScript or JavaScript routines to respond to events. The scripts run in the server as opposed to in the client browser. The server pages are files with an .ASP extension. What provides the power to the Active Server pages are the programming objects like server, application, and session. These objects help to coordinate a user's interaction through various HTTP requests. The Active Server pages have the capability to provide security through the generally accepted crypto-graphic techniques, including certificates and key organization.

Figure 8.1 shows a sample interaction between a Web client and a database through an Active Server page. When you look at the information flow (shown in Figure 8.2) and the architectural block diagram (shown in Figure 8.3) you can see the interaction between OLE automation, Active Data Objects (ADO), OLE DB, and ODBC drivers. Figure 8.4 shows the simplified hierarchy of an Active Server page.

FIG. 8.2

The information flow for data access through Active Server pages shows the interface between the Web browser, Active Server, and the database.

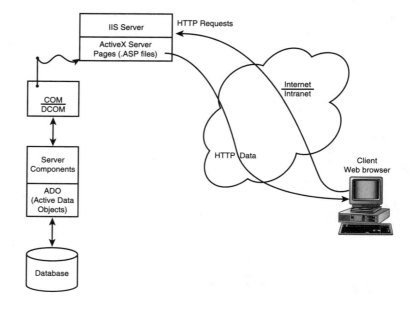

FIG. 8.3

The Active Server Data Access Block Diagram shows the data access through ODBC drivers and OLE DB from IIS and Active pages.

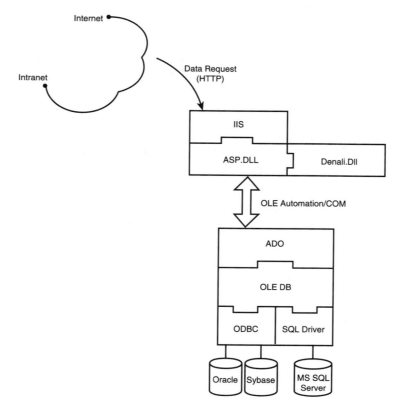

FIG. 8.4
The Active Server pages hierarchy consists of the .ASP files that contain the objects and scripting.

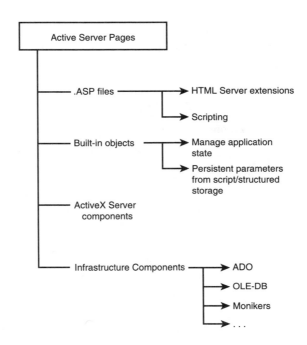

Active Server Page Scripting

Active Server Page scripting is similar to client-side scripting. The language is still VBScript or JavaScript. The Active Server pages have the OnStartPage and OnEndPage events for initialization and termination procedures. You can run a script in any server with the "runat=server" parameter with the script procedure. The built-in objects available in the Active Server Page are: Server, Session, Application, Request, and Response.

Deciding Whether to Use Client-Side or Server-Side Scripting

You should use client-side scripts for error checking, for user interaction, and to connect client-side ActiveX objects. Client-side scripting reduces network traffic (which is a factor for intranet-based applications and is of great importance for Internet-based applications).

Server-side scripting is required when you need to do browser-independent processing or back-end processing like dynamic page generation with the latest data, database access, and so on. Also, with server-side scripting, you can implement security more robustly and possibly more easily. Another reason to go for server-side scripting is to provide access to legacy systems where the server scripting effectively acts as a middleware.

Another point to remember is that usually the server-side scripting will be done by server developers and Webmasters, while client-side scripting will be done by all who are developing Web pages.

Table 8.1 lists the objects and a sample of their properties, events, and methods. This table is by no means meant to be a full reference, but to give you a flavor of what is available with the Active Server page objects.

Table 8.1   Active Server Page Objects

Object	Description
Server	The object to interact with the server. As of now, the Active Server components base set are: advertisement rotator, browser capabilities, database access (ADO), content linking, and file access. These are available from the `Server` object. You would use the script statements like `Server.CreateObject("MSWC.Adrotor")` to create these objects. The Active Server uses OLE automation for implementing many functionalities.
Session	A single browser's interactions viewed from the server. The `Session` object will persist over multiple Web pages and HTTP requests.
Application	Object that can be used at the application level from the server.
Request	Object to get information from the client. The functions include `Request.QueryString`, `Request.Form`, `Request.Cookies`, `Request.ServerVariables`, `Request.ClientCertificate`.
Response	Object to send information to the client browser. For example, `Response.write(<string>)` would output the string to the browser.

Active Server Components

The Active Server components are technically OLE automation servers. They run as an out-of-process COM object on the servers. Since they are COM objects, they can be interfaced using the scripting languages. The Active Server components can live anywhere in the network. The Distributed COM (DCOM) technology provides the location independence for these Active Server components.

The Active Server components make it easy to compartmentalize functionality and distribute it over networks local, intranet or the Internet, depending on the Web applications. In fact, for complex applications, Web servers are backed by many application servers doing indexing, merchant services, messaging, and so on, with the distributed components. You can also have redundant application servers for load balancing and fault tolerance. Systems like merchant servers and search engines should be a 24×7 (or round-the-clock) operation—especially if they are your main business.

IIS Services for the Active Server Framework

In a nutshell, the Microsoft IIS provides the following built-in services under the Active Server framework: Network Services, Active Server Pages, NetShow, FrontPage Services, Internet Services Manager, Index Server, SSL, Crystal Reports, ISAPI, and Data Access. You will recognize many of these services from the block diagrams and descriptions in this chapter. Network services include HTTP, FTP, Gopher, and file protocols. You can extend these services or add a new service.

Microsoft is adding more services to enhance the server support for the intranet Weblications. One such example is the "Viper." In the words of Microsoft, Viper Transaction Server is a "scalable application-partitioning and load-balancing component for flexible deployment and management of Weblications."

What Can Be Done with Active Server?

In the following sections, you will see some of the Active Server component applications. They are all developed as components and can be activated anywhere in your network. As they are scalable, you can combine them in one application server or can have many application servers running the same component with load balancing and possibly content replication.

Data Access Features

One of the good features of the Active Server framework is the data access capabilities. Figure 8.2 showed the various data access layers. Data access is through the ActiveX data objects, or ADO. The ADO helps you write the middle-layer business objects that implement your business rules.

In a sense, ADO objects follow the JDBC and ODBC data abstraction. The first layer ADO object is the connection object, which establishes and manages the interface with a database management system. Once a connection is successfully established, you can open a database and send a query. You can also call a stored procedure. It is always more efficient to use stored procedures rather than raw SQL statements. The recordset object handles the execution and processing of SQL queries, parameters, and so on. The result set is accessed in the script using the field object, which has columns of data. The error object is available to examine and find more details about any errors that occurred during the database interaction.

Which Technology Is Most Suited for Data Access and Publishing?

As you can see, there are many ways of publishing data. How do you decide which one to use? From Microsoft materials, the following guidelines emerge as a first-line strategy:

If you want to quickly publish existing data and don't know HTML, use the dbWeb to provide data access to your users.

If you have existing Access forms, publish them with the Access 97 HTML Form Wizard.

If you want to publish SQL Server data automatically, use SQL Server Web Assistant.

If you want database publishing, the IDC is a suitable approach.

But ...

If you want high-performance dynamic, interactive database Web application, the Active Server Pages are the best choice.

And ...

If you are developing complex n-tier Web applications with sophisticated database interaction, you could be using the Advanced Data Connector, described in the next section.

This gives you a general idea of the positioning of the various database access tools available from Microsoft. The above guidelines are true even if your database is Oracle, Approach, Sybase, or another similar database.

Refer to Part II, Chapter 11, "Publishing Your Database on the Web," for some ideas on publishing your data through the Web.

Advanced Data Connector

The Advanced Data Connector is aimed at complex n-tier Web applications that require cursor-level data manipulation and access to different types of live dynamic data in multiple databases. It is still in preliminary alpha stages. In the words of Microsoft, it "facilitates development of multi-tiered, data-centric applications."

The Advanced Data Connector is the component that you embed in your Web pages. It is a container for data-aware ActiveX controls. The ADC, with the higher level Advanced Data Namespace, manages recordsets that are rows of data. The Advanced Data Namespace manages database connections, SQL, and stored procedures. You can bind many ActiveX controls to one ADC.

The Web database application is developed by connecting these objects, through scripting, in the HTML page. You will be using the normal UI ActiveX controls for user interface.

Information Retrieval System

Another component of the Active Server is the Information Retrieval system. This system is a combination of distributed search servers and index servers. A search server, or a collection of search servers, manages queries from clients and returns the results to clients. The search server is also called the Information Retrieval Web server because it is the HTTP front-end to the client browsers. Indexer servers usually are the back-end processors that index the contents. When you have multiple search servers, the indexes can be updated and kept current by the content replication process. The search and indexing functions can be run on a single machine or distributed across multiple machines dispersed geographically.

Transaction Server

Currently, the transaction server, code-named "Viper," combines the worlds of transaction processing and component development. The transaction server component is an important part of the Active Server model for building mission-critical Internet and intranet servers. The transaction server aims at delivering reliable distribution and execution of the component architecture. For dynamic Web systems, with hundreds of users interacting with online databases, data consistency and reliability is a major issue. For electronic commerce and merchant servers to become successful, load balancing is a required feature.

Transaction servers provide features such as transaction coordination, multithreading, connection and context management, and data consistency.

Active Messaging

Active Messaging is based on the Microsoft Exchange 5.0 and the Internet Information Server 3.0. The Active Messaging components are geared toward e-mail, discussions, team C&S (calendaring and scheduling) including free-time search, information dissemination, and so on. Active Messaging also borders on the groupware and workflow applications like loan processing, sales force automation, calendaring, or help desk and customer service.

N O T E The Active Messaging concepts are pursued by Lotus Notes and Netscape Communicator products, also. Even though they are not called Active Messaging, all these products have OLE capabilities, as well as workflow and messaging functionalities. They can coexist with the Active Server applications as they support the OLE standard. ■

ActiveEDI

ActiveEDI is not only a component, but it is an ActiveX technology-based system that will be of interest to corporate developers. EDI, or Electronic Data Interchange, is business-to-business communication technology. There are many systems available and now you can also use the ActiveX technology to develop EDI systems. The main components of ActiveEDI are the server-manager and the client-manager. The client-manager manages business rule events, data streams, and some GUI. The server-manager takes care of the data stream at the server-side. One innovative approach in the ActiveEDI architecture is the dynamic creation and management of business rules. Business rules can be tied to server or client events and can be developed and stored dynamically. This makes system development and maintenance easier. ActiveEDI also has error objects that can be programmatically manipulated by scripts.

If you are involved with EDI, you should keep an eye on the ActiveEDI as it develops. ●

Java & ActiveX

On first look, Java and ActiveX could seem to be incompatible—Java is a cross-platform language while ActiveX is a Windows-specific technology (at least for now). But this is not true. Java and ActiveX do coexist, and you can choose a strategy which includes both. Having said that, one needs to qualify that statement with a few aspects—some technological, some political, and some marketing.

ActiveX and Java—technology, politics, and marketing

The ActiveX, Java, and Microsoft Java Development Kit (JDK) are in the middle of "100% pure Java initiative" with ActiveX and Java complementing each other.

The Microsoft Java Virtual Machine for Windows

You can interface with ActiveX controls using the Microsoft VM and the Java SDK. The Visual J++ has wizards and other facilities to interface with ActiveX components.

Data Access from Java

You can use the Remote Data Objects (RDO) to access data in servers, and the Data Access Objects (DAO) to access local data in databases from Java programs.

N O T E   The emphasis of this chapter is to give you a perspective and an architectural overview
on interfacing Java with ActiveX. As the discussion roams around the mechanisms of
ActiveX access, some basic Java knowledge is assumed. ■

Technology, Politics, and Marketing

Technologically, ActiveX is based on components with binary interfaces, and Java is a
component-based language (at some level of abstraction). The popular notion is that
ActiveX is a technology while Java is a language. In Microsoft's Java VM implementation,
your Java programs can see ActiveX object's properties, methods, and events. On the
other hand, if you are using Sun's technologies, JavaBeans has an ActiveX bridge through
which you can interact with server-side ActiveX components. The Active Desktop is becoming cross-platform from Mac to UNIX. In the future, your Java programs with embedded ActiveX controls will be able to run on OSs other than Windows.

Politically, it is not all that cozy between the competing technologies. If you mention
Win32 extensions for Java, you will either elicit sharp criticism or a knowing nod, depend-
ing on whom you talk to. JavaSoft's "100% Pure Java" initiative directly counteracts
Microsoft's Java SDK, Win32 extensions for Java, and some of the Java wizards that create
Java code geared specifically to Windows implementation.

In a marketing sense, you need to be involved with Java. You should be developing applications in Java also. Whether you belong to the "100% pure Java" initiative also depends on
the platforms you are developing. As you have come to Chapter 9 in this book, my as-
sumption is that you are catering predominantly to the Windows "crowd." If your intranet
is fully Windows-based PCs, or if your applications are catering to the Microsoft Windows
environment, you can write Java code with ActiveX technology and Win32 extensions. If
your users include other operating systems, your Java applications should use ActiveX
only if the ActiveX desktop is supported in that platform. You should sense the client platform from your Web server and offer alternatative Web pages. For server-side applications, if your platform is Windows NT, you can use all the Win32, COM, ADO, and other
ActiveX technologies from your Java applets. The word is know your users, your applications, and your operating systems (client and server) and then decide accordingly. But
you need not shy away from Java.

The Microsoft Java Virtual Machine for Windows Implementation

First, some theoretical discussion: The Microsoft Java Virtual Machine is implemented as an ActiveX control. From the outside, the Java applet looks like another ActiveX control and, hence, it can be integrated and controlled by scripts and other ActiveX methods. From inside, the Java applet can access other ActiveX controls' properties, methods, and events as it would access any other Java applets. Figure 9.1 shows this concept.

Part

II

Ch

9

FIG. 9.1
The Java applet/bytecode can interact with any ActiveX control through the Microsoft Java VM, which is also an ActiveX control.

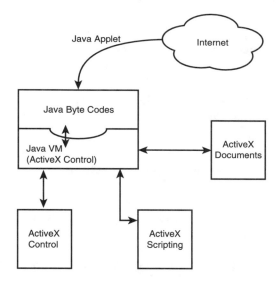

For a Java applet, there is no difference between other Java applets and an ActiveX control. On the other hand, an ActiveX control or a script sees a Java applet as another ActiveX control.

N O T E Even though it is theoretically possible to create an ActiveX control using the Java language, currently it is not easy to produce an ActiveX control using the Visual J++ 1.0 product. With the current version of Visual J++ (1.0), you can create a basic COM object but not a full ActiveX control that can use ActiveX containers as VBCCE or the Control Pad. Hopefully, Microsoft will make the ActiveX control creation as easy as the VBCCE, possibly in the next version of Visual J++. ■

Microsoft SDK for Java

The Java SDK from Microsoft contains tools, utilities, and documentation for writing Java applets with Microsoft Java Virtual Machine, COM, and other Microsoft extensions to the Java class libraries.

You can download the Java SDK, and a lot of other Java-related information, from **http://www.microsoft.com/visualj**. If you are developing database applets, you should download and install the Data Access Objects (DAO), MSSQL, and MSSQLERR help documentation. The Remote Data Objects help is available online for you to read and understand.

The SDK files are in the SDK-JAVA.EXE, and the documentation is in the SDK-DOCS.EXE file. The SDK contains the latest version of the Java Virtual Machine, the Java class library with standard and Microsoft Java class extensions, tools, and utilities. The utilities include the *javatlb* (to convert type library files into Java classes), *jexegen* (to convert Java stand-alone applications to native executable binaries), and c-header files for native code and COM interfaces. The SDK-DOCS.EXE contains the documentation for Java, COM, and so on.

Using ActiveX Controls from Java Applets

To use ActiveX controls in your Java applets, you will need the Java type library compiler. In the Visual J++ development studio, the type library wizard is accessible under the Tools menu as shown in Figure 9.2.

FIG. 9.2
The Java type library wizard, available in the Microsoft Visual J++ (1.0), is used to create a Java type library for ActiveX controls.

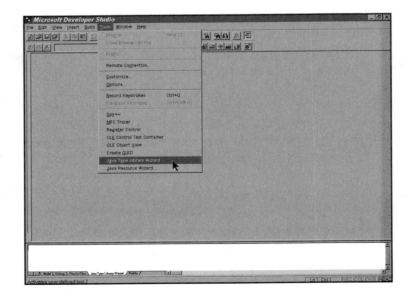

You can select the ActiveX control you want to use from the controls list as shown in Figure 9.3.

FIG. 9.3
Java type library wizard controls list, where you can select an ActiveX control to create the Java type Library files.

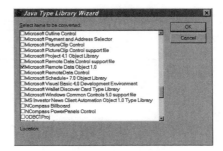

The wizard will generate wrapper classes for the selected ActiveX controls. (It actually uses the `javatlb` program to generate these files.) You will find the class files, as well as a summary .TXT file, in the `%windir%\java\trustlib\<controlname>` sub-directory. In your Java program, you will use the `import <controlname>.*` statement.

Controlling Java Applets from HTML Using Scripting

You can embed an applet in an HTML page and use VBScript or JavaScript to control the applet. The ActiveX runtime for Java makes all the public methods and variables of your embedded Java applets visible to the ActiveX scripting languages.

> **N O T E** Only the public methods and variables in your applet-derived class are visible for scripting. If you want other classes in your applets to be visible for scripting, you should code extra wrapper methods in your applet-derived class. ■

Data Access from Java Applets

Two technologies—Data Access Objects and remote Data Access Objects—are also available from Java language. To use the RDO, you should use the Java type library wizard to generate wrapper classes for the RDO components. It will generate the classes in the **%windir%\java\trustlib\msrdo32** subdirectory. Then you should use the `import msrdo32*.*` statement in your Java programs.

Using RDO from Java Applets The RDO (Remote Data Object) is a very powerful data access tool. It is a thin layer of code over the ODBC API so it can be used to access any database that has ODBC drivers. With RDO, you can develop simple data access applications to complex applications which use cursors and transactions. As the name implies, you are accessing data in server databases.

The only class available for the Remote Data Object is the *rdoEngine* COM class. Figure 9.4 shows the object hierarchy of the *rdoEngine*.

FIG. 9.4
Remote Data Object Hierarchy showing the objects available for programming.

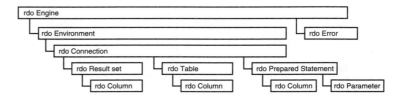

The following list shows all the interfaces available for the *rdoEngine*.

- *rdoEngine*
- *rdoEnvironments*
- *rdoEnvironment*
- *rdoErrors*
- *rdoError*
- *rdoConnections*
- *rdoConnection*
- *rdoResultsets*
- *rdoResultset*
- *rdoTables*
- *rdoTable*
- *rdoPreparedStatements*
- *rdoPreparedStatement*
- *rdoColumns*
- *rdoColumn*
- *rdoParameters*
- *rdoParameter*

Using DAO from Java Applets The DAO (Data Access Object) is used to access local databases in various popular databases including dBase, Access, Excel, Microsoft Jet Database, structured text, and so on.

The top level DAO object is the *DBEngine*, which in turn contains the *workspace* and the *error* object. One *workspace* object can be associated with many databases and many user objects. A database object can contain many *tables*, *resultsets*, and queries.

You can use the DAO data access when you want simple database operations usually in local databases. For such applications, DAO gives you powerful and easy-to-use objects.

The Future of Java and ActiveX

You are seeing the first glimpses of Java and ActiveX integration. You can be assured that Microsoft is working on many aspects of Java to make ActiveX controls use as easy as possible. The Java type library wizard, for example, is a first-generation tool. You will see a lot more development aids in the coming months.

Because the Java Virtual Machine is thread safe and Java itself allows multi-threaded objects, Java is a good language to develop the middle-tier objects for three-tier or n-tier client/server Web applications. In such cases, if your server runs Windows NT with Active Server Pages/IIS 3.0, cross-platform issues do not arise at all. ●

CHAPTER 10

ActiveX and Microsoft Office

One of the greatest challenges for the managers of Web sites is their ability to move valuable content out onto the Web. The novelty of Web sites with a few static images and descriptive HTML pages is over. Users of the Internet now expect real-time data, valuable information, and current reports. After all, a Web site is only as good as its content.

Unfortunately, most of this information can no longer be created by a few HTML programmers copying the company brochure. The information that determines the success of the Web site can only be found in the PCs of the writers, analysts, and others who work with the data on a day to day basis. This information resides in word processors, database applications, spreadsheets, and presentation software.

This leaves the manager of the Web site with no option except to spend time and money having all of this content converted to HTML by hand, right? Wrong.

To address the need of making content of all types easily accessible through the Internet browser, Microsoft has developed a suite of add-ins, browser helper applications, and new document viewing

Convert, edit, and create new HTML documents

Discover the new features and functionality that the Internet Assistant brings toWord.

A wizard that's as quick and easy as pressing a few buttons

The Internet Assistant for Excel will guide you through the steps of placing your spreadsheet into an existing HTML file or creating a new file.

Convert Access objects into HTML documents

The Internet Assistant for Access allows you to move any Access data to a new HTML file without typing in a line of HTML.

A new beta

Internet Assistant for Schedule+ creates a stand-alone HTML file with schedule information for viewing through the Internet.

Converting a PowerPoint presentation to HTML

The Internet Assistant for Power-Point provides a quick and powerful way to get content onto the Web.

Sharing Office documents over the Internet

The Microsoft Office Viewer provides a way to view presentations and documents in their native formats.

technologies. These tools are designed to make the converting of Office documents to HTML format simple, while also allowing for the viewing of almost any content directly through the Web browser.

Microsoft Office Assistants will allow you to convert existing Office documents into Web-ready HTML with the press of a button, while Office viewers, once installed on the client browser, will allow content to be viewed and printed in its native format. And ActiveX documents will allow for the display and editing of Microsoft Office documents (spreadsheets, Word files, and so on) directly through the Web browser. All of these components together (part of ActiveX Internet strategy to make the browser the universal PC interface) will serve to make the publishing and viewing of information over the Internet as simple as a point and click.

For those who are the early users of Microsoft's Office 97, much of the functionality discussed in this chapter will come bundled with the software, but for those who do not upgrade right away, all the tools discussed in this chapter may be downloaded from Microsoft. And for all of you Web site managers out there, you can now breathe a sigh of relief. ■

Internet Assistant for Word

The Internet Assistant for Word is an add-in that allows you to use your existing knowledge of Word to create new HTML documents—as quickly and easily as converting existing Word documents into HTML. It allows you to add HTML features such as hyperlinks, tables, and form fields to your documents. It also provides Word with limited Internet browser capabilities for viewing newly created HTML documents. The Internet Assistant for Word may not be the tool to use if you are trying to create high-graphic, dynamic Web pages. However, it is an extremely effective, efficient, and simple tool to use for creating a new HTML content-intensive document and the conversion of existing Word documents for Web publishing.

Downloading Internet Assistant for Word

Internet Assistant for Word must be downloaded from the Microsoft Web site and installed on your local PC. Microsoft has versions of the Internet Assistant for Word for Windows 95, Windows NT, Windows 3.0, and Macintosh. Not all language versions of Word are currently supported with add-ins and viewers. Therefore, check out the system requirements page when you download. You can download information on these products and more at **http://www.microsoft.com/msdownload/** on Microsoft's Web site.

To download the appropriate version, follow directions from the Microsoft Free Downloads page (see Figure 10.1).

FIG. 10.1
The Microsoft Free Downloads page provides you with instructions on how to download all the Office Assistants and Viewers.

The Office Assistant

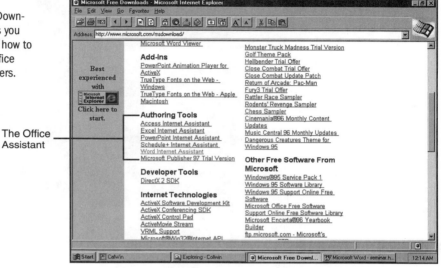

 TIP Save the self-extracting executable files to a temporary folder on your hard drive. After you install each Assistant, you can delete the executable.

Installing Internet Assistant for Word

To use the Internet Assistant for Word, it must first be installed on your PC. To begin the setup process, run the file that you downloaded. This self-extracting executable will unload all the necessary components and lead you through the setup process.

NOTE Continuing the setup process without closing all open applications will prompt a message informing you which applications are still open. You must close all applications to continue with the setup (see Figure 10.2). ■

Once completed, the Internet Assistant for Word allows you to use commands and tools that are built directly into the Word interface to create new HTML documents or to convert existing Word documents into HTML.

FIG. 10.2
It is important to close any other applications before continuing with the setup process.

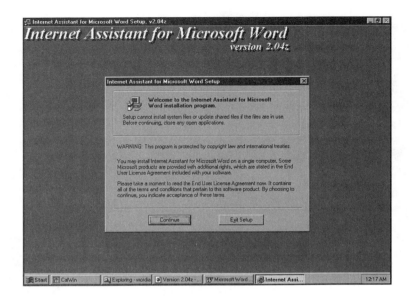

What Is Different in Word

The Internet Assistant interacts with Word by providing additional tools and increased functionality. This is accomplished through the addition of buttons, macros, and templates to your existing Word installation. To see the effects of your Internet Assistant Installation, open up your copy of Word. The immediate change you see is the addition of a button with glasses on it, seen on the left side of the toolbar. The addition of this button indicates that the Internet Assistant has been installed.

This button switches you between Edit View and the newly added Web Browse View as shown in Figure 10.3. Press the button to see the new Web Browse toolbar options (see Figure 10.4).

N O T E Once you are inside the Web Browse View, the image on the button changes from glasses to a pencil. This indicates that you will return to a normal edit mode if you press the button again. ■

Working with Existing Word Documents

Perhaps the single greatest feature of the Internet Assistant for Word is its ability to convert existing Word documents into HTML quickly and easily. In a few simple steps, the Internet Assistant will convert any graphics present in the document and add the HTML tags that most closely match the existing formatting of the document. The resulting document, complete with graphics, tables, bullets, and headings, is ready for movement onto a Web server. All this is done without having to know a single HTML tag.

FIG. 10.3
Once Internet Assistant for Word has been installed, a new button—Web Browse View—will appear on your toolbar.

Web Browse View button

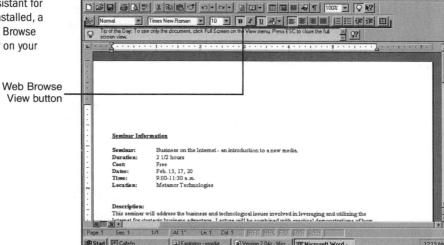

FIG. 10.4
Pressing the Web Browse View button switches you from edit mode to Web Browse mode.

Web browsing buttons

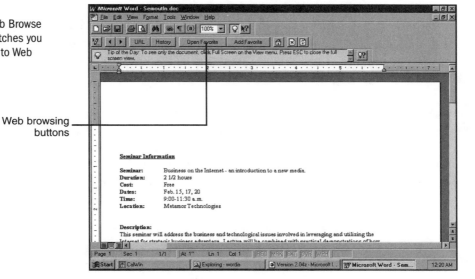

Part
II

Ch
10

Converting Existing Word Documents into HTML   Converting existing Word documents into HTML with the Internet Assistant is as easy as 1-2-3.

1. Open your existing document in Word.

2. Under the **File** menu, select **Save As**.

3. When the Save As dialog box appears, go down to the Save As Type list box, select a type of HTML Document (*.htm), and save the document (as shown in Figure10.5).

N O T E   You have not seen the HTML Document (*.html) file type option before. It was added to Word when the Internet Assistant was installed. ▄

FIG. 10.5

To convert an existing document into HTML, change the Save As Type file to HTML Document.

When the save has completed, you will notice the name of your document has been changed to an .HTM extension.

N O T E   Word gives you the option to save files in the three-character extension of .HTM only. If your content is being published in an environment where four-character extensions are necessary (.HTML), you must first save your file as .HTM and then rename the file to .HTML using File Manager or Explorer. ▄

 T I P   When converting Word documents that have images or graphics, save the resulting .HTM file to an empty directory. When documents are converted to HTML, all images are converted from their native format to .GIF format and saved. When moving your new HTML document to the Web server, you will have to move the .HTM file and all associated .GIF files. By having them all in a clean directory, there will be no confusion as to which graphics are associated with which document.

Viewing HTML Source   Now that your document has been converted into HTML, you can view the HTML codes that the Internet Assistant has added to your document. This is done by selecting HTML Source under the View option on the main toolbar. If you are not familiar with HTML (or even if you are), this page may look very confusing. Fortunately, the Internet Assistant provides a tool that will automatically format the HTML source code to make it a little more understandable.

When viewing your document as a HTML source, you will notice that a new toolbar has appeared. This toolbar, titled HTML, contains two buttons. You will recognize the first button (with the image of a pencil) as the one that will take you back to the edit mode; however, the second button (with the image of writing on it), when pressed, will reformat the HTML in your document. Figure 10.6 shows the HTML source code that was created by converting a Word document with the Internet Assistant.

FIG. 10.6

Viewing the source will ensure that your document was converted into HTML.

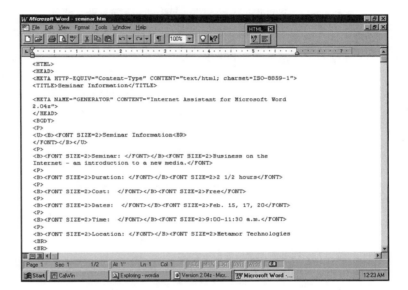

Now, press the Format button to format the source. You will see that the Internet Assistant will highlight and help organize the HTML tags. A dialog box will appear to let you know that the process was successful.

Pressing the button to return you to the edit mode (the button with the pencil) will take you back to your document. Now save and close the document—you are now ready to publish on the Web.

Modifying an HTML Document

This section goes into more detail about the new features and functionality that the Internet Assistant brings to Word. Along with being able to convert existing Word documents into HTML, the Internet Assistant may also be used to edit existing HTML documents or even create new HTML documents.

One of the things that makes the Internet Assistant so easy to use is that HTML pages are built the same way a document is created in Word. For basic HTML page creation, no knowledge of HTML is necessary. Words, tables, and lists are added as they would be for a standard document. The Internet Assistant does the rest.

This section is not designed to be an HTML reference. It will merely give you an overview of the major HTML features that Internet Assistant adds to Word, while providing you with some examples of how to implement some of the more common features.

N O T E   To learn more about HTML tags and uses, search for HTML in your favorite Internet search engine, or check Que's *Special Edition Using HTML*, Third Edition. ■

New Menu Items   Following is a partial listing of the menu items and options that you can use when editing or creating an HTML document with Internet Assistant. If you are planning to use the Internet Assistant to create and modify Web pages, spend some time viewing and learning about all the menu items available (see Table 10.1).

Table 10.1   Menu Options

File	Description
Open URL	Opens remote URL
Browse Web	Switches Word to Web Browse View
HTML Document Info	Provides information on the HTML document
Preview in Browser	Opens the document in a Web browser

Edit	Description
Copy Hyperlink	Copies a hyperlink to the active document to the clipboard

View	Description
Web Browse	Switches Word to Web Browse View
HTML Source	Enables you to view HTML source code

Insert	Description
Hyperlink	Inserts a hyperlink
Horizontal Rule	Inserts a horizontal rule
Marquee	Inserts a marquee
HTML Markup	Inserts new HTML

Format	Description
Background and Links	Modifies properties of background and links
Background Sound	Modifies properties of background sound

Table	Description
Insert Table	Inserts a table
Borders	Sets border properties
Cell Width and Spacing	Sets properties of cell width and spacing
Cell Type	Sets properties of cell type
Align	Sets alignment of table
Caption	Sets caption for table
Background Color	Sets background color of table

Help	Description
Internet Assistant for...	Help file for Internet Assistant

New Toolbar Buttons   Internet Assistant adds several new buttons to the Word toolbars. These new buttons and their functions are described in Table 10.2:

Table 10.2   Word Toolbar Buttons

Button	Name	Function
	Switch to Web	Browse View
	Display/Hide	HTML Tags
	Forward/Back	Navigation
	Preview in Browser	
	Increase/Decrease	Font Size
	Horizontal Rule	
	Insert Picture	

continues

Table 10.2 Continued		
Button	**Name**	**Function**
	Insert Bookmark	
	Add Hyperlink	
	Add/Edit Document	Title

The Forms Toolbar   Forms are often the most difficult part of an HTML document to both build and understand. The Internet Assistant for Word makes the development of forms considerably easier by providing a toolbar with all the standard forms objects. Using this toolbar, you can now build a form without writing a single line of HTML code.

If the Forms toolbar is not visible on your screen, select Toolbars under the View menu option. This will bring up a dialog box listing all the available toolbars. Check the forms box and press OK.

T I P   Right-click a toolbar to display the Toolbar pop-up menu where you can quickly display or hide appropriate toolbars.

N O T E   Remember that designing the form is only half of the work. The front-end form (the interface) is merely a data-collection mechanism for a CGI (Common Gateway Interface), ActiveX component, JavaScript, or VBScript running in the background. Forms that you build with the Internet Assistant will require an application linked to it to perform any sort of function over the Internet or intranet. ■

Selecting the Forms toolbar adds the form creation buttons to your existing toolbars. The Forms toolbar is seen in Figure 10.7, and its functions are listed in Table 10.3.

Table 10.3 Forms Toolbar		
Button	**Name**	**Function**
ab|	Text Form Field	Adds a text box form field
⊠	Check Box Form	Adds a check box form field

Button	Name	Function
	Select List	Adds a select list form field
	Radio Button	Adds a radio button form field
	Hidden Form Field	Adds a hidden form field
	Field Properties	Shows the properties of a selected form field
Submit	Submit Button	Adds a Submit button to the form
Reset	Reset Button	Adds a Reset button to the form
	Form Field Shading	Adds shading to form fields
	Protect Field	Adds protection for the selected field

FIG. 10.7
The Forms toolbar provides
all the form construction
elements you will need.

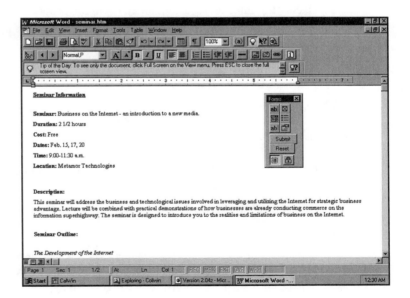

To add form elements to your document, press the appropriate Forms toolbar button and
watch as the elements are added to your document.

Internet Assistant for Excel

The Internet Assistant for Excel is an add-in that allows Excel spreadsheets to be converted into HTML pages and viewed over the Internet. Acting as a "Wizard," the Excel Internet Assistant will guide you through the steps necessary to either create a new HTML file or place your spreadsheet into an existing HTML file.

Downloading the Internet Assistant for Excel

Microsoft Internet Assistant for Excel must be downloaded from the Microsoft Web site and installed on your local PC. The download procedure is the same as the Internet Assistant for Word. The Internet Assistant for Excel should be downloaded and saved on your hard drive. Download information on all of these products can be found at **http://www.microsoft.com/msdownload/** on Microsoft's Web site.

Installing Internet Assistant for Excel

Installing the Internet Assistant for Excel is quick, painless, and will have you publishing your spreadsheet data on the Internet in no time. The installation procedure involves two parts: placing the Internet Assistant for Excel in the proper directory and configuring Excel to recognize the new Assistant Wizard.

Begin the setup process by copying the downloaded file (HTML.XLA) to the Microsoft Excel Library, where it will reside.

N O T E The Excel Library directory is in a different location depending upon which version of Excel you are running. Check your version to see where your Excel Library directory (the location for HTML.XLA) is located. ■

Table 10.4 shows where the Library directory resides within different versions of Excel.

Table 10.4 Location of Library Directory within Excel

Version	Location
Excel 5.0 for Windows	The Library directory sits directly under the Excel directory at C:\EXCEL\LIBRARY.
Excel 5.0 for Macintosh	The Library directory sits directly under the Excel directory at My Computer:Microsoft Excel:Macro Library.
Excel 7.0 and MS Office	The Library directory sits under the MS Office and Excel directories at C:\MSOFFICE\EXCEL\LIBRARY.

Configuring Internet Assistant for Excel

Once you have copied HTML.XLA to the Excel Library directory, you are ready to configure Excel to use the Internet Assistant. From the Tools Menu, select Add-Ins. Check the box titled Internet Assistant Wizard and click OK.

The Internet Assistant for Excel is now configured and ready to help you get your spreadsheet data onto the Web. You can confirm that the process has completed successfully by looking at the Tools menu options. At the bottom of the list you should see a menu item of Internet Assistant Wizard.

Using Internet Assistant for Excel

The Internet Assistant for Excel provides you with a wizard that makes moving Excel spreadsheet data onto the Web as easy as pressing a few buttons. It will automatically convert headings, data and formatting into HTML, and either create a new HTML file, or place your data into an existing HTML file.

The first step to converting Excel data is to open Excel and select the spreadsheet that you want to convert. On the Tools menu, select Internet Assistant Wizard. This will start the wizard, and present you with a dialog box to get you on your way.

The first option that the Internet Assistant Wizard gives you is to select the cell range that you wish to convert. Once you have selected the appropriate cells, click Next.

The Internet Assistant Wizard will then ask you how you want your data converted. Here you have two options. You can have the Internet Assistant create a new HTML file to place the data in, or you can have the data placed into an existing HTML file.

N O T E To place data into an existing HTML file, you need to first edit the destination file. The location for the converted data within the existing HTML file will be determined by placing the tag `<!--##table##-->` in the destination file. If this tag does not exist in the destination HTML file, the Internet Assistant will not be able to insert converted data. ■

Placing Excel Data into a New HTML File If you do not have an existing HTML file for your Excel data, the Internet Assistant will create one for you. By selecting the option to create a new file, the Internet Assistant will create an independent file containing only your spreadsheet data.

To begin this process, select the option to create an independent, ready to view document and press Next (see Figure 10.8).

FIG. 10.8

If you want the Internet Assistant to create a new HTML page for you, select the top option.

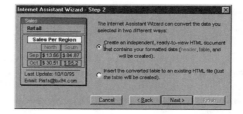

The Internet Assistant now allows you to customize your new HTML page. Fill out the form (as shown in Figure 10.9) with the appropriate information.

FIG. 10.9

The Internet Assistant Wizard lets you customize the look of your page.

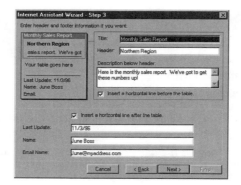

The fields on the form are described in Table 10.5.

Table 10.5   HTML Customization Options

Form Field	Description
Title	Sets the title of the page
Header	Creates a header for the data
Description	Text describing the data
Line Before Table	Places a horizontal line before the data
Line After Table	Places a horizontal line after the data
Last Update	Places a last updated field on the page
Name	Name
E-mail Address	E-mail address

After filling out the appropriate fields, continue by pressing the Next button.

The next option presented involves how much formatting you want the Internet Assistant to do. There are two options: converting as much of the data as possible, and converting only the data (see Figure 10.10).

FIG. 10.10
The Internet Assistant gives you the option of converting all formatting or just the data.

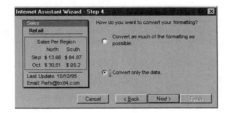

Select an option and press the Next button.

TIP To see what effect the different options will have on the look of your data, select an option and look at the image on the dialog box. The Internet Assistant Wizard will show you what your data will look like.

Next, choose where you want the new HTML file to be saved and press the Finish button.

The process is now complete, and a new HTML file has been created with your data. To view your new file, open it up in your Web browser.

Placing Excel Data in an Existing HTML File   One of the features of the Internet Assistant for Excel is its ability to convert spreadsheet data and place it into an existing HTML file, making it quick and easy to move data onto the Web to supplement existing HTML pages.

To have the Internet Assistant convert your data and place it into an existing HTML file, select Internet Assistant Wizard from the Tools menu. Highlight or type in the cell range that you want to convert and press Next.

Now choose the option to insert the converted table into an existing HTML file and press Next. It is important to remember that you need to make a modification of the destination HTML file for the Internet Assistant to be able to insert your data. The tag `<!--##Table##-->` must be placed in the file where you want your table to be located (see Figure 10.11).

N O T E   Placing an exclamation mark inside an < (`<!`) tells the browser not to display anything inside the arrows. That is why `<!--##table##-->` will not be seen when the page is viewed through a browser. ∎

FIG. 10.11

The tag `<!--##Table##-->` must be placed in the existing HTML file to tell the Internet Assistant where to place the data.

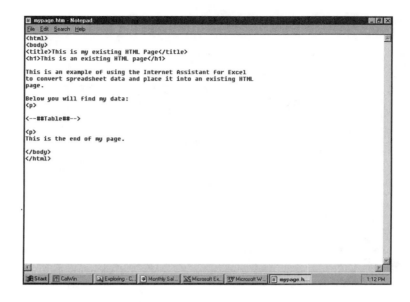

After making sure that you have an HTML file with the tag in it you can select that file for the Internet Wizard to use and press Next (see Figure 10.12).

FIG. 10.12

Make sure that the file that you select has the tag `<!--##Table##-->` in the source.

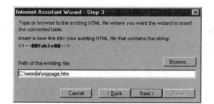

Next, you can choose to have the Internet Assistant convert as much of the formatting as possible, or just the data. Select one of the options, and press the Next button.

The final step is to choose a name to save the newly created HTML file. This file cannot be the same as the source HTML file. Excel will create a new file, merging the source HTML file with the Excel date. Choose a new file name to save this file and press Finish.

Your HTML file is now complete, a combination of text from an existing file and data from your spreadsheet. Open your browser to view your new file (see Figure 10.13.)

FIG. 10.13
You can now view your new file though your browser.

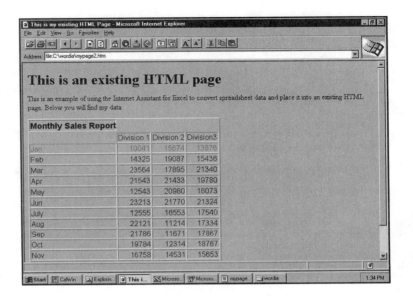

Internet Assistant for Access

The Internet Assistant for Access is an add-in that allows Access objects (tables, queries, form datasheets, and reports) to be converted into HTML documents and viewed over the World Wide Web. Acting as a "Wizard," the Access Internet Assistant will guide you through the steps necessary to create a new HTML file containing your Access data. Templates can even be utilized to give files a common look and feel.

Downloading the Internet Assistant for Access

Microsoft Internet Assistant for Access must be downloaded from the Microsoft Web site and installed on your local PC. The download procedure is the same as that for other Internet Assistants. The Internet Assistant for Access should be downloaded and saved on your hard drive. Download information on all of these products can be found at **http:// www.microsoft.com/msdownload/** on Microsoft's Web site.

Installing the Internet Assistant for Access

The Internet Assistant for Access guides you through the setup process with the help of a setup wizard. To begin the setup, simply run the downloaded executable.

The Install Wizard will copy all the necessary files to your hard drive. When this is completed, you will get a message stating that the install has completed successfully. You are now ready to use the Internet Assistant for Access.

Using the Internet Assistant for Access

Using the Internet Assistant for Access to move converted Access objects, such as tables, queries, form datasheets, or reports, to HTML is extremely easy, thanks to the Wizard that guides you through the process. In a matter of minutes you will be able to move any Access data to a new HTML file without ever typing in a line of HTML.

To begin the process of moving Access data into HTML files, open Access and select the database that you want to work with.

Under the Tools menu, you will see the item Add-ins. Move your mouse over the Add-ins item to see the list of Add-ins that you have installed.

Select Internet Assistant. This will start the Internet Assistant for Microsoft Access Wizard (see Figure 10.14), and present you with an introductory dialog box. Press Next to continue running the Wizard.

FIG. 10.14

The Internet Assistant for Microsoft Access will guide you through the process of converting Access objects into HTML.

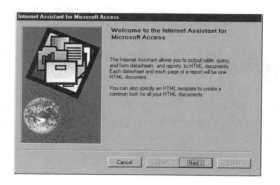

Select the object from the Object Type list box that you want to convert. Then check all the appropriate object names. You can select as many object types and names as you want (see Figure 10.15). When this is completed, press the Next button.

N O T E The Internet Assistant for Access creates a separate HTML file for each object selected, and names the new file as object name .HTM. Selecting multiple objects will result in the creation of multiple new HTML files. Also, only Access data is converted from Access to HTML. Graphs, bitmaps, Microsoft pivot tables, and background images are not converted. ■

Next, you will need to choose whether to use a template for the output of the data. Templates will be discussed later in the chapter. For now, choose not to use a template and press Next (see Figure 10.16).

FIG. 10.15
Select as many objects as
you want to have converted
into HTML.

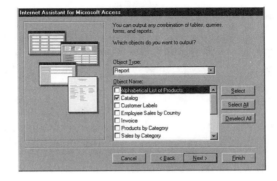

FIG. 10.16
Internet Assistant for Access
gives you the option of
using a template to help
format the HTML page.

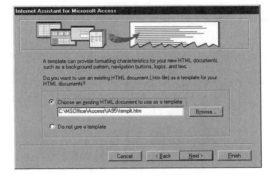

After selecting a directory for Access to place the output HTML files, press the Finish
button.

The Internet Assistant is now complete. Open your browser to take a look at the new
HTML files.

Utilizing Templates   Internet Assistant for Access provides the option of using a template
when converting Access data to HTML. The template essentially provides a format for the
presentation of the data. Data from Access objects can be placed between text on a page
that contains background colors, button bars, and so on.

The Internet Assistant comes with several templates already installed. Two formats of
templates are included—one version for datasheets and one version for reports (templates
with the suffix _R are for reports).

Any .HTML file can be used as a template, and can include items such as background
patterns, graphics, text, and so on. HTML files used as Internet Assistant for Access templates must also have placeholders inserted to identify where data is to be inserted.

Creating Custom Templates   Custom templates can be created with any standard HTML editor. In fact, any HTML file can be turned into a template for the Access Internet Assistant. For any template creation, two versions should be made—one for datasheet views and one for report pages. These templates should have the same name, with the report template having a suffix of _R.

For example, a datasheet template named STUDENTS.HTM should also have a copy for reports called STUDENTS_R.HTM. The report template (STUDENTS_R) will have navigational placeholders inserted to help move between multiple page reports.

Following is a list of Internet Assistant for Access placeholders:

```
<!ACCESSTEMPLATE_TITLE>
```

Access replaces this placeholder with the name of the database object. If this placeholder is omitted, the name of the .HTML file will be used as the title.

```
<!ACCESSTEMPLATE_BODY>
```

Access replaces this placeholder with the output from the query, datasheet, or report. If this placeholder is omitted, Access will replace anything within the <body> tags on the HTML file.

```
<A HREF="<!AccessTemplate_FirstPage">First</A>

<A HREF="<!AccessTemplate_PreviousPage">Previous</A>

<A HREF="<!AccessTemplate_NextPage">Next</A>

<A HREF="<!AccessTemplate_LastPage">Last</A>
```

Access uses these navigational placeholders to link the multiple files created from a multi-page report. If these placeholders are omitted, files created from a multi-page report will not be linked.

Following is a sample of how to use the template placeholders:

```
<HTML>
<TITLE><!ACCESSTEMPLATE_TITLE></TITLE>
<BODY>
Any graphics or text that is to appear before the data is presented.
<P>
<!ACCESSTEMPLATE_BODY>
<P>
Text or graphics that are to appear after the data.
<P>
<A HREF="<!AccessTemplate_FirstPage">First</A>
<A HREF="<!AccessTemplate_PreviousPage">Previous</A>
<A HREF="<!AccessTemplate_NextPage">Next</A>
<A HREF="<!AccessTemplate_LastPage">Last</A>
</BODY>
</HTML>
```

Internet Assistant for Schedule+

Microsoft's Internet Assistant for Schedule+ is a new beta product designed to work as an add-in to Schedule+. The Schedule+ Internet Assistant provides Schedule+ with the ability to export schedule information to an HTML file for viewing through the Internet.

At the time of this writing, the Internet Assistant for Schedule+ is in beta testing, and is only available for Windows 95 and Windows NT 4.0 beta 2 (Intel version only).

Downloading Internet Assistant for Schedule+

Internet Assistant for Schedule+ must be downloaded from the Microsoft Web site and installed on your local PC. The download procedure is the same as that for other Microsoft Internet Assistants. The Internet Assistant for Schedule+ should be downloaded and saved on your hard drive. Download information on all of these products can be found at **http://www.microsoft.com/msdownload/** on Microsoft's Web site.

Part

II

Ch

10

Installing Internet Assistant for Schedule+

To install the Internet Assistant for Schedule+, simply run the downloaded file, SCHIA.EXE. The installation process for Schedule+ is completely automatic, and will require no user input.

Using Internet Assistant for Schedule+

To export schedule information from Schedule+, select the Internet Assistant option found under the File menu. This will bring up the Internet Assistant configuration box. Settings can be modified to customize the resulting HTML file (see Figure 10.7).

FIG. 10.17
The Internet Assistant for Schedule+ can be configured to display schedule information.

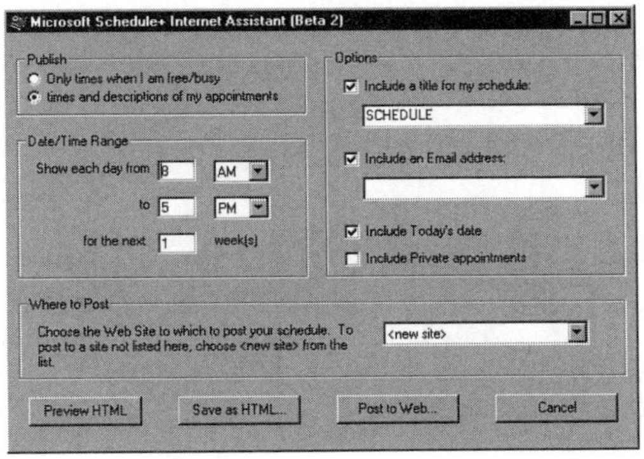

The Publish group gives you two options: the ability to display only schedule times or schedule times and descriptions of appointments.

The Date/Time Range group is used to set the time and date range that will be displayed.

In the Options group, a check box is provided to select if a title should be displayed on the HTML page. A customized title may be added into the text box. A check box also allows for the option of displaying information such as an e-mail address, the current date, and even the listing of private appointments.

The Where to Post group includes a feature that is not currently implemented in this beta of Internet Assistant for Schedule+. When completed, it will provide the functionality of being able to publish schedule information directly to a specific Web site.

Pressing the Preview HTML button will create the HTML file based upon the specification chosen, and launch a local Web browser to display the file.

Pressing the Save as HTML button will save the schedule information to an HTML file.

After you select all the configuration settings and press the Save as HTML button, the Internet Assistant for Schedule+ will create a stand-alone HTML file with schedule information. Open the file in your browser to view your schedule (shown in Figure 10.18).

FIG. 10.18

Internet Assistant for Schedule+ produces an HTML file suitable for viewing on the Internet.

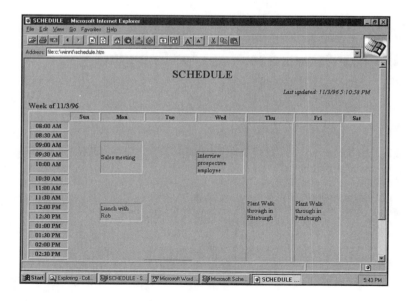

Internet Assistant for PowerPoint

Internet Assistant for PowerPoint is a very powerful tool that will allow you to move full PowerPoint presentations onto the Web without spending hours of image conversion and HTML creation. It also creates full HTML adaptations of PowerPoint presentations while converting them from PowerPoint to HTML in a matter of minutes.

Images in the presentation are converted into either .JPEG or .GIF formats, while HTML pages are created for both the image and notes slides of the presentation. If interactive settings are used in the original creation of the presentation, graphical imagemaps are even created automatically.

Downloading Internet Assistant for PowerPoint

The Internet Assistant for PowerPoint must be downloaded from the Microsoft Web site and installed on your local PC. The download procedure is the same as that for other Internet Assistants. The Internet Assistant for PowerPoint should be downloaded and saved on your hard drive. Download information on all of these products can be found at **http://www.microsoft.com/msdownload/** on Microsoft's Web site.

Installing Internet Assistant for PowerPoint

To install the Internet Assistant for PowerPoint, simply run the downloaded file. The installation process for PowerPoint will walk you through with an installation wizard. The only user input necessary is to agree to the software licensing agreement. Make sure that PowerPoint is not running during installation of the PowerPoint Internet Assistant.

Converting PowerPoint Presentations

Converting a PowerPoint presentation to HTML with the Internet Assistant provides a very quick and powerful way to get content onto the Web. Presentations are converted to hyperlinked HTML files in a single step. To convert a PowerPoint presentation, select the Export as an HTML option found under the File menu. This will bring up the HTML Export Options dialog box.

The Internet Assistant for PowerPoint provides several configuration options (see Figure 10.19). The first of these is the output style of the pages. Pages can be produced in grayscale, or in color. The output format of the images can also be configured, with a choice between .JPEG and .GIF format. If JPEG is selected, the quality of the image resolution can be configured. Finally, a folder needs to be selected where the HTML files and graphics will be saved.

FIG. 10.19
The Internet Assistant for
PowerPoint lets you convert
entire presentations to linked
HTML pages with the touch
of a button.

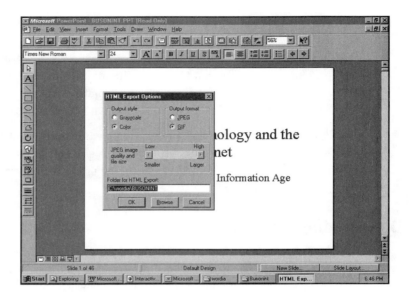

 T I P Choosing between .GIF and .JPEG file formats can make a difference in the file size and clarity
of your images. As a rule, use the .GIF format for images with much text. The images will be
smoother and the text will be clearer. For images such as photographs, JPEG can save you some
size and still be clear and sharp.

Pressing the OK button starts the Internet Assistant conversion process. As slides are
converted, they will show up on your screen. A presentation with many slides could take
several minutes to complete.

 T I P As the slides show up on your screen, they are being converted into .GIF format. Make sure that
you don't move your mouse over the slides while they are being converted or your slides will
display the slideshow Popup Menu button.

To prevent this button from appearing, select Options on the Tools menu, click the View tab, and
clear the Show Popup Menu Button check box.

When the process is completed, you will find that a directory (the one that was specified
in the Configuration dialog box) has been created and filled with graphics and HTML
files. The file entitled INDEX.HTM is the starting point of the presentation and contains
hyperlinks to all the slides. Open INDEX.HTM in your browser to see the results of the
conversion (see Figure 10.20).

FIG. 10.20
PowerPoint's Internet
Assistant creates a title page
that links all the pages.

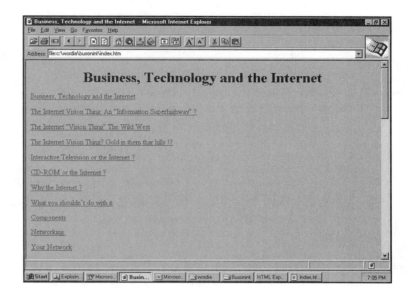

Selecting the first hyperlink (linked to the first page of the presentation) will show the
power of the Assistant. The graphic from the presentation has been converted to a .GIF
format, and hyperlinked buttons have been added to the bottom of the page. Buttons on
the pages are linked to take you to the next page of the presentation, the previous page
of the presentation (if appropriate), back to the index page, and to the notes page (see
Figure 10.21). Click the button with the letter A to view a notes page.

FIG. 10.21
The Internet Assistant
produces HTML pages that
can be viewed and navigated
in both text and graphic
mode.

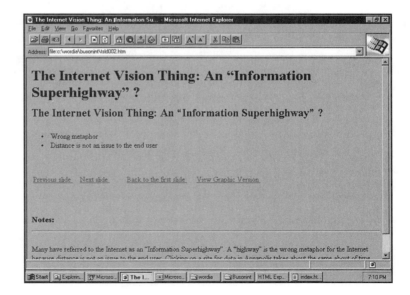

Notice that every page of the presentation can be viewed and navigated through as a notes page or as a graphic page.

 When the Internet Assistant for PowerPoint converts a presentation, it converts all the slides present. Subsequently, any hidden slides you may have had in your presentation will show up in the HTML version. If you are converting a presentation with hidden slides, make a copy of the presentation first, remove the hidden slides, and then convert to HTML.

N O T E The output of HTML pages from the Internet Assistant is controlled by template files found in your PowerPoint folder (extension .TPL). With a little knowledge of HTML, these template files can be modified and customized with a standard text editor. If you are going to modify your .TPL files, always back up the your originals first. ■

Using the PowerPoint Animation Publisher and Player for ActiveX

The PowerPoint Animation Publisher and Player for ActiveX provide another means for publishing and viewing PowerPoint presentations on the Internet. Unlike the PowerPoint Internet Assistant that converts PowerPoint slides into .GIFs and .JPEGs, the PowerPoint Animation Publisher and Player for ActiveX will maintain animations, transitions, build effects, and multimedia effects. Acting as add-ins for PowerPoint and the Web browser, the Publisher and Player work together to enable presentations with full animation to be downloaded and viewed over the Internet without having to have PowerPoint installed.

Downloading and Installing the PowerPoint Animation Player and Publisher   The PowerPoint Animation Player and Publisher can be downloaded together from Microsoft at **http://www.microsoft.com/mspowerpoint/internet/player/installing.htm**. Once downloaded, run the AXPUB.EXE. This will automatically install both components at once. You can also download the player only at the same address.

Creating and Viewing PowerPoint Animation Files   With the PowerPoint Animation Publisher it is easy to create animation for the Web. From the File menu, select Export as PowerPoint Animation, or if you have the Internet Assistant installed, click Export for Internet and then select As PowerPoint Animation.

Give the PowerPoint presentation a name, and continue. This will produce two files: .PPZ file and an .HTM file (with the name you provided).

Open the .HTM file in your browser, follow the links, and enjoy the show.

N O T E When moving .PPZ files to a Web server, remember that you might need to add MIME type mappings to support the .PPZ files. For more information on add MIME types, see the instruction manual for your server. ■

Viewing Native Content on the Internet: The Office Viewers

Along with using Office Internet Assistants to move content from Microsoft Office file formats to HTML, there is another way to share Office documents over the Internet: Office Viewers.

Office viewers are add-ins that when installed work with the browser to display Excel, PowerPoint, and Word files in their native format. Office Viewers allow the viewing and printing of files, but do not support editing. Office Viewers may be a valuable asset when used where content is best preserved in its original format and a full functioning version of the application (Word, Excel, PowerPoint) is not present on client machines.

Part

II

Ch

10

Viewing Content in the Web Browser?

To understand why you need viewers or ActiveX components to display certain types of information over the Internet, you must first grasp how the browser works. One of the things that has made the Web browser one of the premier mechanisms for collecting and viewing information is its simplicity. It is designed to perform a known function (display text, graphics, and so on) when presented with known file types (HTML text, specific graphic formats, and so on). It understands HTML codes, and uses those fairly simple codes to understand how a particular document should be formatted and displayed. Content coming from other sources, however, may contain other codes and formatting instructions specific to that application. The content, however, may only be effective or valuable in its native format. It is for this reason that you need a mechanism for viewing the content in its native format directly through the browser. This is where viewers, assistants, and ActiveX components come into play. The browser can be configured to react to encounters with unknown file types and use a helper application, viewer, or the browser itself, to decipher the application-specific information. This enables the browser to remain the common denominator for platform- and application-independent information distribution, while the Viewers handle individual application's specific instruction. Part of Microsoft's (and Netscape's, for that matter) strategy is to make the browser the universal interface on the PC. While it is already possible to view and edit files, created in Word or Excel, directly through newer versions of Internet Explorer, look for the future to bring more specific file functionality to the Web browser.

Office Viewer for Word

Comparable to the Office Viewer for Excel, the Office Viewer for Word is an application that works with the browser to display Word documents in their native formats. As with all the Office viewers, files can be viewed and printed in their native format, but not edited.

Downloading information for the Office Viewer for Word can be found at **http://www.microsoft.com/msdownload/**.

System requirements are as follows:

- PC with 386DX or higher processor
- Windows 95 or Windows NT 3.51 or later
- 4M of memory for Windows 95 (6M is recommended)
- 12M of memory for Windows NT Workstation
- 3M of hard disk space (6M free needed for installation only)

When downloading the self-extracting executable, make sure to save it in a temporary directory. Do not save it in the same directory that it is going to run out of.

Running the downloaded executable will begin the setup process. The Setup Wizard will prompt you for a location to install the Word Viewer. The default directory is C:\Program Files\WORDVIEW. Click the installation button to install the Viewer.

N O T E   If the setup program detects a version of Word for Windows (version 6.0 or later), it will prompt you to determine which application should open Word documents (.DOC) by default. Choosing Open with Word means the full Word for Windows application. Choosing Open with Viewer means that the Word Viewer will be used by default.

If you choose the Open with Viewer option to restore Word for Windows as the default viewer for .DOC documents, you must run Word for Windows setup program. ■

Office Viewer for Excel

When installed on a client desktop, the Excel viewer functions as a helper application for the browser. The viewer is launched when the browser comes across a file with an Excel extension (.XLS).

The Office Viewer for Excel can be downloaded from Microsoft at **http://www.microsoft.com/msdownload/**. System requirements are as follows:

- PC with 386DX or higher processor
- Windows 95 or Windows NT 3.51 or later
- 4M of memory for Windows 95 (6M is recommended)
- 12M of memory for Windows NT Workstation
- 3M of hard disk space (6M free needed for installation only)

> **CAUTION**
>
> If you already have a full version of Excel installed on your computer, do not install the Microsoft Excel Viewer in the same directory. File conflicts could occur if you do.

Installation is as easy as running the downloaded executable. The Excel Viewer will automatically configure itself as a browser helper application.

To view Excel files located on Web sites, just click any file with the Excel extension.

Part

II

Ch

10

Office Viewer for PowerPoint

The PowerPoint Viewer for Windows 95 is a new application that allows PowerPoint presentations to be viewed with a full set of features, including builds, animation, graphics, and hyperlinks. As with the other Microsoft Office Viewers, the Office Viewer for PowerPoint provides a means to view PowerPoint presentations without requiring a full version of PowerPoint.

Downloading information for the Office Viewer for PowerPoint can be found at **http://www.microsoft.com/msdownload/**.

Running the downloaded executable will begin the setup process. Setting the directory to install the viewer is the only user input necessary to install the viewer.

Clicking files on the Internet with the .PPT extension will automatically launch the viewer.

Overall, the suite of Microsoft Office Internet Assistants and Viewers makes it easy to publish and view Microsoft Office data over the Internet. Whether the content that needs to be converted into HTML (or is best viewed in its native format) is as a Word document, Excel spreadsheet, Access databases, Schedule+, or PowerPoint, the Internet Assistants and Office Viewers make Internet publishing simple and painless. ●

CHAPTER 11

Publishing Your Database on the Web

To develop dynamic Web pages, you need database publishing capability, which is becoming the most common application for ActiveX controls today. This chapter introduces you to mechanisms for feeding the required data to the browser.

This chapter also covers the Microsoft Index Server that will enable you to provide search functions for your Web users to search across data in various formats, such as Excel, Word, PowerPoint, and so on in your servers. ■

Internet Database Connector (IDC)

The IDC, which is a part of the Microsoft Internet Information Server (IIS), is an effective method to dynamically publish data in databases using the ODBC drivers.

SQL Server Web Assistant

The data in the SQL Server databases can be published or triggered by an event such as an update or delete of data in the database or periodically by the SQL Server Web Assistant.

dbWeb

The dbWeb is a graphical tool to develop truly data interactive Web pages that are capable of publishing data, as well as providing update, delete, and add capability to the Web users.

Database Publishing

In the beginning of the Internet/intranet, Web pages were static and the information provided was general in nature. Within a year, the information requirement has galloped to a point where the Internet or Web site has become the primary point of business. Users want to get dynamic information fast, whether it's a Federal Express package or checking the status of an order or a product's price through an online ordering system.

Now, an effective Web site requires interface with back-end data. For example, an online catalog management system will include processes to check product inventory levels and reorder points, display account transaction histories, and update the catalog for product additions, deletions, and so on. In the case of an online merchant system, you need real-time prices, order status, customer information, and so on.

In this chapter, you will look at a few solutions to interface data in databases with the client browser.

Static or Dynamic Publishing?

There are mainly two categories of publishing data in the databases.

The first can be called snap shot model, where the data at a given time is converted into HTML files. This conversion can occur by manual activation, automatically by an event handler, or a timer. The client browsers can view the data, but there are no facilities for interacting with the data. This model is useful for developing catalogues, price lists, telephone directories, or other corporate reference applications.

The second category of applications is the one that interacts dynamically with the data. In these applications, the user will enter part numbers, package IDs, or some selection criteria through a Web browser like Internet Explorer. The system will dynamically generate the data set to be displayed.

Internet Database Connector (IDC)

The Internet Database Connector (IDC) allows the publishing of ODBC compliant databases on the Internet/intranet. IDC is a part of the Microsoft Internet Information Server (IIS), which comes with Windows NT 4.0. With the IDC, one can publish data in SQL Server, Access, ORACLE, Informix, SYBASE, and other ODBC-compliant databases. Microsoft positions IDC as a developer technology that serves as a foundation for developing custom database applications with its Internet Information Server (IIS). Basically, it provides a way to use SQL statements through ODBC drivers and connect the results to a Web page.

> **N O T E** What is this ODBC? ODBC stands for Open Database Connectivity that has become a de facto standard to access data through programs for client/server applications, especially for the Windows platform. ODBC drivers are available for almost all the databases. The advantage of having an ODBC interface is that because the ODBC drivers are already installed in the systems, you can access data from all databases without any additional drivers and other programs. ▨

Using the Internet Data Connector

The Internet Data Connector is an ISAPI DLL named HTTPODBC.DLL. It converses with the Web browsers through the IIS with the HTTP protocol. On the back-end, it talks ODBC. Figure 11.1 shows the schematics of the steps.

FIG. 11.1
IDC interactions with Database and the Web browser.

Part
II

Ch
11

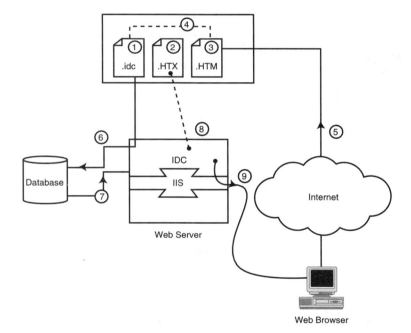

Web Browser

1. Create an Internet data connector file (with an .IDC extension) on the IIS server. This is a text file that specifies an ODBC data source and login information, as well as queries programmed in SQL to retrieve or update data.

2. Create an HTML extension file (with .HTX extension) in the IIS server. This file also is a text file and acts as a formatting template for any retrieved results. Through the IDC file referencing the .HTX file, the database information formats to display in an HTML page.

3. Now create the Web page that passes a reference to a specific .IDC file to connect to and access the database from a Web browser. The Web page (HTML document) can include a form so that users can enter, search, or update information that will be used by the IDC file when executing the SQL statements. If results are returned, they appear in an HTML page that is formatted according to the rules set up in the .HTX file.

4. The HTML Web page document has the HREF link filled with the .IDC file name. For example,

```
<A HREF="http://www.astrix.com/samples/sample1.idc">Sample IDC</A>
```

As the .IDC extension is associated with HTTPODBC.DLL, the .IDC file is passed to the HTTPODBC.DLL. This .IDC file has ODBC data source details including username, password, and data source name, the .HTX template file name, and the SQL query at minimum.

 TIP There are many more fields possible in the .IDC file. Please refer to the IIS product documentation for the .IDC field details.

5. Through a Web browser, the user will activate the HREF object.

6. The query is passed to the HTTPODBC.DLL which issues the ODBC query or statement against the database.

7. The query is run by the DBMS that passes the result back to the IDC.

8. The IDC formats the result using the .HTX file as the template.

9. The now HTML formatted ODBC result is sent to the IIS and the IIS sends the HTML document to the client.

NOTE The IDC is capable of creating interactive forms that can create, modify, and delete SQL data. ■

SQL Server Web Assistant

The SQL Server Web Assistant is positioned as a tool to publish snapshots of data in Microsoft SQL server databases, in the HTML format. The main distinction from other database tools is that the SSWA is a non-interactive process and in that sense it is a truly publishing solution.

In comparison to the IDC that uses the ISAPI gateway to "pull" data from the an SQL server database, the Web Assistant uses the "push" method to deliver data. It updates the Web page as scheduled by the configuration.

The Web Assistant can handle Transact-SQL queries, stored procedures, and extended stored procedures. On a functional level, the Web assistant is an interface to a stored procedure named sp_makewebtask. The HTML file can be updated whenever relevant data changes (by using a trigger). By using SQL Enterprise Manager scheduling, the HTML file can also be updated at scheduled intervals.

dbWeb

The Microsoft dbWeb is another tool to publish database data in the HTML format. dbWeb is implemented through ISAPI DLLs and in that respect, is similar to IDC. The difference is that dbWeb is an end-user tool with graphical, point-and-click, query-by-example (QBE) interface. Similar to IDC, dbWeb connects the Web to ODBC data sources. The dbWeb runs on Windows NT 3.51 with Service Pack 4 installed and now in 4.0. It requires IIS and ODBC 2.5 drivers for the database you want to publish.

You Can Publish Data from Any Database Using the dbWeb

Remember, dbWeb is a very flexible product. It is not limited to Microsoft databases. It can connect to diverse data sources that support 32-bit ODBC. Thus, this product can be used on all the major databases including Oracle, Sybase, and Microsoft Access in addition to SQL server. Even Lotus Notes has an ODBC driver. Also, dbWeb supports dynamic data queries and basic row manipulation which means you cannot only publish data but can manipulate that data.

---

dbWeb Installation

As of today, dbWeb is a downloadable product that is free from Microsoft. Download a copy—it's about 7.7M—from **www.microsoft.com/intdev/dbweb**. The file is named DBWEB11A.EXE. The current version is Version 1.1a. The Web site also contains detailed documentation, an exhaustive tutorial, and FAQs. You should browse through and download the information to view offline. The tutorial is very useful, especially when you begin working with the dbWeb.

NOTE The dbWeb was developed by Aspect Software Engineering Inc., prior to Microsoft acquiring the company. ■

Run the DBWEB11A.EXE to install the dbWeb. Figure 11.2 shows the first screen that gives a choice of components to install.

FIG. 11.2
dbWeb Installation shows
the selection screen for the
components to install.

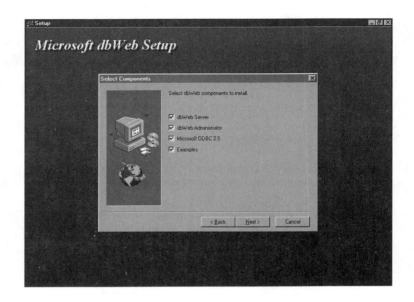

Figure 11.3 shows the directory options window for WWW publishing of the data through
dbWeb.

FIG. 11.3
dbWeb Installation shows
the directories for WWW
publishing of data through
dbWeb.

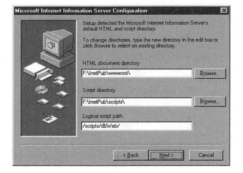

dbWeb Installation Checkout

To verify proper installation, you can access the dbWeb Test Page as shown in Figure
11.4. The installation program creates all the required databases, other files, and ODBC
entries.

From this test page you should be able to access the "pubs" database that shows a successful installation.

FIG. 11.4
This is the dbWeb Installation test page.

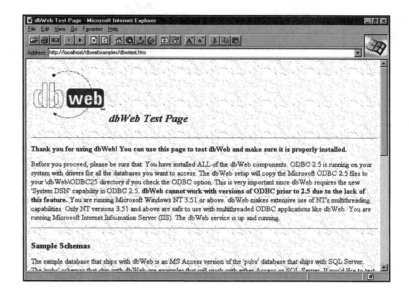

Using dbWeb

The dbWeb consists of two components—the dbWeb service and the dbWeb Administrator. Figure 11.5 shows the dbWeb architecture.

The dbWeb service runs as a 32-bit multi-threaded NT service. The functionality includes processing data retrieval requests and formatting and displaying the results. The results are displayed based on the configurations done using the dbWeb Administrator. The data display including the query fields, the actions permitted (insert, delete, or update records), and so on, can be controlled.

The dbWeb service gets the user requests from the WWW browser, communicates with the ODBC data source, and returns the results to the server which in turn sends it to the client browser.

The dbWeb Administrator is a very powerful GUI front-end for configuring the system. It uses schema to control how the database information is published on the intranet. Schema defines the query and resulting HTML pages displayed on the Web.

The main advantage of dbWeb is that no HTML or ISAPI programming knowledge is necessary to create the dbWeb schema. The dbWeb Administrator provides an interactive Schema Wizard for this purpose. Figures 11.6 and 11.7 show two representative dbWeb Administrator screens.

To set up a data page, the administrator will create a schema that is a collection of data required by the dbWeb to setup queries, data sources, tables, and so on.

FIG. 11.5
This is dbWeb Architecture.

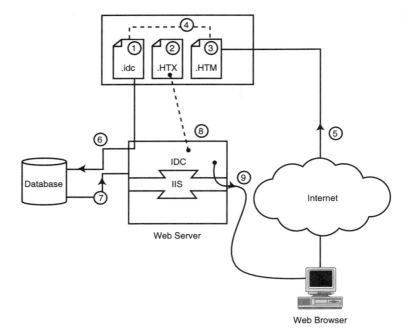

FIG. 11.6
AdbWeb Administrator—a
Schema property page
shows the configuration for
a table to be published.

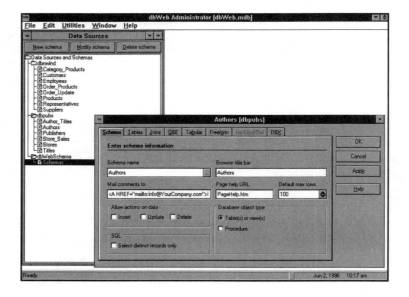

The Schema property page in Figure 11.6 defines the general HTML page layout as well as the actions behind the hot links, such as mail to and help URL. Also, there are options to control user interactions, such as update, add, and delete.

In the Tables property page, shown in Figure 11.7, you can select the tables that will be used in this page. You can also join different tables and create a page as shown in Figure 11.8.

FIG. 11.7
dbWeb Administrator—Table Joins property page

FIG. 11.8
dbWeb Administrator—Tables property page

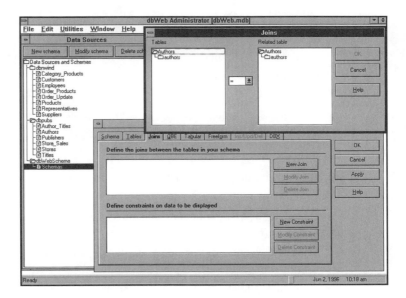

In the QBE property page, you can include the columns the user can use to fill in the Query-By-Example data. QBE is a user-friendly way of getting query data from the user.

FIG. 11.9
dbWeb Administrator—QBE
property page

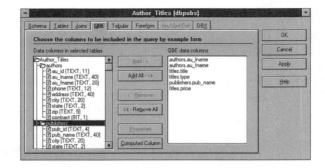

QBE is not limited to existing columns in the database. You can build a computed column as shown in Figure 11.10 for the QBE user form.

FIG. 11.10
dbWeb Administrator—QBE
Computed Column Expression Builder property page

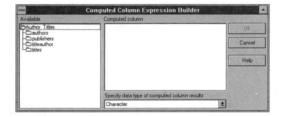

Once the schema is defined, a user can use any WWW browser to interact with the data as defined in the schema. The following list summarizes the main capabilities of dbWeb Administrator:

- Specifies search fields for a Query-By-Example(QBE) Web page
- Chooses the data fields that will appear on a tabular Web page showing a list of the records
- Specifies jumps from the list of records to a single record displayed on a Freeform Web page
- Use Schema GUI to choose data sources, set properties for fields on the Query-By-Example (QBE) Web page, and set properties, such as Automatic Links, to jump to data displayed in other schema, to quickly drill down from a tabular results page to a single record page
- Uses DBX editor to fully customize your Web pages by entering HTML code directly into the specification for the Web page
- Controls the availability of tables and fields for display or update. In the Schema window, you choose fields to appear on your Web pages.

- Sets properties to allow updates, deletes, and inserts on your database
- Writes procedures to enforce business rules
- Supports remote administration using Windows NT 4.0 Server or Windows NT Workstation, a new feature on Version 1.1.A

Indexing Your Web Site

While the database approach gives the users an interactive path to data stored in databases, the Index Server gives the users ability to search through documents stored in the Internet or corporate intranet sites. The Microsoft Index Server works with Windows NT Server 4.0 and Internet Information Server. It also works with the Peer-Web Services available for Windows NT Workstation.

The following list shows some of the features offered by the Microsoft Index Server:

- The Index Server acts as a back end for users to query on documents stored on the Internet or intranet site. The front end is a search form that interacts with the back-end Index Server process.
- The user forms can be customized to suit different user needs and application structure. The Results Page of the query search can also be customized.
- The Index Server has built-in support for documents written in Dutch, English, French, German, Italian, Spanish, and Swedish.
- From a server administration point of view, the Index Server is a "zero maintenance" system with 24–7 availability. This includes automatic updates, index creation and optimization, and crash recovery in case there is a power failure.
- The Index Server counters are accessible from the windows performance monitor for administrators to monitor the system.
- The Index Server works with the Internet News Server to include the news feeds.
- One of the cool features of the Index Server is the "hit highlight"— the words encountered in the result documents are highlighted. This works with all supported document types including HTML, Excel, Word, PowerPoint, and so on.

Part

II

Ch

11

System Requirement

The Index Server runs on the Windows NT 4.0 platform. That means it will run on the Intel Pentium or RISC-based systems such as the Digital Alpha, PowerPC, and the MIPS R4x00.

One of the important requirements is the hard disk space to store the indexes. The index files occupy about 40% of the total size of the indexed documents.

Server memory is another point to be remembered. Even though the 16M for Windows NT and 32M for the RISC systems are recommended, if you are deploying an Index Server for a department or corporate division, you will require a 64M or 80M system.

 TIP The indexer task capacity and speed are directly related to the number of processors and the RAM available.

You can limit the resource usage by the Index Server through registry entries. The controls include maximum and minimum RAM used, disk usage, processor utilization, and also the priority of the various tasks such as indexing, query processing, and so on. The indexer runs as a background task and the status of the indexer can be checked. Periodically, the indexer performs clean up and data structure maintenance to optimize the system. The Web site **http://www.microsoft.com/ntserver/search/docs/reghelp.htm** has an extensive list and description of the registry entries associated with the Index Server.

Installation

The Index Server can be downloaded from the Web site **http://www.microsoft.com/ntserver/search**. The site contains documentation, feature list, and link to download the current version (now version 1.1). The downloaded file is IS11ENU.EXE. Run the file to start the Index Server installation process.

N O T E The file name IS11ENU.EXE is for the Index Server Version 1.1 English U.S. edition. Your file name could be different if you are using another language or country version. ▪

The installation process first stops the Gopher, WWW, and FTP services if they are running. Then it proceeds to get directory information as shown in Figure 11.11.

The installation proceeds after the directory prompts. The program also installs some sample and default query forms during the installation. After the installation is finished, the stopped services are started.

Using the Index Server

The Index Server requires very little administration and maintenance. Server functions such as index updates, optimization, and crash recovery are automatically started and

FIG. 11.11

Index Server Installation
Screen I

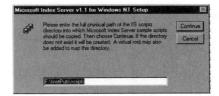

stopped as needed by the Index Server Tasks.

The search is done based on the user's queries. The users fill in their queries in HTML forms. The system can work with the default query forms or the forms can be customized using HTML codes. Index Server assembles query hits into result sets and returns them to the client browser.

 The query forms can be customized for:

- Scope—Where to look for the search including virtual roots and sites, the document collection that can be searched, the directories, and so on

- Restriction—the documents which can be returned, the object properties

- The Result Set—the maximum number of hits returned, the information to be returned as the query result

The Index Server is a very unassuming piece of software. It performs a straightforward function—indexing documents as they are changed and displaying to the user the documents that fit the conditions specified. ●

ActiveX Control and Plug-In Reference

Form Element Controls

One of the basic building blocks of a good graphical user interface (GUI) is a basic control like the CheckBox and Text Box. This chapter concentrates on general controls that are useful to build forms and other GUI elements. For each control, you will follow the usual format. First, you will learn about the control and discover where you can get it. Then you will learn the properties, events, and methods available for use with the control. ■

N O T E A lot of the Microsoft Forms controls discussed in this chapter are as Microsoft implements the HTML forms. When Internet Explorer encounters an `<INPUT TYPE=CHECKBOX>` tag in an HTML document, for example, it calls its CheckBox control to implement it. Therefore, it is not necessary for you to implement HTML form elements by directly accessing the controls, since you can achieve the same thing using standard HTML 3.2.

However, there are instances where you want to use the controls directly. Other reasons are to put form elements into an HTML layout or to use the control to achieve a special effect in these controls that is not possible when using it through standard HTML. ▪

Cal32

This is a flexible control to implement the display of a calendar in your Web pages. It also has buttons to go to next or previous months and years. You can control the display of the buttons, colors, and more, either during design time or from a script. If your Web pages require the display and manipulation of dates, you should take a good look at this control.

Source

Vendor Information:

DameWare Development
http://atlantis.ni-inc.com/~dameware/

FIG. 12.1
Cal32

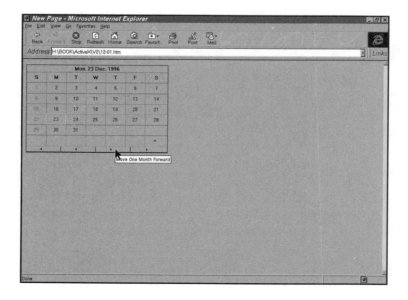

Properties

Table 12.1   Control Properties

Property	Description
BackColor	Background color of the object
BackStyle	Background style of the object—transparent, opaque, and so on
CodeBase	The origin of the control including URL, file type, and version number
ContextMenu	True, to allow context menu
Date	The date value to be displayed
DateCaption	True, to enable caption for the dates
DateCaptionColor	Color of the date caption
DateCaptionFont	The font of the date caption
DateCaptionFormat	The format for the date caption
DateStringFormat	Format string for the date caption
DayFont	Font for the day text
DaysOfWeekFont	Font for the days of week text
DaysOfWeekText	True, to display weekday names
DaysOfWeekTextColor	Color of the weekday names text
DayTextColor	Color of the day text
Draw3D	True, to display a 3-D effect
FocusIndicator	True, to display focus indicator
GridStyle	True, to display the grid
Height	The vertical height of the object
ID	Name of the object or control
Left	The distance between the left edge of the control and the left edge of the HTML layout
MonthYearButtons	True, to display the Next Month and Next Year buttons
OffsetTextCaption	True, to give the caption a 3-D look
OffsetTextColor	Color for the offset (3-D) portion of the caption

continues

Part

III

Ch

12

Table 12.1   Continued

Property	Description
OffsetTextDays	True, to offset the number days text, giving them a 3-D look
OffsetTextWeekdays	True, to offset the weekdays text, giving them a 3-D look
SelectedDayTextColor	Color of the selected day
SingleCharacterDay	True, to display days in single characters
StringDate	The date in string format
TabIndex	The object's tab order position in the HTML layout
ToolTips	True, to display the tool tips
Top	The distance between the top edge of the control and the top edge of the HTML layout
Visible	False, to hide the control
Width	The width of the control in points

Methods

Table 12.2   Control Methods

Method	Description
GetDateString	Retrieves the focused date in string format
GetDateAsFormat	Retrieves the focused date as per format string
GetDateAsDate	Retrieves the focused date as a variable of type DATE
SetCaptionDateFormat	Sets the caption format
SetDateAsDate	Sets focus on a date from a variable of type DATE
SetDateFormat	Sets focus on a date from a variable with a date format
SetDateString	Sets focus on a date from a variable of type STRING

Events

Table 12.3   Control Events

Event	Description
Click	Triggers when a control is clicked with the mouse
DateChanged	Triggers when the focus changes from one date to another
DateStringChanged	Triggers when the StringDate property changes
DblClick	Triggers when a control is double-clicked with the mouse
KeyDown	Triggers when a user presses a control, navigation, or function key
MouseDown	Triggers when a user presses a mouse button
MouseMove	Triggers when the user moves the mouse
ShiftClick	Triggers when the mouse is clicked while the user presses the Shift key

Example

```
<OBJECT ID="Cal321" WIDTH=160 HEIGHT=140
 CLASSID="CLSID:891C9A24-4070-11CF-8E46-00AA006DB209">
    <PARAM NAME="_Version" VALUE="65536">
    <PARAM NAME="_ExtentX" VALUE="3387">
    <PARAM NAME="_ExtentY" VALUE="2963">
    <PARAM NAME="_StockProps" VALUE="33">
    <PARAM NAME="BackColor" VALUE="12632256">
    <PARAM NAME="BorderStyle" VALUE="1">
</OBJECT>
```

Part
III

Ch
12

CheckBox Control

The Microsoft Forms 2.0 CheckBox control implements the check box GUI element. A check box is a three-state (yes/no/null) control with a gray mark for null, blank for no, and a cross mark for yes. This control is used for selecting inclusive options. You can select more than one.

Source

Vendor Information:

Microsoft Corporation
http://www.microsoft.com/activex/gallery/

FIG. 12.2
CheckBox control

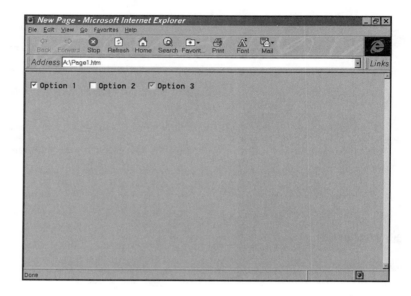

Properties

Table 12.4   Control Properties

Property	Description
Accelerator	The accelerator key
Alignment	Alignment of the caption text
AutoSize	Automatically resize the object to fit the contents
BackColor	Background color of the object
BackStyle	Background style of the object—transparent, opaque, and so on
Caption	The object heading text displayed

Property	Description
CodeBase	The origin of the control, including URL, file type, and version number
Enabled	True, to set the control to get focus and respond to UI
Font	The font for the options text; the font has the following properties: Bold, Charset, Italic, Name, Size, StrikeThrough, Underline, and Weight
ForeColor	Foreground color of the object
GroupName	The group name for the option button
Height	The vertical height of the object
ID	Name of the object or control
Left	The distance between the left edge of the control and the left edge of the HTML layout
Locked	True, to disallow editing through the UI
MouseIcon	The image that appears when the mouse is moved over the object
MousePointer	The mouse pointer that appears when the mouse is moved over the object
Picture	The bitmap or icon to display
PicturePosition	The location of the picture with respect to its caption
SpecialEffect	The visual appearance of the control (flat, border, highlight, and so on)
TabIndex	The object's tab order position in the HTML layout
TabStop	True, to get focus when the user tabs through the controls
Top	The distance between the top edge of the control and the top edge of the HTML layout
TripleState	True, for the control to have three states (yes, no, null)
Value	The content or state of the control object
Visible	False, to hide the control
Width	The width of the control in points
Wordwrap	True, to wrap the lines to fit the width of the control

Method

Any change in the properties will be displayed immediately.

Events

Table 12.5   Control Events

Event	Description
BeforeDragOver	Triggers when a dragged object has reached the drop target
BeforeDropOrPaste	Triggers when an object is about to be dropped or pasted into a control
Change	Triggers when the value of a control changes, either by the UI or from the script; use this event handler to synchronize data between controls
Click	Triggers when a control is clicked with the mouse; also triggers when the user selects a value in a multi-value control, such as the list box
DblClick	Triggers when a control is double-clicked with the mouse
Error	Triggers when a control encounters an error
KeyDown	Triggers when a user presses a control or navigation or function key
KeyPress	Triggers when a key is either pressed by the user or sent from a script by the SendKeys function
KeyUp	Triggers when a user releases a control, navigation, or function key
MouseDown	Triggers when a user presses a mouse button
MouseMove	Triggers when the user moves the mouse
MouseUp	Triggers when a user releases a mouse button

Example

```
<OBJECT ID="CheckBox1" WIDTH=128 HEIGHT=30
 CLASSID="CLSID:8BD21D40-EC42-11CE-9E0D-00AA006002F3">
    <PARAM NAME="BackColor" VALUE="2147483663">
    <PARAM NAME="ForeColor" VALUE="2147483666">
    <PARAM NAME="DisplayStyle" VALUE="4">
    <PARAM NAME="Size" VALUE="2709;635">
    <PARAM NAME="Value" VALUE="True">
    <PARAM NAME="Caption" VALUE="Option 1">
    <PARAM NAME="FontName" VALUE="Fixedsys">
    <PARAM NAME="FontCharSet" VALUE="0">
    <PARAM NAME="FontPitchAndFamily" VALUE="2">
</OBJECT>
<OBJECT ID="CheckBox2" WIDTH=128 HEIGHT=30
 CLASSID="CLSID:8BD21D40-EC42-11CE-9E0D-00AA006002F3">
    <PARAM NAME="BackColor" VALUE="2147483663">
    <PARAM NAME="ForeColor" VALUE="2147483666">
    <PARAM NAME="DisplayStyle" VALUE="4">
    <PARAM NAME="Size" VALUE="2709;635">
    <PARAM NAME="Value" VALUE="False">
    <PARAM NAME="Caption" VALUE="Option 2">
    <PARAM NAME="FontName" VALUE="Fixedsys">
    <PARAM NAME="FontCharSet" VALUE="0">
    <PARAM NAME="FontPitchAndFamily" VALUE="2">
</OBJECT>
<OBJECT ID="CheckBox3" WIDTH=128 HEIGHT=30
 CLASSID="CLSID:8BD21D40-EC42-11CE-9E0D-00AA006002F3">
    <PARAM NAME="BackColor" VALUE="2147483663">
    <PARAM NAME="ForeColor" VALUE="2147483666">
    <PARAM NAME="DisplayStyle" VALUE="4">
    <PARAM NAME="Size" VALUE="2709;635">
    <PARAM NAME="Caption" VALUE="Option 3">
    <PARAM NAME="FontName" VALUE="Fixedsys">
    <PARAM NAME="FontCharSet" VALUE="0">
    <PARAM NAME="FontPitchAndFamily" VALUE="2">
</OBJECT>
```

Part
III

Ch
12

Combo Box Control

The Microsoft Forms 2.0 Combo Box implements a selectable list with capability for adding items by the user. A list of items is displayed for the user, and he or she can choose one or more values from the list. The user can add a value to the list and select that item.

Source

Vendor Information:

Microsoft Corporation
http://www.microsoft.com/activex/gallery/

FIG. 12.3
Combo Box control

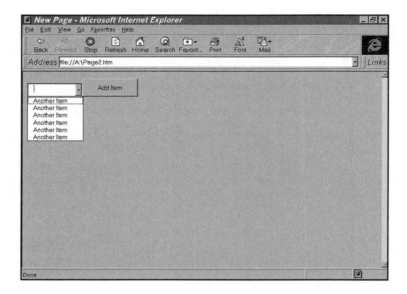

Properties

Table 12.6   Control Properties

Property	Description
AutoSize	Automatically resizes the object to fit the contents
AutoTab	Focus moves to the next control once the maximum input size is reached
AutoWordSelect	Specifies either word or character as the unit of selection
BackColor	Background color of the object
BackStyle	Background style of the object—transparent, opaque, and so on
BorderColor	The object's border color

Property	Description
BorderStyle	The object's border style—none or single
BoundColumn	The stored data column for a multicolumn combo box
CodeBase	The origin of the control, including URL, file type, and version number
Column	Assigns or gets an item from a column
ColumnCount	The number of columns that appear
ColumnHeads	True, to display one row of column heading
ColumnWidths	Sets the column widths
CurTargetX	The x-coordinate of the insertion point relative to the left edge of the control
CurX	The x-coordinate of the insertion point relative to the left edge of the control
DragBehavior	True, to enable drag-and-drop actions
DropButtonStyle	The symbol for the drop button—plain, arrow, ellipsis, or reduce
Enabled	True, to set the control to get focus and respond to UI
Font	The font of the text items
ForeColor	Foreground color of the object
Height	The vertical height of the object
HideSelection	True, to keep the text highlight, even when the control loses focus
ID	Name of the object or control
IMEMode	Runtime mode of the Input Method Editor (left to right or right to left); only for the Far East languages
Left	The distance between the left edge of the control and the left edge of the HTML layout
ListIndex	The index of the currently selected item
ListRows	The rows to be displayed
ListStyle	The list box style (plain or option)
ListWidth	The width of the list box
Locked	True, to disallow editing through the UI

Part
III

Ch
12

continues

Table 12.6   Continued

Property	Description
MatchEntry	The way to match an entry (by first letter, when entry is complete, and so on)
MatchRequired	True, to require a match before the user leaves the field
MaxLength	The maximum number of characters a user can enter into the field
MouseIcon	The image that appears when the mouse is moved over the object
MousePointer	The mouse pointer that appears when the mouse is moved over the object
SelectionMargin	True, to allow the user to select by clicking the left margin region
ShowDropButtonWhen	The situations when the drop button will appear (never, always, focus—when the control has focus)
SpecialEffect	The visual appearance of the control (raised, sunken, flat, etched, bump)
TabIndex	The object's tab order position in the HTML layout
TabStop	True, to get focus when the user tabs through the controls
Text	The string in the control
TextAlign	The alignment of the string information in the control
TextColumn	The column to be displayed for the user
Top	The distance between the top edge of the control and the top edge of the HTML layout
TopIndex	The first item displayed in the list
Value	The content or state of the control object
Visible	False, to hide the control
Width	The width of the control in points

Methods

Table 12.7	Control Methods
Method	**Description**
AddItem	Adds an item to the list
Clear	Deletes the contents of an object or collection
Copy	Copies the selected item text to the clipboard
Cut	Moves the selected item text to the clipboard
Dropdown	Toggles the display of the list portion
Paste	Copies the contents of the clipboard to the object
RemoveItem	Removes an item from the list

Events

Table 12.8	Control Events
Event	**Description**
BeforeDragOver	Triggers when a dragged object has reached the drop target
BeforeDropOrPaste	Triggers when an object is about to be dropped or pasted into a control
Change	Triggers when the value of a control changes either by the UI or from a script; use this event handler to synchronize data between controls
Click	Triggers when a control is clicked with the mouse; also triggers when the user selects a value in a multi-value control, such as the list box
DblClick	Triggers when a control is double-clicked with the mouse
DropButtonClick	Triggers when the drop-down button is clicked
Error	Triggers when a control encounters an error
KeyDown	Triggers when a user presses a control, navigation, or function key

Part

III

Ch

12

continues

Table 12.8   Continued

Event	Description
KeyPress	Triggers when a key is either pressed by the user or sent from a script by the SendKeys function
KeyUp	Triggers when a user releases a control or navigation or function key
MouseDown	Triggers when a user presses a mouse button
MouseUp	Triggers when a user releases a mouse button

Examples

```
<HTML>
<HEAD>
<TITLE>New Page</TITLE>
</HEAD>
<BODY>
    <OBJECT ID="ComboBox1" WIDTH=120 HEIGHT=30
 CLASSID="CLSID:8BD21D30-EC42-11CE-9E0D-00AA006002F3">
    <PARAM NAME="VariousPropertyBits" VALUE="746604571">
    <PARAM NAME="DisplayStyle" VALUE="3">
    <PARAM NAME="Size" VALUE="2540;635">
    <PARAM NAME="MatchEntry" VALUE="1">
    <PARAM NAME="ShowDropButtonWhen" VALUE="2">
    <PARAM NAME="FontCharSet" VALUE="0">
    <PARAM NAME="FontPitchAndFamily" VALUE="2">
</OBJECT>
    <SCRIPT LANGUAGE="VBScript">
<!--
Sub cmdAddComboBoxItem_Click()
ComboBox1.AddItem("Another Item")
end sub
-->
    </SCRIPT>
    <OBJECT ID="cmdAddComboBoxItem" WIDTH=120 HEIGHT=40
     CLASSID="CLSID:D7053240-CE69-11CD-A777-00DD01143C57">
        <PARAM NAME="Caption" VALUE="Add Item">
        <PARAM NAME="Size" VALUE="2540;847">
        <PARAM NAME="FontCharSet" VALUE="0">
        <PARAM NAME="FontPitchAndFamily" VALUE="2">
        <PARAM NAME="ParagraphAlign" VALUE="3">
    </OBJECT>
</BODY>
</HTML>
```

N O T E The Add Item button shown in this example is not part of the Combo Box control. The combo box is a combination of text box and list box. ▩

Command Button Control

As the name implies, the Microsoft Forms 2.0 Command Button gives the Web developers the capability to embed a button in the Web pages.

Source

Vendor Information:

Microsoft Corporation
http://www.microsoft.com/activex/gallery/

FIG. 12.4
Command Button control

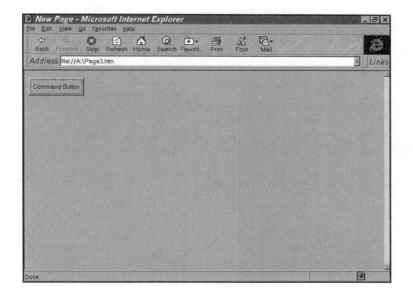

Part
III

Ch

12

Properties

Table 12.9 Control Properties

Property	Description
Accelerator	The accelerator key
AutoSize	Automatically resize the object to fit the contents
BackColor	Background color of the object
BackStyle	Background style of the object—transparent, opaque, and so on
Caption	The object heading text that appears
CodeBase	The origin of the control, including URL, file type, and version number
Enabled	True, to set the control to get focus and respond to UI
Font	The font of the button text
ForeColor	Foreground color of the object
Height	The vertical height of the object
ID	Name of the object or control
Left	The distance between the left edge of the control and the left edge of the HTML layout
Locked	True, to disallow editing through the UI
MouseIcon	The image that appears when the mouse is moved over the object
MousePointer	The mouse pointer that appears when the mouse is moved over the object
Picture	The bitmap or icon to be displayed
PicturePosition	The location of the picture with respect to its caption
TabIndex	The object's tab order position in the HTML layout
TabStop	True, to get focus when the user tabs through the controls
TakeFocusOnClick	True, to get focus to this control when clicked
Top	The distance between the top edge of the control and the top edge of the HTML layout
Visible	False, to hide the control
Width	The width of the control in points
Wordwrap	True, to wrap the button caption to fit the width of the control

Methods

There are no methods for this control.

Events

Table 12.10   Control Events

Event	Description
BeforeDragOver	Triggers when a dragged object has reached the drop target
BeforeDropOrPaste	Triggers when an object is about to be dropped or pasted into a control
Click	Triggers when a control is clicked with the mouse
DblClick	Triggers when a control is double-clicked with the mouse
Error	Triggers when a control encounters an error
KeyDown	Triggers when a user presses a control or navigation or function key
KeyPress	Triggers when a key is either pressed by the user or sent from a script by the SendKeys function
KeyUp	Triggers when a user releases a control or navigation or function key
MouseDown	Triggers when a user presses a mouse button
MouseMove	Triggers when a user moves the mouse
MouseUp	Triggers when a user releases a mouse button

Part
III

Ch
12

Example

```
<OBJECT ID="CommandButton1" WIDTH=120 HEIGHT=40
CLASSID="CLSID:D7053240-CE69-11CD-A777-00DD01143C57">
    <PARAM NAME="Caption" VALUE="Command Button">
    <PARAM NAME="Size" VALUE="2540;846">
    <PARAM NAME="FontCharSet" VALUE="0">
    <PARAM NAME="FontPitchAndFamily" VALUE="2">
    <PARAM NAME="ParagraphAlign" VALUE="3">
</OBJECT>
```

Frame Control

The Microsoft Forms 2.0 Frame control displays a 3-D frame on the Web page. This control can be used to enhance the look of a group of controls—a group of option buttons or check boxes, for example. You can also use it to capture events when a user moves into the frame. Another important use of the frame control is to isolate groups of option buttons. Only one of a set of option buttons can be selected. By placing sets within frames, each separate set can have one option chosen.

Source

Vendor Information:

Microsoft Corporation
http://www.microsoft.com/activex/gallery/

FIG. 12.5
Frame control

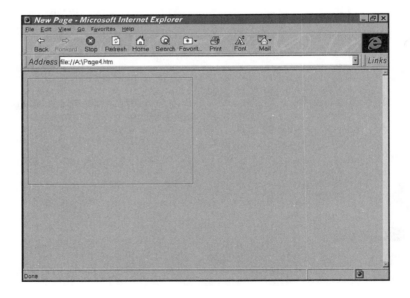

Properties

Table 12.11   Control Properties

Property	Description
ActiveControl	The control that is active in this frame.
BackColor	Background color of the object
BackStyle	Background style of the object—transparent, opaque, and so on
BorderColor	The object's border color
BorderStyle	The object's border style
Caption	The object heading text displayed
CodeBase	The origin of the control, including URL, file type, and version number
Cycle	AllForms or the CurrentForm
Enabled	True, to set the control to get focus and respond to UI
Font	The caption font
ForeColor	Foreground color of the object
ID	Name of the object or control
KeepScrollBarsVisible	The type of scroll bar that appears (none, horizontal, vertical, or both)
Left	The distance between the left edge of the control and the left edge of the HTML layout
MouseIcon	The image that appears when the mouse is moved over the object
MousePointer	The mouse pointer that appears when the mouse is moved over the object
Picture	The bitmap or icon to be displayed
PictureAlignment	The alignment of the background picture
PictureSizeMode	The size of the background image—clip, stretch (enlarge to fit the size), crop, and so on

continues

Part

III

Ch

12

Table 12.11 Continued

Property	Description
PictureTiling	True, to tile the image
ScrollBars	The type (vertical or horizontal or both) of scroll bars displayed
SpecialEffect	The visual appearance of the control (flat, border, highlight, and so on)
TabIndex	The object's tab order position in the HTML layout
TabStop	True, to get focus when the user tabs through the controls
Top	The distance between the top edge of the control and the top edge of the HTML layout
VerticalScrollBarSide	The side to display the vertical scroll bar (right or left)
Visible	False, to hide the control
Width	The width of the control in points

Methods

Table 12.12 Control Methods

Method	Description
Copy	Copies the object contents to the clipboard
Cut	Moves the object contents to the clipboard
Paste	Copies the contents of the clipboard to the object
RedoAction	Performs the undone action
RemoveItem	Removes an item from the list
Repaint	Displays the frame area again
UndoAction	Reverts to the state before the current action

Events

Table 12.13 Control Events

Event	Description
AddControl	Triggers after a control is added into this frame
BeforeDragOver	Triggers when a dragged object has reached the drop target
BeforeDropOrPaste	Triggers when an object is about to be dropped or pasted into a control
Click	Triggers when a control is clicked with the mouse; also triggers when the user selects a value in a multi-value control, such as the list box
DblClick	Triggers when a control is double-clicked with the mouse
Error	Triggers when a control encounters an error
KeyDown	Triggers when a user presses a control, navigation, or function key
KeyPress	Triggers when a key is either pressed by the user or sent from a script by the SendKeys function
KeyUp	Triggers when a user releases a control or navigation or function key
MouseDown	Triggers when a user presses a mouse button
MouseUp	Triggers when a user releases a mouse button
RemoveControl	Triggers when a control is removed from inside the frame
Scroll	Triggers when the scroll bar is moved
Zoom	Triggers when the control is zoomed

Part

III

Ch

12

Example

```
<OBJECT ID="Frame1" WIDTH=360 HEIGHT=240
 CLASSID="CLSID:6E182020-F460-11CE-9BCD-00AA00608E01">
</OBJECT>
```

Hotspot Control

The Microsoft Forms 2.0 Hotspot control implements a region (usually transparent) in the Web page to respond to events. You can make a hotspot control over an image to get a navigator type of user interface. This control has a variety of uses.

Source

Vendor Information:

Microsoft Corporation
http://www.microsoft.com/activex/gallery/

NOTE This is a backend control that works behind the scenes without any direct user interface. The control does not have any visible output as it is invisible at runtime. ▪

Properties

Table 12.14   Control Properties

Property	Description
CodeBase	The origin of the control, including URL, file type, and version number
Enabled	True, to set the control to get focus and respond to UI
Height	The vertical height of the object
ID	Name of the object or control
Left	The distance between the left edge of the control and the left edge of the HTML layout
MouseIcon	The image that appears when the mouse is moved over the object
MousePointer	The mouse pointer that appears when the mouse is moved over the object
TabIndex	The object's tab order position in the HTML layout
TabStop	True, to get focus when the user tabs through the controls
Top	The distance between the top edge of the control and the top edge of the HTML layout
Visible	False, to hide the control
Width	The width of the control in points

Methods

There are no methods for this control.

Events

Table 12.15   Control Events

Event	Description
AfterUpdate	Triggers following the data being updated in a control through the UI
BeforeDragOver	Triggers when a dragged object has reached the drop target
Click	Triggers when a control is clicked with the mouse
DblClick	Triggers when a control is double-clicked with the mouse
Enter	Tiggers just before a control gets focus; similar to GotFocus event
Exit	Triggers just before a control loses the focus; similar to LostFocus event
MouseDown	Triggers when a user presses a mouse button
MouseEnter	Triggers when the mouse pointer moves into the display area occupied by a control
MouseExit	Triggers when the mouse pointer moves out of the display area occupied by a control
MouseMove	Triggers when the user moves the mouse
MouseUp	Triggers when a user releases a mouse button

Part

III

Ch

12

Example

```
<OBJECT ID="HotSpot1"
    CLASSID="CLSID:2B32FBC2-A8F1-11CF-93EE-00AA00C08FDF"
STYLE="TOP:70pt;LEFT:226pt;WIDTH:203pt;HEIGHT:117pt;ZINDEX:0;">
        <PARAM NAME="VariousPropertyBits" VALUE="8388627">
        <PARAM NAME="Size" VALUE="7154;4127">
    </OBJECT>
```

Notes

The HotSpot Control can be added only to an HTML layout.

HTML Layout

The HTML Layout control is one ActiveX control that allows other ActiveX controls to be placed in a layout and be positioned precisely with respect to one another. It also allows other controls (which can include text and graphics through the Label and Image controls) to be layered and overlapped. And, while the most convenient way to create an HTML layout is through the ActiveX Control Pad, it is possible to create one otherwise.

Source

Vendor Information:

Microsoft Corporation
http://www.microsoft.com/activex/gallery/

FIG. 12.6
HTML Layout control

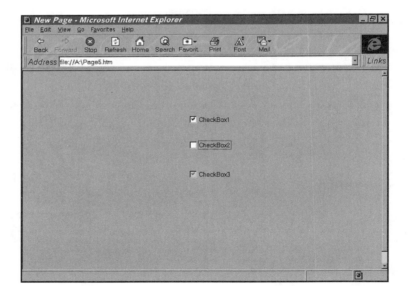

Properties

Table 12.16	Control Properties
Property	**Description**
BackColor	Background color of the object
DrawBuffer	Buffer for off-screen rendering of an HTML Layout
Height	The vertical height of the object
ID	Name of the object or control
Width	The width of the control in points

Methods

There are no methods for this control.

Event

Table 12.17	Control Event
Event	**Description**
OnLoad	Triggers after an HTML layout is created

Examples

```
<HTML>
<HEAD>
<TITLE>New Page</TITLE>
</HEAD>
<BODY>
<OBJECT CLASSID="CLSID:812AE312-8B8E-11CF-93C8-00AA00C08FDF"
ID="Layout1_alx" STYLE="LEFT:0;TOP:0">
<PARAM NAME="ALXPATH" REF VALUE="file:A:\Layout1.alx">
 </OBJECT>
</BODY>
</HTML>
```

The file LAYOUT1.ALX has the following contents:

```
<DIV ID="Layout1" STYLE="LAYOUT:FIXED;WIDTH:454pt;HEIGHT:262pt;">
    <OBJECT ID="HotSpot1"
     CLASSID="CLSID:2B32FBC2-A8F1-11CF-93EE-00AA00C08FDF"
STYLE="TOP:156pt;LEFT:86pt;WIDTH:86pt;HEIGHT:70pt;ZINDEX:0;">
        <PARAM NAME="VariousPropertyBits" VALUE="8388627">
        <PARAM NAME="Size" VALUE="3034;2469">
    </OBJECT>
    <OBJECT ID="WebBrowser1"
     CLASSID="CLSID:EAB22AC3-30C1-11CF-A7EB-0000C05BAE0B"
STYLE="TOP:234pt;LEFT:234pt;WIDTH:289pt;HEIGHT:117pt;ZINDEX:1;">
        <PARAM NAME="Height" VALUE="132">
        <PARAM NAME="Width" VALUE="316">
        <PARAM NAME="AutoSize" VALUE="0">
        <PARAM NAME="ViewMode" VALUE="1">
        <PARAM NAME="AutoSizePercentage" VALUE="0">
        <PARAM NAME="AutoArrange" VALUE="1">
        <PARAM NAME="NoClientEdge" VALUE="1">
        <PARAM NAME="AlignLeft" VALUE="0">
    </OBJECT>
    <OBJECT ID="CheckBox1"
     CLASSID="CLSID:8BD21D40-EC42-11CE-9E0D-00AA006002F3"
STYLE="TOP:47pt;LEFT:211pt;WIDTH:108pt;HEIGHT:18pt;TABINDEX:2;ZINDEX:2;">
        <PARAM NAME="BackColor" VALUE="2147483663">
        <PARAM NAME="ForeColor" VALUE="2147483666">
        <PARAM NAME="DisplayStyle" VALUE="4">
        <PARAM NAME="Size" VALUE="3810;635">
        <PARAM NAME="Caption" VALUE="CheckBox1">
        <PARAM NAME="FontCharSet" VALUE="0">
        <PARAM NAME="FontPitchAndFamily" VALUE="2">
    </OBJECT>
    <OBJECT ID="CheckBox2"
     CLASSID="CLSID:8BD21D40-EC42-11CE-9E0D-00AA006002F3"
STYLE="TOP:78pt;LEFT:211pt;WIDTH:109pt;HEIGHT:23pt;TABINDEX:3;ZINDEX:3;">
        <PARAM NAME="BackColor" VALUE="2147483663">
        <PARAM NAME="ForeColor" VALUE="2147483666">
        <PARAM NAME="DisplayStyle" VALUE="4">
        <PARAM NAME="Size" VALUE="3845;811">
        <PARAM NAME="Caption" VALUE="CheckBox2">
        <PARAM NAME="FontCharSet" VALUE="0">
        <PARAM NAME="FontPitchAndFamily" VALUE="2">
    </OBJECT>
    <OBJECT ID="CheckBox3"
     CLASSID="CLSID:8BD21D40-EC42-11CE-9E0D-00AA006002F3"
STYLE="TOP:117pt;LEFT:211pt;WIDTH:109pt;HEIGHT:23pt;TABINDEX:4;ZINDEX:4;">
        <PARAM NAME="BackColor" VALUE="2147483663">
        <PARAM NAME="ForeColor" VALUE="2147483666">
        <PARAM NAME="DisplayStyle" VALUE="4">
        <PARAM NAME="Size" VALUE="3845;811">
        <PARAM NAME="Caption" VALUE="CheckBox3">
        <PARAM NAME="FontCharSet" VALUE="0">
```

```
            <PARAM NAME="FontPitchAndFamily" VALUE="2">
        </OBJECT>
        <OBJECT ID="Image1"
          CLASSID="CLSID:D4A97620-8E8F-11CF-93CD-00AA00C08FDF"
    STYLE="TOP:156pt;LEFT:70pt;WIDTH:172pt;HEIGHT:70pt;ZINDEX:5;">
            <PARAM NAME="BorderStyle" VALUE="0">
            <PARAM NAME="SizeMode" VALUE="3">
            <PARAM NAME="Size" VALUE="6068;2469">
            <PARAM NAME="PictureAlignment" VALUE="0">
            <PARAM NAME="VariousPropertyBits" VALUE="19">
        </OBJECT>
    </DIV>
```

Image Control

The Microsoft Forms 2.0 Image control can be used to display an image on the Web page. It supports various graphic formats including GIF (87 and 89), JPEG, WMF, and BMP.

Source

Vendor Information:

Microsoft Corporation
http://www.microsoft.com/activex/gallery/

FIG. 12.7
Image control

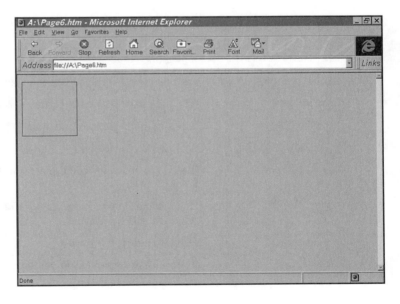

Properties

Table 12.18 Control Properties	
Property	**Description**
AutoSize	Automatically resizes the object to fit the contents
BackColor	Background color of the object
BackStyle	Background style of the object—transparent, opaque, and so on
BorderColor	The object's border color
BorderStyle	The object's border style
CodeBase	The origin of the control, including URL, file type, and version number
Enabled	True, to set the control to get focus and respond to UI
Height	The vertical height of the object
ID	Name of the object or control
Left	The distance between the left edge of the control and the left edge of the HTML layout
MouseIcon	The image that appears when the mouse is moved over the object
MousePointer	The mouse pointer that appears when the mouse is moved over the object
Picture	The bitmap or icon to be displayed
PictureAlignment	The alignment of the background picture
PicturePath	The URL from where the picture should be loaded
PictureSizeMode	The size of the background image
PictureTiling	True, to tile the image
SpecialEffect	The visual appearance of the control (flat, border, highlight, and so on)
Top	The distance between the top edge of the control and the top edge of the HTML layout
Visible	False, to hide the control
Width	The width of the control in points

Methods

There are no methods for this control.

Events

Table 12.19   Control Events

Event	Description
BeforeDragOver	Triggers when a dragged object has reached the drop target
BeforeDropOrPaste	Triggers when an object is about to be dropped or pasted into a control
Click	Triggers when a control is clicked with the mouse
DblClick	Triggers when a control is double-clicked with the mouse
Error	Triggers when a control encounters an error
MouseDown	Triggers when a user presses a mouse button
MouseMove	Triggers when the user moves the mouse
MouseUp	Triggers when a user releases a mouse button

Example

```
<OBJECT ID="Image1" WIDTH=120 HEIGHT=120
    CLASSID="CLSID:4C599241-6926-101B-9992-00000B65C6F9">
        <PARAM NAME="Size" VALUE="2540;2540">
        <PARAM NAME="PicturePath" VALUE="a:\client.gif">
    </OBJECT>
```

Part
III

Ch
12

Label Control

The Microsoft Forms 2.0 Label control displays a text on a Web page. The Label control gives you a lot of flexibility in font, size, color, and scripting. You can change the displayed text dynamically.

Source

Vendor Information:

Microsoft Corporation
http://www.microsoft.com/activex/gallery/

FIG. 12.8
Label control

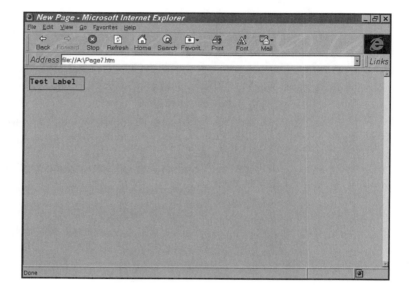

Properties

Table 12.20   Control Properties

Property	Description
Accelerator	The accelerator key
AutoSize	Automatically resizes the object to fit the contents
BackColor	Background color of the object
BackStyle	Background style of the object—transparent, opaque, and so on
BorderColor	The object's border color
BorderStyle	The object's border style
Caption	The label text displayed

Property	Description
CodeBase	The origin of the control, including URL, file type, and version number
Enabled	True, to set the control to get focus and respond to UI
Font	The text font
ForeColor	Foreground color of the object
ID	Name of the control
Left	The distance between the left edge of the control and the left edge of the HTML layout
MouseIcon	The image that appears when the mouse is moved over the object
MousePointer	The mouse pointer that appears when the mouse is moved over the object
Picture	The bitmap or icon to be displayed
PicturePosition	The location of the picture
SpecialEffect	The visual appearance of the control (flat, border, highlight, and so on)
TabIndex	The object's tab order position in the HTML layout
TabStop	True, to get focus when the user tabs through the controls
TextAlign	The alignment of the string information in the control
Top	The distance between the top edge of the control and the top edge of the HTML layout
Visible	False, to hide the control
Width	The width of the control in points
Wordwrap	True, to wrap the lines to fit the width of the control

Part
III

Ch
12

Methods

There are no methods for this control.

Events

Table 12.21 Control Events	
Event	**Description**
BeforeDragOver	Triggers when a dragged object has reached the drop target
BeforeDropOrPaste	Triggers when an object is about to be dropped or pasted into a control
Click	Triggers when a control is clicked with the mouse; also triggers when the user selects a value in a multi-value control, such as the list box
DblClick	Triggers when a control is double-clicked with the mouse
Error	Triggers when a control encounters an error
MouseDown	Triggers when a user presses a mouse button
MouseMove	Triggers when a user moves the mouse
MouseUp	Triggers when a user releases a mouse button

Example

```
<OBJECT ID="Label1" WIDTH=120 HEIGHT=30
CLASSID="CLSID:978C9E23-D4B0-11CE-BF2D-00AA003F40D0">
    <PARAM NAME="Caption" VALUE="Test Label">
    <PARAM NAME="Size" VALUE="2540;635">
    <PARAM NAME="BorderStyle" VALUE="1">
    <PARAM NAME="FontName" VALUE="Fixedsys">
    <PARAM NAME="FontCharSet" VALUE="0">
    <PARAM NAME="FontPitchAndFamily" VALUE="2">
</OBJECT>
```

ListBox Control

The Microsoft Forms 2.0 ListBox control implements the list box GUI capabilities in an ActiveX control. A list of items appears from which the user can choose one or more values.

Source

Vendor Information:

Microsoft Corporation
http://www.microsoft.com/activex/gallery/

FIG. 12.9
ListBox control

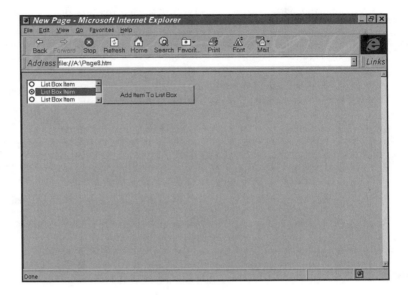

Properties

Table 12.22	Control Properties
Property	**Description**
BackColor	Background color of the object
BorderColor	The object's border color
BorderStyle	The object's border style
BoundColumn	The stored data column for a multicolumn list box
CodeBase	The origin of the control, including URL, file type, and version number

continues

Table 12.22 Continued

Property	Description
Column	An item in a column
ColumnCount	The number of columns to be displayed
ColumnHeads	True, to display one row of column heading
ColumnWidths	The column widths
Enabled	True, to set the control to get focus and respond to UI
Font	The font of the list items text
ForeColor	Foreground color of the object
Height	The vertical height of the object
ID	Name of the object or control
IMEMode	Runtime mode of the Input Method Editor (left to right or right to left); only for the Far East languages
IntegralHeight	True, to fully display the item by resizing the control height
Left	The distance between the left edge of the control and the left edge of the HTML layout
List	A value of an entry in the list box
ListIndex	The index of the currently selected item
ListStyle	The list box style
Locked	True, to disallow editing through the UI
MatchEntry	The way to match an entry (by first letter, when entry is complete, and so on)
MatchFound	True, indicates a match is found between the entry and the contents
MatchRequired	True, to require a match before the user leaves the field
MouseIcon	The image that appears when the mouse is moved over the object
MousePointer	The mouse pointer that appears when the mouse is moved over the object
MultiSelect	True, to allow the user to select more than one item
SpecialEffect	The visual appearance of the control (flat, border, highlight, and so on)
TabIndex	The object's tab order position in the HTML layout

Property	Description
TabStop	True, to get focus when the user tabs through the controls
Text	The value selected in the control
TextColumn	The column to be displayed for the user
Top	The distance between the top edge of the control and the top edge of the HTML layout
TopIndex	The first item displayed in the list
Value	The content of the selected item in the control object
Visible	False, to hide the control
Width	The width of the control in points

Methods

Table 12.23   Control Methods

Method	Description
AddItem	For a single-column list box or combo box, adds an item to the list; for a multicolumn list box or combo box, adds a row to the list.
Clear	Removes all entries in the list
RemoveItem	Removes an item from the list

Events

Table 12.24   Control Events

Event	Description
BeforeDragOver	Triggers when a dragged object has reached the drop target
BeforeDropOrPaste	Triggers when an object is about to be dropped or pasted into a control
Change	Triggers when the value of a control changes either by the UI or from the script; use this event handler to synchronize data between controls

continues

Part

III

Ch

12

Table 12.24   Continued

Event	Description
Click	Triggers when a control is clicked with the mouse; also triggers when the user selects a value in a multi-value control, such as the list box
DblClick	Triggers when a control is double-clicked with the mouse
Error	Triggers when a control encounters an error
KeyDown	Triggers when a user presses a control, navigation, or function key
KeyPress	Triggers when a key is either pressed by the user or sent from a script by the SendKeys function
KeyUp	Triggers when a user releases a control, navigation, or function key
MouseDown	Triggers when a user presses a mouse button
MouseMove	Triggers when the user moves the mouse
MouseUp	Triggers when a user releases a mouse button

Examples

```
<HTML>
<HEAD>
<TITLE>New Page</TITLE>
</HEAD>
<BODY>
    <OBJECT ID="ListBox1" WIDTH=165 HEIGHT=55
 CLASSID="CLSID:8BD21D20-EC42-11CE-9E0D-00AA006002F3">
    <PARAM NAME="ScrollBars" VALUE="3">
    <PARAM NAME="DisplayStyle" VALUE="2">
    <PARAM NAME="Size" VALUE="3492;1166">
    <PARAM NAME="MatchEntry" VALUE="0">
    <PARAM NAME="ListStyle" VALUE="1">
    <PARAM NAME="FontCharSet" VALUE="0">
    <PARAM NAME="FontPitchAndFamily" VALUE="2">
</OBJECT>
    <SCRIPT LANGUAGE="VBScript">
<!--
Sub cmdAddItem_Click()
    ListBox1.AddItem "List Box Item"
end sub
-->
    </SCRIPT>
```

```
<OBJECT ID="cmdAddItem" WIDTH=200 HEIGHT=40
 CLASSID="CLSID:D7053240-CE69-11CD-A777-00DD01143C57">
    <PARAM NAME="Caption" VALUE="Add Item To List Box">
    <PARAM NAME="Size" VALUE="4239;846">
    <PARAM NAME="FontCharSet" VALUE="0">
    <PARAM NAME="FontPitchAndFamily" VALUE="2">
    <PARAM NAME="ParagraphAlign" VALUE="3">
</OBJECT>
</BODY>
</HTML>
```

Option Button

The Microsoft Forms 2.0 Option Button implements the single choice, multi-value option GUI. The user can select only one of the groups of options displayed.

Source

Vendor Information:

Microsoft Corporation
http://www.microsoft.com/activex/gallery/

FIG. 12.10
Option Button control

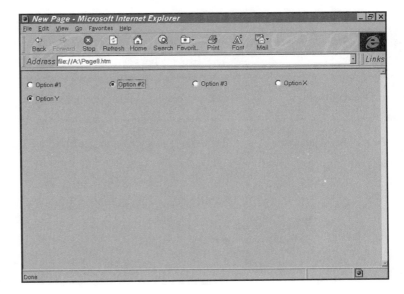

Part
III

Ch
12

Properties

Table 12.25   Control Properties

Property	Description
Accelerator	The accelerator key
Alignment	Alignment of the caption text
AutoSize	Automatically resizes the object to fit the contents
BackColor	Background color of the object
BackStyle	Background style of the object—transparent, opaque, and so on
Caption	The object heading text displayed
CodeBase	The origin of the control, including URL, file type, and version number
Enabled	True, to set the control to get focus and respond to UI
Font	The caption font
ForeColor	Foreground color of the object
GroupName	The group name for the option button
Height	The vertical height of the object
ID	Name of the object or control
Left	The distance between the left edge of the control and the left edge of the HTML layout
Locked	True, to disallow editing through the UI
MouseIcon	The image that appears when the mouse is moved over the object
MousePointer	The mouse pointer that appears when the mouse is moved over the object
Picture	The bitmap or icon to be displayed
PicturePosition	The location of the picture with respect to its caption
SpecialEffect	The visual appearance of the control (flat, border, highlight, and so on)
TabIndex	The object's tab order position in the HTML layout
TabStop	True, to get focus when the user tabs through the controls

Property	Description
Top	The distance between the top edge of the control and the top edge of the HTML layout
TripleState	True, for the button to have three states (Yes, No, Null)
Value	The content or state of the control object
Visible	False, to hide the control
Width	The width of the control in points
Wordwrap	True, to wrap the lines to fit the width of the control

Methods

This control has no methods.

Events

Table 12.26 Control Events

Event	Description
BeforeDragOver	Triggers when a dragged object has reached the drop target
BeforeDropOrPaste	Triggers when an object is about to be dropped or pasted into a control
Change	Triggers when the value of a control changes either by the UI or from the script; use this event handler to synchronize data between controls
Click	Triggers when a control is clicked with the mouse
DblClick	Triggers when a control is double-clicked with the mouse
Error	Triggers when a control encounters an error
KeyDown	Triggers when a user presses a control, navigation, or function key

Part

III

Ch

12

continues

Table 12.26 Continued

Event	Description
KeyPress	Triggers when a key is either pressed by the user or sent from a script by the SendKeys function
KeyUp	Triggers when a user releases a control, navigation, or function key
MouseDown	Triggers when a user presses a mouse button
MouseMove	Triggers when a user moves the mouse
MouseUp	Triggers when a user releases a mouse button

Examples

```
<HTML>
<HEAD>
<TITLE>New Page</TITLE>
</HEAD>
<BODY>
<OBJECT ID="OptionButton1" WIDTH=180 HEIGHT=30
 CLASSID="CLSID:8BD21D50-EC42-11CE-9E0D-00AA006002F3">
    <PARAM NAME="BackColor" VALUE="2147483663">
    <PARAM NAME="ForeColor" VALUE="2147483666">
    <PARAM NAME="DisplayStyle" VALUE="5">
    <PARAM NAME="Size" VALUE="3810;635">
    <PARAM NAME="Caption" VALUE="Option #1">
    <PARAM NAME="GroupName" VALUE="Group1">
    <PARAM NAME="FontCharSet" VALUE="0">
    <PARAM NAME="FontPitchAndFamily" VALUE="2">
</OBJECT>
<OBJECT ID="OptionButton2" WIDTH=180 HEIGHT=30
 CLASSID="CLSID:8BD21D50-EC42-11CE-9E0D-00AA006002F3">
    <PARAM NAME="BackColor" VALUE="2147483663">
    <PARAM NAME="ForeColor" VALUE="2147483666">
    <PARAM NAME="DisplayStyle" VALUE="5">
    <PARAM NAME="Size" VALUE="3810;635">
    <PARAM NAME="Caption" VALUE="Option #2">
    <PARAM NAME="GroupName" VALUE="Group1">
    <PARAM NAME="FontCharSet" VALUE="0">
    <PARAM NAME="FontPitchAndFamily" VALUE="2">
</OBJECT>
<OBJECT ID="OptionButton3" WIDTH=180 HEIGHT=30
 CLASSID="CLSID:8BD21D50-EC42-11CE-9E0D-00AA006002F3">
```

```
        <PARAM NAME="BackColor" VALUE="2147483663">
        <PARAM NAME="ForeColor" VALUE="2147483666">
        <PARAM NAME="DisplayStyle" VALUE="5">
        <PARAM NAME="Size" VALUE="3810;635">
        <PARAM NAME="Caption" VALUE="Option #3">
        <PARAM NAME="GroupName" VALUE="Group1">
        <PARAM NAME="FontCharSet" VALUE="0">
        <PARAM NAME="FontPitchAndFamily" VALUE="2">
</OBJECT>
<OBJECT ID="OptionButton4" WIDTH=180 HEIGHT=30
 CLASSID="CLSID:8BD21D50-EC42-11CE-9E0D-00AA006002F3">
        <PARAM NAME="BackColor" VALUE="2147483663">
        <PARAM NAME="ForeColor" VALUE="2147483666">
        <PARAM NAME="DisplayStyle" VALUE="5">
        <PARAM NAME="Size" VALUE="3810;635">
        <PARAM NAME="Caption" VALUE="Option X">
        <PARAM NAME="GroupName" VALUE="Group2">
        <PARAM NAME="FontCharSet" VALUE="0">
        <PARAM NAME="FontPitchAndFamily" VALUE="2">
</OBJECT>
<OBJECT ID="OptionButton5" WIDTH=180 HEIGHT=30
 CLASSID="CLSID:8BD21D50-EC42-11CE-9E0D-00AA006002F3">
        <PARAM NAME="BackColor" VALUE="2147483663">
        <PARAM NAME="ForeColor" VALUE="2147483666">
        <PARAM NAME="DisplayStyle" VALUE="5">
        <PARAM NAME="Size" VALUE="3810;635">
        <PARAM NAME="Caption" VALUE="Option Y">
        <PARAM NAME="GroupName" VALUE="Group2">
        <PARAM NAME="FontCharSet" VALUE="0">
        <PARAM NAME="FontPitchAndFamily" VALUE="2">
</OBJECT>
</BODY>
</HTML>
```

Part
III

Ch
12

Scroll Bar

The Microsoft Forms 2.0 Scroll Bar implements a way to increase or decrease the value of another control. The user uses the scroll bar to indicate an increase or decrease.

Source

Vendor Information:

Microsoft Corporation
http://www.microsoft.com/activex/gallery/

FIG. 12.11

Scroll Bar control

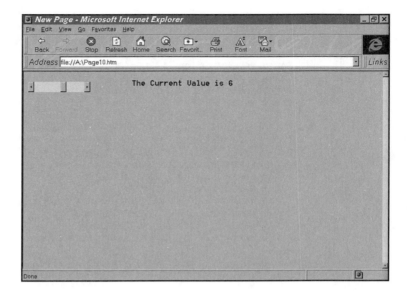

Properties

Table 12.27   Control Properties

Property	Description
BackColor	Background color of the object
CodeBase	The origin of the control, including URL, file type, and version number
Delay	The amount of time between two activation events
Enabled	True, to set the control to get focus and respond to UI
ForeColor	Foreground color of the object
Height	The vertical height of the object
ID	Name of the object or control
LargeChange	The value for the large delta effect when a user clicks between the scroll box and arrow
Left	The distance between the left edge of the control and the left edge of the HTML layout
Max	The upper limit
Min	The lower limit

Property	Description
MouseIcon	The image that appears when the mouse is moved over the object
MousePointer	The mouse pointer that appears when the mouse is moved over the object
Orientation	The orientation (horizontal or vertical)
ProportionalThumb	True, to set the scroll box thumb size proportional to the size of the visible portion
SmallChange	The value for the small delta effect when a user clicks between the scroll box and arrow
TabIndex	The object's tab order position in the HTML layout
TabStop	True, to get focus when the user tabs through the controls
Top	The distance between the top edge of the control and the top edge of the HTML layout
Value	The content of the control object
Visible	False, to hide the control
Width	The width of the control in points

Methods

This control has no methods.

Events

Table 12.28 Control Events

Event	Description
BeforeDragOver	Triggers when a dragged object has reached the drop target
BeforeDropOrPaste	Triggers when an object is about to be dropped or pasted into a control
Change	Triggers when the value of a control changes either by the UI or from the script; use this event handler to synchronize data between controls
Error	Triggers when a control encounters an error
KeyDown	Triggers when a user presses a control, navigation, or function key

continues

Part

III

Ch

12

Table 12.28 Continued

Event	Description
KeyPress	Triggers when a key is either pressed by the user or sent from a script by the SendKeys function
KeyUp	Triggers when a user releases a control, navigation, or function key
Scroll	Triggers when the scroll bar is moved

Examples

```
<HTML>
<HEAD>
<TITLE>New Page</TITLE>
</HEAD>
<BODY>
    <SCRIPT LANGUAGE="VBScript">
<!--
Sub ScrollBar1_Change()
    Label1.Caption = "           The Current Value is " & ScrollBar1.Value
end sub
-->
    </SCRIPT>
    <OBJECT ID="ScrollBar1" WIDTH=135 HEIGHT=23
 CLASSID="CLSID:DFD181E0-5E2F-11CE-A449-00AA004A803D">
    <PARAM NAME="Size" VALUE="2858;494">
    <PARAM NAME="Max" VALUE="10">
</OBJECT>
    <OBJECT ID="Label1" WIDTH=368 HEIGHT=30
 CLASSID="CLSID:978C9E23-D4B0-11CE-BF2D-00AA003F40D0">
    <PARAM NAME="Caption" VALUE="0">
    <PARAM NAME="Size" VALUE="7816;635">
    <PARAM NAME="FontName" VALUE="Fixedsys">
    <PARAM NAME="FontCharSet" VALUE="0">
    <PARAM NAME="FontPitchAndFamily" VALUE="2">
</OBJECT>
</BODY>
</HTML>
```

Spin Button

The Microsoft Forms 2.0 Spin Button is another control (like the Scroll Bar) that increments/decrements the values of other controls. This also gives the user a user-friendly way to change values—numbers, date values, day, month, and so on.

Source

Vendor Information:

Microsoft Corporation
http://www.microsoft.com/activex/gallery/

FIG. 12.12
Spin Button control

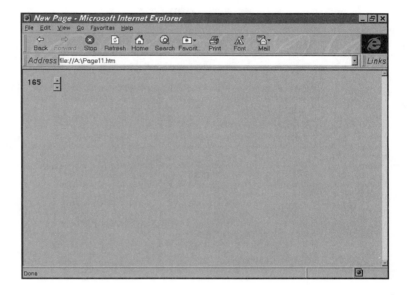

Properties

Table 12.29   Control Properties

Property	Description
BackColor	Background color of the object
CodeBase	The origin of the control, including URL, file type, and version number
Delay	The amount of time between two activation events
Enabled	True, to set the control to get focus and respond to UI
ForeColor	Foreground color of the object
Height	The vertical height of the object
ID	Name of the object or control
Left	The distance between the left edge of the control and the left edge of the HTML layout

continues

Table 12.29   Continued

Property	Description
Max	The upper limit
Min	The lower limit
MouseIcon	The image that appears when the mouse is moved over the object
MousePointer	The mouse pointer that appears when the mouse is moved over the object
Orientation	The orientation (horizontal or vertical)
SmallChange	The increment/decrement value when the user clicks the scroll arrow
TabIndex	The object's tab order position in the HTML layout
TabStop	True, to get focus when the user tabs through the controls
Top	The distance between the top edge of the control and the top edge of the HTML layout
Value	The content or state of the control object
Visible	False, to hide the control
Width	The width of the control in points

Methods

The control has no methods.

Events

Table 12.30   Control Events

Event	Description
BeforeDragOver	Triggers when a dragged object has reached the drop target
BeforeDropOrPaste	Triggers when an object is about to be dropped or pasted into a control
Change	Triggers when the value of a control changes either by the UI or from the script; use this event handler to synchronize data between controls
Error	Triggers when a control encounters an error
KeyDown	Triggers when a user presses a control, navigation, or function key

KeyPress	Triggers when a key is either pressed by the user or sent from a script by the SendKeys function
KeyUp	Triggers when a user releases a control, navigation, or function key
SpinDown	Triggers when the user clicks the spin button arrow to decrease the value (usually the left or the down arrow for horizontal or vertical orientation)
SpinUp	Triggers when the user clicks the spin button arrow to increase the value (usually the right or up arrow for horizontal or vertical orientation)

Examples

```
<HTML>
<HEAD>
<TITLE>New Page</TITLE>
</HEAD>
<BODY>
    <OBJECT ID="Label1" WIDTH=57 HEIGHT=30
     CLASSID="CLSID:978C9E23-D4B0-11CE-BF2D-00AA003F40D0">
        <PARAM NAME="Caption" VALUE="100">
        <PARAM NAME="Size" VALUE="1199;635">
        <PARAM NAME="FontName" VALUE="Fixedsys">
        <PARAM NAME="FontCharSet" VALUE="0">
        <PARAM NAME="FontPitchAndFamily" VALUE="2">
    </OBJECT>
    <SCRIPT LANGUAGE="VBScript">
<!--
Sub SpinButton1_SpinDown()
    Label2.Caption="Spin Down"
end sub
Sub SpinButton1_SpinUp()
    Label2.Caption="Spin Up"
end sub
Sub SpinButton1_Change()
    Label1.Caption=SpinButton1.Value
end sub
-->
    </SCRIPT>
    <OBJECT ID="SpinButton1" WIDTH=17 HEIGHT=32
     CLASSID="CLSID:79176FB0-B7F2-11CE-97EF-00AA006D2776">
        <PARAM NAME="Size" VALUE="353;670">
        <PARAM NAME="Min" VALUE="100">
        <PARAM NAME="Max" VALUE="1000">
        <PARAM NAME="Position" VALUE="100">
    </OBJECT>
    <OBJECT ID="Label2" WIDTH=265 HEIGHT=30
     CLASSID="CLSID:978C9E23-D4B0-11CE-BF2D-00AA003F40D0">
        <PARAM NAME="Size" VALUE="5615;635">
        <PARAM NAME="FontEffects" VALUE="1073741826">
```

Part

III

Ch

12

```
            <PARAM NAME="FontHeight" VALUE="200">
            <PARAM NAME="FontCharSet" VALUE="0">
            <PARAM NAME="FontPitchAndFamily" VALUE="2">
       </OBJECT>
    </BODY>
    </HTML>
```

TabStrip

The Microsoft Forms 2.0 TabStrip control implements a folder GUI in an ActiveX control. The folder concept is very useful when you want to use a lot of controls in your forms. The tab folders in the TabStrip control make it easier to group the controls and put them in many tab strip pages.

Source

Vendor Information:

Microsoft Corporation
http://www.microsoft.com/activex/gallery/

FIG. 12.13
TabStrip control

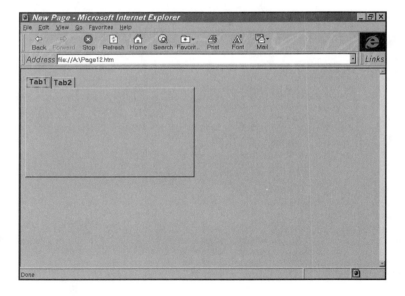

Properties

Table 12.31 Control Properties	
Property	**Description**
BackColor	Background color of the object
CodeBase	The origin of the control, including URL, file type, and version number
Enabled	True, to set the control to get focus and respond to UI
Font	The font for the tab captions
ForeColor	Foreground color of the object
Height	The vertical height of the object
ID	Name of the object or control
Left	The distance between the left edge of the control and the left edge of the HTML layout
MouseIcon	The image that appears when the mouse is moved over the object
MousePointer	The mouse pointer that appears when the mouse is moved over the object
MultiRow	True, to set the control to have more than one tab stop
Style	The tab style—tabs, buttons, and so on
TabFixedHeight	The height of the tab, in points
TabFixedWidth	The width of the tab, in points
TabIndex	The object's tab order position in the HTML layout
TabOrientation	The location of the tab—top, bottom, left, right, and so on
TabStop	True, to get focus when the user tabs through the controls
Top	The distance between the top edge of the control and the top edge of the HTML layout
Value	The content or state of the control object
Visible	False, to hide the control
Width	The width of the control in points

Part

III

Ch

12

Methods

This control has no methods.

Events

Table 12.32   Control Events

Event	Description
BeforeDragOver	Triggers when a dragged object has reached the drop target
BeforeDropOrPaste	Triggers when an object is about to be dropped or pasted into a control
Change	Triggers when the value of a control changes either by the UI or from the script; use this event handler to synchronize data between controls
Click	Triggers when a control is clicked with the mouse
DblClick	Triggers when a control is double-clicked with the mouse
Error	Triggers when a control encounters an error
KeyDown	Triggers when a user presses a control, navigation, or function key
KeyPress	Triggers when a key is either pressed by the user or sent from a script by the SendKeys function
KeyUp	Triggers when a user releases a control, navigation, or function key
MouseDown	Triggers when a user presses a mouse button
MouseMove	Triggers when a user moves the mouse
MouseUp	Triggers when a user releases a mouse button

Example

```
<HTML>
<HEAD>
<TITLE>New Page</TITLE>
</HEAD>
<BODY>
    <OBJECT ID="TabStrip1" WIDTH=368 HEIGHT=227
 CLASSID="CLSID:EAE50EB0-4A62-11CE-BED6-00AA00611080">
    <PARAM NAME="ListIndex" VALUE="0">
    <PARAM NAME="Size" VALUE="7796;4798">
    <PARAM NAME="Items" VALUE="Tab1;Tab2;">
```

```
        <PARAM NAME="MultiRow" VALUE="-1">
        <PARAM NAME="TipStrings" VALUE=";;">
        <PARAM NAME="Names" VALUE="Tab1;Tab2;">
        <PARAM NAME="NewVersion" VALUE="-1">
        <PARAM NAME="TabsAllocated" VALUE="2">
        <PARAM NAME="Tags" VALUE=";;">
        <PARAM NAME="TabData" VALUE="2">
        <PARAM NAME="Accelerator" VALUE=";;">
        <PARAM NAME="FontName" VALUE="Fixedsys">
        <PARAM NAME="FontCharSet" VALUE="0">
        <PARAM NAME="FontPitchAndFamily" VALUE="2">
        <PARAM NAME="TabState" VALUE="3;3">
</OBJECT>
</BODY>
</HTML>
```

TextBox Control

The TextBox is a general purpose input ActiveX control. The user can type values into a text box.

Source

Vendor Information:

Microsoft Corporation

http://www.microsoft.com/activex/gallery/

FIG. 12.14
TextBox control

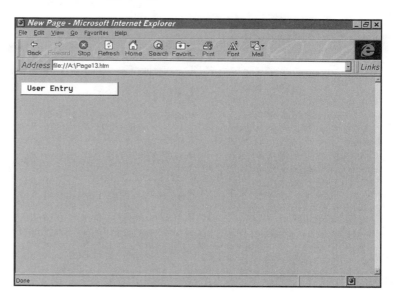

Properties

Table 12.33   Control Properties

Property	Description
AutoSize	Automatically resizes the object to fit the contents
AutoTab	Focus moves to the next control once the maximum input size is reached
AutoWordSelect	Specifies either a word or character as the unit of selection
BackColor	Background color of the object
BackStyle	Background style of the object—transparent, opaque, and so on
BorderColor	The object's border color
BorderStyle	The object's border style
CodeBase	The origin of the control, including URL, file type, and version number
CurLine	The current line in a control, which contains the insertion point
CurTargetX	The x-coordinate of the insertion point relative to the left edge of the control
CurX	The x-coordinate of the insertion point relative to the left edge of the control
DragBehavior	True, to enable drag-and-drop operations
Enabled	True, to set the control to get focus and respond to UI
EnterFieldBehavior	Selection behaviors when the field is entered
EnterKeyBehavior	The effect of pressing the Enter key
Font	The font for the text
ForeColor	Foreground color of the object
Height	The vertical height of the object
HideSelection	True, to keep the text highlighted even when the control loses focus
ID	Name of the object or control
IMEMode	Runtime mode of the Input Method Editor (left to right or right to left); only for the Far East languages

Property	Description
IntegralHeight	True, to fully display the item by resizing the control height
Left	The distance between the left edge of the control and the left edge of the HTML layout
Locked	True, to disallow editing through the UI
MaxLength	The maximum number of characters a user can enter into the field
MouseIcon	The image that appears when the mouse is moved over the object
MousePointer	The mouse pointer that appears when the mouse is moved over the object
MultiLine	True, to allow more than one line to appear
PasswordChar	The character mask displayed for the characters entered
ScrollBars	The type (vertical/horizontal/both) of scroll bars displayed
SelectionMargin	True, to allow the user to select by clicking the left margin region
SelLength	The number of characters selected
SelStart	The starting/insertion point of selection
SelText	The character string selected by the user
TabIndex	The object's tab order position in the HTML layout
TabKeyBehavior	True, to insert a tab character when the Tab key is pressed; false, to move focus to the next control in the tab order
TabStop	True, to get focus when the user tabs through the controls
Text	The string in the control
TextAlign	The alignment of the text inside the control
Top	The distance between the top edge of the control and the top edge of the HTML layout
Value	The content or state of the control object
Visible	False, to hide the control
Width	The width of the control in points
Wordwrap	True, to wrap the lines to fit the width of the control

Part
III

Ch
12

Methods

Method	Description
Table 12.34 Control Methods	
Copy	Copies the selected text to the clipboard
Cut	Moves the selected text to the clipboard
Paste	Copies the contents of the clipboard to the object

Events

Event	Description
Table 12.35 Control Events	
BeforeDragOver	Triggers when a dragged object has reached the drop target
BeforeDropOrPaste	Triggers when an object is about to be dropped or pasted into a control
Change	Triggers when the value of a control changes either by the UI or from the script; use this event handler to synchronize data between controls
DblClick	Triggers when a control is double-clicked with the mouse
DropButtonClick	Triggers when the drop-down button is clicked
Error	Triggers when a control encounters an error
KeyDown	Triggers when a user presses a control, navigation, or function key
KeyPress	Triggers when a key is either pressed by the user or sent from a script by the SendKeys function
KeyUp	Triggers when a user releases a control, navigation, or function key
MouseDown	Triggers when a user presses a mouse button
MouseMove	Triggers when a user moves the mouse
MouseUp	Triggers when a user releases a mouse button

Example

```
<OBJECT ID="TextBox1" WIDTH=213 HEIGHT=30
 CLASSID="CLSID:8BD21D10-EC42-11CE-9E0D-00AA006002F3">
    <PARAM NAME="VariousPropertyBits" VALUE="746604571">
    <PARAM NAME="ScrollBars" VALUE="3">
    <PARAM NAME="Size" VALUE="4514;635">
    <PARAM NAME="SpecialEffect" VALUE="1">
    <PARAM NAME="FontName" VALUE="Fixedsys">
    <PARAM NAME="FontCharSet" VALUE="0">
    <PARAM NAME="FontPitchAndFamily" VALUE="2">
</OBJECT>
```

Toggle Button

The Toggle Button control is a two-state ActiveX button. This can be used to enhance the GUI for showing selected items, options, and the like.

Source

Vendor Information:

Microsoft Corporation
http://www.microsoft.com/activex/gallery/

FIG. 12.15
Toggle Button control

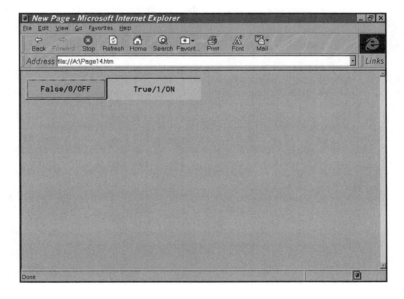

Properties

Table 12.36 Control Properties	
Property	**Description**
Accelerator	The accelerator key
AutoSize	Automatically resizes the object to fit the contents
BackColor	Background color of the object
BackStyle	Background style of the object—transparent, opaque, and so on
Caption	The object heading text
CodeBase	The origin of the control, including URL, file type, and version number
Enabled	True, to set the control to get focus and respond to UI
Font	The font of the caption text
ForeColor	Foreground color of the object
GroupName	The group the control belongs to
Height	The vertical height of the object
ID	Name of the object or control
Left	The distance between the left edge of the control and the left edge of the HTML layout
Locked	True, to disallow editing through the UI
MouseIcon	The image that appears when the mouse is moved over the object
MousePointer	The mouse pointer that appears when the mouse is moved over the object
Picture	The bitmap or icon to be displayed
PicturePosition	The location of the picture with respect to its caption
TabIndex	The object's tab order position in the HTML layout
TabStop	True, to get focus when the user tabs through the controls
Top	The distance between the top edge of the control and the top edge of the HTML layout
TripleState	True, for the button to have three states (Yes, No, Null)
Value	The content or state of the control object (True or False)
Visible	False, to hide the control

Property	Description
Width	The width of the control in points
Wordwrap	True, to wrap the lines to fit the width of the control

Methods

This control has no methods.

Events

Table 12.37   Control Events

Event	Description
BeforeDragOver	Triggers when a dragged object has reached the drop target
BeforeDropOrPaste	Triggers when an object is about to be dropped or pasted into a control
Change	Triggers when the value of a control changes either by the UI or from the script; use this event handler to synchronize data between controls
Click	Triggers when a control is clicked with the mouse
DblClick	Triggers when a control is double-clicked with the mouse
Error	Triggers when a control encounters an error
KeyDown	Triggers when a user presses a control, navigation, or function key
KeyPress	Triggers when a key is either pressed by the user or sent from a script by the SendKeys function
KeyUp	Triggers when a user releases a control, navigation, or function key
MouseDown	Triggers when a user presses a mouse button
MouseMove	Triggers when a user moves the mouse
MouseUp	Triggers when a user releases a mouse button

Part
III

Ch
12

Examples

```
<TITLE>New Page</TITLE>
</HEAD>
<BODY>
```

```
    <SCRIPT LANGUAGE="VBScript">
<!--
Sub ToggleButton1_Change()
    IF ToggleButton1.Value="True" THEN
        ToggleButton1.Caption="True/1/ON"
    ELSE
        ToggleButton1.Caption="False/0/OFF"
    end IF
end sub
Sub ToggleButton2_Change()
    IF ToggleButton2.Value="True" THEN
        ToggleButton2.Caption="True/1/ON"
    ELSE
        ToggleButton2.Caption="False/0/OFF"
    end IF
end sub
-->
    </SCRIPT>
    <OBJECT ID="ToggleButton1" WIDTH=177 HEIGHT=48
 CLASSID="CLSID:8BD21D60-EC42-11CE-9E0D-00AA006002F3">
    <PARAM NAME="BackColor" VALUE="2147483663">
    <PARAM NAME="ForeColor" VALUE="2147483666">
    <PARAM NAME="DisplayStyle" VALUE="6">
    <PARAM NAME="Size" VALUE="3725;1037">
    <PARAM NAME="Value" VALUE="True">
    <PARAM NAME="Caption" VALUE="On">
    <PARAM NAME="FontName" VALUE="Fixedsys">
    <PARAM NAME="FontCharSet" VALUE="0">
    <PARAM NAME="FontPitchAndFamily" VALUE="2">
    <PARAM NAME="ParagraphAlign" VALUE="3">
</OBJECT>
    <OBJECT ID="ToggleButton2" WIDTH=205 HEIGHT=48
 CLASSID="CLSID:8BD21D60-EC42-11CE-9E0D-00AA006002F3">
    <PARAM NAME="BackColor" VALUE="2147483663">
    <PARAM NAME="ForeColor" VALUE="2147483666">
    <PARAM NAME="DisplayStyle" VALUE="6">
    <PARAM NAME="Size" VALUE="4339;1037">
    <PARAM NAME="Value" VALUE="False">
    <PARAM NAME="Caption" VALUE="OFF">
    <PARAM NAME="FontName" VALUE="Fixedsys">
    <PARAM NAME="FontCharSet" VALUE="0">
    <PARAM NAME="FontPitchAndFamily" VALUE="2">
    <PARAM NAME="ParagraphAlign" VALUE="3">
</OBJECT>
</BODY>
</HTML>
```

CHAPTER 13

Web Navigation Controls

When you develop dynamic Web pages with a Web Graphical User Interface, your applications approach the realms of normal desktop systems. The Button-Menu, Popup Menu, Popup Window, View Tracker, and the PreLoader controls enable you to provide your Web application user with an easy, friendly way to navigate through your system.

With static Web pages, the user is limited to the toolbar presented by the Web browser—the navigation is commonly done with the back and forward buttons, while the search, home, and refresh buttons provide a little more functionality.

You can use the Timer control to "actively" interact with the user by trapping the passage of time from your VBScripts. Other controls, described in this chapter as the Stock Ticker and the Payment and Address Selector. are suited for a specific user interface. For developing an effective Web application, these navigation controls rank next to the form and database controls in terms of their usability and importance.

This chapter concentrates on the Graphical User Interface (GUI), particularly the navigation and windowing controls. These controls help you to manage the user navigation from a Web page similar to normal applications.

You will learn about each of these controls and discover where you can get them. Then you will learn about the properties, methods, and events available for use with each control. ■

Microsoft IE30 Button-Menu Control

The Microsoft IE30 Button-Menu control implements a configurable menu for Web pages. This control is simple enough that you can load and display it quickly. It has good functionality to handle menu-related functions from VBScript or JavaScript.

Source

Vendor Information:
Microsoft Corporation
http://www.microsoft.com/activex/gallery/
(Included with the ActiveX Control Pad)
One Microsoft Way
Redmond, WA 98052-6399
(800) 426-9400

FIG. 13.1
Microsoft IE30 Button-Menu control

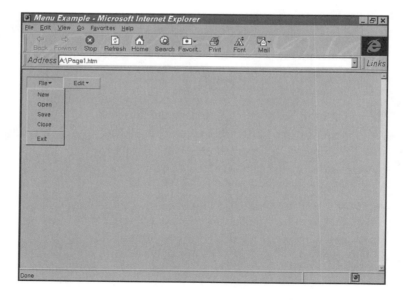

Properties

Table 13.1 Control Properties

Property	Description
Alignment	Aligns the caption of the text
Caption	Menu title
CodeBase	Origin of the control, including URL, file type, and version number
ItemCount	Number of items in the menu
Height	Vertical height of the object
ID	Name of the object or control
MenuItem	Menu item to be displayed
Width	Width of the control in points

Methods

Table 13.2 Control Methods

Method	Description
AboutBox	Displays the About window
Additem	Adds a menu item
Clear	Clears all menu items
GetItem	Fetches the name of the menu item
PopUp	Displays the menu as a pop-up
RemoveItem	Deletes the item from the menu

Events

Table 13.3 Control Events

Event	Description
Click	Triggers when the user clicks the menu. The user has not selected any menu item at this time.
Select	Triggers when the user selects a menu item

Part

III

Ch

13

Example

```
<HTML>
<HEAD>
<TITLE>Menu Example</TITLE>
</HEAD>
<BODY BGCOLOR=#FFFFFF>
<OBJECT ID="mnuFile" WIDTH=80 HEIGHT=25 align=middle
 CLASSID="CLSID:52DFAE60-CEBF-11CF-A3A9-00A0C9034920">
     <PARAM NAME="CODEBASE" VALUE="http://activex.microsoft.com/controls/
iexplorer/btnmenu.ocx#Version=4,70,0,1161">
     <PARAM NAME="_ExtentX" VALUE="1693">
     <PARAM NAME="_ExtentY" VALUE="529">
     <PARAM NAME="Caption" VALUE="File">
     <PARAM NAME="Menuitem[0]" VALUE="New">
     <PARAM NAME="Menuitem[1]" VALUE="Open">
     <PARAM NAME="Menuitem[2]" VALUE="Save">
     <PARAM NAME="Menuitem[3]" VALUE="Close">
     <PARAM NAME="Menuitem[4]" VALUE="">
     <PARAM NAME="Menuitem[5]" VALUE="Exit">
</OBJECT>
<OBJECT ID="mnuEdit" WIDTH=80 HEIGHT=25 align=middle
 CLASSID="CLSID:52DFAE60-CEBF-11CF-A3A9-00A0C9034920">
     <PARAM NAME="CODEBASE" VALUE="http://activex.microsoft.com/controls/
iexplorer/btnmenu.ocx#Version=4,70,0,1161">
     <PARAM NAME="_ExtentX" VALUE="1693">
     <PARAM NAME="_ExtentY" VALUE="529">
     <PARAM NAME="Caption" VALUE="Edit">
     <PARAM NAME="Menuitem[0]" VALUE="Undo">
     <PARAM NAME="Menuitem[1]" VALUE="Redo">
     <PARAM NAME="Menuitem[2]" VALUE="">
     <PARAM NAME="Menuitem[3]" VALUE="Cut">
     <PARAM NAME="Menuitem[4]" VALUE="Copy">
     <PARAM NAME="Menuitem[5]" VALUE="Paste">
</OBJECT>
</BODY>
</HEAD>
```

Microsoft IE30 Popup Menu Control

The Microsoft IE30 Popup Menu control implements a pop-up menu for Web pages. The menu provides a user-friendly Graphical User Interface (GUI) element.

Source

Vendor Information:

Microsoft Corporation

http://www.microsoft.com/activex/gallery/

One Microsoft Way

Redmond, WA 98052-6399

(800) 426-9400

FIG. 13.2
Microsoft IE30 Pop-up Menu
control

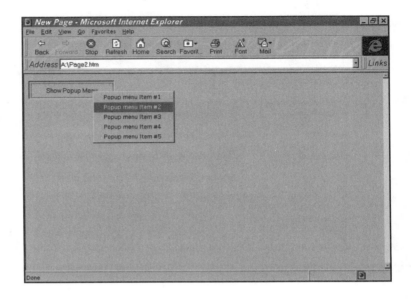

Properties

Table 13.4 Control Properties

Property	Description
Alignment	Aligns the caption of the text
Caption	Menu title
CodeBase	Origin of the control, including URL, file type, and version number
ItemCount	Number of items in the menu
Height	Vertical height of the object
ID	Name of the object or control
MenuItem	Menu item to be displayed
Width	Width of the control in points

Methods

Table 13.5   Control Methods

Method	Description
AboutBox	Displays the About window
Additem	Adds a menu item
Clear	Clears all menu items
GetItem	Fetches the name of the menu item
PopUp	Displays the menu as a pop-up
RemoveItem	Deletes the item from the menu

Events

Table 13.6   Control Events

Event	Description
Click	Triggers when the user clicks the menu by using the mouse. The user has not selected any menu item at this time.
Select	Triggers when the user selects a menu item

Example

```
<HTML>
<HEAD>
<TITLE>New Page</TITLE>
</HEAD>
<BODY>
    <OBJECT ID="IEPOP1" WIDTH=0 HEIGHT=0
 CLASSID="CLSID:7823A620-9DD9-11CF-A662-00AA00C066D2">
    <PARAM NAME="_ExtentX" VALUE="0">
    <PARAM NAME="_ExtentY" VALUE="0">
    <PARAM NAME="Menuitem[0]" VALUE="Popup menu Item #1">
    <PARAM NAME="Menuitem[1]" VALUE="Popup menu Item #2">
    <PARAM NAME="Menuitem[2]" VALUE="Popup menu Item #3">
    <PARAM NAME="Menuitem[3]" VALUE="Popup menu Item #4">
    <PARAM NAME="Menuitem[4]" VALUE="Popup menu Item #5">
</OBJECT>
    <OBJECT ID="btnShowMenu" WIDTH=187 HEIGHT=40
      CLASSID="CLSID:D7053240-CE69-11CD-A777-00DD01143C57">
        <PARAM NAME="Caption" VALUE="Show Popup Menu">
        <PARAM NAME="Size" VALUE="3964;847">
        <PARAM NAME="FontCharSet" VALUE="0">
```

```
        <PARAM NAME="FontPitchAndFamily" VALUE="2">
        <PARAM NAME="ParagraphAlign" VALUE="3">
    </OBJECT>
    <SCRIPT LANGUAGE="VBScript">
Sub btnShowMenu_Click()
    Call IEPOP1.PopUp
end sub
Sub IEPOP1_Click(ByVal x)
    Alert "Menu click on Popup menu item #" & x
End Sub
</SCRIPT>
</BODY>
</HTML>
```

Microsoft IE30 Popup Window Control

The Microsoft IE30 Popup Window control implements a window that appears on command. It displays popup help, tool tips, or a Web page in a window.

> **N O T E** While Web pages can be displayed in the popup window, no hypertext links in those pages will be active, nor will objects such as Java applets or other ActiveX controls work. ■

Source

Vendor Information:
Microsoft Corporation
http://www.microsoft.com/activex/gallery/
One Microsoft Way
Redmond, WA 98052-6399
(800) 426-9400

Part
III

Ch
13

Properties

Table 13.7 Control Properties

Property	Description
Alignment	Aligns the caption of the text
Caption	Menu title
CodeBase	Origin of the control, including URL, file type, and version number
Height	Vertical height of the object

continues

Table 13.7	Continued
Property	**Description**
ID	Name of the object or control
Width	Width of the control in points

FIG. 13.3
Microsoft IE30 Popup
Window control

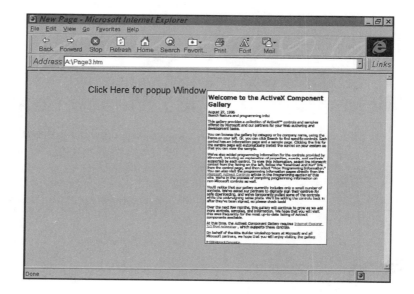

Methods

Table 13.8	Control Methods
Method	**Description**
AboutBox	Displays the About window
PopUp	Displays the pop-up window
Dismiss	Removes the pop-up window from the display

Events

The Microsoft IE30 Popup Window control does not provide any events.

Example

```
<HTML>
<HEAD>
<TITLE>New Page</TITLE>
</HEAD>
<BODY>
    <SCRIPT LANGUAGE="VBScript">
<!--
Sub IeLabel1_Click()
PreVu1.Popup "http://www.microsoft.com/activex/gallery/gallery.htm", True
end sub
-->
    </SCRIPT>
    <OBJECT ID="IeLabel1" WIDTH=500 HEIGHT=50
     CLASSID="CLSID:99B42120-6EC7-11CF-A6C7-00AA00A47DD2">
        <PARAM NAME="_ExtentX" VALUE="0">
        <PARAM NAME="_ExtentY" VALUE="0">
        <PARAM NAME="Caption" VALUE="Click Here for popup Window">
        <PARAM NAME="Angle" VALUE="0">
        <PARAM NAME="Alignment" VALUE="4">
        <PARAM NAME="Mode" VALUE="1">
        <PARAM NAME="FillStyle" VALUE="0">
        <PARAM NAME="FillStyle" VALUE="0">
        <PARAM NAME="ForeColor" VALUE="#000000">
        <PARAM NAME="BackColor" VALUE="#C0C0C0">
        <PARAM NAME="FontName" VALUE="Arial">
        <PARAM NAME="FontSize" VALUE="12">
        <PARAM NAME="FontItalic" VALUE="0">
        <PARAM NAME="FontBold" VALUE="0">
        <PARAM NAME="FontUnderline" VALUE="0">
        <PARAM NAME="FontStrikeout" VALUE="0">
        <PARAM NAME="TopPoints" VALUE="0">
        <PARAM NAME="BotPoints" VALUE="0">
    </OBJECT>
    <OBJECT ID="PreVu1" WIDTH=0 HEIGHT=0
     CLASSID="CLSID:A23D7C20-CABA-11CF-A5D4-00AA00A47DD2">
        <PARAM NAME="_ExtentX" VALUE="0">
        <PARAM NAME="_ExtentY" VALUE="0">
    </OBJECT>
</BODY>
</HTML>
```

Part
III

Ch

13

Microsoft IE30 PreLoader Control

The Microsoft IE30 PreLoader control enables you to preload the existing cache on the user's system, including Web pages, graphics, sounds, or anything else you want. It can be used to speed up a user's time on your pages by preloading information while the user is reading through a page. This control will start downloading a page from an URL when enabled and will trigger the complete event when finished. This is a back-end control—a control that works behind the scenes without any direct user interface and without any visible output, as it is invisible at runtime.

Source

Vendor Information:
Microsoft Corporation
http://www.microsoft.com/activex/gallery/
One Microsoft Way
Redmond, WA 98052-6399
(800) 426-9400

Properties

Table 13.9   Control Properties

Property	Description
Bytes	The amount of data transferred in bytes
CacheFile	The local Web page cache file name
CodeBase	Origin of the control, including URL, file type, and version number
Enable	True to enable the control
ID	Name of the object or control
Percentage	The amount of data transferred in percentage
URL	The download Web page URL

Method

Table 13.10   Control Method

Method	Description
AboutBox	Displays the About window

Events

Table 13.11   Control Events

Event	Description
Complete	Triggers when the Web page download is completed successfully
Error	Triggers when the control encounters an error during downloading

Example

```
<HTML>
<HEAD>
<TITLE>New Page</TITLE>
</HEAD>
<BODY>

<OBJECT ID="PreLoader1" WIDTH=0 HEIGHT=0
  CLASSID="CLSID:16E349E0-702C-11CF-A3A9-00A0C9034920">
    <PARAM NAME="_ExtentX" VALUE="0">
    <PARAM NAME="_ExtentY" VALUE="0">
    <PARAM NAME="URL" VALUE="www.mcp.com">
    <PARAM NAME="enable" VALUE="0">
</OBJECT>

</BODY>
</HTML>
```

Microsoft IE30 Stock Ticker Control

The Microsoft IE30 Stock Ticker control implements the display of continuous data. The main application is the stock market data. The data can be in text or the XRT format. The XRT format is the Microsoft Windows Open Services Architecture Extensions for Real-Time Market Data.

Source

Vendor Information:
Microsoft Corporation
http://www.microsoft.com/activex/gallery/
One Microsoft Way
Redmond, WA 98052-6399
(800) 426-9400

FIG. 13.4
Microsoft IE30 Stock Ticker control

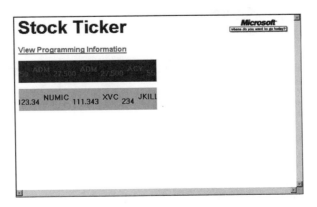

Part
III

Ch
13

Properties

Table 13.12   Control Properties

Property	Description
BackColor	The background color of the control display
CodeBase	Origin of the control, including URL, file type, and version number
DataObjectActive	True, if the control is active
DataObjectName	Data source name
DataObjectNameProperty	The property that has the data name in the data source
DataObjectRequest	The request string to get the data object name
DataObjectValueProperty	The property that has the data object value in the data source
ForeColor	The control's foreground color
Height	Vertical height of the object
ID	Name of the object or control
OffsetValues	Vertical offset, in pixels, of the data from the name
ReloadInterval	The interval to reload the data from the URL
ScrollSpeed	Displays the scroll speed
ScrollWidth	The scroll distance
Width	Width of the control in points

Method

Table 13.13   Control Method

Method	Description
AboutBox	Displays the About window

Events

The Microsoft IE30 Stock Ticker control does not provide any events.

Example

```
<HTML>
<HEAD>
<TITLE>New Page</TITLE>
<OBJECT ID="iexrt1" WIDTH=292 HEIGHT=108
 CLASSID="CLSID:0CA4A620-8E3D-11CF-A3A9-00A0C9034920">
    <PARAM NAME="_ExtentX" VALUE="6181">
    <PARAM NAME="_ExtentY" VALUE="2286">
    <PARAM NAME="DataObjectName" VALUE="H:\BOOK\ActiveX\V1\13-04.xrt">
    <PARAM NAME="DataObjectNameProperty" VALUE="Name">
    <PARAM NAME="DataObjectValueProperty" VALUE="Value">
    <PARAM NAME="DataObjectRequest" VALUE="*">
    <PARAM NAME="ScrollSpeed" VALUE="100">
    <PARAM NAME="ReloadInterval" VALUE="5000">
    <PARAM NAME="ForeColor" VALUE="#FF0000">
    <PARAM NAME="BackColor" VALUE="#0000FF">
    <PARAM NAME="BackColor" VALUE="16711680">
    <PARAM NAME="ScrollWidth" VALUE="5">
    <PARAM NAME="DataObjectActive" VALUE="1">
    <PARAM NAME="DataObjectVisible" VALUE="0">
    <PARAM NAME="OffsetValues" VALUE="10">
</OBJECT>
</HEAD>
<BODY>
</BODY>
</HTML>
```

Microsoft IE30 View Tracker Control

The Microsoft IE30 View Tracker control implements an ActiveX control to recognize events when a user scrolls through a portion of the Web page. That is, the View Tracker control can be placed on a Web page and it will trigger events as the user scrolls through that page.

Part

III

Ch

13

Source

Vendor Information:
Microsoft Corporation
http://www.microsoft.com/activex/gallery/
One Microsoft Way
Redmond, WA 98052-6399
(800) 426-9400

Properties

Table 13.14	Control Properties
Property	**Description**
CodeBase	Origin of the control, including URL, file type, and version number
Height	Vertical height of the object
ID	Name of the object or control
Image	The image to be displayed for the control
Width	Width of the control in points

Method

Table 13.15	Control Method
Method	**Description**
AboutBox	Displays the About window

Events

Table 13.16	Control Events
Event	**Description**
OnHide	Triggers when this control is in the viewing area
OnShow	Triggers when this control is no longer visible

Example

```
<OBJECT ID="IeTrk1" WIDTH=17 HEIGHT=15
 CLASSID="CLSID:1A771020-A28E-11CF-8510-00AA003B6C7E"
 DATA="DATA:application/x-
oleobject;BASE64,IBB3Go6izxGFEACqADtsfiFDNBIIAAAAUwEAAD4BAAAm6gEAAAAAAA==
">
</OBJECT>
```

Microsoft IE30 Timer Control

The Microsoft IE30 Timer control implements a timer function that can be recognized from the script—you set the timer interval and it triggers a periodic event at that fixed interval. Scripts can be used to perform tasks in response to those event. This is a back-end control that works behind the scenes without any direct user interface. The Timer Control does not have any visible output as it is invisible at runtime.

Source

Vendor Information:
Microsoft Corporation
http://www.microsoft.com/activex/gallery/
One Microsoft Way
Redmond, WA 98052-6399
(800) 426-9400

NOTE Even though the control is invisible, it does have size and will take up space on the Web page. The height and width should be set very small to minimize this. ▪

Properties

Table 13.17 Control Properties

Property	Description
CodeBase	Origin of the control, including URL, file type, and version number
Enabled	True, when the Timer Control is active
Height	Vertical height of the object
ID	Name of the object or control
Interval	The time interval, in milliseconds, when the timer event will trigger
Width	Width of the control in points

Part
III

Ch
13

Method

Table 13.18 Control Method

Method	Description
AboutBox	Displays the About window

Event

Table 13.19   Control Event

Event	Description
Timer	Triggers after every unit of time shown by the interval property

Example

```
<HTML>
<HEAD>
<TITLE>New Page</TITLE>
</HEAD>
<BODY>
    <SCRIPT LANGUAGE="VBScript">
<!--
Sub IeTimer1_Timer()
'=========================================
'Some code to respond to the periodic event
'In this case every 30 seconds
'=========================================
end sub
-->
    </SCRIPT>
    <OBJECT ID="IeTimer1" WIDTH=38 HEIGHT=38
     CLASSID="CLSID:59CCB4A0-727D-11CF-AC36-00AA00A47DD2">
        <PARAM NAME="_ExtentX" VALUE="804">
        <PARAM NAME="_ExtentY" VALUE="804">
        <PARAM NAME="Interval" VALUE="30">
    </OBJECT>
</BODY>
</HTML>
```

Payment and Address Selector Control

The Microsoft IE30 Payment and Address Selector control implements the secure address and payment information store at the local machine. You can use this control in your electronic commerce projects as a means to collect, save, and transmit credit card information, address information, and so on.

Source

Vendor Information:
Microsoft Corporation
http://www.microsoft.com/activex/gallery/
One Microsoft Way
Redmond, WA 98052-6399
(800) 426-9400

FIG. 13.5
Payment and Address
Selector control

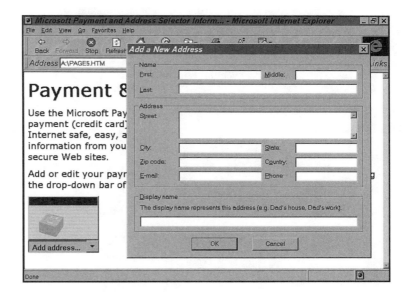

Properties

Table 13.20   Control Properties

Property	Description
AcceptedTypes	The types of cards accepted by the control
CodeBase	Origin of the control, including URL, file type, and version number
DarkShadow3D	The color for the 3-D dark shadow
Face3D	The color for the 3-D face
Font	The font for the control
GrayTextColor	The color for gray text
Height	Vertical height of the object

continues

Table 13.21	Continued
Property	**Description**
Hilight3D	The 3-D highlight color
ID	Name of the object or control
Left	The location of the left corner of the control
Light3D	The color for light 3-D shadow
OrderHash	The order's data hash or signature
Shadow3D	The 3-D shadow color
TextColor	The color for the text foreground
Width	Width of the control in points

Methods

Table 13.22	Control Methods
Method	**Description**
AboutBox	Displays the About window
GetLastError	Fetches the error encountered
GetPaymentValues	Displays the payment form and gets entries from the user
GetValue	Fetches a single element

Events

The Payment and Address Selector control does not provide any events.

Example

```
<HTML>
<HEAD>
<TITLE>New Page</TITLE>
</HEAD>
<BODY>

<OBJECT ID="PaymentSelector1" WIDTH=155 HEIGHT=127
 CLASSID="CLSID:87D3CB66-BA2E-11CF-B9D6-00A0C9083362">
    <PARAM NAME="_ExtentX" VALUE="3281">
    <PARAM NAME="_ExtentY" VALUE="2667">
```

```
        <PARAM NAME="Hilight3D" VALUE="#dae1ed">
        <PARAM NAME="Light3D" VALUE="#b4c3dc">
        <PARAM NAME="Face3D" VALUE="#b4c3dc">
        <PARAM NAME="Shadow3D" VALUE="#587ab1">
        <PARAM NAME="DarkShadow3D" VALUE="#000000">
        <PARAM NAME="TextColor" VALUE="#000000">
        <PARAM NAME="GrayTextColor" VALUE="#587ab1">
        <PARAM NAME="Font" VALUE="MS Sans Serif, 10.0">
        <PARAM NAME="AcceptedTypes" VALUE="">
        <PARAM NAME="Total" VALUE="">
        <PARAM NAME="OrderHash" VALUE="">
    </OBJECT>

    </BODY>
    </HTML>
```

IntraApp

The DameWare IntraApp control implements a virtual desktop or application launcher that enables the user to set up and host local or Web based applications. This can act as a home page for applications, especially for intranet applications. The application icons, title, and so on, are laid out in a configuration file (the format is the same as the Windows INI file).

Source

Vendor Information:
Microsoft Corporation
http://www.microsoft.com/activex/gallery/
One Microsoft Way
Redmond, WA 98052-6399
(800) 426-9400

FIG. 13.6
IntraApp control

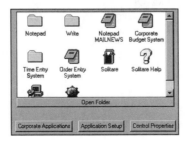

Properties

Table 13.23   Control Properties

Property	Description
BackColor	The background color of the control
BorderStyle	Set to True to enable the border around the control
ButtonText	The text of the run or open folder button
CodeBase	Origin of the control, including URL, file type, and version number
ConfigurationFile	The configuration file that contains the settings
ForeColor	The foreground color of the control
ItemCount	Number of items in the menu
Height	Vertical height of the object
hWND	The window handle of the control window
ID	Name of the object or control
Width	Width of the control in points

Methods

Table 13.24   Control Methods

Method	Description
AboutBox	Displays the About window
DisplayProperties	Displays the Properties dialog box for the items in this control
Execute	Starts an application item in this control

Events

The DameWare IntraApp control does not provide any events.

Example

```
<OBJECT ID="IntraApp1" WIDTH=173 HEIGHT=122
 CLASSID="CLSID:94C31CF1-2698-11D0-B10F-0000F63A6615">
    <PARAM NAME="_Version" VALUE="65536">
    <PARAM NAME="_ExtentX" VALUE="3688">
    <PARAM NAME="_ExtentY" VALUE="2588">
    <PARAM NAME="_StockProps" VALUE="41">
</OBJECT>
```

CHAPTER 14

Database Controls

This chapter contains a collection of controls that are a dream-come-true for a Web-based database application GUI developer. The controls fall under the "formatted control" category. You can use these controls for getting different types of data from the user—for example, the fpCurrency control for getting dollar amount data and the fpBoolean control for option boxes and check boxes.

The controls are chosen for their compactness as well as their functionality. Most of the controls are useful to build the front-end Web forms to interface with Internet and intranet databases. Among the various controls, the fp*xxx* series of controls from FarPoint Technologies are very versatile and simple to use. As you can see from fp*xxx* series' properties, methods, and events, they are powerful enough to handle all your input needs. ■

N O T E   All the controls in this chapter are commercial controls. You can download demo
versions from the ActiveX Gallery Web site or from the developer's Web site. But, if you
plan to use them for your Web applications, you should purchase the controls. ■

fpBoolean

The fpBoolean is a very versatile two- or three-state ActiveX control. This formatted control can be used as a check box or as an option control. This control can be bound to byte,
Boolean, numeric, or text values in the back-end database.

Source

Vendor Information:

FarPoint Technologies, Inc.
http://www.fpoint.com
133 Southcenter Court, Suite 1000
Morrisville, NC 27560
(800) 645-4551
(919) 460-7606

FIG. 14.1
The fpBoolean control

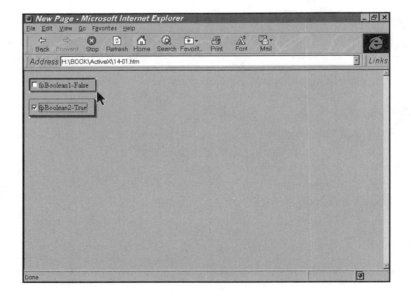

Properties

Table 14.1 Properties of the fpBoolean Control

Property	Description
AlignPictureH	The horizontal alignment of the picture
AlignPictureV	The vertical alignment of the picture
AlignTextH	The horizontal alignment of the text
AlignTextV	The vertical alignment of the text
AllowMnemonic	True, to allow the "&" as a valid character
Appearance	The border look—flat, #D, and so on
AutoToggle	True, to allow the user to toggle the value by using the space bar or clicking
BackColor	The background color of the object
BooleanMode	Two-state, three-state, or button
BooleanPicture	Check box, option button, or user-defined mode
BorderColor	The object's border color
BorderDropShadow	The 3-D shadow for border—none, always, or on focus
BorderDropShadowColor	The border 3-D shadow color
BorderDropShadowWidth	The border 3-D shadow width
BorderGrayAreaColor	The color of the gray area of the 3-D border
BorderStyle	The object's border style
BorderWidth	The object's border width
Caption	The caption for the control
CodeBase	The origin of the control, including the URL, file type, and version number
DataChanged	True, when the data is changed
DataField	The name of the bound column in the DataSource
DataSource	The source of the database to be bound to this control
Enabled	True, to set the control to get focus and respond to UI
Font	The font of the control caption

continues

Part
III

Ch
14

Table 14.1   Continued

Property	Description
ForeColor	The foreground color of the object
GroupID	The group number
GroupSelect	The rule for the controls in a group—no rule, any combination, no more than one, one and only one, one or more
GroupTag	The number inside the group—1, 2, 4, 8, and so on
GroupValue	The value of all the controls in a group
Height	The vertical height of the object
hWND	The handle for the window
ID	The name of the object/control
Left	The distance between the left edge of the control and the left edge of the HTML layout
MarginBottom	The bottom margin in pixels
MarginLeft	The left margin in pixels
MarginRight	The right margin in pixels
MarginTop	The top margin in pixels
MouseIcon	The image that appears when the mouse is moved over the object
MousePointer	The mouse pointer that appears when the mouse is moved over the object
MultiLine	True, to set the text display in more than one line
PictureFalse	The picture that appears with the user-defined BooleanPicture property's False state.
PictureFalseDisabled	The picture that appears with the user-defined BooleanPicture property's False Disabled state
PictureFalseDown	The picture that appears with the user-defined BooleanPicture property's False Down state
PictureGrayed	The picture that appears with the user-defined BooleanPicture property's Grayed state
PictureGrayedDisabled	The picture that appears with the user-defined BooleanPicture property's Grayed Disabled state
PictureGrayedDown	The picture that appears with the user-defined BooleanPicture property's Grayed Down state

Property	Description
PictureTrue	The picture that appears with the user-defined BooleanPicture property's True state
PictureTrueDisabled	The picture that appears with the user-defined BooleanPicture property's True Disabled state
PictureTrueDown	The picture that appears with the user-defined BooleanPicture property's True Down state
ReDraw	Repaint the control
TabIndex	The object's tab order position in the HTML layout
Text	The date in the text format
TextFalse	The text that appears for a False state
TextGrayed	The text that appears for a Grayed state
TextTrue	The text that appears for a True state
ThreeDFrameColor	The color of the 3-D frame
ThreeDFrameWidth	The width of the 3-D frame
ThreeDInsideHighliteColor	The color for the inner border 3-D highlight
ThreeDInsideShadowColor	The color for the inner border 3-D shadow
ThreeDInsideStyle	The style for the inner border 3-D—none, lowered, raised
ThreeDInsideWidth	The width for the inner border 3-D
ThreeDOnFocusInvert	True, to invert the 3-D when the control gets focus
ThreeDOutsideHighliteColor	The color for the outer border 3-D highlight
ThreeDOutsideShadowColor	The color for the outer border 3-D shadow
ThreeDOutsideStyle	The style for the outer border 3-D—none, lowered, raised
ThreeDOutsideWidth	The width for the outer border 3-D
ToggleFalse	The character to toggle the control to False state
ToggleGrayed	The character to toggle the control to Grayed state
ToggleTrue	The character to toggle the control to True state
Top	The distance between the top edge of the control and the top edge of the HTML layout
Value	The numeric value of the state of the control
Visible	False, to hide the control
Width	The width of the control in points

Part
III

Ch
14

Method

Table 14.2   Method of the fpBoolean Control

Method	Description
AboutBox	Displays the About dialog box

Events

Table 14.3   Events of the fpBoolean Control

Event	Description
Advance	Triggers when a valid character is entered at the last position
Change	Triggers when the value of a control changes by either the UI or programmatically; use this event handler to synchronize data between controls
Click	Triggers when a control is clicked with the mouse
DblClick	Triggers when a control is double-clicked
KeyDown	Triggers when a user presses a control, navigation, or function key
KeyPress	Triggers when a key is either pressed by the user or sent from the SendKeys function
KeyUp	Triggers when a user releases a control, navigation, or function key
MouseDown	Triggers when a user presses a mouse button
MouseMove	Triggers when the user moves the mouse
MouseUp	Triggers when a user releases a mouse button
UserError	Triggers when an error occurs

Example

```
<HTML>
<HEAD>
<TITLE>New Page</TITLE>
</HEAD>
<BODY>
    <OBJECT ID="fpBoolean1" WIDTH=148 HEIGHT=32
 CLASSID="CLSID:95C3A8D4-81CB-11CF-ADD0-00AA00A5053A">
    <PARAM NAME="_Version" VALUE="131072">
    <PARAM NAME="_ExtentX" VALUE="3138">
```

```
        <PARAM NAME="_ExtentY" VALUE="662">
        <PARAM NAME="_StockProps" VALUE="68">
        <PARAM NAME="BackColor" VALUE="12632256">
        <PARAM NAME="ForeColor" VALUE="-2147483640">
        <PARAM NAME="ThreeDInsideStyle" VALUE="1">
        <PARAM NAME="ThreeDInsideHighlightColor" VALUE="-2147483633">
        <PARAM NAME="ThreeDInsideShadowColor" VALUE="-2147483642">
        <PARAM NAME="ThreeDInsideWidth" VALUE="1">
        <PARAM NAME="ThreeDOutsideStyle" VALUE="1">
        <PARAM NAME="ThreeDOutsideHighlightColor" VALUE="-2147483628">
        <PARAM NAME="ThreeDOutsideShadowColor" VALUE="-2147483632">
        <PARAM NAME="ThreeDOutsideWidth" VALUE="1">
        <PARAM NAME="ThreeDFrameWidth" VALUE="0">
        <PARAM NAME="BorderStyle" VALUE="2">
        <PARAM NAME="BorderColor" VALUE="-2147483642">
        <PARAM NAME="BorderWidth" VALUE="1">
        <PARAM NAME="AutoToggle" VALUE="-1">
        <PARAM NAME="BooleanStyle" VALUE="0">
        <PARAM NAME="ToggleFalse" VALUE="">
        <PARAM NAME="TextFalse" VALUE="fpBoolean1-False">
        <PARAM NAME="BooleanPicture" VALUE="0">
        <PARAM NAME="AlignPictureH" VALUE="3">
        <PARAM NAME="AlignPictureV" VALUE="1">
        <PARAM NAME="GroupId" VALUE="1">
        <PARAM NAME="GroupTag" VALUE="1">
        <PARAM NAME="GroupSelect" VALUE="0">
        <PARAM NAME="MarginLeft" VALUE="3">
        <PARAM NAME="MarginTop" VALUE="3">
        <PARAM NAME="MarginRight" VALUE="3">
        <PARAM NAME="MarginBottom" VALUE="3">
        <PARAM NAME="MultiLine" VALUE="0">
        <PARAM NAME="AlignTextH" VALUE="0">
        <PARAM NAME="AlignTextV" VALUE="1">
        <PARAM NAME="ToggleTrue" VALUE="">
        <PARAM NAME="TextTrue" VALUE="fpBoolean1-True">
        <PARAM NAME="Value" VALUE="0">
        <PARAM NAME="BooleanMode" VALUE="0">
        <PARAM NAME="ThreeDText" VALUE="0">
        <PARAM NAME="ThreeDTextHighlightColor" VALUE="-2147483633">
        <PARAM NAME="ThreeDTextShadowColor" VALUE="-2147483632">
        <PARAM NAME="ThreeDTextOffset" VALUE="1">
        <PARAM NAME="BorderGrayAreaColor" VALUE="-2147483637">
        <PARAM NAME="ToggleGrayed" VALUE="">
        <PARAM NAME="TextGrayed" VALUE="fpBoolean1-Grayed">
        <PARAM NAME="AllowMnemonic" VALUE="-1">
        <PARAM NAME="ThreeDOnFocusInvert" VALUE="0">
        <PARAM NAME="ThreeDFrameColor" VALUE="-2147483633">
        <PARAM NAME="Appearance" VALUE="0">
        <PARAM NAME="BorderDropShadow" VALUE="1">
        <PARAM NAME="BorderDropShadowColor" VALUE="-2147483632">
        <PARAM NAME="BorderDropShadowWidth" VALUE="3">
</OBJECT>
<P>
    <OBJECT ID="fpBoolean2" WIDTH=148 HEIGHT=43
 CLASSID="CLSID:95C3A8D4-81CB-11CF-ADD0-00AA00A5053A">
```

```
            <PARAM NAME="_Version" VALUE="131072">
            <PARAM NAME="_ExtentX" VALUE="3138">
            <PARAM NAME="_ExtentY" VALUE="917">
            <PARAM NAME="_StockProps" VALUE="68">
            <PARAM NAME="BackColor" VALUE="12632256">
            <PARAM NAME="ForeColor" VALUE="-2147483640">
            <PARAM NAME="ThreeDInsideStyle" VALUE="1">
            <PARAM NAME="ThreeDInsideHighlightColor" VALUE="-2147483633">
            <PARAM NAME="ThreeDInsideShadowColor" VALUE="-2147483642">
            <PARAM NAME="ThreeDInsideWidth" VALUE="1">
            <PARAM NAME="ThreeDOutsideStyle" VALUE="1">
            <PARAM NAME="ThreeDOutsideHighlightColor" VALUE="-2147483628">
            <PARAM NAME="ThreeDOutsideShadowColor" VALUE="-2147483632">
            <PARAM NAME="ThreeDOutsideWidth" VALUE="1">
            <PARAM NAME="ThreeDFrameWidth" VALUE="0">
            <PARAM NAME="BorderStyle" VALUE="2">
            <PARAM NAME="BorderColor" VALUE="-2147483642">
            <PARAM NAME="BorderWidth" VALUE="1">
            <PARAM NAME="AutoToggle" VALUE="-1">
            <PARAM NAME="BooleanStyle" VALUE="0">
            <PARAM NAME="ToggleFalse" VALUE="">
            <PARAM NAME="TextFalse" VALUE="fpBoolean2-False">
            <PARAM NAME="BooleanPicture" VALUE="0">
            <PARAM NAME="AlignPictureH" VALUE="3">
            <PARAM NAME="AlignPictureV" VALUE="1">
            <PARAM NAME="GroupId" VALUE="1">
            <PARAM NAME="GroupTag" VALUE="1">
            <PARAM NAME="GroupSelect" VALUE="0">
            <PARAM NAME="MarginLeft" VALUE="3">
            <PARAM NAME="MarginTop" VALUE="3">
            <PARAM NAME="MarginRight" VALUE="3">
            <PARAM NAME="MarginBottom" VALUE="3">
            <PARAM NAME="MultiLine" VALUE="0">
            <PARAM NAME="AlignTextH" VALUE="0">
            <PARAM NAME="AlignTextV" VALUE="1">
            <PARAM NAME="ToggleTrue" VALUE="">
            <PARAM NAME="TextTrue" VALUE="fpBoolean2-True">
            <PARAM NAME="Value" VALUE="0">
            <PARAM NAME="BooleanMode" VALUE="0">
            <PARAM NAME="ThreeDText" VALUE="0">
            <PARAM NAME="ThreeDTextHighlightColor" VALUE="-2147483633">
            <PARAM NAME="ThreeDTextShadowColor" VALUE="-2147483632">
            <PARAM NAME="ThreeDTextOffset" VALUE="1">
            <PARAM NAME="BorderGrayAreaColor" VALUE="-2147483637">
            <PARAM NAME="ToggleGrayed" VALUE="">
            <PARAM NAME="TextGrayed" VALUE="fpBoolean2-Grayed">
            <PARAM NAME="AllowMnemonic" VALUE="-1">
            <PARAM NAME="ThreeDOnFocusInvert" VALUE="-1">
            <PARAM NAME="ThreeDFrameColor" VALUE="-2147483633">
            <PARAM NAME="Appearance" VALUE="0">
            <PARAM NAME="BorderDropShadow" VALUE="1">
            <PARAM NAME="BorderDropShadowColor" VALUE="-2147483632">
            <PARAM NAME="BorderDropShadowWidth" VALUE="3">
        </OBJECT></BODY>
        </HTML>
```

Notes

This is a very versatile control. It can even have different captions depending on the button state. Additionally, you can make it totally pictorial and have a separate graphic for each state.

fpCurrency

The fpCurrency is a formatted currency and numeric data-entry ActiveX control. It performs validation for invalid characters, a range of values, and so on. This control can be bound to numeric, currency, or text values in the back-end database.

Source

Vendor Information:

FarPoint Technologies, Inc.
http://www.fpoint.com
133 Southcenter Court, Suite 1000
Morrisville, NC 27560
(800) 645-4551
(919) 460-7606

FIG. 14.2
The fpCurrency control

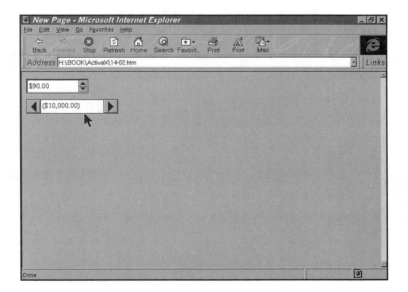

Properties

Table 14.4 Properties of the fpCurrency Control	
Property	**Description**
AlignTextH	The horizontal alignment of the picture
AlignTextV	The vertical alignment of the picture
AllowNull	True, to allow the user the capability to leave this control blank
Appearance	The border look—flat, 3-D, and so on
AutoAdvance	True, to advance to the next control after pressing the Enter key
AutoBeep	True, to sound the beep on user error
BackColor	The background color of the object
BorderColor	The object's border color
BorderDropShadow	The 3-D shadow for border—none, always, on focus
BorderDropShadowColor	The border 3-D shadow color
BorderDropShadowWidth	The border 3-D shadow width
BorderGrayAreaColor	The color of the gray area of the 3-D border
BorderStyle	The object's border style
BorderWidth	The object's border width
ButtonDefaultAction	True, to enable the default action for the spin button
ButtonDisable	True, to disable the buttons on the control
ButtonHide	True, to hide the buttons
ButtonIncrement	The value by which the button index will be increased or decreased
ButtonMax	The upper limit for the button index
ButtonMin	The lower limit for the button index
ButtonStyle	The style of the button—none, spin, slide, and so on
ButtonWidth	The width of the button
ButtonWrap	True, to reset the button index when it crosses the upper or lower limits
CaretInsert	The caret for the insert mode

Property	Description
CaretOverwrite	The overstrike mode caret
CodeBase	The origin of the control, including the URL, file type, and version number
ControlType	The control UI mode—normal, read-only, static, button edit
CurrencyDecimalPlaces	The number of decimal places
CurrencyNegFormat	The appearance when the number is negative
CurrencyPlacement	The placement of the currency symbol
CurrencySymbol	The currency symbol
CurrentPosition	The current position of the cursor
DataChanged	True, when the data is changed
DataField	The name of the bound column in the DataSource
DataSource	The source of the database to be bound to this control
DecimalPoint	The character to be used for decimal point
Enabled	True, to set the control to get focus and respond to UI
FixedPoint	True, to display zeroes to the right of decimal place
Font	The font of the control caption
ForeColor	The foreground color of the object
Height	The vertical height of the object
HideSelection	True, to highlight the selected characters even when the control loses focus
hWND	The handle for the window
ID	The name of the object/control
IncDec	The decimal portion increment when using the button
IncInt	The integer portion increment when using the button
InvalidColor	The background color when the data in the control is invalid
InvalidOption	Action for invalid data when the control loses focus—show data, hide data, clear data
LeadZero	The leading zero display option
Left	The distance between the left edge of the control and the left edge of the HTML layout

continues

Part
III

Ch
14

Table 14.4 Continued

Property	Description
MarginBottom	The bottom margin in pixels
MarginLeft	The left margin in pixels
MarginRight	The right margin in pixels
MarginTop	The top margin in pixels
MaxValue	The upper limit for the control value
MinValue	The lower limit for the control value
MouseIcon	The image that appears when the mouse is moved over the object
MousePointer	The mouse pointer that appears when the mouse is moved over the object
NegToggle	True, to allow the user to enter negative value
NoSpecialKeys	Option for handling keyboard keys
NullColor	The background color when the control contains no value
OnFocusAlignH	Horizontal alignment of the data in the control when it gets focus
OnFocusAlignV	Vertical alignment of the data in the control when it gets focus
OnFocusNoSelect	False, to select the data in the control when it gets focus
OnFocusPosition	The position of the cursor in the data in the control when it gets focus
Separator	The thousands separator character
ReDraw	Repaint the control
SelLength	The number of characters selected
SelStart	The starting/insertion point of selection
SelText	The character string selected by the user
TabIndex	The object's tab order position in the HTML layout
Text	The date in the text format
ThreeDFrameColor	The color of the 3-D frame
ThreeDFrameWidth	The width of the 3-D frame
ThreeDInsideHighliteColor	The color for the inner border 3-D highlight
ThreeDInsideShadowColor	The color for the inner border 3-D shadow

Property	Description
ThreeDInsideStyle	The style for the inner border 3-D—none, lowered, raised
ThreeDInsideWidth	The width for the inner border 3-D
ThreeDOnFocusInvert	True, to invert the 3-D when the control gets focus
ThreeDOutsideHighliteColor	The color for the outer border 3-D highlight
ThreeDOutsideShadowColor	The color for the outer border 3-D shadow
ThreeDOutsideStyle	The style for the outer border 3-D—none, lowered, raised
ThreeDOutsideWidth	The width for the outer border 3-D
Top	The distance between the top edge of the control and the top edge of the HTML layout
UserEntry	Formatted or free format
UseSparator	True, to display the thousands separator character
Visible	False, to hide the control
Width	The width of the control in points

Method

Table 14.5 Method of the fpCurrency Control

Method	Description
AboutBox	Displays the About dialog box

Events

Table 14.6 Events of the fpCurrency Control

Event	Description
Advance	Triggers when a valid character is entered at the last position
ButtonHit	Triggers when a button is pressed by the user
Change	Triggers when the value of a control changes by either the UI or programmatically; use this event handler to synchronize data between controls
ChangeMode	Triggers when the user changes the edit mode between insert and overstrike

Part
III

Ch
14

continues

Table 14.6   Continued

Event	Description
Click	Triggers when a control is clicked with the mouse
DblClick	Triggers when a control is double-clicked
InvalidData	Triggers when the control contains invalid data
KeyDown	Triggers when a user presses a control, navigation, or function key
KeyPress	Triggers when a key is either pressed by ther user or sent from the SendKeys function
KeyUp	Triggers when a user releases a control, navigation, or function key
MouseDown	Triggers when a user presses a mouse button
MouseMove	Triggers when the user moves the mouse
MouseUp	Triggers when a user releases a mouse button
UserError	Triggers when an error occurs

Example

```
<HTML>
<HEAD>
<TITLE>New Page</TITLE>
</HEAD>
<BODY>

<OBJECT ID="fpCurrency1" WIDTH=135 HEIGHT=32
 CLASSID="CLSID:59834660-C0FE-101C-933E-0000C005958C">
    <PARAM NAME="_Version" VALUE="131072">
    <PARAM NAME="_ExtentX" VALUE="2863">
    <PARAM NAME="_ExtentY" VALUE="662">
    <PARAM NAME="_StockProps" VALUE="68">
    <PARAM NAME="BackColor" VALUE="-2147483643">
    <PARAM NAME="ForeColor" VALUE="-2147483640">
    <PARAM NAME="ThreeDInsideStyle" VALUE="1">
    <PARAM NAME="ThreeDInsideHighlightColor" VALUE="-2147483633">
    <PARAM NAME="ThreeDInsideShadowColor" VALUE="-2147483642">
    <PARAM NAME="ThreeDInsideWidth" VALUE="1">
    <PARAM NAME="ThreeDOutsideStyle" VALUE="1">
    <PARAM NAME="ThreeDOutsideHighlightColor" VALUE="-2147483628">
    <PARAM NAME="ThreeDOutsideShadowColor" VALUE="-2147483632">
    <PARAM NAME="ThreeDOutsideWidth" VALUE="1">
    <PARAM NAME="ThreeDFrameWidth" VALUE="0">
    <PARAM NAME="BorderStyle" VALUE="1">
    <PARAM NAME="BorderColor" VALUE="-2147483642">
    <PARAM NAME="BorderWidth" VALUE="1">
```

```
<PARAM NAME="ButtonDisable" VALUE="0">
<PARAM NAME="ButtonHide" VALUE="0">
<PARAM NAME="ButtonIncrement" VALUE="1">
<PARAM NAME="ButtonMin" VALUE="0">
<PARAM NAME="ButtonMax" VALUE="10000">
<PARAM NAME="ButtonStyle" VALUE="1">
<PARAM NAME="ButtonWidth" VALUE="0">
<PARAM NAME="ButtonWrap" VALUE="-1">
<PARAM NAME="ButtonDefaultAction" VALUE="-1">
<PARAM NAME="ThreeDText" VALUE="0">
<PARAM NAME="ThreeDTextHighlightColor" VALUE="-2147483633">
<PARAM NAME="ThreeDTextShadowColor" VALUE="-2147483632">
<PARAM NAME="ThreeDTextOffset" VALUE="1">
<PARAM NAME="AlignTextH" VALUE="0">
<PARAM NAME="AlignTextV" VALUE="0">
<PARAM NAME="AllowNull" VALUE="0">
<PARAM NAME="NoSpecialKeys" VALUE="0">
<PARAM NAME="AutoAdvance" VALUE="0">
<PARAM NAME="AutoBeep" VALUE="0">
<PARAM NAME="CaretInsert" VALUE="0">
<PARAM NAME="CaretOverWrite" VALUE="3">
<PARAM NAME="UserEntry" VALUE="0">
<PARAM NAME="HideSelection" VALUE="-1">
<PARAM NAME="InvalidColor" VALUE="-2147483637">
<PARAM NAME="InvalidOption" VALUE="0">
<PARAM NAME="MarginLeft" VALUE="3">
<PARAM NAME="MarginTop" VALUE="3">
<PARAM NAME="MarginRight" VALUE="3">
<PARAM NAME="MarginBottom" VALUE="3">
<PARAM NAME="NullColor" VALUE="-2147483637">
<PARAM NAME="OnFocusAlignH" VALUE="0">
<PARAM NAME="OnFocusAlignV" VALUE="0">
<PARAM NAME="OnFocusNoSelect" VALUE="0">
<PARAM NAME="OnFocusPosition" VALUE="0">
<PARAM NAME="ControlType" VALUE="0">
<PARAM NAME="Text" VALUE="$0.00">
<PARAM NAME="CurrencyDecimalPlaces" VALUE="-1">
<PARAM NAME="CurrencyNegFormat" VALUE="0">
<PARAM NAME="CurrencyPlacement" VALUE="0">
<PARAM NAME="CurrencySymbol" VALUE="$">
<PARAM NAME="DecimalPoint" VALUE="">
<PARAM NAME="FixedPoint" VALUE="-1">
<PARAM NAME="LeadZero" VALUE="0">
<PARAM NAME="MaxValue" VALUE="100000">
<PARAM NAME="MinValue" VALUE="0">
<PARAM NAME="NegToggle" VALUE="0">
<PARAM NAME="Separator" VALUE="">
<PARAM NAME="UseSeparator" VALUE="-1">
<PARAM NAME="IncInt" VALUE="1">
<PARAM NAME="IncDec" VALUE="1">
<PARAM NAME="BorderGrayAreaColor" VALUE="-2147483637">
<PARAM NAME="ThreeDOnFocusInvert" VALUE="0">
<PARAM NAME="ThreeDFrameColor" VALUE="-2147483633">
<PARAM NAME="Appearance" VALUE="3">
<PARAM NAME="BorderDropShadow" VALUE="0">
```

```
                        <PARAM NAME="BorderDropShadowColor" VALUE="-2147483632">
                        <PARAM NAME="BorderDropShadowWidth" VALUE="3">
                   </OBJECT>
                   <P>
                   <OBJECT ID="fpCurrency1" WIDTH=200 HEIGHT=32
                    CLASSID="CLSID:59834660-C0FE-101C-933E-0000C005958C">
                        <PARAM NAME="_Version" VALUE="131072">
                        <PARAM NAME="_ExtentX" VALUE="4233">
                        <PARAM NAME="_ExtentY" VALUE="670">
                        <PARAM NAME="_StockProps" VALUE="68">
                        <PARAM NAME="BackColor" VALUE="-2147483643">
                        <PARAM NAME="ForeColor" VALUE="-2147483640">
                        <PARAM NAME="ThreeDInsideStyle" VALUE="0">
                        <PARAM NAME="ThreeDInsideHighlightColor" VALUE="-2147483633">
                        <PARAM NAME="ThreeDInsideShadowColor" VALUE="-2147483642">
                        <PARAM NAME="ThreeDInsideWidth" VALUE="1">
                        <PARAM NAME="ThreeDOutsideStyle" VALUE="0">
                        <PARAM NAME="ThreeDOutsideHighlightColor" VALUE="-2147483628">
                        <PARAM NAME="ThreeDOutsideShadowColor" VALUE="-2147483632">
                        <PARAM NAME="ThreeDOutsideWidth" VALUE="1">
                        <PARAM NAME="ThreeDFrameWidth" VALUE="0">
                        <PARAM NAME="BorderStyle" VALUE="1">
                        <PARAM NAME="BorderColor" VALUE="-2147483642">
                        <PARAM NAME="BorderWidth" VALUE="1">
                        <PARAM NAME="ButtonDisable" VALUE="0">
                        <PARAM NAME="ButtonHide" VALUE="0">
                        <PARAM NAME="ButtonIncrement" VALUE="1">
                        <PARAM NAME="ButtonMin" VALUE="0">
                        <PARAM NAME="ButtonMax" VALUE="100">
                        <PARAM NAME="ButtonStyle" VALUE="4">
                        <PARAM NAME="ButtonWidth" VALUE="0">
                        <PARAM NAME="ButtonWrap" VALUE="-1">
                        <PARAM NAME="ButtonDefaultAction" VALUE="-1">
                        <PARAM NAME="ThreeDText" VALUE="0">
                        <PARAM NAME="ThreeDTextHighlightColor" VALUE="-2147483633">
                        <PARAM NAME="ThreeDTextShadowColor" VALUE="-2147483632">
                        <PARAM NAME="ThreeDTextOffset" VALUE="1">
                        <PARAM NAME="AlignTextH" VALUE="0">
                        <PARAM NAME="AlignTextV" VALUE="0">
                        <PARAM NAME="AllowNull" VALUE="0">
                        <PARAM NAME="NoSpecialKeys" VALUE="0">
                        <PARAM NAME="AutoAdvance" VALUE="0">
                        <PARAM NAME="AutoBeep" VALUE="0">
                        <PARAM NAME="CaretInsert" VALUE="0">
                        <PARAM NAME="CaretOverWrite" VALUE="3">
                        <PARAM NAME="UserEntry" VALUE="0">
                        <PARAM NAME="HideSelection" VALUE="-1">
                        <PARAM NAME="InvalidColor" VALUE="-2147483637">
                        <PARAM NAME="InvalidOption" VALUE="0">
                        <PARAM NAME="MarginLeft" VALUE="3">
                        <PARAM NAME="MarginTop" VALUE="3">
                        <PARAM NAME="MarginRight" VALUE="3">
                        <PARAM NAME="MarginBottom" VALUE="3">
                        <PARAM NAME="NullColor" VALUE="-2147483637">
                        <PARAM NAME="OnFocusAlignH" VALUE="0">
```

```
            <PARAM NAME="OnFocusAlignV" VALUE="0">
            <PARAM NAME="OnFocusNoSelect" VALUE="0">
            <PARAM NAME="OnFocusPosition" VALUE="0">
            <PARAM NAME="ControlType" VALUE="0">
            <PARAM NAME="Text" VALUE="$0.00">
            <PARAM NAME="CurrencyDecimalPlaces" VALUE="-1">
            <PARAM NAME="CurrencyNegFormat" VALUE="0">
            <PARAM NAME="CurrencyPlacement" VALUE="0">
            <PARAM NAME="CurrencySymbol" VALUE="">
            <PARAM NAME="DecimalPoint" VALUE=".">
            <PARAM NAME="FixedPoint" VALUE="-1">
            <PARAM NAME="LeadZero" VALUE="0">
            <PARAM NAME="MaxValue" VALUE="10000">
            <PARAM NAME="MinValue" VALUE="-100000">
            <PARAM NAME="NegToggle" VALUE="0">
            <PARAM NAME="Separator" VALUE="">
            <PARAM NAME="UseSeparator" VALUE="-1">
            <PARAM NAME="IncInt" VALUE="1">
            <PARAM NAME="IncDec" VALUE="1">
            <PARAM NAME="BorderGrayAreaColor" VALUE="-2147483637">
            <PARAM NAME="ThreeDOnFocusInvert" VALUE="0">
            <PARAM NAME="ThreeDFrameColor" VALUE="-2147483633">
            <PARAM NAME="Appearance" VALUE="0">
            <PARAM NAME="BorderDropShadow" VALUE="0">
            <PARAM NAME="BorderDropShadowColor" VALUE="-2147483632">
            <PARAM NAME="BorderDropShadowWidth" VALUE="3">
         </OBJECT>

         </BODY>
         </HTML>
```

fpDateTime

The fpDateTime is a formatted date and time data-entry ActiveX control. It performs validation for invalid characters, a range of dates, and so on. This control can be bound to date, time, or text values in the back-end database. One of the interesting features of this control is the capability to select data from a drop-down or popup calendar.

Source

Vendor Information:

FarPoint Technologies, Inc.
http://www.fpoint.com
133 Southcenter Court, Suite 1000
Morrisville, NC 27560
(800) 645-4551
(919) 460-7606

Part

III

Ch

14

FIG. 14.3

The fpDateTime control drop-down calendar

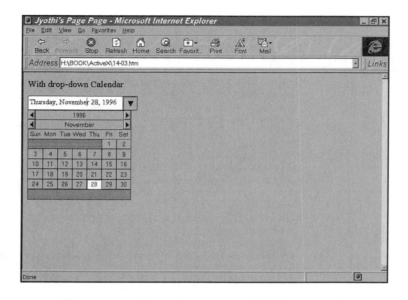

FIG. 14.4

The fpDateTime control popup calendar

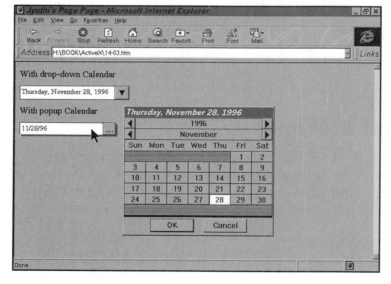

Properties

Table 14.7 Properties of the fpDateTime Control

Property	Description
AlignTextH	The horizontal alignment of the text
AlignTextV	The vertical alignment of the text
AllowNull	True, to allow the user the capability to leave this control blank
Appearance	The border look—flat, 3-D, and so on
AutoAdvance	True, to advance to the next control after pressing the Enter key
AutoBeep	True, to sound the beep on user error
BackColor	The background color of the object
BorderColor	The object's border color
BorderDropShadow	The 3-D shadow for border—none, always, on focus
BorderDropShadowColor	The border 3-D shadow color
BorderDropShadowWidth	The border 3-D shadow width
BorderGrayAreaColor	The color of the gray area of the 3-D border
BorderStyle	The object's border style
BorderWidth	The object's border width
ButtonDefaultAction	True, to enable the default action for the spin button
ButtonDisable	True, to disable the buttons on the control
ButtonHide	True, to hide the buttons
ButtonIncrement	The value by which the button index will be increased or decreased
ButtonMax	The upper limit for the button index
ButtonMin	The lower limit for the button index
ButtonStyle	The style of the button—none, spin, slide, and so on
ButtonWidth	The width of the button
ButtonWrap	True, to reset the button index when it crosses the upper or lower limits

continues

Part

III

Ch

14

Table 14.7 Continued

Property	Description
CaretInsert	The caret for the insert mode
CaretOverwrite	The overstrike mode caret
CodeBase	The origin of the control, including the URL, file type, and version number
ControlType	The control UI mode—normal, read-only, static, button edit
CurrentPosition	The current position of the cursor
DataChanged	True, when the data is changed
DataField	The name of the bound column in the DataSource
DataSource	The source of the database to be bound to this control
DateCalcMethod	The method for calculating missing date and time values—Current Date/Time, User Defined Date/Time, 50/50, Future
DateDefault	The default date displayed when the control is initialized
DateMax	The upper limit for the date entry
DateMin	The lower limit for date entry
DateTimeFormat	The format of the date/time
Day	The day value of the date in the control
Enabled	True, to set the control to get focus and respond to UI
Font	The font of the control caption
ForeColor	The foreground color of the object
Height	The vertical height of the object
HideSelection	True, to highlight the selected characters even when the control loses focus
hWND	The handle for the window
ID	The name of the object/control
InvalidColor	The background color when the data in the control is invalid
InvalidOption	Action for invalid data when the control loses focus—show data, hide data, clear data
Left	The distance between the left edge of the control and the left edge of the HTML layout

Property	Description
MarginBottom	The bottom margin in pixels
MarginLeft	The left margin in pixels
MarginRight	The right margin in pixels
MarginTop	The top margin in pixels
Month	The month value of the date in the control
MouseIcon	The image that appears when the mouse is moved over the object
MousePointer	The mouse pointer that appears when the mouse is moved over the object
NoSpecialKeys	Option for handling keyboard keys
NullColor	The background color when the control contains no value
OnFocusAlignH	Horizontal alignment of the data in the control when it gets focus
OnFocusAlignV	Vertical alignment of the data in the control when it gets focus
OnFocusNoSelect	False, to select the data in the control when it gets focus
OnFocusPosition	The position of the cursor in the data in the control when it gets focus
ReDraw	Repaint the control
SelLength	The number of characters selected
SelStart	The starting/insertion point of selection
SelText	The character string selected by the user
TabIndex	The object's tab order position in the HTML layout
Text	The date in the text format
ThreeDFrameColor	The color of the 3-D frame
ThreeDFrameWidth	The width of the 3-D frame
ThreeDInsideHighliteColor	The color for the inner border 3-D highlight
ThreeDInsideShadowColor	The color for the inner border 3-D shadow
ThreeDInsideStyle	The style for the inner border 3-D—none, lowered, raised
ThreeDInsideWidth	The width for the inner border 3-D
ThreeDOnFocusInvert	True, to invert the 3-D when the control gets focus

Part
III

Ch
14

continues

Table 14.7 Continued

Property	Description
ThreeDOutsideHighliteColor	The color for the outer border 3-D highlight
ThreeDOutsideShadowColor	The color for the outer border 3-D shadow
ThreeDOutsideStyle	The style for the outer border 3-D—none, lowered, raised
ThreeDOutsideWidth	The width for the outer border 3-D
TimeDefault	The default time that appears when the control is initialized
TimeMax	The upper limit for the time entry
TimeMin	The lower limit for date entry
TimeString1159	The string to indicate morning, for example, AM
TimeString2359	The string to indicate evening, for example, PM
TimeStyle	The style for time display: 12-hour, 24-hour, and so on
TimeValue	The value of time in the control
Top	The distance between the top edge of the control and the top edge of the HTML layout
UnFmtText	The control text without any formatting
UserDefinedFormat	The format for display for user-defined format
UserEntry	Formatted or free format
Visible	False to hide the control
Width	The width of the control in points
Year	The year value of the date in the control

Method

Table 14.8 Method of the fpDateTime Control

Method	Description
AboutBox	Displays the About dialog box

Events

Table 14.9   Events of the fpDateTime Control

Event	Description
Advance	Triggers when a valid character is entered at the last position
ButtonHit	Triggers when the user presses a button
Change	Triggers when the value of a control changes by either the UI or programmatically; use this event handler to synchronize data between controls
ChangeMode	Triggers when the user changes the edit mode between insert and overstrike
Click	Triggers when a control is clicked with the mouse
DblClick	Triggers when a control is double-clicked
InvalidData	Triggers when the control contains invalid data
KeyDown	Triggers when a user presses a control, navigation, or function key
KeyPress	Triggers when a key is either pressed by the user or sent from the SendKeys function
KeyUp	Triggers when a user releases a control, navigation or, function key
MouseDown	Triggers when a user presses a mouse button
MouseMove	Triggers when the user moves the mouse
MouseUp	Triggers when a user releases a mouse button
Popup	Triggers when the popup calendar is activated
UserError	Triggers when an error occurs

Example

```
<HTML>
<HEAD>
<TITLE>Jyothi's Page Page</TITLE>
</HEAD>
<BODY>
<P>
<TEXT> With drop-down Calendar</TEXT>
<P>
<OBJECT ID="fpDateTime1" WIDTH=238 HEIGHT=32
```

Part

III

Ch

14

```
CLASSID="CLSID:B8958DE0-BAC9-101C-933E-0000C005958C">
    <PARAM NAME="_Version" VALUE="131072">
    <PARAM NAME="_ExtentX" VALUE="5045">
    <PARAM NAME="_ExtentY" VALUE="670">
    <PARAM NAME="_StockProps" VALUE="68">
    <PARAM NAME="BackColor" VALUE="16777215">
    <PARAM NAME="ForeColor" VALUE="-2147483640">
    <PARAM NAME="ThreeDInsideStyle" VALUE="0">
    <PARAM NAME="ThreeDInsideHighlightColor" VALUE="-2147483633">
    <PARAM NAME="ThreeDInsideShadowColor" VALUE="-2147483642">
    <PARAM NAME="ThreeDInsideWidth" VALUE="1">
    <PARAM NAME="ThreeDOutsideStyle" VALUE="0">
    <PARAM NAME="ThreeDOutsideHighlightColor" VALUE="-2147483628">
    <PARAM NAME="ThreeDOutsideShadowColor" VALUE="-2147483632">
    <PARAM NAME="ThreeDOutsideWidth" VALUE="1">
    <PARAM NAME="ThreeDFrameWidth" VALUE="0">
    <PARAM NAME="BorderStyle" VALUE="1">
    <PARAM NAME="BorderColor" VALUE="-2147483642">
    <PARAM NAME="BorderWidth" VALUE="1">
    <PARAM NAME="ButtonDefaultAction" VALUE="-1">
    <PARAM NAME="ButtonDisable" VALUE="0">
    <PARAM NAME="ButtonHide" VALUE="0">
    <PARAM NAME="ButtonIncrement" VALUE="1">
    <PARAM NAME="ButtonMin" VALUE="0">
    <PARAM NAME="ButtonMax" VALUE="100">
    <PARAM NAME="ButtonStyle" VALUE="3">
    <PARAM NAME="ButtonWidth" VALUE="0">
    <PARAM NAME="ButtonWrap" VALUE="-1">
    <PARAM NAME="ThreeDText" VALUE="0">
    <PARAM NAME="ThreeDTextHighlightColor" VALUE="-2147483633">
    <PARAM NAME="ThreeDTextShadowColor" VALUE="-2147483632">
    <PARAM NAME="ThreeDTextOffset" VALUE="1">
    <PARAM NAME="AlignTextH" VALUE="0">
    <PARAM NAME="AlignTextV" VALUE="0">
    <PARAM NAME="AllowNull" VALUE="0">
    <PARAM NAME="NoSpecialKeys" VALUE="0">
    <PARAM NAME="AutoAdvance" VALUE="0">
    <PARAM NAME="AutoBeep" VALUE="0">
    <PARAM NAME="CaretInsert" VALUE="0">
    <PARAM NAME="CaretOverWrite" VALUE="3">
    <PARAM NAME="UserEntry" VALUE="1">
    <PARAM NAME="HideSelection" VALUE="-1">
    <PARAM NAME="InvalidColor" VALUE="-2147483637">
    <PARAM NAME="InvalidOption" VALUE="0">
    <PARAM NAME="MarginLeft" VALUE="3">
    <PARAM NAME="MarginTop" VALUE="3">
    <PARAM NAME="MarginRight" VALUE="3">
    <PARAM NAME="MarginBottom" VALUE="3">
    <PARAM NAME="NullColor" VALUE="-2147483637">
    <PARAM NAME="OnFocusAlignH" VALUE="0">
    <PARAM NAME="OnFocusAlignV" VALUE="0">
    <PARAM NAME="OnFocusNoSelect" VALUE="0">
    <PARAM NAME="OnFocusPosition" VALUE="0">
    <PARAM NAME="ControlType" VALUE="0">
    <PARAM NAME="Text" VALUE="Thursday, November 28, 1996">
    <PARAM NAME="DateCalcMethod" VALUE="0">
```

```
            <PARAM NAME="DateTimeFormat" VALUE="1">
            <PARAM NAME="UserDefinedFormat" VALUE="">
            <PARAM NAME="DateMax" VALUE="00000000">
            <PARAM NAME="DateMin" VALUE="00000000">
            <PARAM NAME="TimeMax" VALUE="000000">
            <PARAM NAME="TimeMin" VALUE="000000">
            <PARAM NAME="TimeString1159" VALUE="">
            <PARAM NAME="TimeString2359" VALUE="">
            <PARAM NAME="DateDefault" VALUE="00000000">
            <PARAM NAME="TimeDefault" VALUE="000000">
            <PARAM NAME="TimeStyle" VALUE="0">
            <PARAM NAME="BorderGrayAreaColor" VALUE="-2147483637">
            <PARAM NAME="ThreeDOnFocusInvert" VALUE="0">
            <PARAM NAME="ThreeDFrameColor" VALUE="-2147483633">
            <PARAM NAME="Appearance" VALUE="0">
            <PARAM NAME="BorderDropShadow" VALUE="0">
            <PARAM NAME="BorderDropShadowColor" VALUE="-2147483632">
            <PARAM NAME="BorderDropShadowWidth" VALUE="3">
</OBJECT>
<P>
<TEXT> With popup Calendar</TEXT>
<P>
<OBJECT ID="fpDateTime1" WIDTH=213 HEIGHT=32
 CLASSID="CLSID:B8958DE0-BAC9-101C-933E-0000C005958C">
            <PARAM NAME="_Version" VALUE="131072">
            <PARAM NAME="_ExtentX" VALUE="4514">
            <PARAM NAME="_ExtentY" VALUE="662">
            <PARAM NAME="_StockProps" VALUE="68">
            <PARAM NAME="BackColor" VALUE="-2147483643">
            <PARAM NAME="ForeColor" VALUE="-2147483640">
            <PARAM NAME="ThreeDInsideStyle" VALUE="0">
            <PARAM NAME="ThreeDInsideHighlightColor" VALUE="-2147483633">
            <PARAM NAME="ThreeDInsideShadowColor" VALUE="-2147483642">
            <PARAM NAME="ThreeDInsideWidth" VALUE="1">
            <PARAM NAME="ThreeDOutsideStyle" VALUE="0">
            <PARAM NAME="ThreeDOutsideHighlightColor" VALUE="-2147483628">
            <PARAM NAME="ThreeDOutsideShadowColor" VALUE="-2147483632">
            <PARAM NAME="ThreeDOutsideWidth" VALUE="1">
            <PARAM NAME="ThreeDFrameWidth" VALUE="0">
            <PARAM NAME="BorderStyle" VALUE="2">
            <PARAM NAME="BorderColor" VALUE="-2147483642">
            <PARAM NAME="BorderWidth" VALUE="1">
            <PARAM NAME="ButtonDefaultAction" VALUE="-1">
            <PARAM NAME="ButtonDisable" VALUE="0">
            <PARAM NAME="ButtonHide" VALUE="0">
            <PARAM NAME="ButtonIncrement" VALUE="1">
            <PARAM NAME="ButtonMin" VALUE="0">
            <PARAM NAME="ButtonMax" VALUE="100">
            <PARAM NAME="ButtonStyle" VALUE="2">
            <PARAM NAME="ButtonWidth" VALUE="0">
            <PARAM NAME="ButtonWrap" VALUE="-1">
            <PARAM NAME="ThreeDText" VALUE="0">
            <PARAM NAME="ThreeDTextHighlightColor" VALUE="-2147483633">
            <PARAM NAME="ThreeDTextShadowColor" VALUE="-2147483632">
            <PARAM NAME="ThreeDTextOffset" VALUE="1">
            <PARAM NAME="AlignTextH" VALUE="0">
```

```
        <PARAM NAME="AlignTextV" VALUE="0">
        <PARAM NAME="AllowNull" VALUE="0">
        <PARAM NAME="NoSpecialKeys" VALUE="0">
        <PARAM NAME="AutoAdvance" VALUE="0">
        <PARAM NAME="AutoBeep" VALUE="0">
        <PARAM NAME="CaretInsert" VALUE="0">
        <PARAM NAME="CaretOverWrite" VALUE="3">
        <PARAM NAME="UserEntry" VALUE="1">
        <PARAM NAME="HideSelection" VALUE="-1">
        <PARAM NAME="InvalidColor" VALUE="-2147483637">
        <PARAM NAME="InvalidOption" VALUE="0">
        <PARAM NAME="MarginLeft" VALUE="3">
        <PARAM NAME="MarginTop" VALUE="3">
        <PARAM NAME="MarginRight" VALUE="3">
        <PARAM NAME="MarginBottom" VALUE="3">
        <PARAM NAME="NullColor" VALUE="-2147483637">
        <PARAM NAME="OnFocusAlignH" VALUE="0">
        <PARAM NAME="OnFocusAlignV" VALUE="0">
        <PARAM NAME="OnFocusNoSelect" VALUE="0">
        <PARAM NAME="OnFocusPosition" VALUE="0">
        <PARAM NAME="ControlType" VALUE="0">
        <PARAM NAME="Text" VALUE="fpDateTime1">
        <PARAM NAME="DateCalcMethod" VALUE="0">
        <PARAM NAME="DateTimeFormat" VALUE="0">
        <PARAM NAME="UserDefinedFormat" VALUE="">
        <PARAM NAME="DateMax" VALUE="00000000">
        <PARAM NAME="DateMin" VALUE="00000000">
        <PARAM NAME="TimeMax" VALUE="000000">
        <PARAM NAME="TimeMin" VALUE="000000">
        <PARAM NAME="TimeString1159" VALUE="">
        <PARAM NAME="TimeString2359" VALUE="">
        <PARAM NAME="DateDefault" VALUE="00000000">
        <PARAM NAME="TimeDefault" VALUE="000000">
        <PARAM NAME="TimeStyle" VALUE="0">
        <PARAM NAME="BorderGrayAreaColor" VALUE="-2147483637">
        <PARAM NAME="ThreeDOnFocusInvert" VALUE="0">
        <PARAM NAME="ThreeDFrameColor" VALUE="-2147483633">
        <PARAM NAME="Appearance" VALUE="0">
        <PARAM NAME="BorderDropShadow" VALUE="1">
        <PARAM NAME="BorderDropShadowColor" VALUE="-2147483632">
        <PARAM NAME="BorderDropShadowWidth" VALUE="3">
    </OBJECT>

    </BODY>
    </HTML>
```

Notes

This control is essential in the tool box of any Web designer. The user-friendly popup or drop-down calendar is becoming an essential feature for data-entry systems.

fpDoubleSingle

The fpDoubleSingle is a formatted, decimal, numeric data-entry ActiveX control. It performs validation for invalid characters, a range of values, and so on. This control can be bound to numeric or text values in the back-end database.

Source

Vendor Information:

FarPoint Technologies, Inc.
http://www.fpoint.com
133 Southcenter Court, Suite 1000
Morrisville, NC 27560
(800) 645-4551
(919) 460-7606

FIG. 14.5
The fpDoubleSingle control

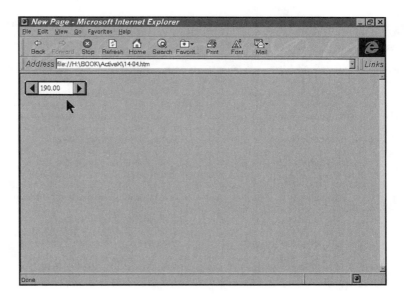

Properties

Table 14.10 Properties of the fpDoubleSingle Control	
Property	**Description**
AlignTextH	The horizontal alignment of the text
AlignTextv	The vertical alignment of the text

continues

Table 14.10   Continued

Property	Description
AllowNull	True, to allow the user the capability to leave this control blank
Appearance	The border look—flat, 3-D, and so on
AutoAdvance	True, to advance to the next control after pressing the Enter key
AutoBeep	True, to sound the beep on user error
BackColor	The background color of the object
BorderColor	The object's border color
BorderDropShadow	The 3-D shadow for border—none, always, on focus
BorderDropShadowColor	The border 3-D shadow color
BorderDropShadowWidth	The border 3-D shadow width
BorderGrayAreaColor	The color of the gray area of the 3-D border
BorderStyle	The object's border style
BorderWidth	The object's border width
ButtonDefaultAction	True, to enable the default action for the spin button
ButtonDisable	True, to disable the buttons on the control
ButtonHide	True, to hide the buttons
ButtonIncrement	The value by which the button index will be increased or decreased
ButtonMax	The upper limit for the button index
ButtonMin	The lower limit for the button index
ButtonStyle	The style of the button—none, spin, slide, and so on
ButtonWidth	The width of the button
ButtonWrap	True, to reset the button index when it crosses the upper or lower limits
CaretInsert	The caret for the insert mode
CaretOverwrite	The overstrike mode caret
CodeBase	The origin of the control, including the URL, file type, and version number
ControlType	The control UI mode—normal, read-only, static, button edit

Property	Description
DataChanged	True, when the data is changed
DataField	The name of the bound column in the DataSource
DataSource	The source of the database to be bound to this control
DecimalPlaces	The number of decimal places in the control
DecimalPoint	The character to be used for decimal point
Enabled	True, to set the control to get focus and respond to UI
FixedPoint	True, to display zeroes to the right of decimal place
Font	The font of the control caption
ForeColor	The foreground color of the object
Height	The vertical height of the object
HideSelection	True, to highlight the selected characters even when the control loses focus
hWND	The handle for the window
ID	The name of the object/control
IncDec	The decimal portion increment when using the button
IncInt	The integer portion increment when using the button
InvalidColor	The background color when the data in the control is invalid
InvalidOption	The action for invalid data when the control loses focus— show data, hide data, clear data
LeadZero	The leading zero display option
Left	The distance between the left edge of the control and the left edge of the HTML layout
MarginBottom	The bottom margin in pixels
MarginLeft	The left margin in pixels
MarginRight	The right margin in pixels
MarginTop	The top margin in pixels
MaxValue	The upper limit for the control value
MinValue	The lower limit for the control value
MouseIcon	The image that appears when the mouse is moved over the object
MousePointer	The mouse pointer that appears when the mouse is moved over the object

continues

Part
III

Ch

14

Table 14.10 Continued

Property	Description
NegFormat	The display format for negative numbers
NegToggle	True, to allow the user to enter negative value
NoSpecialKeys	The option for handling keyboard keys
NullColor	The background color when the control contains no value
OnFocusAlignH	Horizontal alignment of the data in the control when it gets focus
OnFocusAlignV	Vertical alignment of the data in the control when it gets focus
OnFocusNoSelect	False, to select the data in the control when it gets focus
OnFocusPosition	The position of the cursor in the data in the control when it gets focus
Separator	The thousands separator character
ReDraw	Repaint the control
SelLength	The number of characters selected
SelStart	The starting/insertion point of selection
SelText	The character string selected by the user
TabIndex	The object's tab order position in the HTML layout
Text	The date in the text format
ThreeDFrameColor	The color of the 3-D frame
ThreeDFrameWidth	The width of the 3-D frame
ThreeDInsideHighliteColor	The color for the inner border 3-D highlight
ThreeDInsideShadowColor	The color for the inner border 3-D shadow
ThreeDInsideStyle	The style for the inner border 3-D—none, lowered, raised
ThreeDInsideWidth	The width for the inner border 3-D
ThreeDOnFocusInvert	True, to invert the 3-D when the control gets focus
ThreeDOutsideHighliteColor	The color for the outer border 3-D highlight
ThreeDOutsideShadowColor	The color for the outer border 3-D shadow
ThreeDOutsideStyle	The style for the outer border 3-D—none, lowered, raised
ThreeDOutsideWidth	The width for the outer border 3-D

Property	Description
Top	The distance between the top edge of the control and the top edge of the HTML layout
UserEntry	Formatted or free format
UseSparator	True, to display the thousands separator character
Visible	False, to hide the control
Width	The width of the control in points

Method

Table 14.11   Method of the fpDoubleSingle Control

Method	Description
AboutBox	Displays the About dialog box

Events

Table 14.12   Events of the fpDoubleSingle Control

Event	Description
Advance	Triggers when a valid character is entered at the last position
ButtonHit	Triggers when a button is pressed by the user
Change	Triggers when the value of a control changes by either the UI or programmatically; use this event handler to synchronize data between controls
ChangeMode	Triggers when the user changes the edit mode between insert and overstrike
Click	Triggers when a control is clicked with the mouse
DblClick	Triggers when a control is double-clicked
InvalidData	Triggers when the control contains invalid data
KeyDown	Triggers when a user presses a control, navigation, or function key
KeyPress	Triggers when a key is either pressed by the user or sent from the SendKeys function

Part

III

Ch

14

continues

Table 14.12   Continued

Event	Description
KeyUp	Triggers when a user releases a control, navigation, or function key
MouseDown	Triggers when a user presses a mouse button
MouseMove	Triggers when the user moves the mouse
MouseUp	Triggers when a user releases a mouse button
UserError	Triggers when an error occurs

Example

```
<HTML>
<HEAD>
<TITLE>New Page</TITLE>
</HEAD>
<BODY>

<OBJECT ID="fpDoubleSingle1" WIDTH=135 HEIGHT=32
 CLASSID="CLSID:B8958DE5-BAC9-101C-933E-0000C005958C">
    <PARAM NAME="_Version" VALUE="131072">
    <PARAM NAME="_ExtentX" VALUE="2858">
    <PARAM NAME="_ExtentY" VALUE="670">
    <PARAM NAME="_StockProps" VALUE="68">
    <PARAM NAME="BackColor" VALUE="-2147483643">
    <PARAM NAME="ForeColor" VALUE="-2147483640">
    <PARAM NAME="ThreeDInsideStyle" VALUE="0">
    <PARAM NAME="ThreeDInsideHighlightColor" VALUE="-2147483633">
    <PARAM NAME="ThreeDInsideShadowColor" VALUE="-2147483642">
    <PARAM NAME="ThreeDInsideWidth" VALUE="1">
    <PARAM NAME="ThreeDOutsideStyle" VALUE="0">
    <PARAM NAME="ThreeDOutsideHighlightColor" VALUE="-2147483628">
    <PARAM NAME="ThreeDOutsideShadowColor" VALUE="-2147483632">
    <PARAM NAME="ThreeDOutsideWidth" VALUE="1">
    <PARAM NAME="ThreeDFrameWidth" VALUE="0">
    <PARAM NAME="BorderStyle" VALUE="2">
    <PARAM NAME="BorderColor" VALUE="-2147483642">
    <PARAM NAME="BorderWidth" VALUE="3">
    <PARAM NAME="ButtonDisable" VALUE="0">
    <PARAM NAME="ButtonHide" VALUE="0">
    <PARAM NAME="ButtonIncrement" VALUE="1">
    <PARAM NAME="ButtonMin" VALUE="0">
    <PARAM NAME="ButtonMax" VALUE="100">
    <PARAM NAME="ButtonStyle" VALUE="4">
    <PARAM NAME="ButtonWidth" VALUE="0">
    <PARAM NAME="ButtonWrap" VALUE="-1">
    <PARAM NAME="ButtonDefaultAction" VALUE="-1">
    <PARAM NAME="ThreeDText" VALUE="0">
    <PARAM NAME="ThreeDTextHighlightColor" VALUE="-2147483633">
```

```
          <PARAM NAME="ThreeDTextShadowColor" VALUE="-2147483632">
          <PARAM NAME="ThreeDTextOffset" VALUE="1">
          <PARAM NAME="AlignTextH" VALUE="0">
          <PARAM NAME="AlignTextV" VALUE="0">
          <PARAM NAME="AllowNull" VALUE="0">
          <PARAM NAME="NoSpecialKeys" VALUE="0">
          <PARAM NAME="AutoAdvance" VALUE="0">
          <PARAM NAME="AutoBeep" VALUE="0">
          <PARAM NAME="CaretInsert" VALUE="0">
          <PARAM NAME="CaretOverWrite" VALUE="3">
          <PARAM NAME="UserEntry" VALUE="0">
          <PARAM NAME="HideSelection" VALUE="-1">
          <PARAM NAME="InvalidColor" VALUE="-2147483637">
          <PARAM NAME="InvalidOption" VALUE="0">
          <PARAM NAME="MarginLeft" VALUE="3">
          <PARAM NAME="MarginTop" VALUE="3">
          <PARAM NAME="MarginRight" VALUE="3">
          <PARAM NAME="MarginBottom" VALUE="3">
          <PARAM NAME="NullColor" VALUE="-2147483637">
          <PARAM NAME="OnFocusAlignH" VALUE="0">
          <PARAM NAME="OnFocusAlignV" VALUE="0">
          <PARAM NAME="OnFocusNoSelect" VALUE="0">
          <PARAM NAME="OnFocusPosition" VALUE="0">
          <PARAM NAME="ControlType" VALUE="0">
          <PARAM NAME="Text" VALUE="0.00">
          <PARAM NAME="DecimalPlaces" VALUE="-1">
          <PARAM NAME="DecimalPoint" VALUE="">
          <PARAM NAME="FixedPoint" VALUE="-1">
          <PARAM NAME="LeadZero" VALUE="0">
          <PARAM NAME="MaxValue" VALUE="9000000000">
          <PARAM NAME="MinValue" VALUE="-9000000000">
          <PARAM NAME="NegFormat" VALUE="1">
          <PARAM NAME="NegToggle" VALUE="0">
          <PARAM NAME="Separator" VALUE="">
          <PARAM NAME="UseSeparator" VALUE="0">
          <PARAM NAME="IncInt" VALUE="1">
          <PARAM NAME="IncDec" VALUE="1">
          <PARAM NAME="BorderGrayAreaColor" VALUE="-2147483637">
          <PARAM NAME="ThreeDOnFocusInvert" VALUE="0">
          <PARAM NAME="ThreeDFrameColor" VALUE="-2147483633">
          <PARAM NAME="Appearance" VALUE="0">
          <PARAM NAME="BorderDropShadow" VALUE="0">
          <PARAM NAME="BorderDropShadowColor" VALUE="-2147483632">
          <PARAM NAME="BorderDropShadowWidth" VALUE="3">
     </OBJECT>

     </BODY>
     </HTML>
```

fpLongIntegerSingle

The fpLongInteger is a formatted, numeric data-entry ActiveX control. It performs validation for invalid characters, a range of values, and so on. This control can be bound to numeric or text values in the back-end database.

Source

Vendor Information:

FarPoint Technologies, Inc.
http://www.fpoint.com
133 Southcenter Court, Suite 1000
Morrisville, NC 27560
(800) 645-4551
(919) 460-7606

FIG. 14.6
The fpLongInteger control

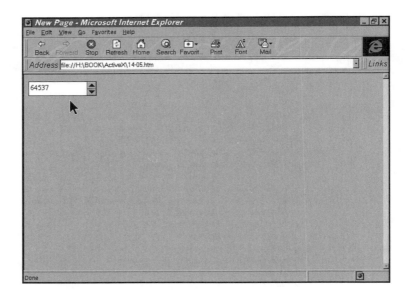

Properties

Table 14.13 Properties of the fpLongInteger Control

Property	Description
AlignTextH	The horizontal alignment of the text
AlignTextV	The vertical alignment of the text
AllowNull	True, to allow the user the capability to leave this control blank
Appearance	The border look—flat, 3-D, and so on
AutoAdvance	True, to advance to the next control after pressing the Enter key

Property	Description
AutoBeep	True, to sound the beep on user error
BackColor	The background color of the object
BorderColor	The object's border color
BorderDropShadow	The 3-D shadow for border—none, always, on focus
BorderDropShadowColor	The border 3-D shadow color
BorderDropShadowWidth	The border 3-D shadow width
BorderGrayAreaColor	The color of the gray area of the 3-D border
BorderStyle	The object's border style
BorderWidth	The object's border width
ButtonDefaultAction	True, to enable the default action for the spin button
ButtonDisable	True, to disable the buttons on the control
ButtonHide	True, to hide the buttons
ButtonIncrement	The value by which the button index will be increased or decreased
ButtonMax	The upper limit for the button index
ButtonMin	The lower limit for the button index
ButtonStyle	The style of the button—none, spin, slide, and so on
ButtonWidth	The width of the button
ButtonWrap	True, to reset the button index when it crosses the upper or lower limits
CaretInsert	The caret for the insert mode
CaretOverwrite	The overstrike mode caret
CodeBase	The origin of the control, including the URL, file type, and version number
ControlType	The control UI mode—normal, read-only, static, button edit
DataChanged	True, when the data is changed
DataField	The name of the bound column in the DataSource
DataSource	The source of the database to be bound to this control
Enabled	True, to set the control to get focus and respond to UI
Font	The font of the control caption

Part
III

Ch

14

continues

Table 14.13   Continued

Property	Description
ForeColor	The foreground color of the object
Height	The vertical height of the object
HideSelection	True, to highlight the selected characters even when the control loses focus
hWND	The handle for the window
ID	The name of the object/control
IncDec	The decimal portion increment when using the button
IncInt	The integer portion increment when using the button
InvalidColor	The background color when the data in the control is invalid
InvalidOption	The action for invalid data when the control loses focus— show data, hide data, clear data
Left	The distance between the left edge of the control and the left edge of the HTML layout
MarginBottom	The bottom margin in pixels
MarginLeft	The left margin in pixels
MarginRight	The right margin in pixels
MarginTop	The top margin in pixels
MaxValue	The upper limit for the control value
MinValue	The lower limit for the control value
MouseIcon	The image that appears when the mouse is moved over the object
MousePointer	The mouse pointer that appears when the mouse is moved over the object
NegFormat	The display format for negative numbers
NegToggle	True, to allow the user to enter negative value
NoSpecialKeys	The option for handling keyboard keys
NullColor	The background color when the control contains no value
OnFocusAlignH	Horizontal alignment of the data in the control when it gets focus
OnFocusAlignV	Vertical alignment of the data in the control when it gets focus

Property	Description
OnFocusNoSelect	False, to select the data in the control when it gets focus
OnFocusPosition	The position of the cursor in the data in the control when it gets focus
Separator	The thousands separator character
ReDraw	Repaint the control
SelLength	The number of characters selected
SelStart	The starting/insertion point of selection
SelText	The character string selected by the user
TabIndex	The object's tab order position in the HTML layout
Text	The date in the text format
ThreeDFrameColor	The color of the 3-D frame
ThreeDFrameWidth	The width of the 3-D frame
ThreeDInsideHighliteColor	The color for the inner border 3-D highlight
ThreeDInsideShadowColor	The color for the inner border 3-D shadow
ThreeDInsideStyle	The style for the inner border 3-D—none, lowered, raised
ThreeDInsideWidth	The width for the inner border 3-D
ThreeDOnFocusInvert	True, to invert the 3-D when the control gets focus
ThreeDOutsideHighliteColor	The color for the outer border 3-D highlight
ThreeDOutsideShadowColor	The color for the outer border 3-D shadow
ThreeDOutsideStyle	The style for the outer border 3-D—none, lowered, raised
ThreeDOutsideWidth	The width for the outer border 3-D
Top	The distance between the top edge of the control and the top edge of the HTML layout
UserEntry	Formatted or free format
UseSparator	True, to display the thousands separator character
Value	The value of the data in the control
Visible	False, to hide the control
Width	The width of the control in points

Part
III

Ch
14

Method

Table 14.14	Method of the fpLongInteger Control
Method	**Description**
AboutBox	Displays the About dialog box

Events

Table 14.15	Events of the fpLongInteger Control
Event	**Description**
Advance	Triggers when a valid character is entered at the last position
ButtonHit	Triggers when a button is pressed by the user
Change	Triggers when the value of a control changes by either the UI or programmatically; use this event handler to synchronize data between controls
ChangeMode	Triggers when the user changes the edit mode between insert and overstrike
Click	Triggers when a control is clicked with the mouse
DblClick	Triggers when a control is double-clicked
InvalidData	Triggers when the control contains invalid data
KeyDown	Triggers when a user presses a control, navigation, or function key
KeyPress	Triggers when a key is either pressed by the user or sent from the SendKeys function
KeyUp	Triggers when a user releases a control, navigation, or function key
MouseDown	Triggers when a user presses a mouse button
MouseMove	Triggers when the user moves the mouse
MouseUp	Triggers when a user releases a mouse button
UserError	Triggers when an error occurs

Example

```
<HTML>
<HEAD>
<TITLE>New Page</TITLE>
</HEAD>
```

```
<BODY>
    <OBJECT ID="fpLongInteger1" WIDTH=148 HEIGHT=32
    CLASSID="CLSID:B8958DEF-BAC9-101C-933E-0000C005958C">
        <PARAM NAME="_Version" VALUE="131072">
        <PARAM NAME="_ExtentX" VALUE="3140">
        <PARAM NAME="_ExtentY" VALUE="670">
        <PARAM NAME="_StockProps" VALUE="68">
        <PARAM NAME="BackColor" VALUE="-2147483643">
        <PARAM NAME="ForeColor" VALUE="-2147483640">
        <PARAM NAME="ThreeDInsideStyle" VALUE="0">
        <PARAM NAME="ThreeDInsideHighlightColor" VALUE="-2147483633">
        <PARAM NAME="ThreeDInsideShadowColor" VALUE="-2147483642">
        <PARAM NAME="ThreeDInsideWidth" VALUE="1">
        <PARAM NAME="ThreeDOutsideStyle" VALUE="0">
        <PARAM NAME="ThreeDOutsideHighlightColor" VALUE="-2147483628">
        <PARAM NAME="ThreeDOutsideShadowColor" VALUE="-2147483632">
        <PARAM NAME="ThreeDOutsideWidth" VALUE="1">
        <PARAM NAME="ThreeDFrameWidth" VALUE="0">
        <PARAM NAME="BorderStyle" VALUE="1">
        <PARAM NAME="BorderColor" VALUE="-2147483642">
        <PARAM NAME="BorderWidth" VALUE="1">
        <PARAM NAME="ButtonDisable" VALUE="0">
        <PARAM NAME="ButtonHide" VALUE="0">
        <PARAM NAME="ButtonIncrement" VALUE="1">
        <PARAM NAME="ButtonMin" VALUE="0">
        <PARAM NAME="ButtonMax" VALUE="100">
        <PARAM NAME="ButtonStyle" VALUE="1">
        <PARAM NAME="ButtonWidth" VALUE="0">
        <PARAM NAME="ButtonWrap" VALUE="-1">
        <PARAM NAME="ButtonDefaultAction" VALUE="-1">
        <PARAM NAME="ThreeDText" VALUE="0">
        <PARAM NAME="ThreeDTextHighlightColor" VALUE="-2147483633">
        <PARAM NAME="ThreeDTextShadowColor" VALUE="-2147483632">
        <PARAM NAME="ThreeDTextOffset" VALUE="1">
        <PARAM NAME="AlignTextH" VALUE="0">
        <PARAM NAME="AlignTextV" VALUE="0">
        <PARAM NAME="AllowNull" VALUE="0">
        <PARAM NAME="NoSpecialKeys" VALUE="0">
        <PARAM NAME="AutoAdvance" VALUE="0">
        <PARAM NAME="AutoBeep" VALUE="0">
        <PARAM NAME="CaretInsert" VALUE="0">
        <PARAM NAME="CaretOverWrite" VALUE="3">
        <PARAM NAME="UserEntry" VALUE="0">
        <PARAM NAME="HideSelection" VALUE="-1">
        <PARAM NAME="InvalidColor" VALUE="-2147483637">
        <PARAM NAME="InvalidOption" VALUE="0">
        <PARAM NAME="MarginLeft" VALUE="3">
        <PARAM NAME="MarginTop" VALUE="3">
        <PARAM NAME="MarginRight" VALUE="3">
        <PARAM NAME="MarginBottom" VALUE="3">
        <PARAM NAME="NullColor" VALUE="-2147483637">
        <PARAM NAME="OnFocusAlignH" VALUE="0">
        <PARAM NAME="OnFocusAlignV" VALUE="0">
        <PARAM NAME="OnFocusNoSelect" VALUE="0">
        <PARAM NAME="OnFocusPosition" VALUE="0">
```

```
<PARAM NAME="ControlType" VALUE="0">
<PARAM NAME="Text" VALUE="fpLongInteger1">
<PARAM NAME="MaxValue" VALUE="2147483647">
<PARAM NAME="MinValue" VALUE="-2147483648">
<PARAM NAME="NegFormat" VALUE="1">
<PARAM NAME="NegToggle" VALUE="0">
<PARAM NAME="Separator" VALUE="">
<PARAM NAME="UseSeparator" VALUE="0">
<PARAM NAME="IncInt" VALUE="1">
<PARAM NAME="BorderGrayAreaColor" VALUE="-2147483637">
<PARAM NAME="ThreeDOnFocusInvert" VALUE="0">
<PARAM NAME="ThreeDFrameColor" VALUE="-2147483633">
<PARAM NAME="Appearance" VALUE="0">
<PARAM NAME="BorderDropShadow" VALUE="0">
<PARAM NAME="BorderDropShadowColor" VALUE="-2147483632">
<PARAM NAME="BorderDropShadowWidth" VALUE="3">
</OBJECT>
</BODY>
</HTML>
```

fpMask

The fpMask is a formatted data-entry ActiveX control. This control can be used for any type of data entry, such as Social Security numbers, phone numbers, and ZIP codes. It performs validation for invalid characters, a range of values, and so on. This control can be bound to any type of value (except binary type) in the back-end database.

Source

Vendor Information:

FarPoint Technologies, Inc.
http://www.fpoint.com
133 Southcenter Court, Suite 1000
Morrisville, NC 27560
(800) 645-4551
(919) 460-7606

FIG. 14.7
The fpMask control

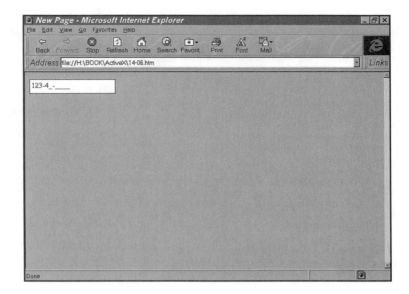

Properties

Table 14.16 Properties of the fpMask Control

Property	Description
AlignTextH	The horizontal alignment of the text
AlignTextV	The vertical alignment of the text
AllowNull	True, to allow the user the capability to leave this control blank
AllowOverflow	True, to allow the user to enter more characters on a full control
Appearance	The border look—flat, 3-D, and so on
AutoAdvance	True, to advance to the next control after pressing the Enter key
AutoBeep	True, to sound the beep on user error
AutoTab	True, to go to next control by using the Tab key
BackColor	The background color of the object
BestFit	True, to accept data that does not fit the mask exactly
BorderColor	The object's border color

Part

III

Ch

14

continues

Table 14.16   Continued

Property	Description
BorderDropShadow	The 3-D shadow for border—none, always, on focus
BorderDropShadowColor	The border 3-D shadow color
BorderDropShadowWidth	The border 3-D shadow width
BorderGrayAreaColor	The color of the gray area of the 3-D border
BorderStyle	The object's border style
BorderWidth	The object's border width
ButtonDisable	True, to disable the buttons on the control
ButtonHide	True, to hide the buttons
ButtonIncrement	The value by which the button index will be increased or decreased
ButtonMax	The upper limit for the button index
ButtonMin	The lower limit for the button index
ButtonStyle	The style of the button—none, spin, slide, and so on
ButtonWidth	The width of the button
ButtonWrap	True, to reset the button index when it crosses the upper or lower limits
CaretInsert	The caret for the insert mode
CaretOverwrite	The overstrike mode caret
ClipMode	Clip data and literals or clip data without literals
CodeBase	The origin of the control, including the URL, file type, and version number
ControlType	The control UI mode—normal, read-only, static, button edit
DataChanged	True, when the data is changed
DataField	The name of the bound column in the DataSource
DataSource	The source of the database to be bound to this control
Enabled	True, to set the control to get focus and respond to UI
FixedPoint	True, to display zeros to the right of decimal place
Font	The font of the control caption
ForeColor	The foreground color of the object

Property	Description
Height	The vertical height of the object
HideSelection	True, to highlight the selected characters even when the control loses focus
hWND	The handle for the window
ID	The name of the object/control
IncDec	The decimal portion increment when using the button
IncInt	The integer portion increment when using the button
InvalidColor	The background color when the data in the control is invalid
InvalidOption	Action for invalid data when the control loses focus—show data, hide data, clear data
Left	The distance between the left edge of the control and the left edge of the HTML layout
MarginBottom	The bottom margin in pixels
MarginLeft	The left margin in pixels
MarginRight	The right margin in pixels
MarginTop	The top margin in pixels
Mask	The edit mask for this control
MouseIcon	The image that appears when the mouse is moved over the object
MousePointer	The mouse pointer that appears when the mouse is moved over the object
NoPrefix	The mode for the entry of the "&" character
NoSpecialKeys	Option for handling keyboard keys
NullColor	The background color when the control contains no value
OnFocusAlignH	Horizontal alignment of the data in the control when it gets focus
OnFocusAlignV	Vertical alignment of the data in the control when it gets focus
OnFocusNoSelect	False, to select the data in the control when it gets focus
OnFocusPosition	The position of the cursor in the data in the control when it gets focus

Part
III

Ch
14

continues

Table 14.16 Continued	
Property	**Description**
PromptChar	The character to indicate placeholder for data
PromptInclude	True, to include the prompt characters when the data is cut or copied
RequireFill	True, to require that all the characters be filled when the control loses focus
ReDraw	Repaint the control
SelLength	The number of characters selected
SelStart	The starting/insertion point of selection
SelText	The character string selected by the user
TabIndex	The object's tab order position in the HTML layout
Text	The date in the text format
ThreeDFrameColor	The color of the 3-D frame
ThreeDFrameWidth	The width of the 3-D frame
ThreeDInsideHighliteColor	The color for the inner border 3-D highlight
ThreeDInsideShadowColor	The color for the inner border 3-D shadow
ThreeDInsideStyle	The style for the inner border 3-D—none, lowered, raised
ThreeDInsideWidth	The width for the inner border 3-D
ThreeDOnFocusInvert	True, to invert the 3-D when the control gets focus
ThreeDOutsideHighliteColor	The color for the outer border 3-D highlight
ThreeDOutsideShadowColor	The color for the outer border 3-D shadow
ThreeDOutsideStyle	The style for the outer border 3-D—none, lowered, raised
ThreeDOutsideWidth	The width for the outer border 3-D
Top	The distance between the top edge of the control and the top edge of the HTML layout
UserEntry	Formatted or free format
Visible	False, to hide the control
Width	The width of the control in points

Method

Table 14.17   Method of the fpMask Control

Method	Description
AboutBox	Displays the About dialog box

Events

Table 14.18   Events of the fpMask Control

Event	Description
Advance	Triggers when a valid character is entered at the last position
ButtonHit	Triggers when a button is pressed by the user
Change	Triggers when the value of a control changes by either the UI or programmatically; use this event handler to synchronize data between controls
ChangeMode	Triggers when the user changes the edit mode between insert and overstrike
Click	Triggers when a control is clicked with the mouse
DblClick	Triggers when a control is double-clicked
InvalidData	Triggers when the control contains invalid data
KeyDown	Triggers when a user presses a control, navigation, or function key
KeyPress	Triggers when a key is either pressed by the user or sent from the SendKeys function
KeyUp	Triggers when a user releases a control, navigation, or function key
MouseDown	Triggers when a user presses a mouse button
MouseMove	Triggers when the user moves the mouse
MouseUp	Triggers when a user releases a mouse button
UserError	Triggers when an error occurs

Part
III

Ch
14

Example

```
<HTML>
<HEAD>
<TITLE>New Page</TITLE>
</HEAD>
```

```
<BODY>

<OBJECT ID="fpMask1" WIDTH=187 HEIGHT=32
 CLASSID="CLSID:1211A3D5-B48E-101C-933E-0000C005958C">
    <PARAM NAME="_Version" VALUE="131072">
    <PARAM NAME="_ExtentX" VALUE="3951">
    <PARAM NAME="_ExtentY" VALUE="670">
    <PARAM NAME="_StockProps" VALUE="68">
    <PARAM NAME="BackColor" VALUE="-2147483643">
    <PARAM NAME="ForeColor" VALUE="-2147483640">
    <PARAM NAME="ThreeDInsideStyle" VALUE="0">
    <PARAM NAME="ThreeDInsideHighlightColor" VALUE="-2147483633">
    <PARAM NAME="ThreeDInsideShadowColor" VALUE="-2147483642">
    <PARAM NAME="ThreeDInsideWidth" VALUE="1">
    <PARAM NAME="ThreeDOutsideStyle" VALUE="0">
    <PARAM NAME="ThreeDOutsideHighlightColor" VALUE="-2147483628">
    <PARAM NAME="ThreeDOutsideShadowColor" VALUE="-2147483632">
    <PARAM NAME="ThreeDOutsideWidth" VALUE="1">
    <PARAM NAME="ThreeDFrameWidth" VALUE="0">
    <PARAM NAME="BorderStyle" VALUE="1">
    <PARAM NAME="BorderColor" VALUE="-2147483642">
    <PARAM NAME="BorderWidth" VALUE="1">
    <PARAM NAME="ButtonDisable" VALUE="0">
    <PARAM NAME="ButtonHide" VALUE="0">
    <PARAM NAME="ButtonIncrement" VALUE="1">
    <PARAM NAME="ButtonMin" VALUE="0">
    <PARAM NAME="ButtonMax" VALUE="100">
    <PARAM NAME="ButtonStyle" VALUE="0">
    <PARAM NAME="ButtonWidth" VALUE="0">
    <PARAM NAME="ButtonWrap" VALUE="-1">
    <PARAM NAME="ThreeDText" VALUE="0">
    <PARAM NAME="ThreeDTextHighlightColor" VALUE="-2147483633">
    <PARAM NAME="ThreeDTextShadowColor" VALUE="-2147483632">
    <PARAM NAME="ThreeDTextOffset" VALUE="1">
    <PARAM NAME="AlignTextH" VALUE="0">
    <PARAM NAME="AlignTextV" VALUE="0">
    <PARAM NAME="AllowNull" VALUE="0">
    <PARAM NAME="NoSpecialKeys" VALUE="0">
    <PARAM NAME="AutoAdvance" VALUE="0">
    <PARAM NAME="AutoBeep" VALUE="0">
    <PARAM NAME="CaretInsert" VALUE="0">
    <PARAM NAME="CaretOverWrite" VALUE="3">
    <PARAM NAME="UserEntry" VALUE="0">
    <PARAM NAME="HideSelection" VALUE="-1">
    <PARAM NAME="InvalidColor" VALUE="-2147483637">
    <PARAM NAME="InvalidOption" VALUE="0">
    <PARAM NAME="MarginLeft" VALUE="3">
    <PARAM NAME="MarginTop" VALUE="3">
    <PARAM NAME="MarginRight" VALUE="3">
    <PARAM NAME="MarginBottom" VALUE="3">
    <PARAM NAME="NullColor" VALUE="-2147483637">
    <PARAM NAME="OnFocusAlignH" VALUE="0">
    <PARAM NAME="OnFocusAlignV" VALUE="0">
    <PARAM NAME="OnFocusNoSelect" VALUE="0">
    <PARAM NAME="OnFocusPosition" VALUE="0">
```

```
        <PARAM NAME="ControlType" VALUE="0">
        <PARAM NAME="AllowOverflow" VALUE="0">
        <PARAM NAME="BestFit" VALUE="0">
        <PARAM NAME="ClipMode" VALUE="0">
        <PARAM NAME="DataFormat" VALUE="27715">
        <PARAM NAME="Mask" VALUE="###-##-####">
        <PARAM NAME="PromptChar" VALUE="_">
        <PARAM NAME="PromptInclude" VALUE="0">
        <PARAM NAME="RequireFill" VALUE="0">
        <PARAM NAME="BorderGrayAreaColor" VALUE="-2147483637">
        <PARAM NAME="NoPrefix" VALUE="0">
        <PARAM NAME="ThreeDOnFocusInvert" VALUE="0">
        <PARAM NAME="ThreeDFrameColor" VALUE="-2147483633">
        <PARAM NAME="Appearance" VALUE="0">
        <PARAM NAME="BorderDropShadow" VALUE="0">
        <PARAM NAME="BorderDropShadowColor" VALUE="-2147483632">
        <PARAM NAME="BorderDropShadowWidth" VALUE="3">
        <PARAM NAME="AutoTab" VALUE="0">
    </OBJECT>

    </BODY>
    </HTML>
```

fpMemo

The fpMemo is a text data-entry ActiveX control. This control can be used to give the user the ability to enter and retrieve large amounts of text data. In database applications, you always need some text entry, such as description and comments. In some applications, you might need to display and get from the user a large amount of text data. This control is useful in such circumstances. This control can be bound to memo fields in the back-end database.

Source

Vendor Information:

FarPoint Technologies, Inc.
http://www.fpoint.com
133 Southcenter Court, Suite 1000
Morrisville, NC 27560
(800) 645-4551
(919) 460-7606

Part
III

Ch
14

FIG. 14.8
The fpMemo control

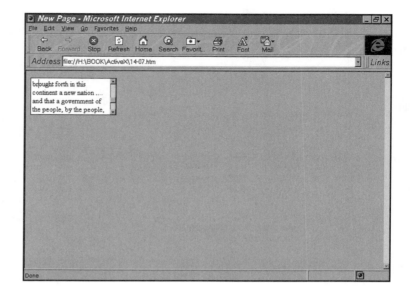

Properties

Table 14.19   Properties of the fpMemo Control

Property	Description
AllowNull	True, to allow the user the capability to leave this control blank
Appearance	The border look—flat, 3-D, and so on
AutoAdvance	True, to advance to the next control after pressing the Enter key
AutoBeep	True, to sound the beep on user error
BackColor	The background color of the object
BorderColor	The object's border color
BorderDropShadow	The 3-D shadow for border—none, always, on focus
BorderDropShadowColor	The border 3-D shadow color
BorderDropShadowWidth	The border 3-D shadow width
BorderGrayAreaColor	The color of the gray area of the 3-D border
BorderStyle	The object's border style
BorderWidth	The object's border width
CaretInsert	The caret for the insert mode

Property	Description
CaretOverwrite	The overstrike mode caret
CodeBase	The origin of the control, including the URL, file type, and version number
ControlType	The control UI mode—normal, read-only, static, button edit
DataChanged	True, when the data is changed
DataField	The name of the bound column in the DataSource
DataSource	The source of the database to be bound to this control
Enabled	True, to set the control to get focus and respond to UI
Font	The font of the control caption
ForeColor	The foreground color of the object
Height	The vertical height of the object
HideSelection	True, to highlight the selected characters even when the control loses focus
hWND	The handle for the window
ID	The name of the object/control
Left	The distance between the left edge of the control and the left edge of the HTML layout
LineLimit	The maximum number of lines allowed
MouseIcon	The image that appears when the mouse is moved over the object
MousePointer	The mouse pointer that appears when the mouse is moved over the object
NoSpecialKeys	The option for handling keyboard keys
NullColor	The background color when the control contains no value
OnFocusNoSelect	False to select all the text in the control when this control gets focus
OnFocusPosition	The position of the cursor when this control gets focus
PageWidth	The width of the display page
ScrollBars	The type of scroll bars displayed
SelBackColor	The background color for the selected text
SelForeColor	The foreground color for the selected text

Part
III

Ch
14

continues

Table 14.19 Continued

Property	Description
SelMode	The selection mode—normal, line, or extended
ShowEOL	Show the End-Of-Line character
ReDraw	Repaint the control
SelLength	The number of characters selected
SelStart	The starting/insertion point of selection
SelText	The character string selected by the user
TabIndex	The object's tab order position in the HTML layout
Text	The date in the text format
ThreeDFrameColor	The color of the 3-D frame
ThreeDFrameWidth	The width of the 3-D frame
ThreeDInsideHighliteColor	The color for the inner border 3-D highlight
ThreeDInsideShadowColor	The color for the inner border 3-D shadow
ThreeDInsideStyle	The style for the inner border 3-D—none, lowered, raised
ThreeDInsideWidth	The width for the inner border 3-D
ThreeDOnFocusInvert	True, to invert the 3-D when the control gets focus
ThreeDOutsideHighliteColor	The color for the outer border 3-D highlight
ThreeDOutsideShadowColor	The color for the outer border 3-D shadow
ThreeDOutsideStyle	The style for the outer border 3-D—none, lowered, raised
ThreeDOutsideWidth	The width for the outer border 3-D
Top	The distance between the top edge of the control and the top edge of the HTML layout
Visible	False, to hide the control
Width	The width of the control in points
WordWrap	True, to automatically wrap the lines

Method

Table 14.20   Method of the fpMemo Control

Method	Description
AboutBox	Displays the About dialog box

Events

Table 14.21   Events of the fpMemo Control

Event	Description
Advance	Triggers when a valid character is entered at the last position
ButtonHit	Triggers when a button is pressed by the user
Change	Triggers when the value of a control changes by either the UI or programmatically; use this event handler to synchronize data between controls
ChangeMode	Triggers when the user changes the edit mode between insert and overstrike
Click	Triggers when a control is clicked with the mouse
DblClick	Triggers when a control is double-clicked
InvalidData	Triggers when the control contains invalid data
KeyDown	Triggers when a user presses a control, navigation, or function key
KeyPress	Triggers when a key is either pressed by the user or sent from the SendKeys function
KeyUp	Triggers when a user releases a control, navigation, or function key
MouseDown	Triggers when a user presses a mouse button
MouseMove	Triggers when the user moves the mouse
MouseUp	Triggers when a user releases a mouse button
UserError	Triggers when an error occurs

Part
III

Ch
14

Example

```
<HTML>
<HEAD>
<TITLE>New Page</TITLE>
</HEAD>
```

```
<BODY>
    <OBJECT ID="fpMemo1" WIDTH=187 HEIGHT=83
    CLASSID="CLSID:A18D4665-91EF-101C-84A6-BA990A365A4E">
        <PARAM NAME="_Version" VALUE="131072">
        <PARAM NAME="_ExtentX" VALUE="3951">
        <PARAM NAME="_ExtentY" VALUE="1764">
        <PARAM NAME="_StockProps" VALUE="68">
        <PARAM NAME="BackColor" VALUE="-2147483643">
        <PARAM NAME="ForeColor" VALUE="-2147483640">
        <PARAM NAME="ThreeDInsideStyle" VALUE="0">
        <PARAM NAME="ThreeDInsideHighlightColor" VALUE="-2147483633">
        <PARAM NAME="ThreeDInsideShadowColor" VALUE="-2147483642">
        <PARAM NAME="ThreeDInsideWidth" VALUE="1">
        <PARAM NAME="ThreeDOutsideStyle" VALUE="0">
        <PARAM NAME="ThreeDOutsideHighlightColor" VALUE="-2147483628">
        <PARAM NAME="ThreeDOutsideShadowColor" VALUE="-2147483632">
        <PARAM NAME="ThreeDOutsideWidth" VALUE="1">
        <PARAM NAME="ThreeDFrameWidth" VALUE="0">
        <PARAM NAME="BorderStyle" VALUE="1">
        <PARAM NAME="BorderColor" VALUE="-2147483642">
        <PARAM NAME="BorderWidth" VALUE="1">
        <PARAM NAME="AllowNull" VALUE="0">
        <PARAM NAME="NoSpecialKeys" VALUE="0">
        <PARAM NAME="AutoAdvance" VALUE="0">
        <PARAM NAME="AutoBeep" VALUE="0">
        <PARAM NAME="CaretInsert" VALUE="0">
        <PARAM NAME="CaretOverWrite" VALUE="3">
        <PARAM NAME="HideSelection" VALUE="-1">
        <PARAM NAME="NullColor" VALUE="-2147483637">
        <PARAM NAME="OnFocusNoSelect" VALUE="-1">
        <PARAM NAME="OnFocusPosition" VALUE="3">
        <PARAM NAME="ControlType" VALUE="0">
        <PARAM NAME="Text" VALUE="fpMemo1">
        <PARAM NAME="WordWrap" VALUE="-1">
        <PARAM NAME="ShowEOL" VALUE="0">
        <PARAM NAME="SelMode" VALUE="0">
        <PARAM NAME="LineLimit" VALUE="2147483647">
        <PARAM NAME="ScrollBars" VALUE="3">
        <PARAM NAME="PageWidth" VALUE="0">
        <PARAM NAME="SelBackColor" VALUE="-2147483635">
        <PARAM NAME="SelForeColor" VALUE="-2147483634">
        <PARAM NAME="BorderGrayAreaColor" VALUE="-2147483637">
        <PARAM NAME="ThreeDOnFocusInvert" VALUE="0">
        <PARAM NAME="ThreeDFrameColor" VALUE="-2147483633">
        <PARAM NAME="Appearance" VALUE="0">
        <PARAM NAME="BorderDropShadow" VALUE="0">
        <PARAM NAME="BorderDropShadowColor" VALUE="-2147483632">
        <PARAM NAME="BorderDropShadowWidth" VALUE="3">
    </OBJECT>
</BODY>
</HTML>
```

fpText

The fpText is a text data-entry ActiveX control. This control can be used to give the user the ability to enter and retrieve text data of length 255 characters or less.

Source

Vendor Information:

FarPoint Technologies, Inc.
http://www.fpoint.com
133 Southcenter Court, Suite 1000
Morrisville, NC 27560
(800) 645-4551
(919) 460-7606

FIG. 14.9
The fpText control

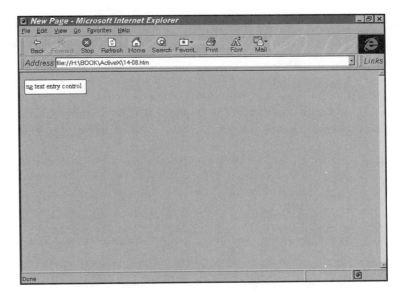

Properties

Table 14.22   Properties of the fpText Control

Property	Description
AlignTextH	The horizontal alignment of the text
AlignTextV	The vertical alignment of the text
AllowNull	True, to allow the user the capability to leave this control blank
Appearance	The border look—flat, 3-D, and so on
AutoAdvance	True, to advance to the next control after pressing the Enter key
AutoBeep	True, to sound the beep on user error
AutoCase	The type of case conversion for display—none, upper, lower, proper
BackColor	The background color of the object
BorderColor	The object's border color
BorderDropShadow	The 3-D shadow for border—none, always, on focus
BorderDropShadowColor	The border 3-D shadow color
BorderDropShadowWidth	The border 3-D shadow width
BorderGrayAreaColor	The color of the gray area of the 3-D border
BorderStyle	The object's border style
BorderWidth	The object's border width
ButtonDefaultAction	True, to enable the default action for the spin button
ButtonDisable	True, to disable the buttons on the control
ButtonHide	True, to hide the buttons
ButtonIncrement	The value by which the button index will be increased or decreased
ButtonMax	The upper limit for the button index
ButtonMin	The lower limit for the button index
ButtonStyle	The style of the button—none, spin, slide, and so on
ButtonWidth	The width of the button
ButtonWrap	True, to reset the button index when it crosses the upper or lower limits

Property	Description
CaretInsert	The caret for the insert mode
CaretOverwrite	The overstrike mode caret
CharPositionLeft	The left index of the characters displayed
CharPositionRight	The right index of the characters displayed
CharValidationText	The valid characters allowed
CodeBase	The origin of the control, including the URL, file type, and version number
ControlType	The control UI mode—normal, read-only, static, button edit
CurrentPosition	The position of the cursor
DataChanged	True, when the data is changed
DataField	The name of the bound column in the DataSource
DataSource	The source of the database to be bound to this control
Enabled	True, to set the control to get focus and respond to UI
Font	The font of the control caption
ForeColor	The foreground color of the object
Height	The vertical height of the object
HideSelection	True, to highlight the selected characters even when the control loses focus
hWND	The handle for the window
ID	The name of the object/control
IncHoriz	The distance the cursor will be moved for slider button
InvalidColor	The background color when the data in the control is invalid
InvalidOption	Action for invalid data when the control loses focus—show data, hide data, clear data
IsNull	True, if the control value is null
IsValid	True, if the control contains a valid entry
Left	The distance between the left edge of the control and the left edge of the HTML layout
MarginBottom	The bottom margin in pixels
MarginLeft	The left margin in pixels

Part
III

Ch
14

continues

Table 14.22 Continued

Property	Description
MarginRight	The right margin in pixels
MarginTop	The top margin in pixels
MaxLength	The maximum number of characters allowed
MouseIcon	The image that appears when the mouse is moved over the object
MousePointer	The mouse pointer that appears when the mouse is moved over the object
MultiLine	True, to display the text in multiple lines
NoSpecialKeys	Option for handling keyboard keys
NullColor	The background color when the control contains no value
OnFocusAlignH	Horizontal alignment of the data in the control when it gets focus
OnFocusAlignV	Vertical alignment of the data in the control when it gets focus
OnFocusNoSelect	False, to select all the text in the control when this control gets focus
OnFocusPosition	The position of the cursor when this control gets focus
PasswordChar	The mask character to appear
ScrollV	True, to allow vertical scrolling
ReDraw	Repaint the control
SelLength	The number of characters selected
SelStart	The starting/insertion point of selection
SelText	The character string selected by the user
TabIndex	The object's tab order position in the HTML layout
Text	The date in the text format
ThreeDFrameColor	The color of the 3-D frame
ThreeDFrameWidth	The width of the 3-D frame
ThreeDInsideHighliteColor	The color for the inner border 3-D highlight
ThreeDInsideShadowColor	The color for the inner border 3-D shadow
ThreeDInsideStyle	The style for the inner border 3-D—none, lowered, raised

Property	Description
ThreeDInsideWidth	The width for the inner border 3-D
ThreeDOnFocusInvert	True, to invert the 3-D when the control gets focus
ThreeDOutsideHighliteColor	The color for the outer border 3-D highlight
ThreeDOutsideShadowColor	The color for the outer border 3-D shadow
ThreeDOutsideStyle	The style for the outer border 3-D—none, lowered, raised
ThreeDOutsideWidth	The width for the outer border 3-D
Top	The distance between the top edge of the control and the top edge of the HTML layout
UserEntry	Formatted or free format
Visible	False, to hide the control
Width	The width of the control in points
WordWrap	True, to automatically wrap the lines

Method

Table 14.23   Method of the fpText Control

Method	Description
AboutBox	Displays the About dialog box

Events

Table 14.24   Events of the fpText Control

Event	Description
Advance	Triggers when a valid character is entered at the last position
ButtonHit	Triggers when a button is pressed by the user
Change	Triggers when the value of a control changes by either the UI or programmatically; use this event handler to synchronize data between controls
ChangeMode	Triggers when the user changes the edit mode between insert and overstrike

Part
III

Ch
14

continues

Table 14.24 Continued

Event	Description
Click	Triggers when a control is clicked with the mouse
DblClick	Triggers when a control is double-clicked
InvalidData	Triggers when the control contains invalid data
KeyDown	Triggers when a user presses a control, navigation, or function key
KeyPress	Triggers when a key is either pressed by the user or sent from the SendKeys function
KeyUp	Triggers when a user releases a control, navigation, or function key
MouseDown	Triggers when a user presses a mouse button
MouseMove	Triggers when the user moves the mouse
MouseUp	Triggers when a user releases a mouse button
UserError	Triggers when an error occurs

Example

```
<HTML>
<HEAD>
<TITLE>New Page</TITLE>
</HEAD>
<BODY>

<OBJECT ID="fpText1" WIDTH=135 HEIGHT=32
 CLASSID="CLSID:CDF3B180-D408-11CE-AE2C-0080C786E37D">
    <PARAM NAME="_Version" VALUE="131072">
    <PARAM NAME="_ExtentX" VALUE="2858">
    <PARAM NAME="_ExtentY" VALUE="670">
    <PARAM NAME="_StockProps" VALUE="68">
    <PARAM NAME="BackColor" VALUE="-2147483643">
    <PARAM NAME="ForeColor" VALUE="-2147483640">
    <PARAM NAME="ThreeDInsideStyle" VALUE="0">
    <PARAM NAME="ThreeDInsideHighlightColor" VALUE="-2147483633">
    <PARAM NAME="ThreeDInsideShadowColor" VALUE="-2147483642">
    <PARAM NAME="ThreeDInsideWidth" VALUE="1">
    <PARAM NAME="ThreeDOutsideStyle" VALUE="0">
    <PARAM NAME="ThreeDOutsideHighlightColor" VALUE="-2147483628">
    <PARAM NAME="ThreeDOutsideShadowColor" VALUE="-2147483632">
    <PARAM NAME="ThreeDOutsideWidth" VALUE="1">
    <PARAM NAME="ThreeDFrameWidth" VALUE="0">
    <PARAM NAME="BorderStyle" VALUE="2">
    <PARAM NAME="BorderColor" VALUE="-2147483642">
    <PARAM NAME="BorderWidth" VALUE="1">
    <PARAM NAME="ButtonDisable" VALUE="0">
```

```
            <PARAM NAME="ButtonHide" VALUE="0">
            <PARAM NAME="ButtonIncrement" VALUE="1">
            <PARAM NAME="ButtonMin" VALUE="0">
            <PARAM NAME="ButtonMax" VALUE="100">
            <PARAM NAME="ButtonStyle" VALUE="0">
            <PARAM NAME="ButtonWidth" VALUE="0">
            <PARAM NAME="ButtonWrap" VALUE="-1">
            <PARAM NAME="ButtonDefaultAction" VALUE="-1">
            <PARAM NAME="ThreeDText" VALUE="0">
            <PARAM NAME="ThreeDTextHighlightColor" VALUE="-2147483633">
            <PARAM NAME="ThreeDTextShadowColor" VALUE="-2147483632">
            <PARAM NAME="ThreeDTextOffset" VALUE="1">
            <PARAM NAME="AlignTextH" VALUE="0">
            <PARAM NAME="AlignTextV" VALUE="0">
            <PARAM NAME="AllowNull" VALUE="0">
            <PARAM NAME="NoSpecialKeys" VALUE="0">
            <PARAM NAME="AutoAdvance" VALUE="0">
            <PARAM NAME="AutoBeep" VALUE="0">
            <PARAM NAME="AutoCase" VALUE="0">
            <PARAM NAME="CaretInsert" VALUE="0">
            <PARAM NAME="CaretOverWrite" VALUE="3">
            <PARAM NAME="UserEntry" VALUE="0">
            <PARAM NAME="HideSelection" VALUE="-1">
            <PARAM NAME="InvalidColor" VALUE="-2147483637">
            <PARAM NAME="InvalidOption" VALUE="0">
            <PARAM NAME="MarginLeft" VALUE="3">
            <PARAM NAME="MarginTop" VALUE="3">
            <PARAM NAME="MarginRight" VALUE="3">
            <PARAM NAME="MarginBottom" VALUE="3">
            <PARAM NAME="NullColor" VALUE="-2147483637">
            <PARAM NAME="OnFocusAlignH" VALUE="0">
            <PARAM NAME="OnFocusAlignV" VALUE="0">
            <PARAM NAME="OnFocusNoSelect" VALUE="0">
            <PARAM NAME="OnFocusPosition" VALUE="0">
            <PARAM NAME="ControlType" VALUE="0">
            <PARAM NAME="Text" VALUE="fpText1">
            <PARAM NAME="CharValidationText" VALUE="">
            <PARAM NAME="MaxLength" VALUE="255">
            <PARAM NAME="MultiLine" VALUE="0">
            <PARAM NAME="PasswordChar" VALUE="">
            <PARAM NAME="IncHoriz" VALUE="0.25">
            <PARAM NAME="BorderGrayAreaColor" VALUE="-2147483637">
            <PARAM NAME="NoPrefix" VALUE="0">
            <PARAM NAME="ScrollV" VALUE="0">
            <PARAM NAME="ThreeDOnFocusInvert" VALUE="0">
            <PARAM NAME="ThreeDFrameColor" VALUE="-2147483633">
            <PARAM NAME="Appearance" VALUE="0">
            <PARAM NAME="BorderDropShadow" VALUE="0">
            <PARAM NAME="BorderDropShadowColor" VALUE="-2147483632">
            <PARAM NAME="BorderDropShadowWidth" VALUE="3">
        </OBJECT>

    </BODY>
</HTML>
```

MhDateInput

The MhDateInput control is specifically aimed at date and time entry. This control has a lot of versatility and includes a built-in spin button for a user-friendly data input.

Source

Vendor information:

MicroHelp, Inc.
http://www.microhelp.com
4211 J.V.L Industrial Park Drive, NE
Marietta, GA 30066
(800) 922-3383
(770) 516-1099

FIG. 14.10
The MhDateInput control

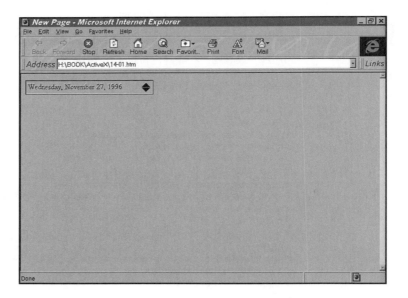

Properties

Table 14.25   Properties of the MhDateInput Control

Property	Description
Alignment	Alignment of the caption text
AllowBlank	True, to allow blank entries

Property	Description
AutoHScroll	True, to scroll automatically for entries that are longer than the control
BackColor	The background color of the object
BevelSize	The 3-D bevel size in points
BevelColor	The color for the 3-D bevel
BorderColor	The object's border color
BorderStyle	The object's border style
CaretColor	Color of the caret, the small current value pointer that points to the day number or month or year
CaretHeight	The height of the caret
CaretInterval	The blink interval for the caret
CaretStyle	The style of the caret
CaretVAlign	The vertical alignment of the caret
CaretVisible	True, to display the caret
CaretWidth	The width of the caret
CodeBase	The origin of the control, including the URL, file type, and version number
DateFormat	The format of the date display—normal, Julian, verbose, verbose with weekday, and so on
Enabled	True, to set the control to get focus and respond to UI
FillColor	The background color
FocusSelect	True, to select the entries when the control gets focus
Font	The font for the date display
ForeColor	The foreground color of the object
Height	The vertical height of the object
hWND	The handle for the window
ID	The name of the object/control
Intent	The pixels between the date and the control border
Language	The language code to display the date
LanguageNumber	The language number to display the date
Left	The distance between the left edge of the control and the left edge of the HTML layout

Part
III

Ch

14

continues

Table 14.25   Continued

Property	Description
LightColor	The light color for the control
MaxDay,MaxMonth,MaxYear	The upper limit for day, month, and year
MinDay,MinMonth,MinYear	The lower limit for day, month, and year
MouseIcon	The image that appears when the mouse is moved over the object
MousePointer	The mouse pointer that appears when the mouse is moved over the object
ReadOnly	True, to make the control non-edit
SelLength	The number of characters selected
SelStart	The starting/insertion point of selection
SelText	The character string selected by the user
ShadowColor	The color for the shadow
Spin	The position of the spin button—left or right
SpinChange	The delta or amount of change when the spin arrow is clicked
SpinDelay	The delay between the first click and start of the repeat
SpinSpeed	The delay between two consecutive spin activation
TabIndex	The object's tab order position in the HTML layout
Text	The date in the text format
TextColor	The color of the date display
Top	The distance between the top edge of the control and the top edge of the HTML layout
Undo	Reverts to the last change made
Valignment	The vertical alignment—top, bottom, center
Visible	False, to hide the control
Width	The width of the control in points

Methods

Table 14.26   Methods of the MhDateInput Control

Method	Description
AboutBox	Displays the About dialog box
Refresh	Repaints the control

Events

Table 14.27   Events of the MhDateInput Control

Event	Description
AutoTerminate	Triggers when a valid character is entered at the last position
Change	Triggers when the value of a control changes by either the UI or programmatically; use this event handler to synchronize data between controls
Click	Triggers when a control is clicked with the mouse; also triggers when the user selects a value in a multi-value control such as the list box
DblClick	Triggers when a control is double-clicked
InvalidEntry	Triggers when the control has a value outside the minimum to maximum range
InvalidSetText	Triggers when invalid text is pasted into the control
KeyDown	Triggers when a user presses a control, navigation, or function key
KeyPress	Triggers when a key is either pressed by the user or sent from the SendKeys function
KeyUp	Triggers when a user releases a control, navigation, or function key
MouseDown	Triggers when a user presses a mouse button
MouseMove	Triggers when the user moves the mouse
MouseUp	Triggers when a user releases a mouse button

Part
III

Ch
14

Example

```
<HTML>
<HEAD>
<TITLE>New Page</TITLE>
</HEAD>
<BODY>

<OBJECT ID="MhDateInput1" WIDTH=252 HEIGHT=32
 CLASSID="CLSID:AFCBCE20-AAF2-11CE-85B2-00AA00575482">
    <PARAM NAME="_Version" VALUE="65536">
    <PARAM NAME="_ExtentX" VALUE="5339">
    <PARAM NAME="_ExtentY" VALUE="670">
    <PARAM NAME="_StockProps" VALUE="77">
    <PARAM NAME="BevelSize" VALUE="1">
    <PARAM NAME="Text" VALUE="Wednesday, November 27, 1996">
    <PARAM NAME="Spin" VALUE="2">
    <PARAM NAME="AutoHScroll" VALUE="-1">
    <PARAM NAME="FontStyle" VALUE="1">
    <PARAM NAME="CaretStyle" VALUE="1">
    <PARAM NAME="DateFormat" VALUE="3">
</OBJECT>
</BODY>
</HTML>
```

MhInput

The MhInput control is a general purpose data input control. The main advantage of this control is the formatted input functionality, such as phone numbers, Social Security numbers, ZIP codes, and so on. You can add more formatted inputs like credit card numbers or ID numbers specific to your application.

Source

Vendor information:

MicroHelp, Inc.
http://www.microhelp.com
4211 J.V.L Industrial Park Drive, NE
Marietta, GA 30066
(800) 922-3383
(770) 516-1099

FIG. 14.11
The MhInput control

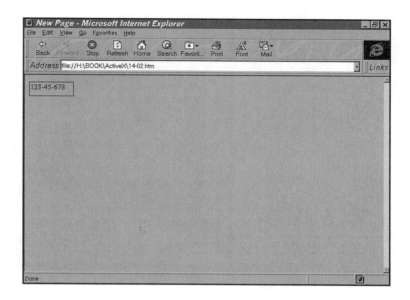

Properties

Table 14.28 Properties of the MhInput Control	
Property	**Description**
_Text	The string value in the control
Alignment	Alignment of the text in the control
BackColor	The background color of the object
BorderStyle	The object's border style
CaretInsert	The caret type during the insert mode
CaretOverstrike	The caret type during the overstrike mode
CodeBase	The origin of the control, including the URL, file type, and version number
DateFormat	The format of the date display—normal, Julian, verbose, verbose with weekday and so on
Enabled	True, to set the control to get focus and respond to UI
FieldType	Preformatted field type—phone number, ZIP code, Social Security, and so on
Font	The font for the text display

Part
III

Ch
14

continues

Table 14.28 Continued

Property	Description
ForeColor	The foreground color of the object
Height	The vertical height of the object
hWND	The handle for the window
ID	The name of the object/control
Intent	The pixels between the text and the control border
Left	The distance between the left edge of the control and the left edge of the HTML layout
Mask	The input mask for data entry
MouseIcon	The image that appears when the mouse is moved over the object
MousePointer	The mouse pointer that appears when the mouse is moved over the object
MultiLine	True, to allow multiple lines data entry
PassChar	The character mask that appears for password-type entries
Position	The current position of the caret
RejectEnter	True, to not pass a press of the Enter key (ASCII 13) to the control
ScrollBars	The scroll bar display—none, vertical, horizontal, both
SelLength	The number of characters selected
SelStart	The starting/insertion point of selection
SelText	The character string selected by the user
TabIndex	The object's tab order position in the HTML layout
Text	The date in the text format
TextDefault	The default text that appears when the control is initialized
TextLen	The maximum length of text allowed
TextRaw	The string without any of the formatting characters
Top	The distance between the top edge of the control and the top edge of the HTML layout
Undo	Reverses the last change made
Visible	False, to hide the control
Width	The width of the control in points
Wordwrap	True, to allow word wrap

Methods

Table 14.29   Methods of the MhInput Control

Method	Description
AboutBox	Displays the About dialog box
Refresh	Repaints the control

Events

Table 14.30   Events of the MhInput Control

Event	Description
AutoTerminate	Triggers when a valid character is entered at the last position
Change	Triggers when the value of a control changes by either the UI or programmatically; use this event handler to synchronize data between controls
KeyDown	Triggers when a user presses a control, navigation, or function key
KeyPress	Triggers when a key is either pressed by the user or sent from the SendKeys function
KeyUp	Triggers when a user releases a control, navigation, or function key
MouseDown	Triggers when a user presses a mouse button
MouseMove	Triggers when the user moves the mouse
MouseUp	Triggers when a user releases a mouse button

Example

```
<HTML>
<HEAD>
<TITLE>New Page</TITLE>
</HEAD>
<BODY>

<OBJECT ID="MhInput1" WIDTH=97 HEIGHT=32
 CLASSID="CLSID:16E88EE0-A62A-11CE-85B2-00AA00575482">
    <PARAM NAME="_Version" VALUE="65536">
    <PARAM NAME="_ExtentX" VALUE="2037">
```

Part
III

Ch

14

```
            <PARAM NAME="_ExtentY" VALUE="662">
            <PARAM NAME="_StockProps" VALUE="77">
            <PARAM NAME="FieldType" VALUE="1">
            <PARAM NAME="Mask" VALUE="999 99 9999">
            <PARAM NAME="Text" VALUE="123-45-6789">
            <PARAM NAME="TextLen" VALUE="11">
            <PARAM NAME="CaretInsert" VALUE="1">
            <PARAM NAME="Indent" VALUE="0">
            <PARAM NAME="TextDefault" VALUE="   -  -    ">
            <PARAM NAME="TextRaw" VALUE="123456789">
    </OBJECT>

    </BODY>
    </HTML>
```

Notes

There is a 50-character text limitation for this control.

IntInput

The IntInput control is specifically aimed at numeric data entry. This control has a lot of versatility and includes a built-in spin button for a user-friendly data input.

Source

Vendor information:

MicroHelp, Inc.
http://www.microhelp.com
4211 J.V.L Industrial Park Drive, NE
Marietta, GA 30066
(800) 922-3383
(770) 516-1099

FIG. 14.12
The IntInput Control

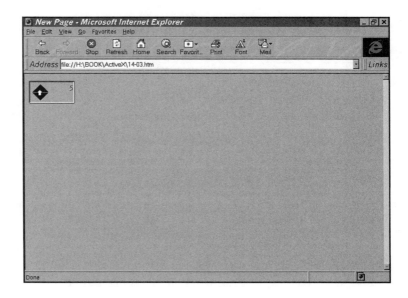

Properties

Table 14.31   Properties of the IntInput Control

Property	Description
Alignment	Alignment of the number
AutoHScroll	True, to scroll automatically for entries that are longer than the control
BackColor	The background color of the object
BevelSize	The 3-D bevel size in points
BevelStyle	The style of the bevel—lowered, raised, chiseled, and so on
BorderColor	The object's border color
BorderStyle	The object's border style
CaretColor	Color of the caret, the small current value pointer that points to the current digit
CaretHeight	Height of the caret
CaretInterval	The blink interval for the caret
CaretStyle	The style of the caret

continues

Part
III

Ch

14

Table 14.31 Continued

Property	Description
CaretVAlign	The vertical alignment of the caret
CaretVisible	True, to display the caret
CaretWidth	The width of the caret
CodeBase	The origin of the control, including URL, file type, and version number
Enabled	True, to set the control to get focus and respond to UI
FillColor	The background color
FocusSelect	True, to select the entries when the control gets focus
Font	The font for the date display
FontStyle	The style of the font—none, raised, raised with more shading, lowered, lowered with more shading
ForeColor	The foreground color of the object
Height	The vertical height of the object
hWND	The handle for the window
ID	The name of the object/control
Intent	The pixels between the date and the control border
Left	The distance between the left edge of the control and the left edge of the HTML layout
LightColor	The light color for the control
Max	The upper limit for the number
Min	The lower limit for the number
MouseIcon	The image that appears when the mouse is moved over the object
MousePointer	The mouse pointer displayed when the mouse is moved over the object
ReadOnly	True, to make the control non-editable
SelLength	The number of characters selected
SelStart	The starting/insertion point of selection
SelText	The character string selected by the user
ShadowColor	The color for the shadow
Spin	The position of the spin button—left or right
SpinChange	The delta or the amount of change when the spin arrow is clicked

Property	Description
SpinDelay	The delay between the first click and start of the repeat
SpinSpeed	The delay between two consecutive spin activations
TabIndex	The object's tab order position in the HTML layout
Text	The date in the text format
TextColor	The color of the date display
Top	The distance between the top edge of the control and the top edge of the HTML layout
Undo	Reverses the last change made
VAlignment	The vertical alignment—top, bottom, center
Visible	False, to hide the control
Width	The width of the control in points

Methods

Table 14.32 Methods of the IntInput Control

Method	Description
AboutBox	Displays the About dialog box
Refresh	Repaints the control

Events

Table 14.33 Events of the IntInput Control

Event	Description
Change	Triggers when the value of a control changes by either the UI or programmatically; use this event handler to synchronize data between controls
Click	Triggers when a control is clicked with the mouse
DblClick	Triggers when a control is double-clicked
InvalidEntry	Triggers when the control has a value outside the minimum to maximum range
InvalidSetText	Triggers when an invalid text is pasted into the control

Part

III

Ch

14

continues

Table 14.33 Continued	
Event	**Description**
KeyDown	Triggers when a user presses a control, navigation, or function key
KeyPress	Triggers when a key is either pressed by the user or sent from the SendKeys function
KeyUp	Triggers when a user releases a control, navigation, orfunction key
MouseDown	Triggers when a user presses a mouse button
MouseMove	Triggers when the user moves the mouse
MouseUp	Triggers when a user releases a mouse button

Example

```
<HTML>
<HEAD>
<TITLE>New Page</TITLE>
</HEAD>
<BODY>

<OBJECT ID="MhIntInput1" WIDTH=100 HEIGHT=50
 CLASSID="CLSID:02B97C10-ED1E-11CD-A08B-00AA00575482">
    <PARAM NAME="_Version" VALUE="65536">
    <PARAM NAME="_ExtentX" VALUE="2117">
    <PARAM NAME="_ExtentY" VALUE="1058">
    <PARAM NAME="_StockProps" VALUE="77">
    <PARAM NAME="BevelSize" VALUE="2">
    <PARAM NAME="BorderColor" VALUE="-2147483640">
    <PARAM NAME="BorderStyle" VALUE="2">
    <PARAM NAME="Max" VALUE="100">
    <PARAM NAME="Min" VALUE="0">
    <PARAM NAME="Spin" VALUE="1">
    <PARAM NAME="AutoHScroll" VALUE="1">
    <PARAM NAME="FontStyle" VALUE="1">
    <PARAM NAME="CaretColor" VALUE="-2147483642">
    <PARAM NAME="CaretStyle" VALUE="2">
</OBJECT>
</BODY>
</HTML>
```

MhMaskedInput

The MhMaskedInput control is aimed at text entry with specific formats. This control has a lot of versatility and can be used for a user-friendly data input.

Source

Vendor information:

MicroHelp, Inc.
http://www.microhelp.com
4211 J.V.L Industrial Park Drive, NE
Marietta, GA 30066
(800) 922-3383
(770) 516-1099

FIG. 14.13
The MhMaskedInput control

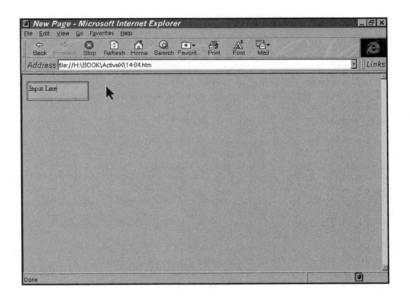

Properties

Table 14.34   Properties of the MhMaskedInput Control

Property	Description
Alignment	Alignment of the caption text
AutoHScroll	True, to scroll automatically for entries that are longer than the control
BackColor	The background color of the object
BevelSize	The 3-D bevel size in points
BevelStyle	The style of the 3-D bevel

Part
III

Ch
14

continues

Table 14.34   Continued

Property	Description
BorderColor	The object's border color
BorderStyle	The object's border style
CaretColor	The color of the caret, the small current value pointer
CaretHeight	The height of the caret
CaretInterval	The blink interval for the caret
CaretStyle	The style of the caret
CaretVAlign	The vertical alignment of the caret
CaretVisible	True, to display the caret
CaretWidth	The width of the caret
Case	The case conversion of the input value—mixed, upper, lower, proper
CMask	The custom mask
CodeBase	The origin of the control, including the URL, file type, and version number
Enabled	True, to set the control to get focus and respond to UI
FillColor	The background color
FocusSelect	True, to select the entries when the control gets focus
Font	The font for the date display
ForeColor	The foreground color of the object
Height	The vertical height of the object
hWND	The handle for the window
ID	The name of the object/control
Intent	The pixels between the date and the control border
INIFile	The INI file where the settings for this control are kept
Left	The distance between the left edge of the control and the left edge of the HTML layout
LightColor	The light color for the control
Mask	The input mask for the text entry

Property	Description
MouseIcon	The image that appears when the mouse is moved over the object
MousePointer	The mouse pointer that appears when the mouse is moved over the object
ReadOnly	True, to make the control non-editable
SelLength	The number of characters selected
SelStart	The starting/insertion point of selection
SelText	The character string selected by the user
ShadowColor	The color for the shadow
TabIndex	The object's tab order position in the HTML layout
Text	The date in the text format
TextColor	The color of the date display
TextDefault	The default text displayed when the control is initialized
TextLength	The maximum length of the text entry
TextRaw	The entered text without and formatting characters and conversion
Top	The distance between the top edge of the control and the top edge of the HTML layout
Undo	Reverses the last change made
Valignment	The vertical alignment—top, bottom, center
Visible	False, to hide the control
Width	The width of the control in points

Methods

Table 14.35	Methods of the MhMaskedInput Control
Method	**Description**
AboutBox	Displays the About dialog box
Refresh	Repaints the control

Events

Table 14.36	Events of the MhMaskedInput Control
Event	**Description**
AutoTerminate	Triggers when a valid character is entered at the last position
Change	Triggers when the value of a control changes by either the UI or programmatically; use this event handler to synchronize data between controls
Click	Triggers when a control is clicked with the mouse
DblClick	Triggers when a control is double-clicked
InvalidEntry	Triggers when the control has an invalid entry
InvalidSetText	Triggers when an invalid text is pasted into the control
KeyDown	Triggers when a user presses a control, navigation, or function key
KeyPress	Triggers when a key is either pressed by the user or sent from the SendKeys function
KeyUp	Triggers when a user releases a control, navigation, or function key
MouseDown	Triggers when a user presses a mouse button
MouseMove	Triggers when the user moves the mouse
MouseUp	Triggers when a user releases a mouse button

Example

```
<HTML>
<HEAD>
<TITLE>New Page</TITLE>
</HEAD>
<BODY>

<OBJECT ID="MhMaskInput1" WIDTH=135 HEIGHT=43
 CLASSID="CLSID:39540F00-F4F8-11CE-86BA-00AA00A25549">
    <PARAM NAME="_Version" VALUE="65536">
    <PARAM NAME="_ExtentX" VALUE="2858">
    <PARAM NAME="_ExtentY" VALUE="917">
    <PARAM NAME="_StockProps" VALUE="77">
    <PARAM NAME="BevelSize" VALUE="2">
    <PARAM NAME="BevelStyle" VALUE="2">
    <PARAM NAME="BorderColor" VALUE="-2147483642">
```

```
        <PARAM NAME="BorderStyle" VALUE="2">
        <PARAM NAME="FillColor" VALUE="-2147483633">
        <PARAM NAME="LightColor" VALUE="-2147483628">
        <PARAM NAME="ShadowColor" VALUE="-2147483632">
        <PARAM NAME="TextColor" VALUE="-2147483630">
        <PARAM NAME="Text" VALUE="MhMaskInput1">
        <PARAM NAME="Indent" VALUE="2">
        <PARAM NAME="AutoHScroll" VALUE="-1">
        <PARAM NAME="CaretColor" VALUE="-2147483642">
        <PARAM NAME="CaretVisible" VALUE="-1">
        <PARAM NAME="VAlignment" VALUE="0">
        <PARAM NAME="INIFile" VALUE="mhmask.ini">
        <PARAM NAME="CharMaskMax" VALUE="-1">
        <PARAM NAME="CaseProperMax" VALUE="-1">
    </OBJECT>
    </BODY>
    </HTML>
```

Notes

This control can also be used with mixed-case formatting.

MhRealInput

The MhRealInput control is specifically aimed at numeric data entry. This control has a lot of versatility and includes a built-in spin button for a user-friendly data input.

Source

Vendor information:

MicroHelp, Inc.
http://www.microhelp.com
4211 J.V.L Industrial Park Drive, NE
Marietta, GA 30066
(800) 922-3383
(770) 516-1099

Part

III

Ch

14

FIG. 14.14
The MhRealInput control

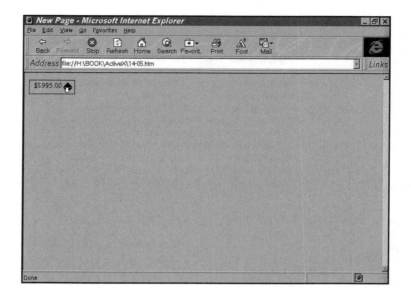

Properties

Table 14.37	Properties of the MhRealInput Control
Property	**Description**
Alignment	Alignment of the number
AutoHScroll	True, to scroll automatically for entries that are longer than the control
BackColor	The background color of the object
BevelSize	The 3-D bevel size in points
BevelStyle	The style of the bevel—lowered, raised, chiseled, and so on
BorderColor	The object's border color
BorderStyle	The object's border style
CaretColor	The color of the caret, the small current value pointer that points to the current digit
CaretHeight	The height of the caret
CaretInterval	The blink interval for the caret
CaretStyle	The style of the caret
CaretVAlign	The vertical alignment of the caret
CaretVisible	True, to display the caret

Property	Description
CaretWidth	The width of the caret
CodeBase	The origin of the control, including the URL, file type, and version number
DecimalPlaces	The number of decimal places
Enabled	True, to set the control to get focus and respond to UI
FillColor	The background color
FocusSelect	True, to select the entries when the control gets focus
Font	The font for the number display
FontStyle	The style of the font—none, raised, raised with more shading, lowered, lowered with more shading
ForeColor	The foreground color of the object
Height	The vertical height of the object
hWND	The handle for the window
ID	The name of the object/control
Intent	The pixels between the date and the control border
Left	The distance between the left edge of the control and the left edge of the HTML layout
LightColor	The light color for the control
MaxReal	The upper limit for the number
MinReal	The lower limit for the number
MoneyFormat	True, to set the currency format
MouseIcon	The image that appears when the mouse is moved over the object
MousePointer	The mouse pointer that appears when the mouse is moved over the object
ReadOnly	True, to make the control non-edit
SelLength	The number of characters selected
SelStart	The starting/insertion point of selection
SelText	The character string selected by the user
Separator	The separator character, usually ","
ShadowColor	The color for the shadow
Spin	The position of the spin button—left or right

Part
III

Ch
14

continues

Table 14.37	Continued
Property	**Description**
SpinChangeReal	The delta or the amount of change when the spin arrow is clicked
SpinDelay	The delay between the first click and start of the repeat
SpinSpeed	The delay between two consecutive spin activations
TabIndex	The object's tab order position in the HTML layout
Text	The number in the text format
TextColor	The color of the number display
Top	The distance between the top edge of the control and the top edge of the HTML layout
Undo	Reverses the last change made
VAlignment	The vertical alignment—top, bottom, center
ValueReal	The number in the control
Visible	False, to hide the control
Width	The width of the control in points

Methods

Table 14.38	Methods of the MhRealInput Control
Method	**Description**
AboutBox	Displays the About dialog box
Refresh	Repaints the control

Events

Table 14.39	Events of the MhRealInput Control
Event	**Description**
Change	Triggers when the value of a control changes by either the UI or programmatically; use this event handler to synchronize data between controls
Click	Triggers when a control is clicked with the mouse

Event	Description
DblClick	Triggers when a control is double-clicked
InvalidEntry	Triggers when the control has a value outside the minimum to maximum range
InvalidSetText	Triggers when an invalid text is pasted into the control
KeyDown	Triggers when a user presses a control, navigation, or function key
KeyPress	Triggers when a key is either pressed by the user or sent from the SendKeys function
KeyUp	Triggers when a user releases a control, navigation, or function key
MouseDown	Triggers when a user presses a mouse button
MouseMove	Triggers when the user moves the mouse
MouseUp	Triggers when a user releases a mouse button

Example

```
<HTML>
<HEAD>
<TITLE>New Page</TITLE>
</HEAD>
<BODY>

<OBJECT ID="MhRealInput1" WIDTH=100 HEIGHT=32
 CLASSID="CLSID:0F1F1505-C40A-101B-AD04-00AA00575482">
    <PARAM NAME="_Version" VALUE="65536">
    <PARAM NAME="_ExtentX" VALUE="2117">
    <PARAM NAME="_ExtentY" VALUE="670">
    <PARAM NAME="_StockProps" VALUE="77">
    <PARAM NAME="BevelStyle" VALUE="3">
    <PARAM NAME="Text" VALUE="10000.000000">
    <PARAM NAME="MaxReal" VALUE="10000">
    <PARAM NAME="MinReal" VALUE="0">
    <PARAM NAME="Spin" VALUE="2">
    <PARAM NAME="CaretColor" VALUE="-2147483642">
    <PARAM NAME="MoneyFormat" VALUE="-1">
</OBJECT>
</BODY>
</HTML>
```

Notes

A good control for quantity and currency inputs.

Part

III

Ch

14

Crystal Report Engine

The Crystal Report Engine gives you the flexibility to add ad hoc reporting capability to your applications. The reporting can be as simple as point-and-shoot printed reports or as complex as a fully user-configurable online report viewer.

Source

Vendor Information;

Seagate Software Information Management Group, Inc.
http://www.img.seagatesoftware.com
3873 Airport Way, P.O. Box 9754,
Bellingham, WA USA 98227-9754
(800) 663-1244
(604) 681-2934

This is a back-end ActiveX control and, hence, has no GUI.

Properties

Table 14.40   Properties of the Crystal Report Engine

Property	Description
BoundReportFooter	The footer for the report
BoundReportHeading	The heading for the report
CodeBase	The origin of the control, including the URL, file type, and version number
Connect	Connects to the data source
CopiesToPrinter	The number of copies when the destination is printer
DataFiles	An array containing the data source file names
DataSource	The bound data control
Destination	The destination of the report—To Window, To Printer, To File
Formulas	An array containing the formulas used in the reports
GroupSelectionFormula	A formula to limit the group of records included in the report
GroupSortFields	The sort fields
LastErrorNumber	The error number of the last error encountered

Property	Description
Height	The vertical height of the object
ID	The name of the object/control
Left	The distance between the left edge of the control and the left edge of the HTML layout
PrintFileName	The file name when the destination is a file
PrintFileType	Record, Tab Separated, DIF, CSV, and so on
ReportFileName	The name of the report definition file
ReportSource	The source for the report; selected files as defined in the report definition file or all files in the data source
SelectionFormula	The record selection formula
Top	The distance between the top edge of the control and the top edge of the HTML layout
UserName	The user name for access database
Width	The width of the control in points

Methods

Table 14.41	Methods of the Crystal Report Engine
Method	**Description**
AboutBox	Displays the About dialog box
PrintReport	Prints the report control

Events

There are no events for the Crystal Report Engine.

Example

```
<HTML>
<HEAD>
<TITLE>New Page</TITLE>
</HEAD>
<BODY>
<OBJECT ID="CrystalReport1" WIDTH=28 HEIGHT=28
 CLASSID="CLSID:00025601-0000-0000-C000-000000000046">
    <PARAM NAME="_ExtentX" VALUE="593">
```

Part
III

Ch
14

```
                <PARAM NAME="_ExtentY" VALUE="593">
                <PARAM NAME="_StockProps" VALUE="0">
                <PARAM NAME="ReportFileName" VALUE="">
                <PARAM NAME="Destination" VALUE="0">
                <PARAM NAME="WindowLeft" VALUE="100">
                <PARAM NAME="WindowTop" VALUE="100">
                <PARAM NAME="WindowWidth" VALUE="490">
                <PARAM NAME="WindowHeight" VALUE="300">
                <PARAM NAME="WindowTitle" VALUE="">
                <PARAM NAME="WindowBorderStyle" VALUE="2">
                <PARAM NAME="WindowControlBox" VALUE="-1">
                <PARAM NAME="WindowMaxButton" VALUE="-1">
                <PARAM NAME="WindowMinButton" VALUE="-1">
                <PARAM NAME="CopiesToPrinter" VALUE="1">
                <PARAM NAME="PrintFileName" VALUE="">
                <PARAM NAME="PrintFileType" VALUE="0">
                <PARAM NAME="SelectionFormula" VALUE="">
                <PARAM NAME="GroupSelectionFormula" VALUE="">
                <PARAM NAME="Connect" VALUE="">
                <PARAM NAME="UserName" VALUE="">
                <PARAM NAME="ReportSource" VALUE="0">
                <PARAM NAME="BoundReportHeading" VALUE="">
                <PARAM NAME="BoundReportFooter" VALUE="0">
        </OBJECT>
        </BODY>
        </HTML>
```

Notes

The Crystal Report Engine is part of a group of products from Seagate Software aimed at flexible reporting and querying functions. The products are positioned as workgroup-decision support applications and are rightfully so.

Another related product from Seagate Software is the CrystalINFO, which has all the features required to design, develop, and deploy report (online, offline, or both) generating client/server applications. Because it can connect to a variety of databases, including MS SQL Server, Sybase, Oracle, and Btrieve, the CrystalINFO product can be used to access data from legacy and other applications.   ●

CHAPTER 15

Imaging and Portable Document Controls

ActiveX imaging and portable document controls can change the way you display information and graphics on your Web pages. ActiveX imaging and portable document controls enable you to build Web pages that contain graphics that act and react with clear and sharp images, and documents and forms that maintain their original formatting and layout. Many different companies have created ActiveX controls that permit viewing of their imaging and document formatting over the Web. Several of these imaging and portable document controls are discussed here. ■

Using ActiveX Imaging Controls

There are many different ActiveX imaging controls on the market with new ones being released daily. ActiveX imaging controls developed by third-party software companies can help you to display and manipulate images created in file formats that are not usually recognized by HTML (.GIF or .JPG). This chapter takes a look at several of these controls, describing control properties, actions, and events. Additional information and a complete list of ActiveX controls may be found on Microsoft's Web site at **http://www.microsoft.com/activex/controls**.

Portable Document Format Controls

Many of the documents used daily, such as expense reports, purchase requisitions, and most importantly, vacation requests, contain a combination of rich text, graphics and specific formatting. Unfortunately, many of these documents lose their luster when they are converted into HTML and placed on a Web page. To solve this problem, utilize the Portable Document Format. By generating a code that preserves all of the original formatting information of a document, the portable document format can ensure that all of the rich text formatting and layout of a document are maintained and displayed properly. Several companies have now created ActiveX controls that allow you to display portable document formatted files directly in HTML pages.

Following the standard format, descriptions of the controls will be provided along with the properties, methods, and events. Controls discussed in this chapter incude:

- Acrobat Control for ActiveX
- Tumbleweed Software Envoy Control for ActiveX
- Sax Canvas Control for ActiveX

Acrobat Control for ActiveX

Perhaps the company known best for helping you to utilize portable document formatting, Adobe Systems, Inc., now has an ActiveX control available. The Acrobat Control for ActiveX provides a mechanism to view and print complete Adobe .PDF files from directly within an HTML page. With the Acrobat Control for ActiveX, .PDF files may be both viewed and printed through Microsoft Internet Explorer 3.0. .PDF (Portable Document Format) files are created from Adobe Acrobat files, and are often used to display documents that require rich text, strict formatting, and layout control.

Source

Vendor Information:

Adobe Systems, Inc.
http://www.adobe.com/
345 Park Avenue
San Jose, CA 95110-2704 USA
(408) 536-6000
(408) 537-6000 (fax)

FIG. 15.1
Acrobat Control for ActiveX

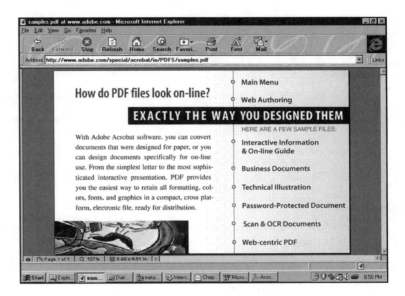

Properties

Table 15.1 summarizes all of the properties available in the Acrobat Control for ActiveX.

Table 15.1   Properties of the Acrobat Control for ActiveX

Property	Description
SRC	Specifies the URL for the PDF file to be downloaded and rendered. Relative or absolute URLs may be used.

Methods

The only methods available in the Acrobat Control allow for printing and displaying the control's "About" box.

Table 15.2   Methods of the Acrobat Control for ActiveX

Method	Description
Print	Invokes the Acrobat print dialog to allow users to print the PDF document.
AboutBox	Invokes the Acrobat Control's "About" box.

Examples

The following HTML code will insert a PDF file directly into an HTML page.

```
<OBJECT CLASSID="clsid:CA8A9780-280D-11CF-A24D-444553540000"
WIDTH=423
HEIGHT=333
ID=Pdf1
CODEBASE="rdrx32b.exe#Version=1,3,0,0">
<PARAM NAME = "SRC"
VALUE="../test.pdf">
</OBJECT>
```

The following HTML code and Visual Basic Script will add an Acrobat Print button to an HTML page.

```
<!-- Visual Basic Script -->
<SCRIPT LANGUAGE="VBSCRIPT">
Sub BtnPrint_OnClick
Pdf1.Print
End Sub
</SCRIPT>

<!--The Print button is below-->
<INPUT TYPE=submit SIZE=20 MAXLENGTH=256 NAME="BtnPrint" VALUE="Print">
```

Tumbleweed Software Envoy Control for ActiveX

Similar to the Acrobat Control, the Tumbleweed Software Envoy Control for ActiveX allows you to create and embed a customized viewer for documents in the Envoy portable document format directly in an HTML page. Through this viewer, Envoy formatted documents will maintain their original formatting even as they are viewed, printed, and zoomed in on through a Web browser. VBScripts attached to HTML forms buttons may be used to provide interaction, such as the showing and hiding of toolbars and navigation through the pages displayed through the control.

Source

Vendor Information:

Tumbleweed Software
http://www.tumbleweed.com
2010 Broadway
Redwood City, CA 94063

FIG. 15.2
Tumbleweed Software Envoy Control for ActiveX

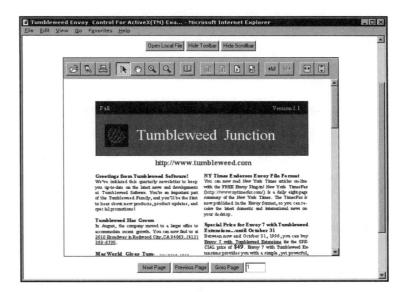

CAUTION
The Envoy Control for ActiveX is available from Tumbleweed Software as freeware, as are its other Envoy document viewers. However, if you wish to use the control to present Envoy format documents in your HTML documents, you will need to contact Tumbleweed Software to obtain the necessary licensing information.

Properties

The properties of the Tumbleweed Software Envoy Control for ActiveX are shown in Table 15.3.

Table 15.3 Properties for the Tumbleweed Software Envoy Control for ActiveX	
Property	**Description**
CurrentPage	The page of the Envoy document being displayed
CurrentTool	The current mouse tool
DocumentName	The file name of the current document
GreekPointSize	The point size below which to greek text
RightClickMenuState	Boolean, True to enable pop-up menu
Scroll	Boolean, True if scrollbars are displayed
SelectionStyle	Used to enable text and graphics selection
Toolbar	Boolean, True if the toolbar is displayed
ViewStyle	Selects between normal and thumbnail viewing
ViewZoom	Current zoom level

Methods

The methods of the Tumbleweed Software Envoy Control for ActiveX are shown in Table 15.4.

Table 15.4 Methods for the Tumbleweed Software Envoy Control for ActiveX	
Method	**Description**
AboutBox	Displays About box
CommandExecute	Executes Envoy Control command
FindText	Starts a text search
GetDocumentFirstVisiblePage	Returns page number of first visible page
GetDocumentInfo	Retrieves document information
GetDocumentLastVisiblePage	Returns page number of last visible page
GetDocumentPageCount()	Returns number of pages in current document

Method	Description
GetSelectedText	Copies selected text to a string
GetTotalHitCount	Returns the number of hits of a search
IsCommandChecked	Checks whether a predefined command is checked in the control
IsCommandEnabled	Checks whether a predefined command is enabled in the control
OpenFile	Opens local Envoy document
PrintPage	Prints page(s) of the current document
Refresh	Refreshes the screen

Many of the functions of the Envoy Control for ActiveX are accessed through the CommandExecute(*command_number*) method. These functions are accessed through the use of the appropriate command number. Table 15.5 shows some of these command numbers, along with a description of what they do.

**Table 15.5   Command Number Argument to the Envoy Control
CommandExecute Method**

Command Number	Description
0	Null command
1	Queries and opens local Envoy document
2	Closes current document
3	Calls standard print dialog to print all or part of document
4	Switches to the selection tool
5	Switches to the scroll tool
6	Switches to the zoom-in tool
7	Switches to the zoom-out tool
8	Fits page width to the width of the control
9	Fits page height to the height of the control
10	Fits entire page into the control
11	Begins text search
12	Finds next
13	Finds previous

continues

Table 15.5   Continued

Command Number	Description
14	Brings up Goto Page dialog
15	Goes to first page
16	Goes to last page
17	Goes to previous page
18	Goes to next page
19	Copies selection to clipboard
20	Goes to bookmark
21	Goes to previous view
22	Goes to next view
23	Clears current selection

Example

Listing 15.1, based on one of the examples available through the Tumbleweed site at **http://www.tumbleweed.com/eax.htm,** shows how to use HTML forms buttons and VBScript to construct a custom user interface for the Envoy Control for ActiveX.

Listing 15.1   Example.HTML—Create Your Own Interface with HTML Forms and VBScript

```
<HTML>
<HEAD>
<TITLE>Tumbleweed Envoy Control For ActiveX Example</TITLE>
<SCRIPT LANGUAGE="VBScript" >
<!-- Hide script from incompatible browsers...
Sub BtnOpen_onClick
   EnvoyControl.CommandExecute 1 'File Query and Open
   EnvoyControl.CommandExecute 8 'Fit Page to Width
End Sub

Sub BtnTool_onClick
   If EnvoyControl.Toolbar = TRUE Then
      EnvoyControl.Toolbar = FALSE
      BtnTool.Value="Show Toolbar"
   Else
      EnvoyControl.Toolbar = TRUE
      BtnTool.Value = "Hide Toolbar"
   End If
End Sub
```

```
Sub BtnScroll_onCLick
   If EnvoyControl.Scroll Then
      EnvoyControl.Scroll = False
      BtnScroll.Value = "Show Scrollbar"
   Else
      EnvoyControl.Scroll = True
      BtnScroll.Value = "Hide Scrollbar"
   End If
End Sub

Sub BtnNextPage_onClick
   EnvoyControl.CommandExecute 18 'Goto Next Page
   EnvoyControl.CommandExecute  8 'Fit Page to Width
End Sub

Sub BtnPrevPage_onClick
   EnvoyControl.CommandExecute 17 'Goto Previous Page
   EnvoyControl.CommandExecute  8 'Fit Page to Width
End Sub

Sub BtnGotoPage_onClick
   EnvoyControl.CurrentPage = EditPageNum.Value - 1
   EnvoyControl.CommandExecute  8 'Fit Page to Width
End Sub

Sub EnvoyControl_HyperCommandClick(Processor,Command)
   If Processor = "External Link" Then
      If Right(Command,4) = ".evy" Then
         EnvoyControl.OpenFile Command
      Else
         Location.Href = Command
      End If
   End If
End Sub

Sub EnvoyControl_ProgressChange(Percent,Status_String)
   Status = StatusString
End Sub
-->
</SCRIPT>
</HEAD>
<BODY BGCOLOR=#FFFFFF>
<CENTER>
<H1>Tumbleweed Envoy Control For ActiveX Example</H1>
<HR>
<OBJECT CLASSID="CLSID:5220cb21-c88d-11cf-b347-00aa00a28331">
<PARAM NAME="LPKPath" VALUE="evyactx.lpk">
</OBJECT>
<INPUT TYPE=BUTTON VALUE="Open Local File" NAME="BtnOpen">
<INPUT TYPE=BUTTON VALUE="Hide Toolbar"    NAME="BtnTool">
<INPUT TYPE=BUTTON VALUE="Hide Scrollbar"  NAME="BtnScroll">
<HR>
<OBJECT ID=EnvoyControl
   CLASSID="clsid:92B54588-AE4A-11CF-A1DD-004095E18035"
   CODEBASE="http://www.tumbleweed.com/ftp/evyactx.cab#version=1,0,0,141"
   HEIGHT=450 WIDTH=100%>
```

continues

Listing 15.1   Continued

```
<PARAM NAME="DocumentName" VALUE="document.evy">
<PARAM NAME="Toolbar"      VALUE=TRUE>
<PARAM NAME="Scroll"       VALUE=TRUE>
</OBJECT>
<HR>
<INPUT TYPE=BUTTON VALUE="Next Page"      NAME="BtnNextPage">
<INPUT TYPE=BUTTON VALUE="Previous Page"  NAME="BtnPrevPage">
<INPUT TYPE=BUTTON VALUE="Goto Page"      NAME="BtnGotoPage">
<INPUT TYPE=TEXT   VALUE="1"              NAME="EditPageNum" SIZE=5>
</CENTER>
</BODY>
</HTML>
```

Remember, to use the Envoy Control for ActiveX to display Envoy documents in your own Web pages, you will need to have the proper licensing of the control. You should note the following from the example listing:

- There are two sets of <OBJECT>...</OBJECT> tags. The first is used to verify the licensing of the control; the file evyactx.lpk must reside on your Web server. The second object is the Envoy Control itself.

- The various VBScript subroutines attached to the HTML forms buttons' onClick events use the Envoy Control methods (primarily the CommandExecute method in this example) to implement their functions.

- HyperCommandClick is an event fired by the Envoy Control when a command is selected through the control toolbar or pop-up menu. In this case, the VBScript subroutine that runs in response to this command allows us to treat selected external links properly—if they are Envoy documents, the Envoy Control is directed to open them, otherwise the Web browser itself is used.

Illustration Controls

Illustration controls work with you to provide real-time, interactive drawing capabilities on your HTML page. The illustration control provides an interactive canvas, and works with VBScript or JScript drawing commands to interact with the user.

Creating Graphics Like the Pros—Almost

Creating great graphics used to be the secret of the design schools, and the tricks of the trade were practiced in the loft spaces of advertising agencies and design firms. But access to the Internet—along with advances in graphics software—began a proliferation of graphics tools that were so easy to use that even non-designers could produce "professional" looking graphics.

The Internet has provided a new breed of graphics developers—anyone who can download a shareware program and perform simple Windows-based commands—access to hundreds of thousands of images, and the tools to change their shape, color, and texture. Now for the professional graphics designers out there, there is no need to worry. All the easy-to-use tools in the world cannot replace true technical training. But the realm of graphics design has been opened, and users of all levels will be layering images and changing colors. For more information on the graphics tools that the pros use, search for graphic tools in your favorite search engine.

Sax Canvas Control for ActiveX

The Sax Canvas Control for ActiveX from Sax Software, Inc. allows you to use VBScript or JScript drawing instructions to draw directly from within the browser. Script commands are executed and the canvas is updated in a seamless, dynamic fashion.

Source

Vendor Information:

Sax Software Corporation
http://www.saxsoft.com
950 Patterson Street
Eugene, OR 97401 USA
(541) 344-2235
(541) 344-2459 (fax)

Properties of the Sax Canvas Control for ActiveX

Table 15.6 summarizes all of the properties available in the Sax Canvas Control for ActiveX.

Table 15.6 Properties of the Sax Canvas Control for ActiveX	
Property	**Description**
Back Color	Sets the background color
Border Color	Sets the border color
Border Width	Sets the border width
Code Base	Sets the location of page to download control

continues

Table 15.6   Continued

Property	Description
Current X	Sets the current X coordinate
Current Y	Sets the current Y coordinate
Fill Color	Sets the fill color
Fill Style	Sets the fill style
Font	Sets the font
Fore Color	Sets the fore color
Height	Sets the height of the frame
ID	Sets the ID of the control (SaxCanvas1)
Left	Sets the left position of the canvas
Top	Sets the top position of the frame
Visible	Sets the canvas to visible
Width	Sets the width of the canvas

FIG. 15.3
Sax Canvas Control for
ActiveX

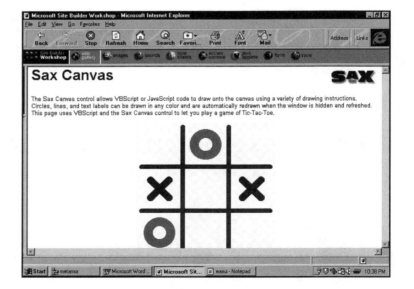

Methods of the Sax Canvas Control for ActiveX

Table 15.7 contains the Methods of the Sax Canvas Control for ActiveX.

Table 15.7   Methods of the Sax Canvas Control for ActiveX

Method	Description
AboutBox	Invokes the Sax about box
Clear	Clears the canvas

Events of the Sax Canvas Control for ActiveX

Table 15.8 summarizes the Events of the Sax Canvas Control for ActiveX.

Table 15.8   Events of the Sax Canvas Control for ActiveX

Events	Actions
Click	Performs action upon mouse click
DblClick	Performs actions upon mouse double-click
MouseDown	Performs actions upon moving the mouse down
MouseUp	Performs actions upon moving the mouse up
MouseMove	Performs actions upon moving the mouse over the control.

Example

The following code will insert the Sax Canvas Control, allowing you to display your VB-Script and JScript drawing instructions on an HTML page.

```
<OBJECT ID="SaxCanvas1" WIDTH=100 HEIGHT=61
 CLASSID="CLSID:1DF67C43-AEAA-11CF-BA92-444553540000">
    <PARAM NAME="_Version" VALUE="65536">
    <PARAM NAME="_ExtentX" VALUE="2646">
    <PARAM NAME="_ExtentY" VALUE="1623">
    <PARAM NAME="_StockProps" VALUE="13">
    <PARAM NAME="ForeColor" VALUE="0">
    <PARAM NAME="BackColor" VALUE="16776960">
</OBJECT>
```

The following VBScript used in conjunction with the Sax Canvas Control lets you play an interactive game of tic tac toe. This code and more examples of using VBScript with the Sax Canvas Control may be found on the Sax Web site as previously listed.

```
<SCRIPT LANGUAGE="VBScript">
<!--

Sub window_onLoad()
    InitBoard
```

```
End Sub

' Module level variables
Dim Field

' Draw initial board and empty field
Sub InitBoard()
    Field = "          "
    ' Draw board
    Canvas.Clear
    Canvas.BorderColor = 128
    Canvas.BorderWidth = 10
    Canvas.MoveTo 100, 10
    Canvas.LineTo 100, 290
    Canvas.MoveTo 200, 10
    Canvas.LineTo 200, 290
    Canvas.MoveTo 10, 100
    Canvas.LineTo 290, 100
    Canvas.MoveTo 10, 200
    Canvas.LineTo 290, 200
End Sub

' Make player's move and respond with your own
Sub Canvas_MouseDown(Button, Shift, x, y)
    If Field = "" Then InitBoard

    If MakeMove("X", x \ 100, y \ 100) Then
        Do
            myX = Rnd * 300
            myY = Rnd * 300
        Loop Until MakeMove("O", myX \ 100, myY \ 100)
    End If
End Sub

' Draw move and update Field variable
' Check if won, and if so, display message
' If bord full or won, clear bord
Function MakeMove(Player, X, Y)
    ' If the board is full, start over
    If Instr(Field, " ") = 0 Then InitBoard
    ' Check to see if it's a valid move.
    If FieldItem(X,Y) <> " " Then
        MakeMove = False
        Exit Function
    End If
    Field = Left(Field, X + 3 * Y) + Player + Mid(Field, X + 3 * Y + 2)

    If Player = "X" Then
        Canvas.BorderWidth = 16
        Canvas.BorderColor =  16711680
        Canvas.MoveTo X * 100 + 30, Y * 100 + 30
        Canvas.LineTo (X + 1) * 100 - 30, (Y + 1) * 100 - 30
        Canvas.MoveTo (X + 1) * 100 - 30, Y * 100 + 30
        Canvas.LineTo X * 100 + 30, (Y + 1) * 100 - 30
    Else
```

```
                    Canvas.BorderWidth = 20
                    Canvas.BorderColor = 255
                    Canvas.FillColor = 11206655
                    Canvas.FillStyle = 0
                    Canvas.MoveTo (X * 100) + 50, (Y * 100) + 50
                    Canvas.Circle 25
            End If
            If CheckMove(X, Y) Then
                    If Player = "X" Then MsgBox "Congratulations!", 0, "Tic-Tac-Toe"
                    ➥else MsgBox "I'm smarter than you...", 0, "Tic-Tac-Toe"
                    Field = "XXXXXXXXX"            ' Force new game next time
            End If
            MakeMove = True
    End Function

    ' Returns item at a certain position ("X", "O", or " ")
    Function FieldItem(X, Y)
            FieldItem = Mid(Field, 1 + X + Y * 3, 1)

    End Function

    ' Check if if all the items in a row are the same value
    Function CheckLine(X, Y, dX, dY, Value)
            If (FieldItem(X, Y) = Value) and (FieldItem(X + dX, Y + dY) = Value) and
    (FieldItem(X + 2 * dX, Y + 2 * dY) = Value) Then
                    CheckLine = True
        else
                    CheckLine = False
        End If
    End Function

    ' Check if rows at a certain position contain three in a row
    Function CheckMove(X, Y)
            CheckMove = CheckLine(0, Y, 1, 0, FieldItem(X, Y))  or CheckLine(X, 0,
            ➥0, 1, FieldItem(X, Y)) or CheckLine(0, 0, 1, 1, FieldItem(X, Y)) or
            ➥CheckLine(0, 2, 1, -1, FieldItem(X, Y))
    End Function

    -->
        </SCRIPT>
```

CHAPTER 16

Animation Controls

Back in the olden days of the Web (about one year ago), animation (or any image sequencing) was achieved by placing images on separate Web pages and requiring the user to navigate from page to page via hyperlinks or imagemaps. Working slightly worse than those old-fashioned flipbooks, many of the creators of this animation felt much of the effect of their hard work was lost in the method. New methods followed and developers began utilizing new techniques, such as server push, where the Web server sends the client a series of images in a row. Although this method produced the desired effect for the fading in and out of images, it was too slow and cumbersome for the display of true animation.

Today there are several different methods for achieving animation over the Web, including Java, animated gifs, and now ActiveX controls. These methods have graphic artists, Web artists, and end users jumping for joy. In this chapter, several of the more popular ActiveX controls that will help you provide high-quality animation on your Web site are discussed. ■

FutureSplash Player Control for ActiveX

The FutureSplash Player Control for ActiveX from Future Wave Software, Inc. (**http:// www.futurewave.com**) allows you to integrate and display Web animations created with the FutureSplash Animator within HTML page (see Figure 16.1).

Source

Vendor Information:

FutureWave Software Inc.
http://www.futurewave.com
9909 Huennekens St. Ste. 210
San Diego, CA 92121 USA
619-552-7680
619-552-7680 (fax)

FIG. 16.1
FutureSplash Player Control
for ActiveX

Properties of the FutureSplash Player Control for ActiveX

Table 16.1 summarizes all of the properties available in the FutureSplash Player Control for ActiveX.

Table 16.1   Properties of the FutureSplash Player Control for ActiveX

Property	Description
Align Mode	Sets the alignment of the frame
Background Color	Sets the background color of the frame
Code Base	Sets the location of the page to download the control
FrameNum	Sets the number of frames in the Animation
Height	Sets the Height of the frame
ID	Sets the ID of the control (FutureSplash1)
Left	Sets the left orientation of the frame
Loop	Sets the movie to loop
Movie	Sets the name and path of the movie
Playing	Sets the movie to automatically begin playing
Quality	Sets the image quality to high or low
Top	Sets the top location of the frame
Visible	Sets the animation to visible
Width	Sets the width of the frame

Methods of the FutureSplash Player Control for ActiveX

Table 16.2 lists the events of the FutureSplash Player Control for ActiveX.

Table 16.2   Methods of the FutureSplash Player Control for ActiveX

Method	Description
Back	Moves the animation backward one frame
Current Frame	Sets the current frame of the animation
Forward	Moves the animation one frame forward
IsPlaying	Sets the state of the animation
PercentLoaded	States the percent of the animation loaded
Play	Plays the animation
Rewind	Rewinds the animation to the first frame
SetZoomRect	Sets the size of the zoom frame

continues

Table 16.2 Continued	
Method	**Description**
Stop	Stops the animation
StopPlay	Stops the playing of the animation on the current frame
Zoom	Sets the zoom percentage for the animation

Events of the FutureSplash Player Control for ActiveX

Table 16.3 lists the events of the FutureSplash Player Control for ActiveX.

Table 16.3 Events of the FutureSplash Player Control for ActiveX	
Event	**Actions**
FS Command	Accepts FutureSplash command options
On Progress	Sends a signal prompting the progress of an animation
OnReadyStateChange	Sends a signal prompting a change of state

Example

The following code enables you to view FutureSplash animations and images through an HTML page.

```
<OBJECT ID="FutureSplash1" WIDTH=127 HEIGHT=71
 CLASSID="CLSID:D27CDB6E-AE6D-11CF-96B8-444553540000">
    <PARAM NAME="_ExtentX" VALUE="3360">
    <PARAM NAME="_ExtentY" VALUE="1879">
    <PARAM NAME="Movie" VALUE="MyMovie">
    <PARAM NAME="Loop" VALUE="-1">
    <PARAM NAME="Play" VALUE="0">
    <PARAM NAME="Quality" VALUE="AutoLow">
    <PARAM NAME="SAlign" VALUE="_">
    <PARAM NAME="DeviceFont" VALUE="0">
    <PARAM NAME="Menu" VALUE="-1">
</OBJECT>
```

mBED Player Control for ActiveX

The mBED Player Control for ActiveX from mBED Software allows you to incorporate interactive animation into your Web site by displaying "mBEDlets" through the mBED player (see Figure 16.2).

Source

Vendor Information:

mBED Software
http://www.mbed.com
185 Berry Street
Suite 3807
San Francisco, CA 94107 USA
415-778-0930
415-778-0933 (fax)

FIG. 16.2
mBED Player Control for
ActiveX

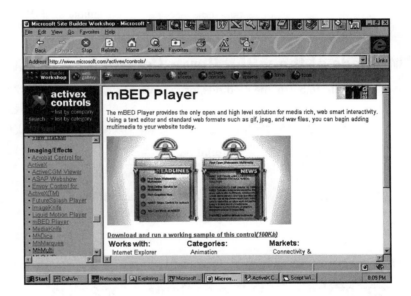

Properties of the mBED Player Control for ActiveX

Table 16.4 summarizes all of the properties available in the mBED Player Control for ActiveX.

Table 16.4   Properties of the mBED Player Control for ActiveX

Property	Description
Codebase	Sets the location of the page to download the control
Height	Sets the height of the player frame

continues

Table 16.4	Continued
Property	**Description**
ID	Sets the ID of the control (MbedPlayer1)
Left	Sets the left position of the player
Name	Sets the name of the mBEDlet to display
Top	Sets the top position of the player frame
Visible	Sets the animation to visible
Width	Sets the width of the player frame
Src	Sets the source path of the animation .MBD file

Methods of the mBED Player Control for ActiveX

Table 16.5 lists the methods for the mBED Player Control for ActiveX.

Table 16.5	Methods of the mBED Player Control for ActiveX
Method	**Description**
AboutBox	Invokes the mBED About box
Action	Sets the action of the animation
Start	Starts the animation
Stop	Stops the animation

Event of the mBED Player Control for ActiveX

Table 16.6 shows the event of the mBED Player Control for ActiveX.

Table 16.6	Event of the mBED Player Control for ActiveX
Event	**Description**
CallBack	Sets the current call back state of the animation

Example

The following code inserts the mBED Player Control, allowing you to display animated "mbeblets" on your HTML page.

```
<OBJECT ID="MbedPlayer1" WIDTH=127 HEIGHT=137
 CLSID="CLSID:873237C3-C440-11CF-B4B6-00A02429C7EF">
<PARAM NAME="_ExtentX" VALUE="3360">
<PARAM NAME="_ExtentY" VALUE="3625">
<PARAM NAME="src" value="my.mbd">
<EMBED SRC="my.mbd" height=535 width=325>
</OBJECT>
```

Sizzler Control for ActiveX

The Sizzler Control for ActiveX from Totally Hip Software allows you to incorporate streamed animation into your Web site by displaying Sizzler animation files (see Figure 16.3).

Source

Vendor Information:

Totally Hip Software
http://www.totallyhip.com
Suite #301
1224 Hamilton Street
Vancouver, BC V6B-2S8 Canada
(604) 685-6525
(604) 685-4057 (fax)

FIG. 16.3
Sizzler Control for ActiveX

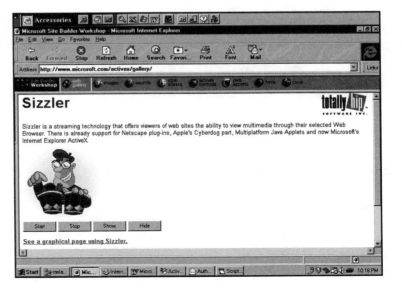

Properties of the Sizzler Control for ActiveX

Table 16.7 summarizes all of the properties available in the Sizzler Control for ActiveX.

Table 16.7	Properties of the Sizzler Control for ActiveX
Property	**Description**
CodeBase	Sets the location of page to download control
Height	Sets the height of the frame
ID	Sets the ID of the control (Sizzler1)
Image	Sets the path of the Sizzler file to display
Left	Sets the left position of the frame
Top	Sets the top position of the frame
Visible	Sets the viewer to visible
Width	Sets the width of the frame

Methods of the Sizzler Control for ActiveX

Table 16.8 shows the methods for the Sizzler Control for ActiveX.

Table 16.8	Methods of the Sizzler Control for ActiveX
Method	**Description**
AboutBox	Invokes the Sizzler About box
Hide	Hides the current object
Show	Shows the current object
Start	Starts the animation
Stop	Stops the animation

Events of the Sizzler Control for ActiveX

Table 16.9 lists the events of the Sizzler Control for ActiveX.

Table 16.9 Events and Actions of the Sizzler Player Control for ActiveX

Event	Description
OnHidden	Performs action when object state is hidden
OnNewFile	Performs action when new file is opened
OnProgress	Performs action when state of animation is in progress
OnReadyStateChange	Performs action when animation state is about to change
OnShown	Performs action when object is shown
OnStopped	Performs action when animation is stopped

Example

The following code inserts your HTML page.

```
<OBJECT ID="Sizzler1" WIDTH=137 HEIGHT=83
 CLASSID="CLSID:088D8100-C496-11CF-B54A-00C0A8361ED8"
 DATA="DATA:application/x-
oleobject;BASE64,AIGNCJbEzxG1SgDAqDYe2CFDNBIIAAAAKQ4AAHoIAABOYbwAAAAAAA==
">
<PARAM NAME="Image" VALUE="my.spr">
</OBJECT>
```

CHAPTER 17

VRML Controls

Glide off a Web page into a virtual world through a VRML ActiveX control. Virtual worlds began appearing on the Web following the release of the first version of the Virtual Reality Modeling Language (VRML 1.0) in late 1995. Since then, VRML worlds have evolved into places that include animated virtual objects, three-dimensional sound, and time. Immerse yourself in state-of-the-art Internet virtual realities or present your own virtual worlds by using VRML ActiveX controls.

In this chapter, you will review several of the leading ActiveX controls and Netscape plug-ins that are available for creating your own VRML world.

You will learn all about each of the controls introduced and discover where you can get them. Then you will learn about the properties, events, and methods available for use with each control. ■

Using VRML

You explore virtual worlds by walking or flying through three-dimensions, which is in sharp contrast to the way you encounter Web pages. Virtual worlds and Web pages are defined using different languages. Virtual worlds on the Internet are typically defined using the Virtual Reality Modeling Language (VRML), whereas Web pages are defined using the Hypertext Markup Language (HTML). Each language requires its own interpreter; which requires a separate browser to view the virtual worlds and Web pages; that is, until VRML ActiveX controls and Netscape plug-ins appeared on the scene.

A VRML ActiveX control or a Netscape plug-in adds a VRML interpreter to your Web browser so that the browser can display both virtual worlds and Web pages. In fact, your browser can display a virtual world in a Web page! Your Web browser switches between the VRML and HTML interpreters, depending on the Internet file's extension (the three letters after the period in the file name). If the file's extension is WRL, your Web browser sends the file's contents through the VRML interpreter provided by the installed VRML ActiveX control or Netscape plug-in. Otherwise, if the file's extension is HTM, the file's contents are interpreted by the browser's own HTML interpreter.

Once you've installed a VRML ActiveX control or Netscape plug-in, virtual worlds appear in your Web browser automatically when you click a hyperlink to a VRML file. However, the different VRML ActiveX controls and Netscape plug-ins that are provided by different companies vary in the details of their implementations. Which VRML ActiveX control or Netscape plug-in you prefer is a matter of taste. You may like how one company implements controls for flying through a world over another company's implementation of these controls. More importantly, they may be compatible with one of two VRML versions, VRML 1.0 or VRML 2.0.

VRML 1.0 worlds are static, three-dimensional spaces filled with static, three-dimensional objects, whereas VRML 2.0 worlds include animated, three-dimensional objects that exhibit behavior. Clearly, VRML 2.0 worlds are more exciting. Also, ActiveX controls and Netscape plug-ins that are VRML 2.0 compatible can display VRML 1.0 virtual worlds, but only ActiveX controls and Netscape plug-ins that are VRML 1.0 compatible cannot display VRML 2.0 worlds.

The Microsoft VRML 1.0 ActiveX Control

The Microsoft VRML 1.0 ActiveX control is an excellent control to start with. It's free and it's easy to download from the Microsoft Web site. Also, because it's free, it's probably the most widely used VRML ActiveX control. This control's main limitation is that it's only compatible with VRML 1.0. In the ActiveX Control Pad, this control is called the

`VrmlViewer` object. The Microsoft VRML 1.0 ActiveX control is available for free at Microsoft's Web site.

Source

Vendor Information:

Microsoft Corporation
http://www.microsoft.com/ie/download/ieadd.htm
One Microsoft Way
Redmond, WA 98052-6399
(800) 426-9400

FIG. 17.1
The Microsoft VRML 1.0
ActiveX control

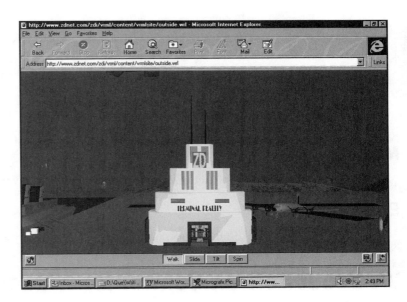

Properties

Table 17.1   Microsoft VRML 1.0 ActiveX Control Properties

Property	Description
CodeBase	The URL where the Microsoft VRML 1.0 ActiveX control resides. Installation is automatically initiated if the user doesn't already have the control installed on their computer.
DataPath	The URL where the VRML file resides.
Height	The height of the ActiveX control's window.

continues

Table 17.1	Continued
Property	**Description**
ID	A name that identifies the particular instance of a control on your Web page. Use this ID in scripts.
Left	The amount of space between the left edge of the Web page and the left edge of the ActiveX control's window.
TabIndex	Sets the tab index. The tab index determines the order in which tab stops are visited. If TabStop is set to True, a TabIndex of "0" indicates this is the first tab stop. A TabIndex of "1" indicates this is the second tab stop, and so on.
TabStop	Set to True if you want the control window to be a tab stop; otherwise, set it to False.
Top	The amount of space between the top of the Web page and the top of the ActiveX control's window.
Visible	Set to True if you want the control window to be visible; otherwise, set it to False.
Width	The width of the ActiveX control's window.

Methods

The Microsoft VRML 1.0 ActiveX control does not provide any methods.

Events

The Microsoft VRML 1.0 ActiveX control does not provide any events.

VR Scout ActiveX Control for Windows 95 and Windows NT

The VR Scout ActiveX control provides the same properties as the Microsoft VRML 1.0 ActiveX control listed in Table 17.1. The only difference is that the DataPath property is named the VrmlFile property in VR Scout. VR Scout has an excellent rendering engine. The VR Scout ActiveX control is called the VRScoutCtl Object in the ActiveX Control Pad. You can download the VR Scout ActiveX control and try it free for 30 days. Then you must buy the control to keep using it. Download the control from the Chaco Web site.

Source

Vendor Information:

Chaco Communications, Inc.
http://www.chaco.com/
10164 Parkwood Dr., Suite 8
Cupertino, CA 95014
(408) 996-1115
(408) 865-0571 fax

FIG. 17.2
The VR Scout ActiveX
control for Windows 95
and Windows NT

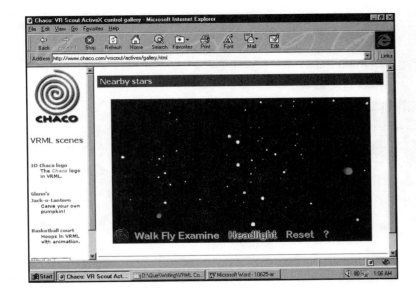

Properties

Table 17.2   VR Scout ActiveX Control Properties

Property	Description
CodeBase	The URL where the VR Scout ActiveX control resides. Installation is automatically initiated if the user doesn't already have the control installed on their computer.
Height	The height of the ActiveX control's window.
ID	A name that identifies the particular instance of a control on your Web page. Use this ID in scripts.
Left	The amount of space between the left edge of the Web page and the left edge of the ActiveX control's window.

continues

Table 17.2	Continued
Property	**Description**
TabIndex	Sets the tab index. The tab index determines the order in which tab stops are visited. If TabStop is set to True, a TabIndex of "0" means that this is the first tab stop. A TabIndex of "1" means that this is the second tab stop, and so on.
TabStop	Set to True if you want the control window to be a tab stop; otherwise, set it to False.
Top	The amount of space between the top of the Web page and the top of the ActiveX control's window.
Visible	Set to True if you want the control window to be visible; otherwise, set it to False.
VrmlFile	The URL where the VRML file resides.
Width	The width of the ActiveX control's window.

Methods

Table 17.3	VR Scout ActiveX Control Methods
Method	**Description**
AboutBox	Displays a dialog box that describes the VR Scout ActiveX control.
Navigate	Takes a fully qualified URL to a virtual world.

Event

Table 17.4	VR Scout ActiveX Control Event
Event	**Description**
OnProgress	The control fires progress status events so that you can show a progress message.

WIRL 1.20 ActiveX Control

The WIRL 1.20 ActiveX control provides more properties than Microsoft's VRML 1.0 ActiveX control. One of these properties allows you to turn the display of WIRL's control panel interface on and off. WIRL has a long list of options that you can set from a menu. WIRL's 1.20 ActiveX control is called the Wirlocx Control in the ActiveX Control Pad. Download WIRL 1.20 from the VREAM Web site.

Source

Vendor Information:

VREAM, Inc.
http://www.vream.com
223 West Erie Street, Suite 600
Chicago, Illinois 60610
(312) 337-5164
(312) 337-5264 fax

FIG. 17.3
The WIRL 1.20 ActiveX control

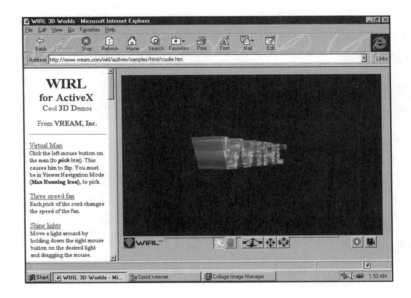

Part

III

Ch

17

Properties

Table 17.5   WIRL 1.2 ActiveX Control Properties

Property	Description
CodeBase	The URL where the WIRL 1.2 ActiveX control resides. Installation is automatically initiated if the user doesn't already have the control installed on their computer.
Control Panel	Set to True if you want WIRL's control panel displayed; otherwise, set it to False.
Height	The height of the ActiveX control's window.

continues

Table 17.5	Continued
Property	**Description**
ID	A name that identifies the particular instance of a control on your Web page. Use this ID in scripts.
Left	The amount of space between the left edge of the Web page and the left edge of the ActiveX control's window.
Renderer	This property remains exposed but is no longer implemented. (It was used to switch between different rendering libraries.)
TabIndex	Sets the tab index. The tab index determines the order in which tab stops are visited. If TabStop is set to True, a TabIndex of "0" means that this is the first tab stop. A TabIndex of "1" means that this is the second tab stop and so on.
TabStop	Set to True if you want the control window to be a tab stop; otherwise, set it to False.
Top	The amount of space between the top of the Web page and the top of the ActiveX control's window.
Visible	Set to True if you want the control window to be visible; otherwise, set it to False.
Width	The width of the ActiveX control's window.
World	The URL where the VRML file resides.

Method

Table 17.6	WIRL 1.20 ActiveX Control Method
Method	**Description**
AboutBox	Displays a dialog box that describes the WIRL 1.20 ActiveX control.

Events

The WIRL 1.20 ActiveX control does not provide any events. ●

Conferencing Controls

Collaborating over a network is one of the many possibilities available to Internet users with ActiveX conferencing controls. Collaboration can take many forms. In this chapter, you will take a look at a diverse (though a bit eclectic) group of controls.

For each control, you will follow the usual format. First, you will learn about the control and discover where you can get it. Then you will learn the properties, events, and methods available for use with the control. Note also that Microsoft has created a product called NetMeeting. NetMeeting is not an ActiveX control; therefore, it is not covered in this book. However, if you are interested, check it out on the Web at **http://www.microsoft.com/netmeeting/**. ■

The ASAP WebShow Control

ASAP WebShow is an ActiveX control for delivering presentations over the Internet. With the ASAP WebShow control, users can view, download, print, and even listen to presentation content. ASAP WebShow is a companion product of ASAP WordPower presentation software developed by Software Publishing Corporation. The WebShow control uses VCR buttons as the metaphor for permitting users to move forward and backward through a slide show. Presentations can also be configured to cycle through a set of slides. Audio support that is synchronized to the presentation is provided through the RealAudio Player.

Source

The ASAP WebShow ActiveX control is available for free download over the Internet.

Vendor Information:

Software Publishing Corporation
http://www.spco.com
111 North Market St.
San Jose, CA 95113 USA
408-537-3000
408-537-3500 (fax)

FIG. 18.1
The ASAP WebShow control

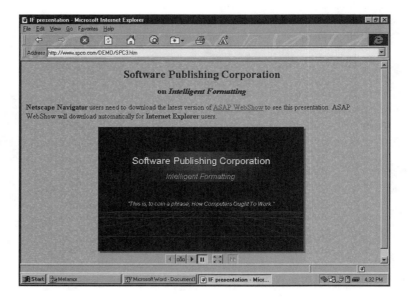

Properties

Table 18.1 Properties of the ASAP WebShow Control

Property	Description
AutoAdvance	Determines whether the slides will automatically cycle or not. The value is either True or False.
Border	Indicates the style of border to surround the presentation with. Valid values include raised, recessed, slide, shadowed, simple, and none
CodeBase	Describes the version of the ActiveX control to be used. An example entry would be svideo.cab#version=1,0,0,180 where SVIDEO.CAB is the installation cabinet file.
DelayTime	Indicates the amount of time in seconds to pause on each slide. This value is relevant when AutoAdvance is True.
Effect	Sets the transition style to use when slides cycle. Valid values include none, default, fade, rain replace, blinds horizontal, blinds vertical, close horizontal, close vertical, iris in, iris out, open, scroll up, scroll down, scroll left, scroll right, wipe up, wipe down, wipe left, wipe right, peel upper right, and peel lower left.
File	Indicates the URL of the presentation file to be presented.
Height	Indicates the height of the space to be covered by the control.
ID	Indicates a name that refers to the current instance of the control.
LoopBack	Determines whether the slides will be shown one time through when AutoAdvance is True or whether the slides will continuously loop.
NavBar	Turns the navigation button bar on or off.
NavButtons	Turns the navigation buttons on or off.
Orientation	Sets the orientation of the presentation. Typically, you will set this to freeform.
Pause	Indicates whether the slide show is paused or not.
PauseButton	Turns the pause button on or off.
Sound	Displays the URL for the sound.
StatusButtons	Turns the status buttons on or off.
ZoomButtons	Turns the zoom buttons on and off.

Part
III

Ch
18

Method

Table 18.2	Method of the ASAP WebShow Control
Method	**Description**
AboutBox	Displays a dialog box that describes the ASAP WebShow control.

Events

The ASAP WebShow control does not expose any events.

Code Example

The following listing shows the code required to create the screen displayed in Figure 18.1.

Listing 18.1   HTML for Declaration of the ASAP WebShow Control

```
<OBJECT ID="AXASAP1"
    CLSID="CLSID:EA28C303-C2DB-11CF-83E6-00608C5B8AAD"
    CODEBASE="http://www.spco.com/codebase/asap/axasap.cab"#Version=1,0,0,4
    HEIGHT="305" WIDTH="450">
<PARAM NAME="File" VALUE="SPC3.asp">
<PARAM NAME="Border" VALUE="shadowed">
<PARAM NAME="NavBar" VALUE="on">
<PARAM NAME="Orientation" VALUE="freeform">
<PARAM NAME="AutoAdvance" VALUE="on">
<PARAM NAME="DelayTime" VALUE="4">
<PARAM NAME="Loopback" VALUE="on">
</OBJECT>
```

Note that the AutoAdvance is turned on. This ensures that the presentation cycles through each slide, pausing 4 seconds on each slide (as indicated in DelayTime).

The CyberGO Control

The CyberGO control is a networked version of one of the world's oldest strategy games. The objective in GO is to conquer a larger part of the board than your opponent. Though the rules for GO are simple, the strategy of the game is quite complex. With the CyberGO control, you can find partners to play over the Internet using a game server.

Source

The CyberGO ActiveX control is available for free download over the Internet.

Vendor Information:

Brilliance Labs, Inc.
http://www.brlabs.com
700 SW 62nd Blvd., Suite H105
Gainesville, FL 32607 USA
352-336-5909
352-336-5909

FIG. 18.2
The CyberGO ActiveX control

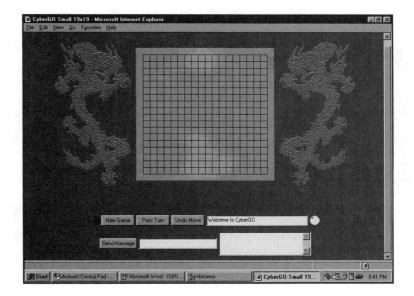

Properties

Table 18.3   Properties of the CyberGO ActiveX Control

Property	Description
BoardImage	The URL of the image to use for the board.
BoardSize	The relative size of the board. (Note that a 19×19 matrix will be scaled and rendered within the size specified.)
ClickSound	The URL of the sound to use when the board is clicked.

continues

Table 18.3 Continued	
Property	**Description**
CodeBase	The version of the ActiveX control to be used. An example entry would be cybergo.cab#ver=1,0,0,7.
ErrorSound	The URL of a sound to be played when the user commits an error.
Height	The height of the space to be covered by the control.
ID	A name that refers to the current instance of the control.
ServerURL	The URL of the game server that conferences two players together.

Methods

Table 18.4 Methods of the CyberGO Control	
Method	**Description**
AboutBox	Displays a dialog box that describes the cyberGO control.
MessageOut	Sends a message.
NewGame	Starts a new game.
PassMove	Permits the current player to pass this turn.
UndoMove	Reverses a mistaken move.

Events

Table 18.5 Events of the CyberGO Control	
Event	**Description**
Messages	Fires when messages are present. Related to MessageOut method.
ReadyStateChange	Triggers when the value of ReadyState changes.
Status	Occurs when status is set.

Code Example

The following listing shows the code required to create the screen displayed in Figure 18.2.

Listing 18.2 HTML for Declaration of the CyberGO Control

```
<OBJECT ID=cybergo
        classid="clsid:538843C4-E0D3-11CF-B0E5-204C4F4F5020"
        CODEBASE="cybergo.cab#ver=1,0,0,7"
        TYPE="application/x-oleobject"
        BORDER=0 ALIGN=center VSPACE=5 WIDTH=300 HEIGHT=300>
        <param name="BoardImage" value="media/boards19.gif">
        <param name="ClickSound" value="media/click.wav">
        <param name="ErrorSound" value="media/pop.wav">
        <param name="BoardWidth" value=300>
        <param name="ServerURL" value="http://www.brlabs.com/cgi-bin/brlabs/
        cybergo.pl">
    </OBJECT>
```

As you can see the ErrorSound, ClickSound, and BoardImage are all relative URLs (although you are free to use absolute URLs as well). The ServerURL is an absolute URL. The Web site shown in ServerURL is a meeting place hosted by the manufacturer of the CyberGO game.

Part
III

Ch
18

The Look@Me Control

The Look@Me control presents us with an opportunity to look into the future of the Internet. Bill Gates once remarked that someday users who encounter a problem using a piece of software would be able to click on a "Customer Support" menu and auto-magically connect with a support representative. Once connected to Customer Support, the technician could examine the user's computer and determine the problem. The Look@Me control takes the technology a step closer to this vision.

Look@Me allows you to observe another user's screen anywhere in the world, in real time, over the Internet. Look@Me is based on Farallon Communications's Timbuktu Pro package and leverages Timbuktu's more robust screen-sharing feature. You can use these tools to troubleshoot and fix problems over the network. Look@Me allows the support professional to solve a remote Internet user's problem. Look@Me can view the desktop of any other Look@Me- or Timbuktu Pro-equipped Windows or Macintosh computer over the Internet.

Source

The Look@Me control is available for free download over the Internet.

Vendor Information:

Farallon Communications, Inc.
http://www.farallon.com
2470 Marriner Square Loop
Alameda, CA 94501 USA
510-814-5000
510-814-5020 (fax)

FIG. 18.3
The Look@Me control

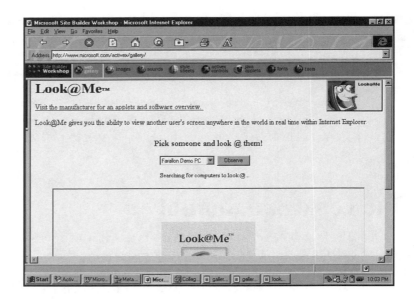

Properties

Table 18.6   Properties of the Look@Me Control

Property	Description
AllowGuests	Determines whether the user will permit an observer or not.
BackColor	Selects the background color.
CodeBase	Describes the version of the ActiveX control to be used. For this control, the proper entry is `http://collaborate.farallon.com/www/look/ie/lookatme.cab#Version=1,0,0,14` where LOOKATME.CAB is the installation cabinet file.

Property	Description
Height	Indicates the height of the space to be covered by the control.
ID	Indicates a name that refers to the current instance of the control.
RemoteAddress	Indicates either the address of the machine that is observing this one or the address of the machine being observed.
Service	Specifies the Look@Me service being used. Currently only the "observe" service is implemented.
ShowAsPopUp	Sets whether the observe session is displayed in a floating pop-up window or within a Web page.
UserName	Specifies the name users will see when observing your computer.

Methods

Table 18.7 Methods of the Look@Me Control

Method	Description
AboutBox	Displays a dialog box that describes the Surround Video control.
Disconnectallusers	Ends an observation session.
GetMyAddress	Returns your IP address as a string.
IsConnected	Returns True, if there is an observation session underway.
OpenConnection	Opens a connection with the specified IP address for observation.

Events

Table 18.8 Events of the Look@Me Control

Event	Description
OnChangedAllowGuests	Triggered when the AllowGuests property is changed.
StatusUpdate	Fires when the status of the connection changes.

Code Example

The following listing shows the code required to create the screen displayed in
Figure 18.3.

Part
III

Ch

18

Listing 18.3 HTML for Declaration of the Look@Me Control

```
<OBJECT ID="LookAtMe1" WIDTH=90% HEIGHT=90%
 CLASSID="CLSID:CF1C1ECB-9925-11CF-B396-0000C5384B10"
 CODEBASE="http://collaborate.farallon.com/www/look/ie/
 lookatme.cab#Version=1,0,0,14">
    <PARAM NAME="BackColor" VALUE="&Hffffff">
    <PARAM NAME="ShowAsPopup"    VALUE=FALSE>
    <PARAM NAME="AllowGuests"    VALUE=TRUE>
    <PARAM NAME="SERVICE"        VALUE="Observe">
    <PARAM NAME="RemoteAddress" VALUE="">
</OBJECT>
```

Note that the RemoteAddress field is blank in this case. Before a connection is made to a distant computer, this value remains blank. After connecting to a computer over the network, this field will contain the target machine's IP address.

The EarthTime Control

The EarthTime ActiveX control tracks time for communications across time zones. The EarthTime user interface includes a world map, clocks for eight cities, time difference calculator, and database of telephone codes, currencies, and other data. The EarthTime control includes in excess of 375 world locations in its database. EarthTime even calculates time differences and graphically displays seasonal changes in daylight and dark cycles. The EarthTime control is perfect for World Wide Web applications used for scheduling appointments, conducting conferences, or engaging in Internet chats.

Source

The EarthTime ActiveX control is available for free download over the Internet.

Vendor Information:

Starfish Software, Inc.
http://www.starfishsoftware.com
1700 Green Hills Road
Scotts Valley, CA 95066 USA
408-461-5800
408-461-5900 (fax)

FIG. 18.4
The EarthTime control

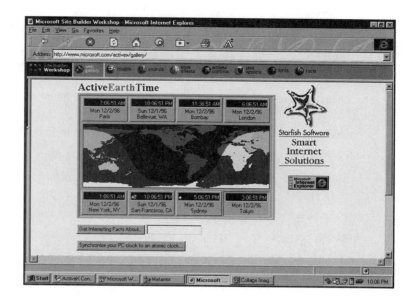

Properties

Table 18.9   Properties of the EarthTime Control

Property	Description
CodeBase	Describes the version of the ActiveX control to be used. An example entry would be cabs/et.cab#version=1,0,0,7 where ET.CAB is the installation cabinet file.
Height	Indicates the height of the space to be covered by the control.
ID	Indicates a name that refers to the current instance of the control.

Methods

Table 18.10   Methods of the EarthTime Control

Method	Description
AboutBox	Displays a dialog box that describes the EarthTime control.
CenterMapBySelectedClock	Causes the displayed map to be centered on the part of the world indicated by the selected clock.

continues

Table 18.10   Continued

Method	Description
ChangeCity	Changes the selected city.
ChooseAsHomeClock	Selects a city as the home clock for time difference calculations.
ChooseAsLocalClock	Selects a city as the local clock.
FactsAboutTheCity	Returns a set of facts concerning a given city.
ModifyCityInformation	Presents a dialog box for modifying the city information databases.
SyncClock	Exercises the Internet time synchonization feature.
TimeDifference	Presents a dialog box to calculate time differences between two cities.

Events

Table 18.11   Events of the EarthTime Control

Event	Description
CityChanged	Triggers when the user changes cities.
Click	Fires when the control is clicked.
DblClick	Triggers when the control is double-clicked.
MouseMove	Occurs when the mouse is moved.

Code Example

The following listing shows the code required to create the screen displayed in Figure 18.4.

Listing 18.4   HTML for Declaration of the EarthTime Control

```
<OBJECT CLASSID="clsid:9590092D-8811-11CF-8075-444553540000"
WIDTH="430"
HEIGHT="280"
codebase="cabs/et.cab#version=1,0,0,7"
Id="et">
</OBJECT>
```

CHAPTER 19

Audio Plug-Ins

Adding sound files, background music, speeches, or just plain-old-fashioned ramblings to your Web site is a relatively painless task when using the right software. This chapter will familiarize you with a variety of ActiveX controls and plug-ins available for the delivery of audio on the Internet. ■

Crescendo ActiveX Control

The Crescendo ActiveX control is ideal for playing MIDI music online. It has a CD-like control panel and a digital counter. This plug-in requires no special server. The HTML document will have <EMBED> tag pointing to the audio file which will be loaded and the HTML file using the HTTP server. The Crescendo Plug-in is available for free download over the Internet.

Source

Vendor Information:

LiveUpDate
http://www.liveupdate.com

FIG. 19.1
Crescendo ActiveX control

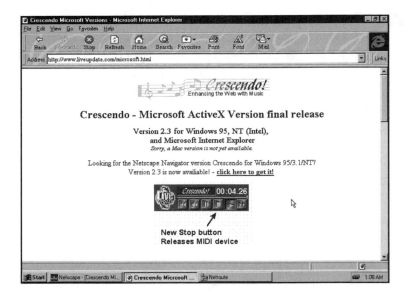

Properties of ActiveX Control

Table 19.1 Properties of Crescendo ActiveX Control

Property	Description
AutoStart	Determines if the audio file starts playing automatically
bgcolor	Sets the background color for the control using RGB values
ClassID	Sets the class ID for the <OBJECT>
CodeBase	Describes the Version of the ActiveX control to be used and activates the auto install of upgrades. The current **CODEBASE="ftp://ftp1.liveupdate.com/labtech/beta/cplus/cres.cab#Version=2,2,0,6"** specifies the version number to use. If you have an older one, the auto installer will install the more recent one on your computer
Height	Height of the control
ID	Refers to the current <OBJECT> name
Loop	Describes the loop behavior
Param Name	Determines the relative attribute "Song" and location of file VALUE="filename.mid"
txtcolor	Sets the RGB color values for the song counter
Width	Width of the control

Methods of Crescendo ActiveX Control

Table 19.2 Methods of Crescendo

Method	Description
AboutBox	Displays a dialog box that describes the Crescendo ActiveX control
Fast Forward	Advances the play position of the file
Pause	Pauses the Audio file playback at the current position
Play	Starts the audio playback
Rewind	Rewinds the audio playback
Rewind to Start	Causes the Crescendo control to restart the audio playback from the beginning of the file

Part
III

Ch
19

Event of Crescendo ActiveX Control

Table 19.3 Event of Crescendo

Method	Description
Automatic Update	Activates when the user opens a page using the Crescendo control

Example

Add the following code to your HTML files, replacing VALUE="yourmidfile.mid" with the filename of your Crescendo audio file.

Listing 19.1 Object—In The Crescendo control

```
<HTML>
<BODY>
<H1>Crescendo Control</H1>
<P>The contents of the page.</P>
<OBJECT ID=Crescendo
CLASSID="clsid:0FC6BF2B-E16A-AB23-0080AD08A326"
HEIGHT=55
WIDTH=200
CODEBASE=ftp://ftp1.liveupdate.com/labtech/beta/cplus/cres.cab#Version2,2,0,6">
<PARAM NAME="Song" VALUE="yourmidfile.mid">
</OBJECT>
</BODY>
</HTML>
```

N O T E The code in Listing 19.1 comes from the Crescendo ActiveX Authoring page accessible from the Crescendo's home page at **http://www.liveupdate.com/**. Be sure to check this page for more on ActiveX authoring for Crescendo. ■

EchoSpeech Plug-In

Echo Speech Corporation offers two distinct Internet audio products: EchoSpeech and EchoSpeech Broadcast. The EchoSpeech Plug-in allows continuous streaming at connections as low as 14.4Kbps. This is one of the most accessible audio plug-ins available on the Net, featuring low speed connection and processor requirements.

TIP EchoSpeech will work on a 486SX-33 using a 14.4Kbps modem.

Compression ratio is 18.5:1.

EchoSpeech users can download a compressed EchoSpeech File and listen to the site in just a few seconds. The EchoSpeech Plug-in, Encoder, and Server are available for free download over the Internet.

Source

Vendor Information:

Echo Speech Corporation
http://www.EchoSpeech.com/
6460 Via Real
Carpinteria, CA 93013
(805) 684-4593

FIG. 19.2
The EchoSpeech icon appears when a file can be heard by clicking the icon

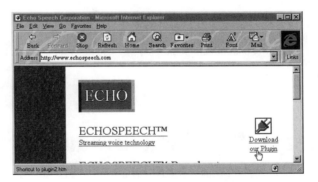

Properties of EchoSpeech Plug-In

There are no properties available for EchoSpeech since there is no user interface. The plug-in runs unseen in the background.

Methods of EchoSpeech Plug-In

There are no methods available for EchoSpeech since there is no user interface. The plug-in runs unseen in the background.

Events of EchoSpeech Plug-In

There are no events available for EchoSpeech since there is no user interface. The plug-in runs unseen in the background.

Example

N O T E The EchoSpeech plug-in will decode files that were created and compressed using the EchoSpeech coder. This plug-in uses HTTP servers. ■

Listing 19.2   Embed Code for EchoSpeech

```
<HTML>
<BODY>
<EMBED SRC="yourfile.es" img src="echo.gif">
<P>Click the echoSpeech Icon to play an EchoSpeech audio file</P>
</BODY>
</HTML>
```

EchoSpeech Real Time Broadcast

Remember when you were a kid and you wanted to run your own radio station? Well maybe not, but with the EchoSpeech Real Time Broadcast plug-in, you can listen to the attempts of those who did. As with EchoSpeech, the Real Time Broadcast version can deliver a smooth multimedia-quality audio presentation over a 14.4 modem.

The EchoSpeech Real Time Broadcast will deliver quality sounds over the Internet in full duplex if you are using a 28.8-or-faster modem. You can have a telephone-like conversation with someone else on the Internet/intranet. The EchoSpeech Broadcast plug-in is available for free download over the Internet.

Source

Vendor Information:

Echo Speech Corporation
http://www.EchoSpeech.com/
6460 Via Real
Carpinteria, CA 90313
(805) 684-4593

Properties of EchoSpeech Real Time Broadcast

There are no properties available for EchoSpeech Broadcast since there is no user interface. The plug-in runs unseen in the background.

Methods of EchoSpeech Real Time Broadcast

There are no methods available for EchoSpeech Broadcast since there is no user interface. The plug-in runs unseen in the background.

Events of EchoSpeech Real Time Broadcast

There are no events available for EchoSpeech Broadcast since there is no user interface. The plug-in runs unseen in the background.

Example

N O T E The EchoSpeech Real Time Broadcast plug-in will only decode files that were created and compressed using the EchoSpeech coder and served through the EchoSpeech Real Time Server.

Listing 19.3   Embed Code for EchoSpeech

```
<HTML>
<BODY>
<EMBED SRC="yourfile.es" >
<P>Click the echoSpeech Icon to play an EchoSpeech audio file</P>
</BODY>
</HTML>
```

Part
III

Ch
19

Koan ActiveX Control

Koan, similar to Crescendo and EchoSpeech, uses lower compression rates and requires no special server. Koan will load the audio file and play it without any prompting from you. A rather special feature of Koan is that it can use sound fonts for the audio files. The Koan ActiveX control is available for free download over the Internet.

Source

Vendor Information:

Sseyo, Inc.
http://www.sseyo.com/
Pyramid House
(011)44 1344 712017
(011)44 1344 712005 fax

FIG. 19.3
Koan ActiveX control

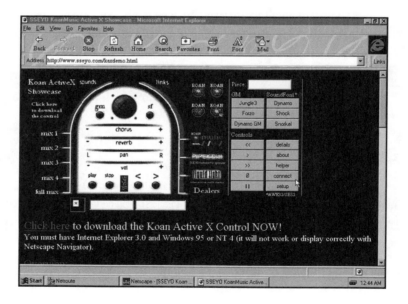

Properties of Koan ActiveX Control

Table 19.4 Properties of Koan ActiveX Control

Property	Description
autostart	Determines if the audio file starts automatically when the page is loaded
embed	Tells the browser to load the item included (audio file) using the properties that are included in the embed tag
Height	Sets the height
Width	Sets the width

Methods of Koan ActiveX Control

This control has no methods.

Events of Koan ActiveX Control

This control has no events.

Example

Listing 19.4 Embed Koan Audio Files—Instant Playback

```
<EMBED SRC="yourmidfile.skp" height=32 width=32 autostart=true>
```

Part
III

Ch
19

Listing 19.5   Koan ActiveX—Script Required

```
<HTML>
<HEAD>

<SCRIPT Language="VBScript">
Sub MyOnLoad
  parent.sitemus1.KoanAX.KoanFile = "http://www.sseyo.com/images/gmjun3t2.skp"
end sub

Sub MyOnUnload
  parent.sitemus1.KoanAX.KoanStop()
end sub

Sub OnBtnStart
 parent.sitemus1.KoanAX.KoanPlay()
End Sub

Sub OnBtnStop
 parent.sitemus1.KoanAX.KoanStop()
End Sub
</SCRIPT>

<SCRIPT for="BtnStart" event="onClick" language="VBScript">
  rem Handle the click event !
  OnBtnStart()
</SCRIPT>

<SCRIPT for="BtnStop" event="onClick" language="VBScript">
  rem Handle the click event !
  OnBtnStop()
</SCRIPT>
</HEAD>
<OBJECT
TYPE="application/x-oleobject"
CLASSID="clsid:984926A3-2D0D-11D0-BF10-444553540000"
height=32
width=32
ID=KoanAX>
</OBJECT>
</BODY></HTML>
```

Listing 19.6   Embed MIDI Files—Instant Playback

```
<HTML>
<HEAD><TITLE>MIDI EXAMPLE<TITLE></HEAD>
<BODY>
<EMBED SRC="yourmidfile.mid" height=32 width=32 autostart=true>
<P>A MIDI file will automatically be loaded, and begin playing, when you load
➥this document.</P>
</BODY>
</HTML>
```

MidPlug

MidPlug, by Yamaha, has a built-in Soft Synthesizer with many GM-compatible voices, reverb, and drum kits. The high quality compact MIDI audio files are set up for maximum efficiency and speed on the Web. Although no extra equipment is required to use this plug-in, the option is available for adding an XG sound module or a daughtercard. The MidPlug plug-in is available for free download over the Internet.

Source

Vendor Information:

Yamaha
http://www.yamaha.co.jp/english/xg/html/

FIG. 19.4
MidPlug

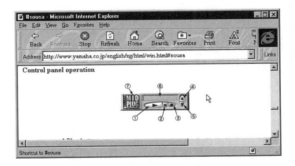

Properties of MidPlug

Table 19.5	Properties of MidPlug
Property	**Description**
autostart	Determines if the audio file is played when the page is loaded
height	Sets the height of the control
panel	Determines the color scheme to use for the Control Panel
repeat	Sets the repeat value
text	Provides alternative text in the display section of the control panel
width	Sets the width of the control

Methods of MidPlug

Table 19.6 Methods of MidPlug	
Method	**Description**
Aboutbox	Displays a dialog box that contains information about MidPlug
display	Displays the name of the current selection
information	Goes to the MidPlug home page
initialize	Automatically initializes the tone generator
MIDIMapper	Opens the MIDI mapper
pause	Pauses the playback at the current position
play	Begins playback
synthesizerSetup	Opens the SGMP Driver control panel
stop	Stops playback of audio file
tempoDown	Decreases the tempo level
tempoReset	Resets the tempo level
tempoUp	Increases the tempo level
volumeDown	Decreases the volume level
volumeUp	Increases the volume level
SGMPDriver	Displays all MIDI drivers available

Events of MidPlug

This control has no events.

Example

Listing 19.7   Embed—In The MidPlug Control

```
<HTML>
<HEAD><TITLE>MIDI EXAMPLE<TITLE></HEAD>
<BODY>
<EMBED SRC="yourfile.mid"      <!— location of MIDPLUG file —>
HEIGHT=40
```

```
WIDTH=150
PANEL=0             <!-- 0/light  1/dark -->
AUTOSTART=true      <!-- true/start false/wait for user action.-->
REPEAT=true         <!-- true/loop false/no-loop -->
TEXT=your message!>     <!-- text replaces midi file name -->
<P>A MIDIPLUG file will automatically be loaded, and begin playing, when you
load this document.</P>
</BODY>
</HTML>
```

RapidTransit Player

RapidTransit uses a proprietary technology called Adaptive Wavelets Transform (AWT) to achieve Hi-Fi music/CD-quality sound at very high compression rates. The RapidTransit Player decompresses the files and passes the decompressed audio file to your operating systems audio feature—Media Player in Windows 95— to play. The RapidTransit Plug-in is available for free download over the Internet.

Source

Vendor Information

FastMan, Inc.
http://www.monsterbit.com/rapidtransit/
1613 Capitol of Texas Hwy. S.
Austin, TX 78748
(512) 328-9088

Part
III

Ch
19

Properties of RapidTransit

There are no properties available for RapidTransit since there is no user interface. This plug-in is a download-and-play type.

Methods of RapidTransit

There are no methods available for RapidTransit since there is no user interface. This plug-in is a download-and-play type.

Events of RapidTransit

There are no events available for RapidTransit since there is no user interface. This plug-in is a download-and-play type.

Example

Listing 19.8   Embed Code for RapidTransit

```
<EMBED SRC="yourfile.1cc" >
```

RealAudio Player 3.0

RealAudio Player 3.0 is ideal for the 28.8 modem or faster—ISDN and LAN—connections. You can expect to receive near-stereo sound at 28.8 and near-CD quality using the faster connections. The RealAudio .RA .RAM files can be served through the RealAudio Server, which makes the audio a streaming Audio file downloaded in packets as they are required. RealAudio files can also be delivered through the HTTP server.

Older versions of RealAudio work fine with a 14.4 modem connection. The RealAudio Player 2.0 information site is accessible from **www.realaudio.com**; go there to find out more about version 2.

N O T E RealAudio with HTTP   If the RealAudio server is not being used, you will have to do a few things so you can listen to the audio file. Once the RealAudio file downloads to your hard drive:

- Use the browser's File to select Open File
- Locate the RealAudio file and click OK.

The RealAudio player will open and play the audio file. You can still control the RealAudio Player panel using this method. The RealAudio plug-in is available for free download over the Internet. ■

Source

Vendor Information:

Progressive Networks
http://www.realaudio.com

FIG. 19.5
RealAudio

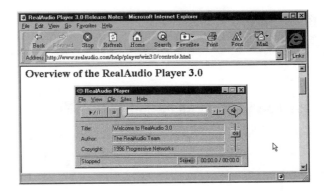

Properties of RealAudio Player 3.0

There are no properties available for RealAudio.

Methods of RealAudio Player 3.0

Table 19.7   Methods of RealAudio

Method	Description
elapsedTime	Displays the elapsed time for the current selection
forward	Fast forwards the audio file
play/pause	Starts or pauses playback
positionSlider	Jumps to any position in the audio file
rewind	Rewinds the clip
statusBar	Displays the current status of the audio file
stereoIndicator	Determines if the file being played is mono or stereo
stop	Stops the playback
volumeControl	Controls the volume level

Part
III

Ch
19

Events of Real Audio Player 3.0

There are no events available for RealAudio.

Example

Using .RAM META files with the RealAudio Server

First, create your META file which has a .RAM extension. In the META file, you place the URL for the RealAudio .RA file

```
pnm://www.yourhost.com/yourfile.ra
```

Now put a hyperlink in your HTML file that will call up the .RAM file when the user clicks it.

```
<A HREF="yourfile.ram" >
<IMG SRC="/pics/ralogo.gif" align=left></a>
```

Using the RealAudio logo makes it easier for the user to identify and activate the audio file.

Using .RAM META files Without the RealAudio Server

You must use the RealAudio Server. You can work around not having the server by linking to someone else's .RAM file and server.

```
<A HREF="http://www.realaudio.com/hello1.ram" >
<IMG SRC="/pics/ralogo.gif" align=left></a>
```

Shockwave Audio

Shockwave is a commercial development program. The player plug-in is available for free download from the Macromedia Web site for anyone wishing to take advantage of sites using Shockwave technology. Before downloading, consider connecting at a minimum of 28.8. Using Shockwave with a slower connection is known to cause systems to crash.

Source

Vendor Information:

Macromedia, Incorporated
http://www.macromedia.com
600 Townsend St.
San Francisco, CA 94103
(415) 252-2000
(415) 626-0554 fax

Macromedia Europe (UK & Benelux)
Pyramid House
East Hampstead Road
Bracknell
Berkshire
RG12 1NS England, UK
44 1 344 458 600
44 1 344 458 666 fax

FIG. 19.6
Shockwave Audio player

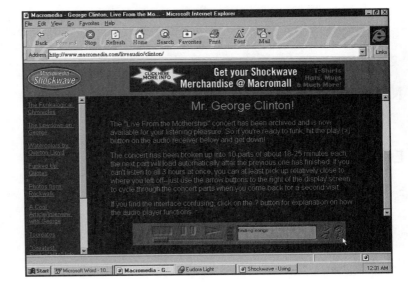

Part
III

Ch
19

Properties of Shockwave Audio

Table 19.8 Properties of Shockwave Audio Player

Property	Description
swPreLoadTime	To permit a portion of the song to be preloaded, you must specify the exact amount of playing time in seconds. This has nothing to do with the wait time for the download, but an "amount" of the SWA file to preload. The default preload time is three seconds.
swText	Specifies what text to include in the text area of the Shockwave Audio Player. The default is "Audio Streaming Over the Internet."
sw1	Debugger, the default is off. It is recommended by Macromedia that you leave the debugger on its default setting.
sw2	Options are 1 & 0. Option 1 tells Shockwave to begin playing the audio file automatically. Use option 0 if you want the playback to begin only after the user has pressed play.
sw3	(0/1) When the user clicks the Shockwave logo of the player, option 0 causes the audio to play or stop, and option 1 (the default setting) causes the audio to play or pause.
sw4	(0/1) Only necessary if you wish to have an infinite loop. Option 0 (the default setting) causes the file to play once and quit at the end of the single loop, and option 1 causes the file to loop.

Methods of Shockwave Audio

Shockwave Audio has no methods.

Events of Shockwave Audio

Shockwave Audio has no events.

Listing 19.9 Shockwave Audio Player

```
<HTML>
<HEAD>
<TITLE>the SWA Player</TITLE>
</HEAD>
<BODY BGCOLOR="#666666">
```

```
<!----Shockwave Audio Player HTML---->
<center>
<embed
width=416
height=32
SRC="http://audio.server.com/player.dcr"
sw1=off
swURL="http://audio.server.com/classic.swa"
swTEXT="Audio Streaming Over the Internet"
swPreLoadTime=3
sw2=0
sw3=1
sw4=0>
<!----sw1= debugger, sw2= Autoplay, sw3= LogoMode, sw4=Autoloop---->
</center>
</BODY>
</HTML>
```

N O T E You can find out more information about using the Shockwave Audio Player from the
Macromedia Developers site:

`http://www.macromedia.com/support/technotes/shockwave/developer/`

Talker Plug-In (for the Mac)

Talker is an Apple plug-in designed to allow users the opportunity to "have their say" on
the Net. It is a very simple text-to-voice application. To use it, simply create a text file
containing your message, save it with a .TALK extension, and, using the HTML <EMBED>
tag, point to the location of the .TALK file. The Talker plug-in is available for free download
over the Internet.

Source

Vendor Information:

MVP Solutions
http://www.mvpsolutions.com/

FIG. 19.7
The Talker icon tells users
there is a talker file available

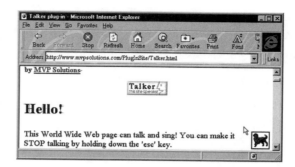

Properties of Talker Plug-In

There are no properties available for Talker since there is no user interface. The plug-in runs unseen in the background.

Methods of Talker Plug-In

There are no methods available for Talker since there is no user interface. The plug-in runs unseen in the background.

Events of Talker Plug-In

There are no events available for Talker since there is no user interface. The plug-in runs unseen in the background.

Example

- Create your text. The first step is to create a text file that includes the message you want heard on the Net.

- To make a .TALK file, you must save the text file you created with a .TALK extension. This extension will tell the Talker plug-in to read the contents of the file.

- Embed the file using the HTML <EMBED> tag, and then point to the location of the .TALK file. This embeded callout will tell the server to automatically serve up the .TALK file along with the HTML document.

- The completed HTML file and .TALK file are placed in your home page directory.

Listing 19.10   Embed—Talker

```
<HTML>
<HEAD><TITLE>MIDI EXAMPLE<TITLE></HEAD>
<BODY>
<EMBED SRC="yourfile1.talk"
HEIGHT=40
WIDTH=150>
</BODY>
</HTML>
```

ToolVox Plug-In

As a powerful little program with a compression ratio of up to 53:1, this plug-in offers one of the fastest real-time download streaming rates. It works on your existing HTTP server, so you don't need to worry about downloading and installing a special server. The ToolVox plug-in is available for free download over the Internet.

Source

Vendor Information:

VoxWare
http://www.voxware.com/
305 College Road East
Princeton, NJ 08540
(609) 514-4100 / (888)TOOLVOX
(609) 514-4101 fax

Part
III

Ch
19

FIG. 19.8
ToolVox

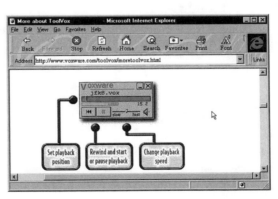

Properties of ToolVox Plug-In

Table 19.9	Properties of ToolVox
Property	**Description**
height	Sets the height of the control
width	Sets the width

Methods of ToolVox Plug-In

Table 19.10	Methods of ToolVox
Method	**Description**
pause/play	Starts or pauses playback
position	Moves to another spot forward or back in the clip
rewind	Rewinds the audio file
speed	Changes the speed of the audio file

Events of ToolVox Plug-In

This plug-in has no events.

TrueSpeech Plug-In

The TrueSpeech plug-in is automatically loaded when you install the TrueSpeech Player. The TrueSpeech plug-in is available for free download over the Internet.

Source

Vendor Information:

DSP Group, Inc.
http://www.dspg.com/
3120 Scott Blvd.
Santa Clara, CA 95054-3317
(408) 986-4300
(408) 986-4323 fax

FIG. 19.9
True Speech

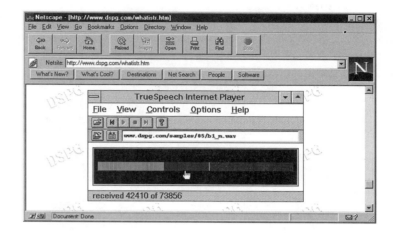

Properties of TrueSpeech Plug-In

This plug-in has no properties.

Methods of TrueSpeech Plug-In

Table 19.11	Methods of TrueSpeech
Method	**Description**
forward	Fast forwards the audio file
play/pause	Starts or pauses playback
rewind	Rewinds the clip
stop	Stops the playback

Part
III

Ch
19

Events of TrueSpeech Plug-In

This plug-in has no events.

Example

```
<HTML>
<HEAD><TITLE>MIDI EXAMPLE<TITLE></HEAD>
<BODY>
<a href="sounds/welcome.tsp"><img src=" images/TS.gif "></a>
</BODY>
</HTML>
```

FIG. 19.10
Web Tracks

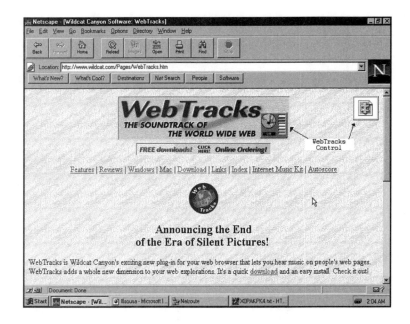

WebTracks Plug-In

WebTracks uses a proprietary music compression format. It will begin playing Web pages immediately when you reach a Web site that has WebTracks files included. In addition to the WebTracks files, it will also play MIDI files. The WebTracks plug-in is available for free download over the Internet.

Source

Vendor Information:

WildCat Canyon Software
http://www.wildcat.com/

Properties of WebTracks Plug-In

This plug-in has no properties.

Methods of WebTracks Plug-In

This plug-in has no methods.

Events of WebTracks Plug-In

This plug-in has no events. ●

CHAPTER 20

Video Controls

One of the most exciting possibilities for delivery of content over the Internet is the prospect of live video on demand. Not only are traditional broadcasters such as ABC and HBO salivating at the prospect of delivering targeted videos to consumers over the Internet, telecommunication companies and software companies are anxious to get into the content delivery market. With ActiveX controls (and other dynamic content rendering engines, such as Netscape Plug-Ins and Java applications), content providers are beginning to acquire the tools to deliver video over the Internet. In this chapter, you will review several of the leading ActiveX controls that are available for the delivery of video content.

For each control, you will follow the usual format. First, you will learn about the control and discover where you can get it. Then you will learn the properties, events, and methods available for use with the control. ■

The Surround Video Control

The Surround Video Control is a unique combination of virtual reality and full motion video. Imagine you are standing on top of the Sears Tower in Chicago and looking out over the city. Unless there are low-lying clouds or overcast skies (a sight seen all too often in the Windy City), you can spin 360 degrees and see all around the city. The Surround Video Control permits you to experience the same effect in a Web page over the Internet. The Surround Video Control allows you to add 360° panoramic images to your Web site. The images shown in a Surround Video Control are either taken by using a special rotating camera or generated by several 3-D software rendering tools.

Source

http://www.bdiamond.com—The Surround Video ActiveX Control is available for free download over the Internet from Black Diamond Consulting, Inc.

The control can easily be used in a Web page. Figure 20.1 shows what you see when you use the Surround Video Control.

FIG. 20.1
The Surround Video Control

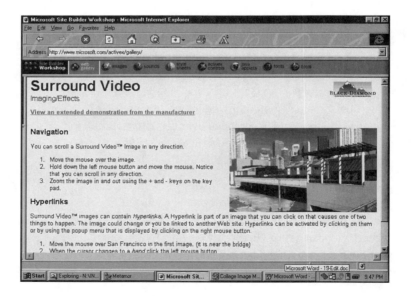

Properties

Table 20.1   Properties of the Surround Video Control

Property	Description
CodeBase	Describes the version of the ActiveX control to be used. An example entry would be **svideo.cab#version=1,0,0,180** where svideo.cab is the installation cabinet file
DataSourceName	Stores the file name of the panoramic photograph to be displayed by the control
DefaultLocation	The default location for the control
EnableHyperLinks	Determines whether the Surround Video being displayed contains hyperlinks that should be honored and acted on when clicked
Height	The height of the space to be covered by the control
ID	Refers to the current instance of the control
MouseManipulation	Determines whether the panoramic video can be navigated using the mouse
RotationFactors	Determines the amount to rotate when the mouse is moved and MouseManipulation is turned on
ZoomFactor	The distance to zoom in and out when the zoom in and out key is pressed
ZoomKeySet	Keys used for zooming in and out. By default the + and – keys are used for zooming

Method

Table 20.2   The Surround Video Control Method

Method	Description
AboutBox	Displays a dialog box that describes the Surround Video Control

Part
III

Ch
20

Events

Table 20.3   Events of the Surround Video Control

Event	Description
OnProgress	Control fires progress status events so that you can show a progress message
OnReadyStateChange	Throws an event when the control is about to change states so that you may notify the user as well

Example

Listing 20.1 shows how this control would be used in a typical Web page.

Listing 20.1   NONE—Surround Video Control

```
<OBJECT ID=SVideo
        CLASSID="clsid:7142BA01-8BDF-11CF-9E23-0000E8A37440"
        CODEBASE="svideo.cab#version=1,0,0,180"
        HEIGHT=190 WIDTH=320 HSPACE=5 VSPACE=0 ALIGN="right">
        <PARAM NAME="DataSourceName" VALUE="marin.svh">
        <PARAM NAME="MouseManipulation" VALUE="1">
        <PARAM NAME="DefaultLocation" VALUE="800000">
        <PARAM NAME="RotationFactors" VALUE="0">
        <PARAM NAME="ZoomKeySet" VALUE="0">
        <PARAM NAME="EnableHyperlinks" VALUE="1">
</OBJECT>
```

Toward World Wide Video on Demand

It's been said that computers, television, information, and entertainment are converging on a collision course. Computer networks such as the Internet, for instance, are rapidly adding a diverse set of content types for distribution, including the infancy of useful real-time video. The television industry, on the other hand, is experimenting heavily with so-called interactive television. Interactive television is intended to allow the user to play along with a game show or ask for additional information about an advertised product. In addition, cable television operators are selling movies on a pay-per-view basis. In the information age, users want to have their entertainment and information where they want it, when they want it, and how they want it. Video content will be a tremendously important part of information and entertainment products and services in the future. Video on-demand on your television and at your computer will be a part of many of these products and services. Unfortunately neither the television industry nor Internet content providers are yet ready to deliver video on-demand services over the net. Internet users, in general, connect to the Internet with too little bandwidth to do video really well. Many have attempted to solve this problem with video compression, which, while helpful, is no panacea and, unfortunately, makes significant picture quality compromises. The broadcast television industry, on the other hand, does not have the infrastructure in place to distribute true on-demand video on a wide-scale basis. While the ActiveX controls discussed in this chapter are by no means sufficient for the kind of real time video-on-demand services that will be available in the future, they provide an early glimpse of this future and can add pizzazz to your Web pages.

The VDOLive Video Control

The VDOLive Video Control is a player for full motion video. Because video files are often quite large, the folks at VDOnet Corporation have done two things to make video easier to use over the Internet. First, they've provided some compression technology. Second, the VDOLive Video Control provides server based streaming of video content. Streaming generally implies a buffering process where the video data is downloaded just in time to be played. All tech talk aside, the best part of VDO is that you can actually use video in your Internet applications without requiring that your users buy an ISDN (integrated service digital network) line.

Source

http://www.vdo.net—The VDOLive Video ActiveX Control is available for free download-ing over the Internet from VDOnet Corp. The control is a great tool for inserting video into a Web page. Figure 20.2 shows what you see when you use the VDOLive Control.

FIG. 20.2
The VDOLive Video Control

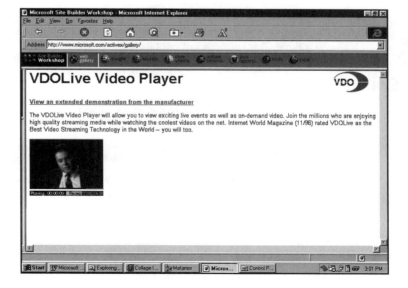

Properties

Table 20.4   Properties of the VDOLive Video Control

Property	Description
AutoStart	Determines whether the video starts up automatically or waits for the users to start it
CodeBase	Describes the version of the ActiveX control to be used. An example entry would be **=ftp://ftp.vdo.net/pub/vdoax20.exe**
Height	The height of the space to be covered by the control
ID	Refers to the current instance of the control
Loop	Tells whether the video will loop or be played just once
Src	Provides the name of the video file to play
Stretch	Sets whether the video display window can be stretched or not

Method

Table 20.5   The VDOLive Video Control Method

Method	Description
AboutBox	Displays a dialog box that describes the VDOLive Video Control

Events

The VDOLive Control does not contain any events.

Example

Listing 20.2 shows how this control would be used in a typical Web page.

Listing 20.2   NONE—VDOLive Control

```
<OBJECT
        CLASSID="clsid:58A00AC3-777B-11CF-827D-0020AFF5FF72"
        CODEBASE="ftp://ftp.vdo.net/pub/vdoax20.exe"
        WIDTH=160 HEIGHT=128 NAME="VDOOCX">
        <PARAM NAME="SRC" VALUE="http://www.vdo.net/vdofiles/asafdemo.vdo">
        <PARAM NAME="Autostart" VALUE="FALSE">
</OBJECT>
```

The VivoActive Video Control

Unlike the VDOLive Control which requires a special server, VivoActive from Vivo Software is a serverless streaming video product. Even without the server component, users can watch uninterrupted streaming audio/video content that starts to play when clicked. The VivoActive Control relies on special compression to speed the download process. This special compression tool is called VivoActive Producer. VivoActive Producer converts windows-based .AVI files and Mac-based QuickTime .MOV files into the compressed VIVO formatted (.VIV) file.

Source

http://www.vivo.com—The VivoActive ActiveX Control is available for free download over the Internet from Vivo Software, Inc.

FIG. 20.3
The VivoActive Video Control

Part
III

Ch
20

Properties

Table 20.6 Properties of the VivoActive Video Control

Property	Description
CodeBase	Describes the version of the ActiveX control to be used. An example entry would be **http://www.vivo.com/ie/vvweb.cab** where vvweb.cab is the installation cabinet file

continues

Table 20.6 Continued	
Property	**Description**
Height	The height of the space to be covered by the control
ID	Refers to the current instance of the control
URL	The URL from which the Vivo video file can be downloaded
AutoStart	Determines whether the video starts playing automatically or not

Methods

Table 20.7 Methods of the Surround Video Control	
Method	**Description**
AboutBox	Displays a dialog box that describes the Surround Video Control
Pause	Pauses the video playback
Play	Starts the video playback

Event

Table 20.8 Event of the Surround Video Control	
Event	**Description**
Click	This event is triggered when the user clicks the control with the mouse

Example

Listing 20.3 shows how this control would be used in a typical Web page.

Listing 20.3   NONE—Vivo Active Control

```
<OBJECT CLASSID="clsid:02466323-75ed-11cf-a267-0020af2546ea#Version=1,0,0,0"
        WIDTH=176 HEIGHT=144
        CODEBASE="http://www.vivo.com/ie/vvweb.cab">
        <PARAM NAME="URL" VALUE="../videos/msoft.viv">
        <PARAM NAME="AUTOSTART" VALUE="TRUE">
        <PARAM NAME="VIDEOCONTROLS" VALUE="ON">
        <EMBED SRC="../videos/msoft.viv" width=176 height=144 autostart=true>
</OBJECT>
```

The MhAVI Video Control

Like the VivoActive Control which does not require a special server, MhAVI from MicroHelp is another serverless video control. The MhAVI Control plays .AVI video content. Unlike the other video controls discussed in this chapter, the MhAVI provides a very robust degree of control over the display of the video content.

Source

http://www.microhelp.com—The MhAVI ActiveX Control is available for free download over the Internet from MicroHelp, Inc.

Notice the "Select File" command button, slider, and play button controls at the bottom of Figure 20.4. The MhAVI ActiveX Control pictured here reflects how the control looks before a video file is loaded. A file can be loaded using the Select File command button. The play of the video can be commenced by pressing the "Play" button. The slider will mark progress of play through the video or can be used to select a starting point within the video.

FIG. 20.4
The MhAVI Video Control

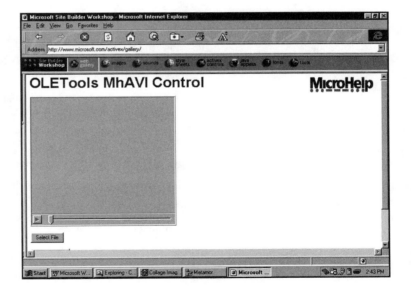

Part
III

Ch
20

Properties

Table 20.9   Properties of the MhAVI Video Control

Property	Description
Action	Stores the current action that is underway. Possible values include `None`, `Stop`, `Play`, and `PlayReverse`
Alignment	Sets the alignment of the video inside the video frame
Autosize	Tells whether the video frame will automatically be fit to the size of the video
BevelSize	Represents the video frame
BevelSizeInner	The size of the inner edge of the bevel
BevelStyle	Sets the beveling style for the video frame. Possible values include `Lowered`, `Raised`, and `Chiseled`
BevelStyleInner	Sets the inner beveling style for the video frame. Possible values include `Raised` and `Lowered`
BorderStyle	Selects the type of border for the control
Caption	Describes the control when no video is present
CodeBase	Describes the version of the ActiveX control to be used. An example entry would be **http://www.vivo.com/ie/vvweb.cab** where vvweb.cab is the installation cabinet file
ControlBox	Indicates whether the control box is displayed or not
FileName	Stores the name of the .AVI file to be displayed by the control
FillColor	Color that fills the video screen when no video is playing
Font	Displays the caption with the font indicated here
FontStyle	Modifies the font for shadowing and other treatments
Height	Space to be covered by the control
ID	Refers to the current instance of the control
LightColor	Color for highlights
MaxButton	Indicates whether there is a useful maximize button
MDI	Indicates that the control can be displayed in an MDI window
MinButton	Indicates whether there is a useful minimize button
PlayBar	Determines whether there is a play bar present
ShadowColor	Color for shadows

Property	Description
ShowTitle	Determines whether the title text will be displayed
Sizeable	True, when the control can be resized
TextColor	The color used when displaying text
TitleHeight	Height of the title to be displayed
TitleText	The text used for the title
Valignment	Describes how the video should be aligned inside the frame
Volume	Sets the volume of the audio track

Methods

Table 20.10   Methods of the Surround Video Control

Method	Description
AboutBox	Displays a dialog box that describes the Surround Video Control
Clear	Clears the current status of the control
Refresh	Causes a control Refresh

Events

Table 20.11   Events of the Surround Video Control

Event	Description
Click	Triggers when the user clicks the control with the mouse
PositionChanged	Fires when the position of the window is changed

Part
III

Ch
20

Example

Listing 20.4 shows how this control would be used in a typical Web page.

Listing 20.4   NONE—MhAvi Control

```
<OBJECT ID="mhavi1" WIDTH=317 HEIGHT=292
 CLASSID="CLSID:D1BCA8E0-F392-11CE-8F33-00AA00B46FE8"
 CODEBASE="/devtools/samples/mhavi32inf.cab">
    <PARAM NAME="_Version" VALUE="65536">
    <PARAM NAME="_ExtentX" VALUE="6703">
```

```
    <PARAM NAME="_ExtentY" VALUE="6174">
    <PARAM NAME="_StockProps" VALUE="38">
    <PARAM NAME="Caption" VALUE="MhAVI1">
    <PARAM NAME="Filename" VALUE="">
    <PARAM NAME="Action" VALUE="0">
    <PARAM NAME="BevelSize" VALUE="1">
    <PARAM NAME="BevelSizeInner" VALUE="2">
    <PARAM NAME="BevelStyle" VALUE="1">
    <PARAM NAME="BevelStyleInner" VALUE="0">
    <PARAM NAME="MDI" VALUE="0">
    <PARAM NAME="Sizeable" VALUE="0">
    <PARAM NAME="ControlBox" VALUE="0">
    <PARAM NAME="MinButton" VALUE="0">
    <PARAM NAME="MaxButton" VALUE="0">
    <PARAM NAME="Autosize" VALUE="0">
    <PARAM NAME="Speed" VALUE="1000">
    <PARAM NAME="Volume" VALUE="1000">
    <PARAM NAME="Position" VALUE="0">
    <PARAM NAME="TitleHeight" VALUE="0">
    <PARAM NAME="ShowTitle" VALUE="0">
    <PARAM NAME="TextColor" VALUE="0">
    <PARAM NAME="ShadowColor" VALUE="11619930">
    <PARAM NAME="LightColor" VALUE="16777215">
    <PARAM NAME="FontStyle" VALUE="0">
    <PARAM NAME="Alignment" VALUE="0">
    <PARAM NAME="VAlignment" VALUE="0">
    <PARAM NAME="TitleText" VALUE="">
</OBJECT>
```

The ActiveMovie Video Control

The ActiveMovie Video Control by Microsoft provides services for the playback of MPEG movie files. With ActiveMovie, you can deliver active content with synchronized audio, video, and special effects. ActiveMovie includes state-of-the-art MPEG playback for full-screen, television-quality video. Over the Internet, the ActiveX control provides streaming so that the user does not have to wait for the entire file to download. ActiveMovie is capable of playing back MPEG movies at 24 frames-per-second with 11 KHz stereo. Best of all, ActiveMovie is integrated with and included in the Microsoft Internet Explorer, enabling Internet users to play back popular media formats on the Web efficiently, including MPEG Audio and Video, .AVI files, QuickTime, AU, .WAV, and AIFF.

Source

http://www.microsoft.com—The ActiveMovie ActiveX Control is available for free download over the Internet from Microsoft.

Figure 20.5 shows how the ActiveMovie Control appears in a Web page. The play of the video can be commenced by pressing the "Play" button. The slider will mark progress of play through the video or can be used to select a starting point within the video.

FIG. 20.5
The ActiveMovie Video
Control

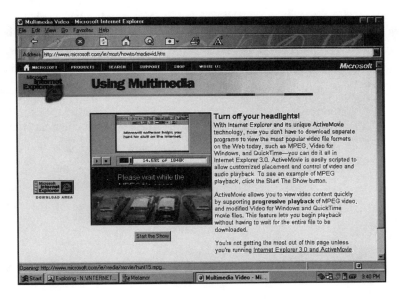

Properties

Table 20.12   Properties of the ActiveMovie Video Control

Property	Description
AllowHideControls	Determines whether the user can hide the controls or not
AllowHideDisplay	Determines whether the user can hide the display or not
Appearance	Sets the appearance of the display to be either 3-D or flat
AutoStart	Set to true, if you want the video to start automatically
AutoRewind	Set to true, if you want the video to rewind automatically when stopped
Balance	Indicates the balance for audio
BorderStyle	Stores the border type to surround the control with

Part
III

Ch
20

continues

Table 20.12 Continued

Property	Description
CodeBase	Describes the version of the ActiveX control to be used. An example entry would be **http://www.vivo.com/ie/ vvweb.cab** where vvweb.cab is the installation cabinet file
DisplayBackColor	Color to use for the background
DisplayForeColor	Color to use for the foreground
DisplayMode	Indicates whether the counter display will show the current position in time or in frame count
EnableContextMenu	Set to true, to enable the context menu
EnablePositionControls	Set to true, to enable the controls that are used to manipulate position
EnableSelectionControls	Set to true, to enable the controls that are used to make a selection
EnableTracker	Enables the Tracker Control
FileName	Stores the name of the MPEG file to be displayed by the control
FullScreenMode	Equal to true, when the control is in full screen mode
Height	Space to be covered by the control
ID	Refers to the current instance of the control
MovieWindowSize	The size to which the original movie will be scaled
PlayCount	Number of times to play the movie
SelectionEnd	Set to the time or frame count of the end of the selection
SelectionStart	Set to the time or frame count of the start of the selection
ShowControls	True, if the controls are shown
ShowDisplay	True, if the display is shown
ShowPositionControls	True, if the position controls are shown
ShowSelectionControls	True, if the selection controls are shown
ShowTracker	True, if the Tracker Control is shown
Volume	Sets the volume of the audio track

Methods

Table 20.13   Methods of the ActiveMovie Control

Method	Description
AboutBox	Displays a dialog box that describes the ActiveMovie Video Control
Pause	Pauses the playback of the video
Run	Starts the playback of the video
Stop	Stops the video playback

Events

Table 20.14   Events of the ActiveMovie Video Control

Event	Description
Click	Triggers when the user clicks the control with the mouse
DblClick	Fires when the user double-clicks the control
Error	Thrown when the control encounters an error
KeyDown	Fires when a key is pressed down
KeyPress	Occurs when a key is pressed
KeyUp	Fires when a key comes up after being pressed
MouseDown	Triggered when the mouse button is pressed down
MouseMove	Fires when the mouse is moved
MouseUp	Fires when the mouse button is released
OpenComplete	Occurs when the MPEG movie has been opened
PositionChanged	Fires when the position of the window is changed
StateChange	Triggers when the control changes state
Timer	Fires when the timer goes off

Part
III

Ch
20

Example

Listing 20.5 shows how this control would be used in a typical Web page.

Listing 20.5 NONE—ActiveMovie Control

```
<OBJECT ID="ActiveMovie" WIDTH=200 HEIGHT=120 CLASSID="CLSID:05589FA1-C356-11CE-
BF01-00AA0055595A">
        <PARAM NAME="FileName" VALUE="/ie/media/movie/hunt15.mpg">
        <PARAM NAME="AutoStart" VALUE="1">
        <PARAM NAME="ShowControls" VALUE="1">
        <PARAM NAME="ShowDisplay" VALUE="0">
    </OBJECT>
```

CHAPTER 21

Other Controls

This chapter is a conglomerate of controls that do not fit strictly into any categories. Most of the controls are communication-related such as the TCP/IP, MIME, SMTP, and so on. These controls will be useful when you want to develop systems such as electronic drop-in boxes, Web presence, interface to legacy systems, and even specialized electronic mail systems. ■

Internet Explorer

The Microsoft Internet Explorer Web browser object theoretically cannot be inserted into your Web page by using the ActiveX Control Pad; however, you can program this object as any other control in your VBScript or JavaScript. Usually, the Internet Explorer object is the parent object for all your controls.

Source

Vendor: Microsoft Corporation.

http://www.microsoft.com/activex/gallery

FIG. 21.1
The Internet Explorer control

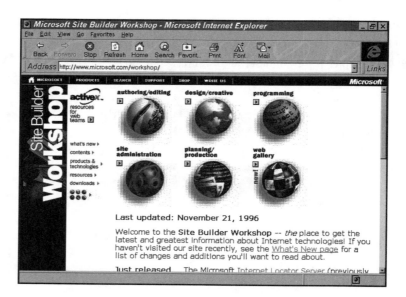

Properties

Table 21.1 Properties of the Internet Explorer Control Object

Property	Description
Application	The control container OLE automation object
Busy	The state of the object
Container	The container application of the control, if any
Document	The OLE automation/active document of the object

Property	Description
FullName	The full name of the executable that contains this control/object
FullScreen	The state indicating whether the screen is maximized or minimized
Height	The vertical height of the object
hWND	The handle of the Internet Explorer main window
Left	The distance between the left edge of the browser and the left edge of the container
LocationName	The name of the current page location
LocationURL	The URL where the current page is located
MenuBar	True, if the menu is visible
Name	The name of the application
Parent	The next upper-level object, if any
Path	The full path name of the application
StatusBar	Set these properties to True to make the status bar visible
StatusText	Set to True to make the Status bar text visible
Width	The width of the control, in points

Methods

Table 21.2   Methods of the Internet Explorer Control Object

Method	Description
ClientToWindow	Converts the coordinates that are relative to the top-left corner of the IE client area to the top-left corner of the window
GetProperty	Gets the value of a property of the object
GoBack	Navigates to the previous URL in the history list
GoForward	Navigates to the next URL in the history list
GoHome	Navigates to the home/start URL
GoSearch	Navigates to the search URL
Navigate	Navigates to a specified URL
PutProperty	Assigns or changes the property value of an object
Quit	Closes the Internet Explorer Web browser object
Refresh	Reloads the current Web page

Part
III

Ch
21

continues

Table 21.2   Continued

Method	Description
Refresh2	Reloads the current Web page (with more control through the VBScript or JavaScript)
Stop	Halts the current and pending Web operations

Events

Table 21.3   The Events of the Internet Explorer Control Object

Event	Description
OnBeginNavigate	Triggers when the Web browser starts to navigate to an URL
OnCommandStateChange	Triggers when a command changes state
OnDownloadBegin	Triggers just before the start of a Web page downloading
OnDownloadComplete	Triggers just after a Web page is downloaded
onLoad	Triggers after an HTML layout is created
OnNavigate	Triggers when the Web browser navigates to an URL
OnNewWindow	Triggers just before a new display window is created by the Web browser
OnProgress	Triggers when the progress of a download operation is updated by the Web browser
OnPropertyChange	Triggers when the PutProperty method changes the value of a property
OnQuit	Triggers when the Internet Explorer object is ready to quit
OnStatusTextChange	Triggers after the text in the status bar is changed
OnWindowActivated	Triggers at the activation of the Internet Explorer object's main window
OnWindowMove	Triggers after the Internet Explorer object's main window is moved
OnWindowSized	Triggers when the Internet Explorer object's main window is resized

Examples

```
<HTML>
<HEAD>
<TITLE>New Page</TITLE>
</HEAD>
<BODY>
    <SCRIPT LANGUAGE="VBScript">
<!--
Sub WebBrowser1_ProgressChange(Progress, ProgressMax)
' You can build a progress bar with the ProgressMax
' as the width and the Progress as the current progress
' value
end sub
Sub WebBrowser1_Quit(Cancel)
' Some code before the browser object closes
end sub
-->
    </SCRIPT>
    <OBJECT ID="WebBrowser1" WIDTH=525 HEIGHT=278
     CLASSID="CLSID:EAB22AC3-30C1-11CF-A7EB-0000C05BAE0B">
        <PARAM NAME="Height" VALUE="278">
        <PARAM NAME="Width" VALUE="525">
        <PARAM NAME="AutoSize" VALUE="0">
        <PARAM NAME="ViewMode" VALUE="1">
        <PARAM NAME="AutoSizePercentage" VALUE="0">
        <PARAM NAME="AutoArrange" VALUE="1">
        <PARAM NAME="NoClientEdge" VALUE="1">
        <PARAM NAME="AlignLeft" VALUE="0">
    </OBJECT>
</BODY>
</HTML>
```

Notes

This is the top-level object.

FTP Control

The Crescent Internet ToolPak File Transfer Protocol (CIFTP) control implements the RFC 959 FTP in an ActiveX control. With the FTP control, you can build customized FTP applications to copy files to and from FTP servers, monitor and recognize FTP sites for changes, and so on. The CIFTP has events, methods, and properties that give access to low-level FTP interactions such as opening an FTP site, providing a password, and so on. The CIFTP also supports high-level aggregate functions or tasks such as downloading a file from an FTP server or getting a directory listing from the FTP server.

Part
III

Ch
21

Source

Vendor: Crescent Software, a Division of Progress Software

http://crescent.progress.com

This is a back-end control, so there is no graphic for this control during the runtime.

Properties

Table 21.4   Properties of the FTP Control

Property	Description
AccessPort	The control channel port number
Codebase	The origin of the control, including the URL, file type, and version number
DataPort	The data channel port number
DirectoryListBoxName	The list box to populate a remote FTP server directory
EventState	The current status of the control
FileListBoxName	The list box populated by remote FTP server file names
Height	The vertical height of the object
HostAddress	The IP address of the FTP server
HostName	The DNS name of the FTP server
ID	The name of this FTP control
Left	The distance between the left edge of the control and the left edge of the HTML layout
LocalFileName	The full path and file name for the client
LoginName	The FTP logon name
MethodState	The ID of the currently running method
Password	The FTP password
RemoteFileName	The file name at the FTP server
RepresentationType	The data stream type (A-ACCII, B-Binary, E-EBCDIC)
ServerOSType	The FTP server's operating system
Top	The distance between the top edge of the control and the top edge of the HTML layout
Width	The width of the control, in points
WorkingDirectory	The FTP server's current working directory

Methods

Table 21.5   Methods of the FTP Control

Method	Description
CDUP	Moves the current directory up one; no effect if the current directory is the root
CleanupConnection	Closes the socket and cleans up the WINSOCK. For normal operations, you should use the QUIT method. This is used only as a final resort
ConnectToAccessControlChannel	Establishes a connection to an FTP server control channel
ConnectToDataChannel	Establishes a connection to the data channel of an FTP server
CWD	Changes the current working directory in the remote FTP server
GetDirectory	Gets a directory listing from the FTP server; this is a higher-level function
GetFile	Retrieves a file from the FTP server; this is a higher-level function
LIST	Gets a directory of the current working directory in the FTP server
PASS	Sends the password to the FTP server
PASV	Gets a data port from the FTP server
PutFile	Sends a local file to the FTP server; this is a higher-level function.
PWD	Gets the present working directory in the FTP server
QUIT	Ends an FTP session with an FTP server
RETR	Updates a local file from the FTP server
SendFTPCommand	Sends an arbitrary FTP command (not implemented by this control) to the server
STOR	Sends a local file to the FTP server
SYST	Gets the system name from the FTP server
TYPE	Sets binary or ACSII stream type
USER	Sends a user name to the FTP server
Zorder	The object is positioned in the container at the front or back

Part
III

Ch
21

Events

Table 21.6 Events for the FTP Control	
Event	**Description**
AccessControlChannelClosed	Triggers when the FTP connection is closed
AccessControlChannelConnection	Triggers when the FTP connection to a control channel is established
AccessControlPacketReceived	Triggers when a control packet is received across the control channel
AccessControlPacketSent	Triggers when a control packet is sent across the control channel
DataControlChannelClosed	Triggers when a data channel is closed
DataControlChannelConnection	Triggers when the FTP connection to a data channel is established
DataControlPacketReceived	Triggers when a packet is received across the data channel
DataPortSet	Triggers when the PASV method populates the DataPort property
EventStateChanged	Triggers when the EventState property of any of the events change
FileClosed	Triggers when the local file stream is closed
GotDirectory	Triggers when the GetDirectory method successfully completes
GotFile	Triggers when the GetFile method successfully completes
InternetError	Triggers when an error occurs in the high level methods
ListBoxesPopulated	Triggers when a DirectoryListBox or FileListBox object is populated
MethodStateChanged	Triggers when any of the method state changes
PutFile	Triggers when the PutFile method successfully completes
SocketClosed	Triggers after a socket is closed

Event	Description
TotalFileBytesReceived	Triggers after every data packet is received with the updated bytes received value
WSAError	Triggers when the FTP control encounters a WINSOCK error

Example

```
<OBJECT ID="CIFTP1" WIDTH=100 HEIGHT=50
 CLASSID="CLSID:3E222583-0E36-11CF-8576-0080C7973784">
    <PARAM NAME="_Version" VALUE="65536">
    <PARAM NAME="_ExtentX" VALUE="2117">
    <PARAM NAME="_ExtentY" VALUE="1058">
    <PARAM NAME="_StockProps" VALUE="0">
    <PARAM NAME="AccessChannelConnectionWAV" VALUE="">
    <PARAM NAME="AccessChannelClosedWAV" VALUE="">
    <PARAM NAME="DataChannelConnectionWAV" VALUE="">
    <PARAM NAME="DataChannelClosedWAV" VALUE="">
    <PARAM NAME="FileClosedWAV" VALUE="">
    <PARAM NAME="ListBoxesPopulatedWAV" VALUE="">
    <PARAM NAME="SocketClosedWAV" VALUE="">
    <PARAM NAME="WSAErrorWAV" VALUE="">
    <PARAM NAME="HostName" VALUE="ftp://ftp.mcp.com">
    <PARAM NAME="HostAddress" VALUE="">
    <PARAM NAME="RemoteFileName" VALUE="">
    <PARAM NAME="LoginName" VALUE="">
    <PARAM NAME="Password" VALUE="">
    <PARAM NAME="RepresentationType" VALUE="">
    <PARAM NAME="WorkingDirectory" VALUE="">
</OBJECT>
```

HTTP Control

The Crescent Internet HTTP (CIHTTP) control provides a very versatile Web browser object. Its functionality includes the capability to retrieve and send data to any Web site as well as get header and other information about the Web sites. The CIHTTP also has capabilities to parse the retrieved data and to pipe the data to other controls.

The CIHTTP control is well-suited for Web crawler applications, Web data retrieval and data-entry back-end applications, and so on.

Source

Vendor: Crescent Software, a Division of Progress Software

http://crescent.progress.com

Part

III

Ch

21

Properties

Table 21.7   Properties of the HTTP Control

Property	Description
Codebase	The origin of the control, including the URL, file type, and version number
EventState	The ID of the control event in progress
Height	The vertical height of the object
HostAddress	The IP address of the HTTP server
HostName	The DNS name of the HTTP server
HTMLPageTextWithoutTags	The parsed Web page without HTML formatting tags
HTMLPageTextWithTags	The parsed Web page with HTML formatting tags
HTTPPort	The port used for the HTTP access
ID	The name of this HTTP control
Left	The distance between the left edge of the control and the left edge of the HTML layout
LocalFileName	The full path and file name for the client
MethodState	The ID of the currently running method
ParseIncomingData	Set to True, to parse the Web data based on HTML codes
ProxyServerAddress	IP address of the Web proxy server, which is usually a firewall
ProxyServerName	The DNS name of the Web proxy server, which is usually a firewall
Top	The distance between the top edge of the control and the top edge of the HTML layout
URL	The URL for the current request
Width	The width of the control, in points
WWWSiteName	The name of the current Web page

Methods

Table 21.8   Methods of the HTTP Control

Method	Description
CleanupConnection	Closes the socket and cleans up the WINSOCK; for normal operations, you should use the QUIT method; this is used only as a final resort
ConnectToHTTPServer	Establishes a connection to an HTTP server
GET	Retrieves a Web page
HEAD	Retrieves the header information from a Web site
POST	Sends data to an HTTP server
SendHTTPCommand	Sends an arbitrary HTTP command (not implemented by this control) to the server
Zorder	The object is positioned in the container at the front or back

Events

Table 21.9   Events of the HTTP Control

Event	Description
EventStateChanged	Triggers when the EventState property of any of the events change
FileClosed	Triggers when the local file stream is closed
HTTPServerConnectionClosed	Triggers when a connection to the HTTP server is closed
HTTPServerConnection	Triggers when a connection to the HTTP server is established
ListBoxesPopulated	Triggers when an AnchorListBox, ImageListBox, or TagListBox object is populated
MethodStateChanged	Triggers when any of the method state changes
PacketReceived	Triggers when a data packet is received from the HTTP server
PacketSent	Triggers when a data packet is sent to the HTTP server
SocketClosed	Triggers after a socket is closed

continues

Part
III

Ch
21

Table 21.9   Continued

Event	Description
TotalFileBytesReceived	Triggers after every data packet is received with the updated bytes received value
WSAError	Triggers when the HTTP control encounters a WINSOCK error

Example

```
<OBJECT ID="CIHTTP1" WIDTH=100 HEIGHT=50
CLASSID="CLSID:DE90AEA3-1461-11CF-858F-0080C7973784">
    <PARAM NAME="_Version" VALUE="65536">
    <PARAM NAME="_ExtentX" VALUE="2117">
    <PARAM NAME="_ExtentY" VALUE="1058">
    <PARAM NAME="_StockProps" VALUE="0">
    <PARAM NAME="FileClosedWAV" VALUE="">
    <PARAM NAME="HTTPServerConnectionWAV" VALUE="">
    <PARAM NAME="HTTPServerConnectionClosedWAV" VALUE="">
    <PARAM NAME="ListBoxesPopulatedWAV" VALUE="">
    <PARAM NAME="PacketReceivedWAV" VALUE="">
    <PARAM NAME="PacketSentWAV" VALUE="">
    <PARAM NAME="SocketClosedWAV" VALUE="">
    <PARAM NAME="WSAErrorWAV" VALUE="">
    <PARAM NAME="URL" VALUE="">
    <PARAM NAME="HostName" VALUE="">
    <PARAM NAME="HostAddress" VALUE="">
    <PARAM NAME="ProxyServerName" VALUE="">
    <PARAM NAME="ProxyServerAddress" VALUE="">
</OBJECT>
```

MIME Control

The Crescent Internet ToolPak MIME control implements the MIME capabilities as per RFCs 1521 and 1522. The control can be used to encode and decode files according to the MIME standard.

Source

Vendor: Crescent Software, a Division of Progress Software

http://crescent.progress.com

Properties

Table 21.10   Properties of the MIME Control

Property	Description
Codebase	The origin of the control, including the URL, file type, and version number
ContentType	The type of the data
DestinationFileName	The full path and file name for the result file
DestinationFileSize	The size of the result file
FileStatus	Set to True to trigger encoded and decoded events
SourceFileName	The source file name for encode or decode operations
SourceFileSize	The size of the source file

Methods

Table 21.11   Methods of the MIME Control

Method	Description
MIMEDecode	Code a file using the MIME standards
MEMEDecode	Decode a MIME-coded file

Events

Table 21.12   Events of the MIME Control

Event	Description
Decoded	Triggers after a MIME file is converted
DecodingFinished	Triggers at the end of the decoding process
DecodingStarted	Triggers at the beginning of the decoding process
Encoded	Triggers after a file is converted as per MIME standards
EncodingFinished	Triggers at the end of the encoding process
EncodingStarted	Triggers at the beginning of the encoding process

Part
III

Ch
21

Example

```
<OBJECT ID="CIMIME1" WIDTH=100 HEIGHT=50
 CLASSID="CLSID:22E7B463-8C01-11CF-A07E-444553540000">
    <PARAM NAME="_Version" VALUE="65536">
    <PARAM NAME="_ExtentX" VALUE="2117">
    <PARAM NAME="_ExtentY" VALUE="1058">
    <PARAM NAME="_StockProps" VALUE="0">
    <PARAM NAME="SourceFilename" VALUE="">
    <PARAM NAME="DestinationFilename" VALUE="">
</OBJECT>
```

NNTP Control

The Crescent Internet ToolPak Network News Transfer Protocol (CINEWS) control implements RFC 977 in an ActiveX control. With the CINEWS control, you can build customized news retrieval, posting, and other news feed applications.

Source

Vendor: Crescent Software, a Division of Progress Software

http://crescent.progress.com

Properties

Table 21.13   Properties of the NNTP Control

Property	Description
ArticleBody	The contents of one news item
ArticleHeader	The header of one news item
ArticleNumber	The sequence number of the article to be retrieved
Codebase	The origin of the control, including the URL, file type, and version number
Date	The news date
Distributions	List of news subjects for which news can be retrieved
EventState	The current status of the control
FirstArticle	The number of the topmost article in the requested group
Height	The vertical height of the object

Property	Description
HostAddress	The IP address of the news server
HostName	The DNS name of the news server
ID	The name of this control
LastArticle	The number of the bottommost article in the requested group
Left	The distance between the left edge of the control and the left edge of the HTML layout
ListGroupNamesOnly	This property has to be set to True to list only the newsgroup names
LocalFileName	The full path and file name for the client news file
MessageID	The message ID of the news article
MethodState	The ID of the currently running method
NewsGroup	The newsgroup name
NNTPPort	The news port name
ParseIncomingData	This property has to be set to True to parse the incoming data
Time	The news time
Top	The distance between the top edge of the control and the top edge of the HTML layout
TotalArticles	The number of articles in the current newsgroup
TotalGroups	The number of groups available in the news server
Width	The width of the control, in points

Methods

Table 21.14 Methods of the NNTP Control

Method	Description
Article	Fetches the article header and body
Body	Fetches the body of an article
CleanupConnection	Closes the socket and cleans up the WINSOCK; for normal operations, you should use the QUIT method; this is used only as a final resort
ConnectToNNTPServer	Establishes a connection to a news server

Part

III

Ch

21

continues

Table 21.14   Continued

Method	Description
Group	Fetches the group counters—FirstArticle, LastArticle, and TotalArticles
Head	Fetches the head of a news article
Last	Sets the news pointer to the previous article
List	Fetches a list of groups
NewsGroups	Fetches the list of groups created since the specified date and time
NewNews	Fetches the news list created since the specified date and time
Next	Sets the news pointer to the next news article
POST	Sends a news article to a group
QUIT	Ends connection with a news server
RETR	Updates a local file from the NNTP server
Slave	Sends a notification that the client is a slave server, not an individual user
STAT	Sets the news pointer to a specified news article
Zorder	The object is positioned in the container at the front or back

Events

Table 21.15   Events of the NNTP Control

Event	Description
ArticleReceived	Triggers when a news article is received
EventStateChanged	Triggers when the EventState property of any of the events changes
FileClosed	Triggers when the local file stream is closed
GroupInformationReceived	Triggers when the FirstArticle, LastArticle, and TotalArticles properties are refreshed
MethodStateChanged	Triggers when any of the method state changes
NNTPConnection	Triggers after a news server connection is established
NNTPConnectionClosed	Triggers after a news server connection is closed

Event	Description
PacketReceived	Triggers when a data packet is received from the news server
PacketSent	Triggers when a data packet is sent to the news server
SocketClosed	Triggers after a socket is closed
WSAError	Triggers when the NNTP control encounters a WINSOCK error

Example

```
<OBJECT ID="CINEWS1" WIDTH=100 HEIGHT=50
 CLASSID="CLSID:168663E3-186D-11CF-859F-0080C7973784">
    <PARAM NAME="_Version" VALUE="65536">
    <PARAM NAME="_ExtentX" VALUE="2117">
    <PARAM NAME="_ExtentY" VALUE="1058">
    <PARAM NAME="_StockProps" VALUE="0">
    <PARAM NAME="FileClosedWAV" VALUE="">
    <PARAM NAME="NNTPServerConnectionWAV" VALUE="">
    <PARAM NAME="NNTPServerConnectionClosedWAV" VALUE="">
    <PARAM NAME="ListBoxesPopulatedWAV" VALUE="">
    <PARAM NAME="PacketReceivedWAV" VALUE="">
    <PARAM NAME="PacketSentWAV" VALUE="">
    <PARAM NAME="SocketClosedWAV" VALUE="">
    <PARAM NAME="WSAErrorWAV" VALUE="">
    <PARAM NAME="Distributions" VALUE="">
    <PARAM NAME="ArticleNumber" VALUE="">
    <PARAM NAME="MessageID" VALUE="">
    <PARAM NAME="ArticleHeader" VALUE="">
    <PARAM NAME="ArticleBody" VALUE="">
    <PARAM NAME="HostName" VALUE="">
    <PARAM NAME="HostAddress" VALUE="">
    <PARAM NAME="NewsGroup" VALUE="">
    <PARAM NAME="Date" VALUE="">
    <PARAM NAME="Time" VALUE="">
</OBJECT>
```

POP Control

The Crescent Internet ToolPak Post Office Protocol (CIPOP) control implements RFC 959's POP3 in an ActiveX control. With the POP control, you can build customized mail applications.

Part

III

Ch

21

Source

Vendor: Crescent Software, a Division of Progress Software

http://crescent.progress.com

Properties

Table 21.16	Properties of the POP Control
Property	**Description**
Codebase	The origin of the control, including the URL, file type, and version number
HostAddress	The IP address of the POP server
HostName	The DNS name of the POP server
ID	The name of this POP control
Left	The distance between the left edge of the control and the left edge of the HTML layout
LocalFileName	The full path and file name for the client
MailPort	The port address for the mail service
Message	The mail message
MessageBody	The body part of the mail message
MessageDate	The date of the mail message
MessageHeader	The header part of the mail message
MessageNumber	The sequence number of the mail message
MessageSubject	The subject part of the mail message
Password	The mailbox password
RecvTimeout	The time in milliseconds to wait before triggering a timeout during receive operations
Sender	The sender of the mail message
SendTimeout	The time in milliseconds to wait before triggering a timeout during send operations
TotalMessages	The number of messages in the connected mailbox
UserName	The mailbox user name

Property	Description
Top	The distance between the top edge of the control and the top edge of the HTML layout
Width	The width of the control, in points

Methods

Table 21.17   Methods of the POP Control

Method	Description
CleanupConnection	Closes the socket and cleans up the WINSOCK; for normal operations, you should use the QUIT method; this is used only as a final resort
ConnectToPOPServer	Establishes a connection to a POP server
DELE	Deletes a mail message
LIST	Fetches the message size
NOOP	Gets the connection status to a mail server
PASS	Sends the mail password to the mail server and verifies that it is correct
QUIT	Ends a POP session with a mail server
RETR	Fetches a mail message
RSET	Resets the state of the mailbox
STAT	Fetches the TotalMessages property
USER	Sends the user name to the mail server
Zorder	The object is positioned in the container at the front or back

Events

Table 21.18   Events of the POP Control

Event	Description
MessageReceived	Triggers after a message is received and parsed by the control
PacketReceived	Triggers when a data packet is received from the mail server
PacketSent	Triggers when a data packet is sent to the mail server

continues

Table 21.18   Continued

Event	Description
SocketClosed	Triggers after a socket is closed
STATReceived	Triggers when the TotalMessages property is refreshed
WSAError	Triggers when the POP control encounters a WINSOCK error

Example

```
<OBJECT ID="CIPOP1" WIDTH=100 HEIGHT=50
 CLASSID="CLSID:25F737F7-0D72-11CF-856B-0080C7973784">
    <PARAM NAME="_Version" VALUE="65536">
    <PARAM NAME="_ExtentX" VALUE="2117">
    <PARAM NAME="_ExtentY" VALUE="1058">
    <PARAM NAME="_StockProps" VALUE="0">
    <PARAM NAME="POPServerConnectionWAV" VALUE="">
    <PARAM NAME="POPServerConnectionClosedWAV" VALUE="">
    <PARAM NAME="MessageReceivedWAV" VALUE="">
    <PARAM NAME="STATReceivedWAV" VALUE="">
    <PARAM NAME="PacketReceivedWAV" VALUE="">
    <PARAM NAME="PacketSentWAV" VALUE="">
    <PARAM NAME="SocketClosedWAV" VALUE="">
    <PARAM NAME="WSAErrorWAV" VALUE="">
    <PARAM NAME="LocalFileName" VALUE="">
    <PARAM NAME="HostAddress" VALUE="">
    <PARAM NAME="HostName" VALUE="">
    <PARAM NAME="MessageNumber" VALUE="">
    <PARAM NAME="Password" VALUE="">
    <PARAM NAME="UserName" VALUE="">
</OBJECT>
```

SMTP Control

The Crescent Internet ToolPak Simple Mail Transfer Protocol (CISMTP) control implements RFC 821's SMTP in an ActiveX control. With the SMTP control, you can build customized mail applications.

Source

Vendor: Crescent Software, a Division of Progress Software

http://crescent.progress.com

Properties

Table 21.19   Properties of the SMTP Control

Property	Description
BC	The address to which a blind copy of the message will be sent
CC	The address to which a carbon copy of the message will be sent
Codebase	The origin of the control, including the URL, file type, and version number
DomainName	The domain name of the SMTP server
HostAddress	The IP address of the SMTP server
HostName	The DNS name of the SMTP server
ID	The name of this SMTP control
Left	The distance between the left edge of the control and the left edge of the HTML layout
MailList	The mail list whose members are being viewed
MailPort	The port address for the mail service
MessageBody	The body part of the mail message
MessageSubject	The subject part of the mail message
Recipient	The address of the mail recipient
RecvTimeout	The time in milliseconds to wait before triggering a timeout during receive operations
Sender	The sender of the mail message
SendTimeout	The time in milliseconds to wait before triggering a timeout during send operations
Top	The distance between the top edge of the control and the top edge of the HTML layout
Width	The width of the control, in points

Methods

Table 21.20   Methods of the SMTP Control

Method	Description
CleanupConnection	Closes the socket and cleans up the WINSOCK; for normal operations, you should use the QUIT method; this is used only as a final resort
ConnectToSMTPServer	Establishes a connection to an SMTP server
DATA	Sends the message to the SMTP server
EXPN	Fetches the list of mail list subscribers
ExpandMailList	High-level function (ConnectToSMTPServer, HELO, EXPN, and QUIT) to get a mail list
HELO	Identifies the sender's SMTP server to the recipient's SMTP server
MAIL	Sends the server value to the SMTP server
NOOP	Gets the connection status to a mail server
QUIT	Ends an SMTP session with an SMTP server
RCPT	Sends the recipient value to the SMTP server
RETR	Fetches a mail message
RSET	Resets the state of the current mail transaction
SendMail	High-level call (ConnectToSMTPServer, HELO, RCPT, MAIL, DATA, and QUIT) to send a mail message to the SMTP server
VRFY	Verifies whether a name exists in the system
Zorder	The object is positioned in the container at the front or back

Events

Table 21.21   Events of the SMTP Control

Event	Description
PacketReceived	Triggers when a data packet is received from the mail server
PacketSent	Triggers when a data packet is sent to the mail server
SocketClosed	Triggers after a socket is closed
WSAError	Triggers when the control encounters a WINSOCK error

Example

```
<OBJECT ID="CISMTP1" WIDTH=100 HEIGHT=50
 CLASSID="CLSID:25F737F3-0D72-11CF-856B-0080C7973784">
    <PARAM NAME="_Version" VALUE="65536">
    <PARAM NAME="_ExtentX" VALUE="2117">
    <PARAM NAME="_ExtentY" VALUE="1058">
    <PARAM NAME="_StockProps" VALUE="0">
    <PARAM NAME="SMTPServerConnectionWAV" VALUE="">
    <PARAM NAME="SMTPServerConnectionClosedWAV" VALUE="">
    <PARAM NAME="ListBoxPopulatedWAV" VALUE="">
    <PARAM NAME="PacketReceivedWAV" VALUE="">
    <PARAM NAME="PacketSentWAV" VALUE="">
    <PARAM NAME="SocketClosedWAV" VALUE="">
    <PARAM NAME="WSAErrorWAV" VALUE="">
    <PARAM NAME="HostName" VALUE="">
    <PARAM NAME="HostAddress" VALUE="">
    <PARAM NAME="DomainName" VALUE="">
    <PARAM NAME="Sender" VALUE="">
    <PARAM NAME="Recipient" VALUE="">
    <PARAM NAME="MailList" VALUE="">
    <PARAM NAME="MessageBody" VALUE="">
    <PARAM NAME="MessageSubject" VALUE="">
    <PARAM NAME="CC" VALUE="">
    <PARAM NAME="BC" VALUE="">
</OBJECT>
```

TCP Control

The Crescent Internet ToolPak TCP/IP Protocol (CITCP) control implements the TCP/IP protocol in an ActiveX control. With the TCP control, you can build customized messaging and database applications on a TCP/IP backbone structure.

Source

Vendor: Crescent Software, a Division of Progress Software

http://crescent.progress.com

Properties

Table 21.22	Properties of the TCP Control
Property	Description
Codebase	The origin of the control, including the URL, file type, and version number

continues

Table 21.22   Continued

Property	Description
HostAddress	The IP address of the TCP/IP host server
HostName	The DNS name of the TCP/IP host server
ID	The name of this TCP control
Left	The distance between the left edge of the control and the left edge of the HTML layout
Port	The port address for the TCP/IP service
ServiceName	Service name provided by the port
Socket	The socket used by this control
Top	The distance between the top edge of the control and the top edge of the HTML layout
Width	The width of the control, in points

Methods

Table 21.23   Methods of the TCP Control

Method	Description
bGetHostByAddress	Fetches the host name when given a host address
bGetHostByName	Fetches the host address when given a host name
bGetHostName	Fetches the name of the local machine
bGetServiceByName	Fetches the port number of a service
bGetServiceByPort	Fetches the service name associated with a port
CloseSocket	Closes the current socket
ConnectToHost	Establishes a TCP/IP connection
ListenForConnection	Waits on a port for connection requests from clients
ListenForDatagram	Waits on a port for a datagram TCP/IP packet
Send	Sends a TCP/IP packet to a host
SendDatagram	Sends a datagram packet to a host
Zorder	The object is positioned in the container at the front or back

Events

Table 21.24   Events of the TCP Control

Event	Description
BlockingFunctionCompleted	Triggers when a blocking operation is completed
Connection	Triggers when a TCP/IP connection is established
ConnectionClosed	Triggers when a TCP/IP connection is closed
PacketReceived	Triggers when a TCP/IP packet is received
PacketSent	Triggers when a TCP/IP packet is sent
PropertyChanged	Triggers when a property is refreshed
WSAError	Triggers when the TCP control encounters a WINSOCK error

Example

```
<OBJECT ID="CITCP1" WIDTH=100 HEIGHT=50
 CLASSID="CLSID:168663EB-186D-11CF-859F-0080C7973784">
    <PARAM NAME="_Version" VALUE="65536">
    <PARAM NAME="_ExtentX" VALUE="2117">
    <PARAM NAME="_ExtentY" VALUE="1058">
    <PARAM NAME="_StockProps" VALUE="0">
    <PARAM NAME="HostName" VALUE="">
    <PARAM NAME="HostAddress" VALUE="">
    <PARAM NAME="ServiceName" VALUE="">
</OBJECT>
```

UUEncode/Decode Control

The Crescent Internet ToolPak UUEncode/Decode Control (CIUU) implements the encoding and decoding capabilities as per RFCs 1521 and 1522. The control can be used to encode and decode files as per the MIME standard.

Source

Vendor: Crescent Software, a Division of Progress Software

http://crescent.progress.com

Part
III

Ch
21

Properties

Table 21.25	Properties of the UUEncode/Decode Control
Property	**Description**
Codebase	The origin of the control, including the URL, file type, and version number
DestinationFileName	The full path and file name for the result file
DestinationFileSize	The size of the result file
FireStatus	This property needs to be set to True to trigger encoded and decoded events
SourceFileName	The source file name for an encode or decode operation
SourceFileSize	The size of the source file

Methods

Table 21.26	Methods of the UUEncode/Decode Control
Method	**Description**
UUDecode	Codes a file using the MIME standards
UUEncode	Decodes a MIME-coded file

Events

Table 21.27	Events of the UUEncode/Decode Control
Event	**Description**
Decoded	Triggers after a MIME file is converted
DecodingFinished	Triggers at the end of the decoding process
DecodingStarted	Triggers at the beginning of the decoding process
Encoded	Triggers after a file is converted as per MIME standards
EncodingFinished	Triggers at the end of the encoding process
EncodingStarted	Triggers at the beginning of the encoding process

Example

```
<OBJECT ID="CIUU1" WIDTH=100 HEIGHT=50
 CLSID="CLSID:C27DB763-51D0-11CF-83A1-444553540000">
    <PARAM NAME="_Version" VALUE="65536">
    <PARAM NAME="_ExtentX" VALUE="2117">
    <PARAM NAME="_ExtentY" VALUE="1058">
    <PARAM NAME="_StockProps" VALUE="0">
    <PARAM NAME="SourceFilename" VALUE="">
    <PARAM NAME="DestinationFilename" VALUE="">
</OBJECT>
```

Certificate Enrollment Control

The Microsoft Certificate Enrollment control (Certenroll) is an ActiveX control (implemented as a DLL) that can be used to create certificate-related functions. The control has methods to generate the public/private key pair, build a certificate request in the PKCS #10 format, and accept and install certificates (of the PKCS #7 format). The control has a built-in enrollment wizard to perform all these functions.

Source

Vendor: Microsoft Corporation

http://www.microsoft.com/intdev/security/csa/enroll-f.htm

Properties

There are no properties for the Certificate Enrollment control.

Methods

Table 21.28   Methods for the Certificate Enrollment Control

Method	Description
AcceptCredentials	Accepts the certificate and puts it in an appropriate place on the local machine for future reference
GenerateKeyPair	Generates a public/private key pair and a PKCS #10 request
GetCredentialsLocation	This is the file where the current credentials are associated
SetSessionInfoIfNeeded	Sets the location of the PVK file

Part
III

Ch
21

Events

There are no events for the Certificate Enrollment Control.

Example

```
<OBJECT
    classid="clsid:33BEC9E0-F78F-11cf-B782-00C04FD7BF43"
    codebase=certenr3.dll
    id=certHelper>
</OBJECT>
```

TAPI Dial Control

The Dameware Telephony API Dial control is an ActiveX control that can be used to add telephone dialing capabilities to any Web application.

Source

Vendor: Dameware Development

http://www.mi-inc.com/~dameware

Properties

Table 21.29   Properties of the TAPI Dial Control

Property	Description
Codebase	The origin of the control, including the URL, file type, and version number
Height	The height of this control, in points
ID	The name of this TAPI Dial control
Left	The distance between the left edge of the control and the left edge of the HTML layout
Top	The distance between the top edge of the control and the top edge of the HTML layout
Width	The width of the control, in points

Methods

Table 21.30   Methods of the TAPI Dial Control

Method	Description
`Dial`	Dials a number
`DialUsing`	Displays the Dial dialog box and dials as per the user entries
`DialProperties`	Displays the native TAPI properties dialog box
`DialPropertiesNumber`	Displays the TAPI properties dialog box for a specific number

Events

Table 21.31   Events of the TAPI Dial Control

Event	Description
`Click`	Triggers when a control is clicked with the mouse; also triggers when the user selects a value in a multi-value control such as the list box
`DblClick`	Triggers when a control is double-clicked
`KeyDown`	Triggers when a user presses a control, navigation, or function key
`KeyUp`	Triggers when a user releases a control, navigation, or function key
`KeyPress`	Triggers when a key is either pressed by the user or sent from the `SendKeys` function

Example

```
<OBJECT ID="TapiDial1" WIDTH=32 HEIGHT=32
 CLASSID="CLSID:1CF8F5D9-DF22-11CF-B0B6-0000F63A6615">
    <PARAM NAME="_Version" VALUE="65536">
    <PARAM NAME="_ExtentX" VALUE="677">
    <PARAM NAME="_ExtentY" VALUE="677">
    <PARAM NAME="_StockProps" VALUE="0">
</OBJECT>
```

RAS Dial Control

The Dameware RAS Dial control is an ActiveX control that can be used to add remote network dialing and access capabilities to any Web application.

Part
III

Ch
21

Source

Vendor: Dameware Development

http://www.mi-inc.com/~dameware

FIG. 21.2
The RAS Dial control

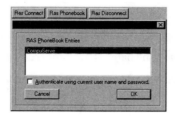

Properties

Table 21.32   Properties of the RAS Dial Control

Property	Description
Codebase	The origin of the control, including the URL, file type, and version number
Height	The height of this control, in points
ID	The name of this RAS Dial control
Left	The distance between the left edge of the control and the left edge of the HTML layout
RASEntry	The name of the current RAS connection
RASUseCurrentUser	Logon with the current user profile
Top	The distance between the top edge of the control and the top edge of the HTML layout
Width	The width of the control, in points

Methods

Table 21.33   Methods of the RAS Dial Control

Method	Description
RASConnect	Dials the current RASEntry
RASDiagConfig	Displays the phone book form

Method	Description
RASShutDown	Disconnects the current RAS connection
GetIPAddress	Fetches the IP address of the current session

Events

Table 21.34 Events of the RAS Dial Control

Event	Description
Click	Triggers when a control is clicked with the mouse; also triggers when the user selects a value in a multi-value control such as the list box
DblClick	Triggers when a control is double-clicked
KeyDown	Triggers when a user presses a control, navigation, or function key
KeyUp	Triggers when a user releases a control, navigation, or function key
KeyPress	Triggers when a key is either pressed by the user or sent from the SendKeys function

Example

```
<OBJECT ID="RasDial1" WIDTH=32 HEIGHT=32
 CLASSID="CLSID:ED29373B-DF14-11CF-B0B6-0000F63A6615">
    <PARAM NAME="_Version" VALUE="65536">
    <PARAM NAME="_ExtentX" VALUE="677">
    <PARAM NAME="_ExtentY" VALUE="677">
    <PARAM NAME="_StockProps" VALUE="0">
</OBJECT>
```

Part
III

Ch
21

CHAPTER 22

The Future of ActiveX

A wise economist once said, "It is very difficult to predict, especially the future." With those words in mind, instead of predicting "in the next one year, ActiveX will…," this chapter will elaborate on some of the forces and emerging technologies that will shape the future of ActiveX Technology. ■

The ActiveX working group

Microsoft has entrusted the ActiveX technologies to a public group. This chapter describes the technologies, the group organization, and the charter.

Design-Time controls

These are another type of ActiveX control, more applicable as wizards and design-aids, that generate HTML or text-based script code.

Multimedia ActiveX, new HTML tags, and IE 4.0

These are some of the initiatives and products that you will see and use within the next six to twelve months' time frame.

Integrated visual Web development tools

A new breed of development tools is coming to the market to aid Web developers in designing, developing, and managing Web sites.

Web-based enterprise management

Recent developments lean toward an integrated management and administration of hardware and software, systems from the Web through the Internet and intranets.

The ActiveX Working Group

Microsoft has entrusted the ActiveX specification and technologies to an independent standards body called the ActiveX working group. This group is comprised of about 80-90 of the major companies in the computer industry. You can find all the details at the URL **www.activex.org**. Microsoft contributed the specification as well as source-code reference implementation. The technologies include the Component Object Model (COM), the Distributed Component Object Model (DCOM), and the ActiveX trademarks.

This working group can make the COM and ActiveX technology function across platforms and thus lead to possible wide acceptance. At a minimum, in the future you should find COM, DCOM, and ActiveX implementations in the Macintosh platform as well as in popular UNIX platforms. In the future, these technologies also should become less vendor-dependent, with companies other than Microsoft writing some of the implementations.

N O T E   Regarding cross-platform implementations, Microsoft already has the ActiveX SDK functioning on Macs. ■

The Burton Group hosted the first meeting of the ActiveX Working Group in New York on October 1, 1996. At that meeting, the majority present elected the Open Group (**www.opengroup.org**.) as the guardian responsible for evolving and deploying the ActiveX core technologies.

N O T E   The Open Group is the parent organization of the Open Software Foundation (OSF) and X/Open Company Ltd. (X/Open). The main charter of these organizations is the advancement of multivendor information systems. In that respect, the ActiveX technologies are in the right hands. ■

The Open Group will form a sub-group called the ActiveX Group to manage the ActiveX technologies across all platforms. The ActiveX Group's charter includes discussions obtaining feedback and commerce from the public, licensing, testing, and locating other sources of technology. The key goals can be summarized as follows:

- Promote the availability and compatibility of ActiveX technologies across systems and architectures
- Enhance ActiveX interoperability with the Distributed Computing Environment (DCE)
- Accelerate the evolution of ActiveX technologies through the collaborative development process

ActiveX Group Structure

The ActiveX Group is structured as a steering committee to direct development of ActiveX technology, cross-platform use, and market growth.

Technologies Managed by the ActiveX Group

Microsoft has entrusted the ActiveX Group with the technologies listed in Table 22.1. The technologies are packaged as a Pre-Structured (PST) proposal to the group.

Table 22.1   Technologies Managed by the ActiveX Group

Technology	Description
Component Object Model (COM) and Distributed COM (DCOM)	Provides the underlying object model used by all ActiveX components
Microsoft Remote Procedure Call (MS-RPC), including Microsoft Interface Definition Remote Language (MIDL), excluding transports	An optimized version of the Distributed Computing Environment-Procedure Call (DCE-RPC) that provides scalability, marshalling and privacy, and support for pluggable network transports (protocols)
NTLM Standard Security Provider Interface (SSPI)	Allows objects to be invoked securely with user authentication
Structured Storage	Provides a structured file format that can be implemented on multiple operating systems
Registry	Provides a database of ActiveX objects on a given system
Monikers	Allows objects to be invoked and communication between objects to be maintained asynchronously
Automation	Allows method invocation and programmability of objects

Observations

The public consensus agrees that the transfer of the ActiveX standards to an independent group is a good thing. But many in the industry—notably Netscape and, to an extent, Sun—are not exactly pleased with the current state of the ActiveX technology.

N O T E One of the criticisms against the ActiveX Group is that many of the core technologies (the Win32 APIs, OLE DB, and other technologies) are still with Microsoft and, hence, are single-vendor, Windows-specific. Microsoft rebuts this criticism with the response that, as the technologies mature, they also might go into the ActiveX Group realm. ▪

On the other hand, the ActiveX Group promises to be a fully vendor-independent, interoperable technology group. One of the major tasks ahead of the group is to provide interoperability between the Internet Inter-ORB Protocol (IIOP) and DCOM. Netscape is the major force behind the IIOP. A bridge between the DCOM and the IIOP will be a major victory for all concerned. As a user and developer of these technologies, you definitely require alternatives and competing technologies.

Design-Time Controls

Another development to watch for is the design-time ActiveX controls. Design-time controls are a function-rich type of ActiveX control that provide properties, design capabilities, and more during design-time. But the Web browser clients will get only HTML code and text-based scripting, making these controls browser-independent. The client need not download and keep the code for design-time functionality, thus making the controls smaller and more efficient from the client's point of view. In this context, design-time means the Web page authoring time.

N O T E The next release of Microsoft's Web design-time Control SDK will include support for more design-time control features. ▪

The main use of design-time controls is as wizards to aid the developer when creating scripts or HTML objects, including full Web pages.

N O T E Technically speaking, the ActiveX control with the design-time interface will implement the IActiveDesigner and the IServiceProvider COM interfaces. ▪

A good example of a design-time ActiveX Control is the Data Command control in the Visual InterDev ("Internet Studio") product. The Data Command control, during design-time, enables the developer to construct complex SQL queries against databases visually by displaying the objects in the database including tables, stored procedures, data elements, and so on. Once the query is visually generated, the control generates the scripts for executing the query and handling the result-set data. If a client downloads a page that uses this control, the client will get the SQL query, and not the visual SQL generator.

The design-time control concept will be applied by the control and tool vendors. Many future tools will employ design-time control technology. This means the user receives controls that are easy to design—as well as content management—while keeping the client download time to a minimum. Also, the client-side controls will be less complex in multiple ways. The Design-Time Control SDK is available at Microsoft's Web site. This site includes the SDK, technical documentation, and sample code. It also includes the beta version of the ActiveX Control Pad, called the WebDC ActiveX Control Pad, which can work with design-time controls.

Source

Vendor Information

Microsoft Corporation
http://www.microsoft.com/interdev/sdk/dtcrl/

Creating a Design-Time Control

The Design-Time controls can be created by using any popular C++ compilers, including Visual C++, Symantec C++, Borland C++, or Delphi, or by using the Visual Basic Control Creation Edition (VBCCE).

As an example, look at the steps required to create a design-time control using the Visual Basic Control Creation Edition.

After creating a project and the control interface in the VBCCE, you add the normal run-time interfaces required by your control. Now you are ready to add the interfaces and code for the design-time support. Select Project-references and add the reference to the "Microsoft Web Design-Time Control Type Library." The library file name is WEBDC.TLB. Then implement the design-time functionalities you want to give to your designers in the IActiveDesigner interface.

Multimedia ActiveX

After rich graphic pictures, the next evolution of ActiveX is audio and video over the Internet. The multimedia ActiveX controls are aimed at just this market—developing Weblications with rich audio and video components.

The application of this technology includes online broadcasting (known as live multi-casting) and on-demand streaming of audio and video content. These applications encompass entertainment, visual instruction materials, training, product demos, multimedia catalogs, and various other marketing applications. The multimedia controls can also be used for multi-site, multi-personnel video enhanced meetings. For corporate developers, this slogan translates into better corporate communication at reduced costs; for Webmasters, the appeal is rich multimedia experience for their Web sites.

Microsoft and other companies are already developing authoring and conversion tools for content development, and administration tools to manage deployment and content delivery. The Internet Audio and NetMeeting controls are already available in beta form. Microsoft is moving toward a NetShow server and the NetShow audio/video client for delivering audio/video content, plus an SDK for developers.

The ActiveX multimedia streaming format (ASF) specification has been submitted and the ActiveX controls are under development. The ASF will run under Windows NT as an ASF service and clients will have ActiveX playback control. Some features of the ActiveX streaming controls include a jitter control to compensate for network delays, and streaming of audio and video with progressive display/playback. The client UI will have functionality similar to a VCR, with the familiar play, stop, forward, and reverse buttons (minus the blinking 12:00 time). The ASF technology is being developed by Microsoft specifically for delivery of synchronized, multimedia content over the Internet/intranet, with enhanced error-correction schemes.

If you start seeing ActiveX controls on your TV controller, it's time to conclude that the technology is here to stay.

New HTML Tags

The next release of browsers, from Microsoft as well as Netscape, will support enhanced HTML syntax-comparable style sheets, image layering, dynamic image rendering, absolute position technology, and more. Both companies are also pushing for their own standards. This is not good for the developer community. Thus, the W3C is looking at an Editorial Review Board as a forum for HTML extensions.

The next version of HTML—HTML 4.0—will have a lot of enhancements to make the Web developers' jobs easier. One example in the HTML syntax is the <OBJECT> tag. The following table shows the proposed <OBJECT> tag syntax. As you can see, it already incorporates Java and ActiveX. More such HTML extensions will make the technologies more prevalent and easier to use.

Table 22.2   The <*Object*> Tag

Code	Description
<OBJECT>	
DECLARE	
ID	Document ID
CLASSID	ActiveX Control GUID or Java Class name
CODEBASE	Load/implementation URL
DATA	URL for object data
TYPE	Object Data type
CODETYPE	The CLASSID code
STANDBY	Text to display while the object is being loaded
ALIGN	
HEIGHT	
WIDTH	
BORDER	
HSPACE	
VSPACE	
SHAPES	
NAME	Form name
<PARAM NAME=...VALUE=...>	Persistent object initialization properties

Source

Vendor Information

Microsoft Corporation
http://www.w3.org/pub/WWW/TR/WD-object.html

The W3C's site has the working drafts of the <object> tag proposal.

IE 4.0 and ActiveDesktop (Active Themes) Features

Microsoft is working on a lot of client and server features for IE 4.0. One of the first no-
ticeable features will be the integration of the Web with the explorer shell, providing
multi-pane viewing capability. The three-pane view is not exactly new—the new Lotus
Notes version 4.0 and some mail programs offer this capability. It is also similar to the
three-pane frames in HTML pages. The enhancement is the integration with the Web for a
seamless "exploration," with built-in features such as line shortcuts, history, and favorites.
Another feature is the offline reader and WebCheck that notifies the user when a Web
page changes. The WebCheck also will have features such as idle time downloading, size
and time limits for offline reader refreshing, and scheduled downloading, which will enable you to have an automatically updated local cache of your favorite Web pages.

Revolutionary features being developed are the Desktop, Ticker, and Screensaver chan-
nels on which multimedia content with information (and, of course, advertisements) will
be piped to your computer in real-time. These are revolutionary because they are built
into Internet Explorer and, possibly, as part of the windows operating system. The Desktop channel will be used for headlines and information, while the Ticker will be used for
stock market quotes, sports scores, and so on.

Integrated Visual Web Site Developers

The next wave of tools will be for the visual development of a Web site (as opposed to
visual development of a page or one component). Borland's Intrabuilder and Microsoft's
Visual InterDev (Internet Studio) fall in this class. Many other companies are also developing significant products in this category. All these products aim at bringing the RAD
technology to develop full-fledged Web applications. You should watch for products in this
category as these tools will be very useful for intranet developers and Webmasters.

As a representative product in this category, look at the Microsoft Visual InterDev, the
latest Web site development environment from Microsoft. The code name for this product
was "Internet Studio." It is in the beta stage now. This product enables developers to build
a Web site consisting of client pages, active server pages, data access to back-end databases, and multimedia content.

Some useful features for developing dynamic Web pages are the visual database tools,
which include a dataview window that enables you to see and interact with the objects
(including queries, tables, and relationships) in the back-end database, the ODBC query

designer, the SQL database designer, the stored procedure editor for Oracle, the SQL Server, SYBASE and other popular databases, database wizards to develop forms with data plug-ins, and so on. These tools enable you to do database design inside the Web development environment and to incorporate the data design in your Web pages, real advancement in the Web development tools.

Another feature, which represents the evolution of the tools, is the IDE with integrated site management, site-visualization, and content development features. It even keeps track of links between the different objects in the Web site and takes care of repairing broken links due to a name change, object removal, additions, and so on.

Web-Based Enterprise Management Initiative

The Web-Based Enterprise Management Initiative (WBEMI) is an aggregation of Internet/ intranet principles and concepts aimed at the management and administration of the enterprise resources using Web-based applications. The resources include servers, networks, desktop machines, and applications. The proponents of this initiative include BMC Software Inc., Cisco Systems, Compaq Computer Corp, Intel, and Microsoft. This effort will integrate technologies such as DMI (Desktop Management Interface) for servers and desktop machines, and SNMP for networks open to HTTP monitoring and administration.

Source

http://wbem.freerange.com/   This URL contains press releases, a protocol overview, a demo of the WBEMI for an enterprise computing resource, definitions, and so on.

Two technologies that fall under this initiative, the HMMS (HyperMedia Management Schema) data model and the HMMP (HyperMedia Management Protocol) communication protocol specifications, are already at the IETF level.

You should watch this initiative for total system monitoring and administration over the Web. This will become more important as organizations start acquiring applications and application servers to build Web-based business systems. ●

Appendixes

ActiveX Controls Index

The following list will help you find a particular control you are looking for as well as provide a quick reference to the controls covered in this book. ■

The controls are organized into the following categories which are based on the chapters in Part III of this book:

Form Element Controls

Web Navigation Controls

Database Controls

Imaging and Portable Document Controls

Animation Controls

VRML Controls

Conferencing Controls

Audio Plug-Ins

Video Controls

Other Controls

Form Element Controls

Cal32

CheckBox

Combo Box

Command Button

Frame

Hotspot

HTML Layout

Image

Label

ListBox

Option Button

Scroll Bar

Spin Button

TabStrip

TextBox

Toggle Button

Web Navigation Controls

IntraApp

Microsoft IE30 Button-Menu

Microsoft IE30 Popup Menu

Microsoft IE30 Popup Window

Microsoft IE30 PreLoader

Microsoft IE30 Stock Ticker

Microsoft IE30 Timer

Microsoft IE30 View Tracker

Payment and Address Selector

Database Controls

Crystal Report Engine

fpBoolean

fpCurrency

fpDateTime

fpDoubleSingle

fpLongIntegerSingle

fpMask

fpMemo

fpText

IntInput

MhDateInput

MhInput

MhMaskedInput

MhRealInput

Imaging and Portable Document Controls

Acrobat

Sax Canvas for ActiveX

Tumbleweed Software Envoy for ActiveX

Animation Controls

FutureSplash Player for ActiveX

mBED Player for ActiveX

Sizzler for ActiveX

VRML Controls

The Microsoft VRML 1.0 ActiveX

VR Scout for Windows 95 and Windows NT

WIRL 1.20

Conferencing Controls

ASAP WebShow

CyberGO

EarthTime

Look@Me

Audio Plug-Ins

Crescendo ActiveX

EchoSpeech

EchoSpeech Real-Time Broadcast

Koan ActiveX

MidPlug

RapidTransit Player

RealAudio Player 3.0

Shockwave Audio

Talker (for the Mac)

ToolVox

TrueSpeech

WebTracks

Video Controls

ActiveMovie Video

MhAVI Video

Surround Video

VDO Live Video

VivoActive Video

Other Controls

Certificate Enrollment

FTP

HTTP

Internet Explorer

MIME

NNTP

POP

RAS Dial

SMTP

TAPI Dial

TCP

UUEncode/Decode

What's on the CD?

The CD-ROM included with this book is packed full of ActiveX utilities, ActiveX controls, and plug-ins. This appendix gives you an overview of the contents of the CD-ROM. For more detailed information, load the CD-ROM in your CD-ROM drive and open the INDEX.HTM file in Internet Explorer.

NOTE   Every effort has been made to ensure that this list matches the exact content of the CD-ROM. However, last minute changes could result in this list and the CD-ROM contents being different. ■

ActiveX Utilities

ActiveX Control Pad

Visual Basic Control Creation Edition & Documentation

All the Office Internet Assistants

Word, Excel, PowerPoint, Access, and Schedule+

Microsoft Java SDK

ActiveX Controls

The following ActiveX Controls are on the CD-ROM. Browse the CD-ROM and follow the instructions for installing each control.

Adobe

Acrobat Control

Black Diamond Consulting

Surround Video Control

Catalyst Development Corporation

Socket Tools

Chaco Communications, Inc.

VR Scout Control

Crescent Software

FTP Control

HTTP Control

Mime Control

NNTP Control

POP Control

SMTP Control

TCP Control

UUEncode/Decode Control

Crescent Software Division of Progress Software

FTP Control

HTTP Control

MIME Control

News Control

POP Control

RAS Control

SMTP Control

TCP Control

UUEncode/Decode Control

DameWare

Cal32

Dameware

IntrApp

RAS Dial Control

DameWare Development

ChkList

NetList

Data Dynamics, Ltd.

DynamiCube

DSP Group Inc

TrueSpeech

Farallon Communciations, Inc.

Look@Me

FutureWave

Future Splash Player

InterCAP Graphics Systems Inc

ActiveCGM Viewer

Live Update

Crescendo ActiveX Control

malbury

mBED Software

mBED control

MicroHelp

MhDateInput

MhInput

InInput

MhMaskedInput

MhRealInput

MhAVI Video Control

MicroHelp, Inc.

MhHistograph

Mh3dCalendar

Mh3dCheckbox

Mh3dCombo

Mh3dDirectory

Mh3dDriveList

Mh3dFile

Mh3dFrame

Mh3dGauge

Mh3dGroup

Mh3dKeyState

Mh3dLabel

Mh3dList

Mh3dOptionButton

Mh3dTextbox

MhAlarm

MhCardDeck

MhClock

MhCommand

MhDateInput

MhDial

MhDice

MhFileList

MhInput

MhIntegerInput

MhMarquee

MhMaskedInput

MhMulti

MhOddPic

MhRealInput

MhRollUp

MhSlider

MhTimeInput

MhTimer

MhAvi

MicroHelp, Inc.

Mh3dButn

MVP Solutions

Talker

ProtoView Development Co.

Calendar Control

DataTable Grid Component

TreeView Control

DateEdit Control

Dial Control

Font Selection Control

InterAct

MultiButton Control

Numeric Edit Control

Percent Bar Control

TimeEdit Control

ProtoView Development Co.

Button Control

http://www.quecorp.com

Sax Software

Sax Canvas Control for ActiveX

Softoholic

Softoholic OGL ActiveX Control

Starfish Software

The EarthTime Control

Superscape VR Plc

Viscape for ActiveX

Totally Hip Software

Sizzler Control for ActiveX

Tumbleweed

Envoy Control

VDOnet Corp

VDO Live Control

VREAM, Inc.

WIRL for ActiveX

Yamaha

MidiPlug

Plug-Ins

NOTE   Some of the included plug-ins may not work properly with Internet Explorer. Consult each plug-in's documentation for more information. ■

VRML Plug-Ins

CyberGate (Black Sun Interactive)

CyberPassage (Sony)

Express VR

Liquid Reality (Dimension X)

Paragraph 3D

Terraform (Brilliance Labs)

Topper

Traveler (Onlive Technologies)

Viscape (SuperScape)

Voyager (Virtus)

V-Realm (IDS)

VRML Add-in for Microsoft Internet Explorer VR Scout (Chaco Communications)

VRweb (IICM/NCSA/University of Minnesota)

WebSpace (Silicon Graphics and TGS)

WIRL (VREAM)

Multimedia/Sound Plug-Ins

TrueSpeech

Crescendo and Crescendo Plus

RapidTransit

Arnaud Masson's MIDI Plugin

MidiShare

Koan

ToolVox

EchoSpeech

Talker

William H. Tudor's Speech Plug-In

Bill Noon's ListenUp

Digital Dream's ShockTalk

Multimedia/Graphics Plug-Ins

FIGleaf Inline

ViewDirector

Autodesk's WHIP!

DWG/DXF Viewer

Corel CMX

SoftSource SVF

InterCAP InLine

FutureSplash's CelAnimator

Lightning Strike

FIF Viewer

Summus Wavelet Viewer

Shockwave

Micrografx's QuickSilver

Johnson-Grace's ART Press

Vertigo

WebXpresso

Web-Active and WebActive 3D

WurlPlug

Multimedia/Video Plug-Ins

VDOLive

CoolFusion

Vosaic

VivoActive Player

QuickTime

MacZilla

MovieStar

Iván Cavero Belaúnde's ViewMovie

TEC Player

Kevin McMurtrie's Multimedia Plugin

Open2U's Action MPEG

InterVU's PreVU

Xing StreamWorks

Sizzler

Emblaze

FutureSplash

Deltapoint's Web Animator

Heads Off's Play3D

Shockwave

ASAP WebShow

Astound Web Player

mBED

Rad Technologies

Asymetrix's Neuron

mFactory

7TH LEVEL Top Gun

Powersoft's media.splash

SCREAM

Productivity Plug-Ins

Acrobat

Envoy

Formula One/NET

Word Viewer

KEYview

PointPlus

PowerPoint Plug-in

Texture Viewer

Techexplorer

QuickView Plus

Navigational Aids Plug-Ins

HindSite (ISYS)

AnchorPage Client Plug-In (Iconovex) HistoryTree

HotPage (DocuMagix)

Remote PC Access:

Carbon Copy/Net

Look@Me

Miscellaneous Plug-Ins

EarthTime (Starfish Software)

PointCast

Argus Map Viewer

Globalink

JetForm Filler

Concerto (Alpha Software)

NET-Install

ICHAT IRC

Groupscape Notes Browser

Galacticomm Worldgroup

NCompass (ExCITE)

OpenScape

QuickServer

WinFrame

WebBASIC (Amara)

Index

Check out Que® Books on the World Wide Web
http://www.quecorp.com

As the biggest software release in computer history, Windows 95 continues to redefine the computer industry. Click here for the latest info on our Windows 95 books

Make computing quick and easy with these products designed exclusively for new and casual users

Examine the latest releases in word processing, spreadsheets, operating systems, and suites

The Internet, The World Wide Web, CompuServe®, America Online®, Prodigy® —it's a world of ever-changing information. Don't get left behind!

Find out about new additions to our site, new bestsellers and hot topics

In-depth information on high-end topics: find the best reference books for databases, programming, networking, and client/server technologies

A recent addition to Que, Ziff-Davis Press publishes the highly-successful *How It Works* and *How to Use* series of books, as well as *PC Learning Labs Teaches* and *PC Magazine* series of book/disc packages

Stay on the cutting edge of Macintosh® technologies and visual communications

Find out which titles are making headlines

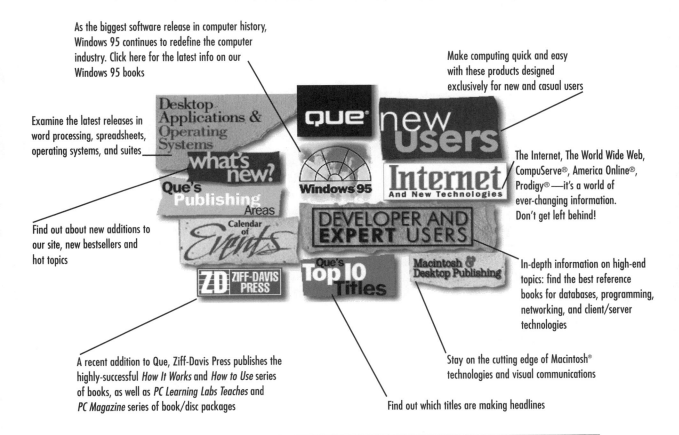

With 6 separate publishing groups, Que develops products for many specific market segments and areas of computer technology. Explore our Web Site and you'll find information on best-selling titles, newly published titles, upcoming products, authors, and much more.

- Stay informed on the latest industry trends and products available
- Visit our online bookstore for the latest information and editions
- Download software from Que's library of the best shareware and freeware

Complete and Return this Card
for a *FREE* Computer Book Catalog

Thank you for purchasing this book! You have purchased a superior computer book written expressly for your needs. To continue to provide the kind of up-to-date, pertinent coverage you've come to expect from us, we need to hear from you. Please take a minute to complete and return this self-addressed, postage-paid form. In return, we'll send you a free catalog of all our computer books on topics ranging from word processing to programming and the Internet.

Mr. ☐   Mrs. ☐   Ms. ☐   Dr. ☐

Name (first) ☐☐☐☐☐☐☐☐☐☐☐☐☐☐ (M.I.) ☐   (last) ☐☐☐☐☐☐☐☐☐☐☐☐☐☐☐☐

Address ☐☐☐☐☐☐☐☐☐☐☐☐☐☐☐☐☐☐☐☐☐☐☐☐☐☐☐☐☐☐☐☐☐

☐☐☐☐☐☐☐☐☐☐☐☐☐☐☐☐☐☐☐☐☐☐☐☐☐☐☐☐☐☐☐☐☐

City ☐☐☐☐☐☐☐☐☐☐☐☐☐☐☐☐☐☐☐☐☐   State ☐☐   Zip ☐☐☐☐☐ ☐☐☐☐

Phone ☐☐☐ ☐☐☐ ☐☐☐☐   Fax ☐☐☐ ☐☐☐ ☐☐☐☐

Company Name ☐☐☐☐☐☐☐☐☐☐☐☐☐☐☐☐☐☐☐☐☐☐☐☐☐☐☐☐☐☐☐☐

E-mail address ☐☐☐☐☐☐☐☐☐☐☐☐☐☐☐☐☐☐☐☐☐☐☐☐☐☐☐☐☐☐☐☐

1. Please check at least (3) influencing factors for purchasing this book.

Front or back cover information on book .... ☐
Special approach to the content .... ☐
Completeness of content .... ☐
Author's reputation .... ☐
Publisher's reputation .... ☐
Book cover design or layout .... ☐
Index or table of contents of book .... ☐
Price of book .... ☐
Special effects, graphics, illustrations .... ☐
Other (Please specify): _____ ☐

2. How did you first learn about this book?

Saw in Macmillan Computer Publishing catalog .... ☐
Recommended by store personnel .... ☐
Saw the book on bookshelf at store .... ☐
Recommended by a friend .... ☐
Received advertisement in the mail .... ☐
Saw an advertisement in: _____ ☐
Read book review in: _____ ☐
Other (Please specify): _____ ☐

3. How many computer books have you purchased in the last six months?

This book only .... ☐   3 to 5 books .... ☐
2 books .... ☐   More than 5 .... ☐

4. Where did you purchase this book?

Bookstore .... ☐
Computer Store .... ☐
Consumer Electronics Store .... ☐
Department Store .... ☐
Office Club .... ☐
Warehouse Club .... ☐
Mail Order .... ☐
Direct from Publisher .... ☐
Internet site .... ☐
Other (Please specify): _____ ☐

5. How long have you been using a computer?

☐ Less than 6 months   ☐ 6 months to a year
☐ 1 to 3 years   ☐ More than 3 years

6. What is your level of experience with personal computers and with the subject of this book?

	With PCs	With subject of book
New	☐	☐
Casual	☐	☐
Accomplished	☐	☐
Expert	☐	☐

Source Code ISBN: 0-7897-1062-5

7. Which of the following best describes your job title?

Administrative Assistant .... ☐
Coordinator .... ☐
Manager/Supervisor .... ☐
Director .... ☐
Vice President .... ☐
President/CEO/COO .... ☐
Lawyer/Doctor/Medical Professional .... ☐
Teacher/Educator/Trainer .... ☐
Engineer/Technician .... ☐
Consultant .... ☐
Not employed/Student/Retired .... ☐
Other (Please specify): _____ ☐

8. Which of the following best describes the area of the company your job title falls under?

Accounting .... ☐
Engineering .... ☐
Manufacturing .... ☐
Operations .... ☐
Marketing .... ☐
Sales .... ☐
Other (Please specify): _____ ☐

9. What is your age?

Under 20 .... ☐
21-29 .... ☐
30-39 .... ☐
40-49 .... ☐
50-59 .... ☐
60-over .... ☐

10. Are you:

Male .... ☐
Female .... ☐

11. Which computer publications do you read regularly? (Please list)

_____
_____
_____
_____
_____
_____
_____
_____
_____
_____

Comments: _____
_____
_____

Fold here and scotch-tape to mail.